Practical AUTO RESTORATION

In
953 Photographs

**The resurrection of Vicky,
a 1955 Ford
Crown Victoria hardtop**

Motorbooks International
Publishers & Wholesalers Inc
Osceola, Wisconsin 54020, USA ®

This edition first published in 1988 by Motorbooks International Publishers & Wholesalers Inc.,
P.O. Box 2, 729 Prospect Ave., Osceola, WI 54020 USA.

Copyright Amos Press Inc., 1988.

Previously published by Amos Press Inc. under the title of THE RESURRECTION OF VICKY.
Compiled by the staff of Cars & Parts Magazine,
Amos Press Inc., 911 Vandemark Rd., Sidney, OH 45365.

Printed and bound in the United States of America.

The information in this book is true and complete to the best of our knowledge. All recommendations
are made without any guarantee on the part of the author or publisher, who also disclaim any liability
incurred in connection with the use of this data or specific details.

We recognize that some words, model names and designations, for example, mentioned herein are
the property of Ford Motor Co. We use them for identification purposes only. This is not an official
publication of Ford Motor Co.

Library of Congress Cataloging-in-Publication Data
Practical auto restoration in 953 photographs.
Previously published as: The Resurrection of Vicky.
1. Automobiles — Conservation and restoration.
2. Ford automobile — Conservation and restoration.
I. Cars & Parts. II. Title.
TL152.2.R47 1988   629.28'722   88-8420
ISBN 0-87938-330-5 (pbk.)

Motorbooks International books are also available at discounts in bulk quantity for industrial or sales-
promotional use. For details write to Special Sales Manager at the Publisher's address.

Introduction

More than two years ago, in early 1986, the staff of *Cars & Parts* Magazine decided to restore a car from the fifties or sixties. Our goal was to use the project car as a means of producing a series of restoration articles for the magazine that would have lasting value for our readers. We narrowed the choice of project car down to two, either a 1955-56 Ford Crown Victoria hardtop or a 1963-64 Chevrolet Impala SS convertible. Since our object was not to do a one-make "how-to" series, we wanted a popular car that would be similar to most postwar collector vehicles. Either one, we felt, would be a good choice.

Our search began quietly, with small advertisements. But the right car didn't surface, nor did it appear at large car shows. Finally, we had to send staffers on the road. Just about the time it seemed we never would find the right car, we found a '55 Ford Crown Victoria. Quickly dubbed Miss Vicky, then simply Vicky, she soon became one of the most well-known old cars in the country as our series of articles began in the spring of 1987.

The series quickly gained a large following amongst readers, many of whom volunteered parts, materials and their services to aid in Vicky's restoration. Most of them have been mentioned in the various articles, but it is appropriate to thank them again though space prevents us from naming everyone who contributed.

We would be remiss, though, in not singling out one organization. We could not have restored Vicky without their assistance, nor without the enthusiastic work by the many skilled and talented people at Classic Car Centre, Warsaw, Ind., Vicky's main restoration shop.

Part of the interest in Vicky, of course, was that she was being offered as the grand prize in a sweepstakes. Our goal from the beginning was to share Vicky with the readers of *Cars & Parts*, both in the articles and by giving her away. As this book goes to press, the identity of the lucky recipient is still unknown. The winner will be announced on June 12, 1988, at Springfield '88, *Cars & Parts*' annual car show and swap meet in Springfield, Ohio.

Whoever wins Vicky will receive a car that has undergone one of the most well-documented frame-off restorations in the history of the hobby. Thanks to the constant intimate exposure, many readers — even those who say they're not Ford fans — have come to feel a special relationship with Vicky over the months. It's been a pleasure to watch visitors to various meets at which we've shown Vicky during her restoration. They smile, carefully scrutinize work that's been done, ask questions, then caution us to take care of "their" car. We've had people walk up to us at coffee stops on the road, in motel parking lots and other places. They all called her Vicky, as if they had known her for years.

Many of Vicky's fans have thanked us for taking on the project, and for presenting the series in the magazine. Many have suggested that we turn the series into a book. We listened, obviously. But rather than simply repackage the original series in the order in which it first appeared, we decided to do it right. We reorganized the articles into groups that made sense together — the

"Star Search" part, the body restoration and painting part, etc. We added new articles — speedometer restoration, steering box rebuild, restoring wheels and hubcaps, six to 12-volt conversion, and post-restoration reflections — that have not appeared in print before.

But *The Resurrection of Vicky* also has been reorganized and made more complete as a means of making the entire series a useful reference guide, whether your interest is in restoring a '55 Ford or any other collector car. We also added an index to help you find, say, the page where we talk about silicone brake fluid. In addition, we have added a substantial appendix that lists enormous numbers of sources for restoration supplies and services for all collector cars.

As was our intention in the original series, our goal with this book has been to serve the needs of old car hobbyists for authoritative, well-documented, and useful restoration articles and information. We think this book fulfills our purposes admirably. But it's not the end of *Cars & Parts* Magazine's commitment to provide the hobbyist with the best in restoration literature. *The Resurrection of Vicky* is the first in what will be a continuing series of restoration projects and publications.

And now, a word about the *Cars & Parts* people behind the Vicky project. Though many people were involved, perhaps the single most important individual contribution was made by Art Director Ken New. Not only did he write the lion's share of the articles, he took most of the photos, and spent innumerable days and nights shepherding Vicky's progress through various restoration phases at the main restoration facility, Classic Car Centre, and elsewhere from Indiana to Pennsylvania. Day in and day out, Vicky was Ken's "baby", as the piles of Vicky parts in his office made clear.

Other staffers also contributed, of course. Editor Bob Stevens wrote a number of the early articles, and also took many pictures. He, too, spent many hours with Vicky, including the final detailing session where he and New applied the last crowning touches. Assistant Editor Jim Scott arrived near the end of the main work, but edited a number of articles in the series, wrote several new articles for this book, and served as the project editor for this book. Joe Taylor of the art staff helped design a large number of the articles, and Beverly Martin and Sharon Fair were instrumental in proofreading, typesetting and other necessary editorial tasks.

The accomplishment that *The Resurrection of Vicky* represents, however, could not have happened without the support of Amos Press, Inc., which owns *Cars & Parts*. Senior Vice President Wayne Lawrence is a long-time car collector who appreciated the value of the undertaking to hobbyists everywhere. He and Publisher Paula L. Garret almost never flinched when the bills came due for various phases of Vicky's restoration. Whatever the cost, though, we think you'll agree with us that it was worth it.

The Editors
Sidney, Ohio
May 1988

Contents

PART ONE

Star Search

WANTED TO BUY

1963-64 CHEVY SS CONVERTIBLE OR

1955-56 FORD CROWN VICTORIA

Car must be in good, solid restorable condition: all original and complete. No junk please! Prefer within 300 miles of Dayton, Ohio.

STAR SEARCH

Cars & Parts looks for a 'special' automobile

1. *Cars & Parts launched its search for a project car with this advertisement placed in several issues in mid-1986. Numerous responses from Crown Victoria owners were received, but not a single Chevy Impala SS convertible owner answered our wanted-to-buy ad. An associate in Dayton, Ohio screened prospects for us, enabling us to conceal our identity for several reasons: If the seller knew who he was dealing with, it might adversely influence the price of his car; competitors didn't need to know exactly what we were planning; and Cars & Parts staffers didn't want to have everyone with a car for sale tracking them down at car shows, visiting the home office, or phoning.*

It all started out innocently enough. It was during one of our routine staff meetings involving the editorial, advertising and circulation people assigned to *Cars & Parts*. Our monthly brainstorming sessions are normally routine: We evaluate our status in terms of editorial profile, circulation, the competition, display and classified advertising, etc., and review various proposals for improving our lot on all scores.

It was during one of the more inspirational meetings that a rather unusual suggestion was tabled in response to editorial projects. A major portion of our staff meetings is devoted to gauging reader interests and responding to any changes we detect in the direction of the hobby and the basic interests of our readers. One particular item that surfaces repeatedly in reader surveys, correspondence and phone conversations is the growing and already substantial interest in vintage car and truck restoration. Identifying this special area of reader interest and activity is not the difficult part, but satisfying it on a regular, ongoing basis certainly is. Resto-

ration articles, especially the very helpful "how-to" pieces, are among the more taxing to develop.

Consequently, our editorial staff is faced with the problem of meeting a major, well-defined reader need for restoration features, and a tremendous difficulty in acquiring and/or developing such articles on a regular basis.

Our publisher, Wayne Lawrence, our art director, Ken New, and the author are all car enthusiasts and collectors, and we frequently use our own vehicles as test subjects for different restoration projects. But this still does not insure a steady supply of restoration articles. As a solution, the publisher recommended that we consider the purchase and renovation of a collector car, developing stories on the various facets of vehicle restoration as our project car progresses along the road to recovery.

After months of deliberation, discussion and problem-solving, it was agreed that *Cars & Parts* would acquire a desirable collector car and have the subject vehicle restored to street-driver-show condition. We wanted to wind up with a nice, re-

stored automobile in good presentable condition — one good enough to compete in local show competition but not a true show car. On a scale of 1 to 10, we decided a good 7 or 8 would be sufficient to achieve our goals in producing a complete series of restoration articles, yet not so nice that it would cost a fortune and end up too nice to drive.

The next decision, of course, was what car to restore. Since *Cars & Parts* is a general interest magazine within the car collector hobby, we quickly determined that our project car had to be a Ford or Chevy, simply because of the overwhelming popularity of America's top two marques. We have staff members whose allegiance goes to Chrysler, American Motors, Studebaker, Packard, Hudson and other notable marques, but Chevy and Ford clearly dominate the old car hobby and we wanted to produce a series of restoration articles with the broadest possible appeal. Also, we really didn't want to spend a lot of time and money searching for super rare parts. Parts, both new-old-stock and reproduction, as well as used and rebuilt, are generally plentiful for America's number one and two selling automobiles, regardless of vintage. This is especially true since we had also decided to focus our search on a post-war model to capitalize on the hobby's dramatic and massive shift into the 1950s and '60s. And, again, numerous articles and even books have been published on restoring a Model A Ford, etc.

Each staff member then drafted a list of potential candidates. The lists were combined in order of popularity and, after a couple of models were discounted because they'd already been covered in magazine articles or book form, we settled on two finalists. The first was a Chevy, a 1963-64 Impala Super Sport convertible. The second contestant was a 1955 or '56 Ford Crown Victoria, either the solid top or glasstop edition.

Launching the search, we soon discovered that our task would be a bit more difficult than originally anticipated. We attended most major national meets, and numerous local shows in the Ohio-Michigan-Indiana region. We also placed advertisements in *Cars & Parts*, including one rather large "wanted to buy" ad that appeared in the Ford and Chevy sections for several issues during 1986. To shield our identity, an associate in nearby Dayton, Ohio agreed to serve as a clearinghouse for all responses to our ads.

The vast majority of the responses to the ads were not quite on target. The cars being offered were either already restored, or far enough along in the restoration process to prove unsuitable. A few presented more of a challenge than we were capable of handling within the prescribed limits of our budget and project deadlines.

We were searching for a car that would require a certain level of restoration in all major areas: Body and paint; engine and powertrain; and the interior. This way we could show restoration of all major and most supplemental components and systems in a vintage car. Again, though, we were looking for a solid and fairly complete automobile, but one requiring some work in each of the designated areas.

Unfortunately, most of the responses to our ad were from owners of nicely restored Crown Vics or cars that were worn and weathered a bit beyond the scope of our imagination. Surprisingly, practically no responses were received from owners of 1963-64 Chevy SS convertibles. A couple of regular convertibles and a few hardtops were uncovered, but not the magical Super Sport and convertible combination. (As one might expect, a week or so after the successful completion of our car search mission, a decent, restorable 1963 Chevy Super Sport convertible with a "409" V-8 and four-speed manual transmission surfaced for sale just a few miles from the *Cars & Parts* office; it sold quickly).

Other considerations in purchasing a car included logistics (we didn't want to travel

2. *One of the first responses to our wanted-to-buy ad came from a veteran reader and super nice hobbyist, Don Stickler, Berlin Center, Ohio. Stickler is seen here (left) talking to some friends. His Crown Victoria, a red-and-white '55 model with a non-original 390 Ford V-8 (correct 272-cid V-8 could be added to a package deal), was displayed in Stickler's swap space at Spring Carlisle '86.*

3. *Inside Stickler's '55 Ford we found a complete but well used and battered interior. Still, it was a decent buy for someone with a lot of time, patience and skill. Hopefully, an adventurous hobbyist has by now adopted the car and is treating it to a full restoration.*

4. *The weathered old Crown Vic also had incorrect wheels, but that didn't bother us. The car just represented too ambitious a project for us, although the $2,500 asking price was certainly in the ballpark.*

halfway around the globe to bring this beauty home) and color (we wanted a car with a bright original color scheme; preferably two-tone in the Crown Victoria). Brightly colored cars photograph much better and provide much more flash than cars painted black or some other dark color.

With this criteria, we launched our search.

The first few responses to our advertisement sparked varying degrees of interest. One good prospect was a 1956 Crown Victoria in solid, original condition. Equipped with the factory continental kit and fresh out of 15 years of storage, the car was offered by Karl Mueller, Indianapolis, Ind., for the reasonable sum of $4,500. Apparently it seemed reasonably priced to someone else, because the car sold before we could get there to look it over. That car was advertised in our September, 1986 issue and was in subscriber hands by the first of August. In line with company policy, we could not and did not respond to the ad until the September issues had been received by our subscribers. Obviously, someone was a bit quicker off the mark.

Before the Mueller car, we had checked out numerous leads, most of which came to us thru our ad in *Cars & Parts*. All of them, though, were rejected for one reason or another. They were either too nice, needed too much, or were priced too high.

There were a couple of candidates that we didn't get to see because of the logistics involved. We simply weren't traveling in those areas and couldn't personally inspect the cars. One was a '55 Crown located in Gallatin, Tenn. But it was fairly well restored with new paint and new interior, although it did have a modest price of $6,000. Another car that we didn't view in person was a 1956 Crown Victoria owned by Ken Amstutz, Muskegon, Mich. He'd owned the two-tone, turquoise-and-white car for 15 years and it showed some 61,000 miles on its odometer. It had a stick shift and a 272-cid V-8. It was on our list, but as things turned out we never did make a trip into his area prior to finding a car.

A really nice Crown Victoria, an all-white '56 with 43,000 miles on it, was located in Portage, Ind. It sported a host of desirable options, including power steering and brakes, automatic transmission, 312-cid V-8, power windows, etc. It was way too nice for our purposes, however, and priced a bit beyond the limits of our budget. Owner Jim Price was asking a very reasonable $9,000 for his super straight Crown Vic.

One of our earliest leads involved a Crown Victoria offered by one of our most loyal readers, Don Stickler, Berlin Center, Ohio. We reviewed photos and descriptive materials, but decided to reserve judgement on the car until we had an opportunity to look it over in person at Spring Carlisle, the popular swap meet held annually in Carlisle, Pa. Stickler had mentioned in his letter sent in response to our ad that he would have the car on sale at Spring Carlisle. The '55 Crown Victoria was fitted with the wrong engine (a newer Ford 390-cid V-8) and incorrect wheels. It was restorable and priced right ($2,500), but it just represented too much of a project for us. We wanted a bit more to start with than this particular car offered. It was the right colors (red and white) and Stickler did have a correct engine he'd throw in with the car. Still, we decided to pass.

Looking for something a little more substantial, we reviewed responses from a few other readers, including one from R.R. Rutter in Fraser, Mich. His 1955 Ford Crown Victoria was a black and white gem priced in the $10,000 range. Again, it was too much of a car for our project, but it did have the rare glasstop.

Our next prospect took us south to Kentucky, where one Charles R. Davis, of Glasgow, had a '55 black Crown Vic for sale. It also proved not quite right for us, as did two other Crown Victorias in Glasgow — a poorly restored red-and-white example priced at $7,500 and an unrestored turquoise and white Crown Vic with the wrong engine. All three were decent buys, but they simply did not suit our situation.

A nice car, but once again one too nice for our purposes, was then located in West Bend, Wis. This nice '55 glasstop with continental kit was priced at $10,000 firm. The green-and-white Ford appeared to be a decent buy and well worth the money, but it

5. One of the nicest cars offered as a direct result of our ad in Cars & Parts was this sharp '55 black and white Crown Vic glasstop owned by Dick Rutter, Fraser, Mich. The car was equipped with automatic transmission, radio, heater, skirts, tinted glass, wheel covers, etc. Priced at $10,000, it was certainly worth the money. But it was a bit steep for us, plus the fact that black and white weren't the best colors for our project car. This particular example was stored in New Jersey, so we never did examine it in person.

6. Turquoise and white Crown Victoria, a '55 glasstop, was offered by Ken Wegener, West Bend, Wis. The car was a bit too nice for us and the price, $10,000 firm, was beyond our budget, but certainly reasonable for a nice, solid glasstop.

7. One of the very nicest cars uncovered in our search was this 1956 all-white Crown Victoria owned by Jim and Sandy Rice in Portage, Ind. The car appeared to be exceptionally solid and clean and was truly loaded, sporting the following equipment: 312 Thunderbird engine, automatic transmission, power steering, power brakes, power windows, skirts, radio, clock,

5

6

7

8

9

10

whitewalls, etc. It showed only 43,000 miles on its odometer, and had just had its dash pad replaced. It could use paint, the owner said, and the original color combo was pink and white. It was priced at $9,000.

8. We found very few candidates at car shows, even the major ones. This '55 Crown Victoria was one of two we spotted at the AACA Fall Hershey meet in Hershey, Pa. It was painted a very weak purple and white, although it was originally pink and white. It was reasonably well equipped with a 292-cid V-8, automatic, power steering, and a radio. A Pennsylvania car dealer had it for sale in the white field with an asking price

of $2,950. We decided that it was a little more than we wanted to tackle. It needed considerable restoration as the body showed evidence of severe rust and a lot of body filler. Reluctantly, we passed, hoping to find something a bit more solid.

9. The Hershey Crown Vic received considerable thought and deliberation before it was rejected as too much of an undertaking. The car did sell at Hershey, so someone, somewhere is now knee-deep in a major restoration project. There was a second Crown Victoria at Hershey, but it was restored and priced at $13,000.

10. What could have been a real winner for us was

this 1955 Crown Victoria owned by Robert Haas, Livonia, Mich. It was priced at $3,800 (within our budget), was the right color combination (red and white), was reasonably well equipped (V-8, automatic, radio, etc.), and was within our target range (200 miles away). We made a tentative appointment to view the car while talking with Haas at the AACA Fall Hershey meet, confirmed our visit the following week and arrived in Detroit the Friday after Hershey only to find that the car had sold the preceding evening to a hobbyist in Northville, Mich., who also owned three other Crown Victorias. Foiled, again!

was a bit out of our price range.

Another lead, also in response to our ad, took us to Hubbard, Ohio, where we surveyed a 1955 Crown Victoria with a white over black paint treatment. The car had a non-stock 390 Ford V-8 from the mid-sixties and was in just fair condition with quite a bit of plastic filler in the body and lots of bad chrome. It was priced on the high side at $4,700. The car had been taken as part downpayment on a house. We passed on it and moved on to another one located by a friend in Dayton, Ohio.

The car was discovered by Bill Kurrek, an employee of Amos Press, which publishes *Cars & Parts*. Kurrek found the car, a 1955 Crown Victoria, near his home in Dayton, Ohio, some 40 miles south of Sidney, Ohio, where *Cars & Parts* is headquartered. The car, equipped with a 272-cid V-8 was originally tropical rose and snowshoe white, an attractive color combination. Unfortunately, it was rougher body-wise than we had envisioned. The floor was in desperate need of replacement and extensive body work was required, much more than we wanted to handle, or have handled for us.

The car, owned by Terry Tackett, Dayton, was intriguing, but we didn't dare drag it home. It needed someone with a bit more ambition and skill than we had, and someone with a lot more vision. Tackett, a friendly sort, also introduced us to a second car, a sedan parts car that really wasn't all that bad. In fact, we decided that it was a bit more restorable than its fancier stablemate, the Crown Vic. We passed on both of them but made a mental note of the two cars as potential parts sources for our elusive project car.

At this point, our search was grinding to an end-of-season halt with no feasible prospects in sight. We attended the Hoosier Auto Show in Indianapolis and didn't find a single candidate. There were two Crown Victorias offered in the huge cars for sale lot at Hoosier, but both were simply too nice. We still needed a car that required some degree of restoration work in all the major areas: Body, paint, chrome, interior, engine, transmission, etc. Surprisingly, we also came up empty-handed at Fall Carlisle — not a single prospect.

11. A '55 Crown Vic located in Hubbard, Ohio, was offered by a realtor who had taken the car as a partial downpayment on a house. The black and white Ford didn't look too bad at a distance.

12. The Thompson car had a powerful surprise under the hood in the form of a mid-'60s vintage 390 Ford V-8. This would have necessitated a search for a correct engine.

13. Deciphering a 1955 Ford data plate is simple enough once you know the different codes. For example, this plate from the '55 Crown Vic discovered in Hubbard, Ohio, shows 64A, which denotes the Fairlane Crown Victoria hard top (64B would identify a Fairlane Crown Victoria transparent top). The next code, AE, is the paint number, which translates into raven black for the lower body and snowshoe white for the upper body.

The following entry, AT, indicates the trim scheme, white vinyl and black bodycloth. The balance of the code, 16 M 7025, indicates that this particular car was assembled on the 16th day of December (M) and that it was the 7,025th car produced. There is considerable controversy within Ford circles as to the interpretations of the last entry, the production code. The serial number (top), which is U5GW116370 in this case, translates as follows: U - 272-cid V-8 engine; 5 - model year (55); G - built at the Chicago assembly plant; W - body style (Crown Victoria); and 116370 - production sequence. We decided to pass on this Crown Vic primarily because of the massive amount of body filler, poor chrome and trim, and the many non-original items on the car.

14. The Crown Vic from Hubbard was basically

complete, but had a number of modifications, including '55 or '56 Mercury Montclair side trim and a Ford 390 engine with Hurst floor shift.

15. Except for the stuffed animal hanging from the mirror, the "big foot" accelerator pedal and the accessory gauges mounted under the dash, the interior (except seat fabric) maintained a basically stock appearance.

16. Up close the Crown Vic from northeastern Ohio suddenly didn't look all that neat, as evidenced by this badly weathered and pitted hood ornament.

17. The Crown Vic owned by Bob Thompson, Hubbard, Ohio, had a number of factors in its favor, including many neat and rare options, such as power windows.

18. The interior was pretty ratty, but the four-way power seat was a definite plus.

19

20

21

22

19. *A fellow employee at Amos Press, which publishes Cars & Parts, spotted this Crown Victoria for sale in his home neighborhood in Dayton, Ohio.*

20. *In addition to his Crown Vic, Tackett was offering a 1956 sedan parts car as part of the package. The parts car was in much better overall condition than the Crown Vic and would make a super parts car for any '56 Ford restoration.*

21. *The floorboard was well ventilated, requiring total replacement, or at least a major patch job.*

22. *The body on the Dayton car was really gone in several spots. New panels would have been required all around.*

23. *The '55 Crown Victoria was originally tropical rose and snowshoe white, a pleasant and vibrant color combination.*

24. *Terry Tackett, Dayton, had the trim moldings for his Crown Vic in the trunk. About everything was there, but in need of total restoration.*

Our last shot of the year, as far as major shows were concerned, was the granddaddy of swap meets, the fall AACA meet in Hershey, Pa. We had a bit more luck at Hershey, but still didn't find that special car. Two Crown Vics were spotted at Hershey. One, located in the blue field, was a gem, but it was restored and priced at $13,000. The second possibility, found at a car dealer's spot in the white field, was pretty well ravaged by rust, but was basically complete and restorable. Also, it was priced at a reasonable $2,950, or offer. We examined the car thoroughly and decided that it was just a tad more than we bargained for when we started our search. It certainly had the right original color combination, that outrageous pink and white scheme that everyone remembers so well, but it was extensively patched and needed more body and interior work than we were able to justify. The car sold before Hershey ended, so someone obviously felt the car had potential.

With Hershey signaling the end of the show season, at least in respect to the major circuit, we were more or less limited to only a couple of remaining prospects, but they were located a good distance from Ohio.

We'd pretty much exhausted all of our leads, including a few supplied by Toby and Sandy Gorny, New Bryan, Ohio. Toby and Sandy own and operate the Ford Parts Store, which specializes in 1955-59 Ford parts. They're also very active in the Crown Victoria Assn.; Sandy as president and Toby as one of the club's two original founders. These active hobbyists volunteered to help us locate a restorable example of the 1955-56 Ford Crown Victoria, and to serve as consultants in authenticating our project car and its restoration. From the start of our search, this knowledgeable couple guided us through the maze of Ford codes, parts numbers, etc., and helped educate us to the various color combinations, equipment options, etc. Unfortunately, the leads they provided didn't work out, primarily because of our inability to move quickly enough to beat other hobbyists to a car. Our heavy show schedule and stringent deadlines often prevented us from reacting swiftly enough to a lead. A couple of good ones got away as a result.

At Toby's invitation, we attended the Crown Victoria Assn. national convention in Columbus, Ohio last August. There were, of course, numerous Crown Victorias on display at the CVA show, but all were nicely restored to street or show condition, and none of them were for sale. It was a very pleasant day and one well invested as we met many Ford enthusiasts, viewed a number of very nice and very authentic cars and learned more and more about the Crown Victoria of 1955-56. But we once again returned home without a car and, as previously mentioned, the big fall trio (Hoosier, Carlisle & Hershey) would not yield a candidate fitting the profile of our proposed project car.

The search would continue ... but this time we'd invest our time and resources in a week-long trip to the west and south in search of our special automobile.

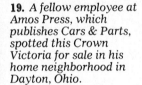

23

24

STAR SEARCH

Picking up a trailer to haul that special car

Since our enthusiasm for the 1963-64 Chevy SS Impala convertible had been dampened by the lack of response to our ad and the complete disappearance of these cars in the car corrals at major car meets, we had more or less reduced our search for a project car to the Ford Crown Victoria of 1955-56.

With this in mind, we had zeroed in on two hobbyists, one in Missouri and one in Arkansas, both of whom specialize in our favorite breed of Ford. We scheduled a trip westward to view the many cars they had; we would leave right after our return from the fall antique car meet in Hershey, Pa.

Before heading west, though, we pointed our *Cars & Parts* van due south in the direction of Bowling Green, Ky., where we were scheduled to pick up a trailer being leased from Trailer World, the former Feldman Trailers long familiar to old car hobbyists.

The weather was gloomy, an ominous sign of what awaited us on our first day out. We arrived safely and on schedule in Bowling Green, all ready to hitch up our new trailer and travel west. But, ill prepared as we were, the day would not go as planned, to say the least.

To begin with, the Trailer World staff almost laughed at our Class II trailer hitch, which was a genuine Reese unit that had worked well enough towing our little vendor trailer. But the small *Cars & Parts* show trailer, even when loaded, wouldn't come close to a fully loaded 22-ft. car hauler in terms of size, weight, etc. After a brief glance at our hitch, Feldman joked:

"It's apparent that *Cars & Parts* wants to test its liability insurance." We were amused, and also a little concerned. We had brought the correct size hitch ball, 2 5/16", but that was about the only thing we got right.

After a tour of Trailer World's impressive new facility in Bowling Green, we determined that the experts were right and we needed the larger, stronger, and higher rated Class III hitch. We examined one at Trailer World and bought it, along with a brake control unit to hook up the trailer's electric brakes. The folks at Trailer World were in the process of settling into their new quarters, however, and they were unable to handle the installation of the hitch and brake control, so we were politely directed to the local U-Haul dealer.

The U-Haul Center of Bowling Green (Ky.) is a huge, well equipped and well staffed rental, sales and service center. Larger and better equipped than many major-franchise new car dealers, the center had little trouble handling our hitch installation, including the new wiring to connect the trailer's light system and the Kelsey brake control to activate the trailer's electric brakes.

The installation, handled by two of the U-Haul Center's skillful and experienced mechanics, Rick Leitz and Homer Cosby, was completed without any major problems. And it was done in a timely and orderly fashion, although it did shoot most of the balance of the day. It was dark by the time we returned to Trailer World, which was located only a few miles from the U-Haul Center, so we decided to spend the night in Bowling Green.

Bowling Green is a hospitable city and one sheltering a lot of automotive activity. We met and talked with numerous hobbyists active in antique, special interest and other collector cars, plus vintage trucks,

1. *The trip south to Bowling Green, Ky., to pick up a car hauler was a relaxing, pleasant freeway drive. We arrived at the new headquarters facility of Trailer World right on time, anxious to look at the hauler that would be at our disposal for the duration of our car project.*

2. *The new, spacious building now housing Trailer World accommodates the firm's service operation, parts and accessories showroom, and offices. Adjacent to the new structure is a fenced area where the trailer inventory is securely stored. There's lots of room for future expansion, too.*

street rods, etc. It was an enjoyable stay, heightened by the fact that Bowling Green is also the relatively new home for the Corvette. Chevy's little fiberglass-bodied sports car experienced a transfer in production facilities from St. Louis, Mo., to Bowling Green in 1982. Chevrolet has reported that the relocation was a good one.

The next morning we were up early and ready to get going. We were about a half day behind schedule, but things weren't critical yet. We rushed over to Trailer World's headquarters, anxious to hook up the trailer and try out our new hauling tandem. While Monday had been a cold, damp and cloudy day, Tuesday dawned

3. The Trailer World staff was in the process of moving into their new quarters the week we visited, yet it seemed to be business as usual as the company's crew was busy recovering from the recent Fall Carlisle and Hershey meets. The new location is convenient to a major freeway, 65.

4. Richard Feldman (left), owner of Trailer World, talks with Ken New, art director of Cars & Parts. Feldman and his associates, Don Owen and Mike Dixon, afforded the magazine's crew a warm reception. Owen was quite helpful in nursing us through the ordeal that was to follow.

5. The author looks over the new trailer in the storage yard at Trailer World. Car haulers always look so much larger in real life than one envisions from reading a spec sheet and looking at catalog photos. The tandem axle trailer assigned to us had an overall length of 22 feet and a bed length of 18 feet, adequate for virtually any collector car. It measured 78 inches between the fenders, weighed 1,560 pounds and boasted a gvw (gross vehicle weight) rating of 6,800 pounds. This left a very comfortable margin with a hauling weight of about 5,240 pounds.

6. The author gets excited over a "real" trailer hitch assembly, one considerably stronger than the unit that was on the Cars & Parts van upon our arrival in Bowling Green. The folks at Trailer World almost laughed at the tiny Reese hitch we had planned to use in towing up to 7,000 pounds across America's mid-section.

7. The new Class III hitch (left) dwarfed the little Class II hitch (right) that had originally been on the van. We hadn't planned on installing a new hitch, but the delay was well worth it from a safety as well as practical standpoint. The Class II hitch, we were advised, was capable of efficiently and safely pulling the trailer, but not with a car on board. The old hitch had a gross rating of about 3,000 pounds.

8. Trailers for virtually any application, from transporting horses and livestock to moving collector cars and heavy equipment, are retailed by Trailer World from its Bowling Green, Ky., headquarters. Open and closed units are offered in a range of models and sizes, including custom made-to-order hauling systems.

9. The open trailer designated for our use made a good first impression. Obviously of high quality materials and construction, the trailer instilled confidence — it looked like it could handle any hauling chore we'd ever muster. Painted a gleaming black with red striping for accents, it's also a very handsome unit.

10. Trailer World, which was formerly known as Feldman Trailers, makes and sells a wide range of haulers. This little beauty is an open aluminum trailer. The light weight and anti-corrosion characteristics of aluminum, coupled with the material's high strength qualities, are making the aluminum trailer a popular choice for many car hobbyists, although there is a definite price premium over the standard steel unit.

11

12

13

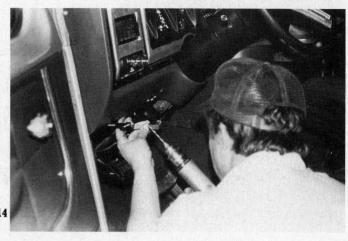

14

11. Since Trailer World was in the process of relocating its operation into new quarters, and its manufacturing operation was temporarily closed, Feldman's staff couldn't handle the mounting of a new hitch. We were directed to the local U-Haul dealer, a huge rent-all center with a full staff of trained service personnel. Rick Leitz, a mechanic at the U-Haul Center of Bowling Green in Bowling Green, Ky., is shown here mounting the new hitch.

12. Homer Cosby, another mechanic at the U-Haul Center of Bowling Green, wires up the rear plug for the trailer lights.

13. The new setup is installed and ready for service. It certainly looks a lot beefier.

14. Cosby installs the control unit for the new Kelsey brake control system, which was a must with the size trailer we had and the potential loads we could be hauling. The trailer was fitted with electrical brakes. Cosby used 12-gauge electrical wire in hooking up the brake control setup. We bought the hitch and the brake system from Trailer World, and both worked perfectly.

15. The brake control unit is connected to the host vehicle's master brake cylinder. The installation was handled quickly and efficiently.

bright and sunny, and considerably warmer. Our luck was bound to improve!

We encountered a small problem getting the nut off the hitch ball. *Cars & Parts'* dynamic duo — Editor Bob Stevens and Art Director Ken New — got a welcome bit of help from one large and very muscular truck driver, Wayne Steinman, who rigged a helper bar and finally pried the old nut loose. With the new ball firmly secured to the new hitch (a Reese-type Class III unit called Quality S, made by Hitch Manufacturing, Phoenix, Ariz), we were ready, or so we thought. After hooking up the electrical lifeline, which activated lights and the trailer's brakes, we bid our friendly hosts adios and headed for the state highway that would carry us to Missouri. We didn't get far.

About a mile away from Trailer World, we encountered our first stop, one of the main intersections of Bowling Green's business district. As we approached the red light, the brakes were applied and the electric-actuated binders on the trailer locked up. With the tires laying rubber, we screeched to a halt, totally under control, but embarrassed beyond belief. Every motorist and gas station attendant within earshot was glaring at us as if we'd committed some great sin. It was embarrassing, but we did learn that the brakes were operative ... and did they work!

One giant U-turn and we were on our way back to Trailer World. As we pulled up at the company's manufacturing complex, the trailer brakes once again locked

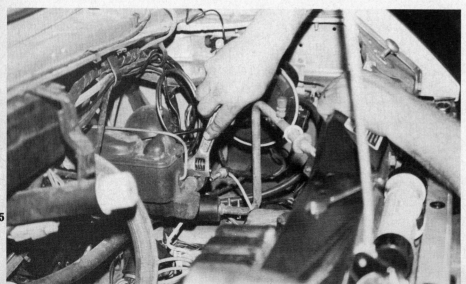

15

up and we pulled to a stop amidst squealing brakes and smoking tires. Richard Feldman himself came to our aid. First he reminded us that those special Goodyear trailer tires sold for about $80 each. He recommended that we return to his showroom on the other side of town and install a variable resistor, which would modulate the brakes in accordance to the load being carried. This resistor would match braking pressure to our load, assuring smoother, safer and certainly quieter stops.

Back at the new Trailer World showroom, we picked up a variable resistor and Don Owen helped us install it. With this in place, we again departed Trailer World, and this time we wouldn't be back. The resistor worked as advertised and we were finally on our way west.

The folks at Trailer World had been great during our lengthy and somewhat strenuous stay; and Richard Feldman and Don Owen were very cooperative. They're both very knowledgeable about their products, and trailering in general, and we certainly learned a lot during our 24 hours in Bowling Green.

Once out of Bowling Green and on our way to southwestern Missouri, we got an opportunity to really experience the trailer as a towing partner to our one-year-old Ford stretch van. We also had a chance to really look it over (our stay in Bowling Green had been dominated by our trou-

16. Once the new hitch and brake control were mounted, we returned to Trailer World to pick up the new car hauler. Our first problem involved the mounting of the ball on the new hitch. We had a devil of a time breaking loose the nut, finally resorting to a large pipe wrench and an impromptu "breaker bar". It finally broke loose, thanks to the volunteer help of a Trailer World truck driver, Wayne Steinman.

17. Warning labels affixed to the trailer near the tires caution that the wheel lugs should be periodically checked and tightened as

necessary, keeping them torqued to 90-95 ft./lbs. The lugs will loosen with use, we discovered, so it is very important to follow this safety recommendation.

18. The new trailer was finally about to be hauled away by our eager adventurers. In the days and weeks ahead we would discover that this very handsome unit would roll along with or without load as beautifully as it looked.

19. The special trailer service tires, F78-14ST Goodyear whitewalls, carry 50 pounds of pressure and are mated to

stylish automotive-type wheels. Being a tandem axle rig, there are, of course, four tires to monitor and four wheels to check regularly.

20. Grease fittings are easily accessible. The trailer should be lubed every 1,000 miles or three months.

21. New, Steinman and Owen hook up the trailer for its maiden voyage.

22. New (left) and Owen double check the rig after the trailer tongue and hitch are securely partnered and the safety chains hooked up.

bles with the hitch, the variable resistor, etc.).

The trailer performed better than we had expected. Our towing experience was admittedly somewhat limited, but both of us had driven a few rigs with trailers in tow. But this particular unit tracked with precision and handled bumps with ease, a tribute to its suspension system. The trailer is fitted with continuous service four-inch dropped axles with slipper springs. Special trailer service tires are mated to white spoke wheels with a standard automotive lug pattern.

The trailer's main frame consists of lightweight but high strength 2x6 box tubing. The entire trailer is dipped in a phosphoric acid bath before priming. After a primer coat, two layers of automotive-quality acrylic enamel are applied. Painted pinstripes then complete the cosmetic package.

Standard features on the tandem axle steel trailer include: Grease fittings on the equalizers for simplified lubrication; self-storing 6'3"x11" ramps with 21" of adjustment per ramp to accommodate narrow and wide track cars; electric brakes on one axle (optional on both axles for an extra $125); jack; four tiedown rings; color-coded wiring in conduit with a connector for hooking up to the tow vehicle; safety chains, 2" or 2⁵⁄₁₆" ball coupler; and black or red finish.

The basic trailer, as described, retails for about $2,200 in the 18-foot version (22-foot overall length). This is a nice size unit capable of handling most collector cars, large and small, with ease. The 78-inch spread between the fenders and the 6,800-pound gvw are more than adequate for most trailer needs.

In addition to the standard equipment and features already mentioned, Trailer World offers a number of options with its open trailers. In addition to brakes on both axles, there are 15" tires (14" standard); hydraulic surge brakes on one or both axles; full floor; ratchet tiedowns; spare wheel and tire; mount for spare wheel and tire; aluminum ramps; a wide range of winches; custom colors; tire racks (single or double row); electric brake control; variable resistor; stake pockets; tool box; wheel for jack in lieu of sand pad; diamond plate tracks; etc.

Trailer World also offers custom engineered and manufactured trailers for special applications.

The trailer assigned to *Cars & Parts* isn't loaded with options. The only accessories on this rig are the ratchet tiedowns, electric brake control, and the variable resistor.

But then the basic open steel trailer carries enough in the way of standard features to easily satisfy our needs. As it turned out in the days and weeks ahead, we were in for a pleasant experience with our new hauling partner.

With the van and trailer teamed together and working in unison, we headed west.

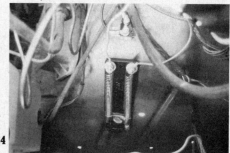

23. With everything checked out and in seemingly good order, we bid our hosts farewell and headed for the Kentucky state road that would carry us west. After locking up our trailer brakes at the first traffic light we hit in Bowling Green, we decided to return to Trailer World and install a variable resistor. This would afford more flexibility in adjusting brake action in response to trailer weight. Richard Feldman (right) explains the steps involved in installing a resistor, while Ken New listens attentively.

24. New (left) and Owen do a little under the hood work, installing the variable resistor. It took only 10 or 15 minutes.

25. The resistor, which was attached to the inner fender on the left side of the Cars & Parts van, is easily adjustable throughout a full range from "no load" to "heavy load". It worked extremely well and solved our problem permanently, as we would later confirm.

26. Don Owen (left) and Ken New perform a final check on the rig and its various fittings.

27. Richard Feldman (left) and Ken New pose for a final shot before the C&P crew heads west for the next leg in our journey. We weren't excited about the delay at Bowling Green caused by our inadequate preparations, but it was certainly an enriching learning experience, and one that would insure thousands of miles of trouble-free, safe and efficient trailering.

STAR SEARCH

Acres of Crown Victorias in Missouri and Arkansas

The weather was gorgeous, the scenery was spectacular and the van-trailer tandem performed flawlessly. The second day of our field mission was shaping up nicely. Yet we still had a lot of time to make up thanks to the extra 20 hours spent in Bowling Green, Ky. Before leaving town, though, we stopped at an auto parts store and picked up a four-way lug wrench (another item we'd failed to include in our travel gear).

With good roads and great weather, it really wasn't much of a problem expediting our travel between Bowling Green, Ky., and Branson, Mo., where we would spend Tuesday night. The scenery, especially the mountainous terrain of southwestern Missouri, was gorgeous. The Ozark Mountains were impressive, even at night.

Earlier in the day, the trip had been punctuated by an exhilarating trip across the mighty Mississippi River. We had a few anxious moments at first as we adjusted our position on the narrow two-lane roadway bridging the wide river to make sure we didn't crowd oncoming traffic or tangle with the mean-looking steel barrier lining the side of the road. Once a happy medium was established the rig tracked beautifully across the narrow structure. One dare not daydream when snaking an extra wide rig through tight quarters such as those presented by a bridge or tunnel. One can quickly gain sympathy and respect for those hearty men and women who drive the big rigs over all kinds of roads and in all types of weather.

We were religiously following all recommendations on the trailer, checking it regularly. All systems remained in proper order. We did tighten the wheel lug nuts periodically as prescribed by the manufacturer. Apparently everything was seating properly because the more we drove, the less we had to tighten the lug nuts. It would soon become merely a daily chore, and even at that very little tightening was needed. The trailer had truly impressed us with its tracking ability, its quiet operation, its seemingly unexcitable suspension system and its smooth running tires. Everything on the trailer appeared to be well engineered and manufactured. Nothing loosened up, other than the wheel lug nuts, which was expected, and everything remained intact.

We arrived in Branson in the Ozarks very late Tuesday night, checking into the modern, well endowed Branson Inn. We didn't have a trailer lock, so we backed the rig up tight against the building to help protect the trailer from traffic and possible thieves.

Wednesday morning brought us another wave of gorgeous weather, at least for mid-October. The air was crisp and clear and the sun was shining brightly. An hour or so of touring through the mountains

brought us to our destination, Lampe. This small town in southwestern Missouri is home to Ernie Peter, an old car collector, parts dealer and enthusiast with a real passion for 1955-56 Fords. He loves them all, and owns about 60 of them, including a number of Crown Victorias. Most of Peter's cars are parts cars, while some are restored and others are partially restored or in the process of restoration. A half dozen or so fully or partially restored 1955-56 Fords line the lawn to the front of his place. It's an impressive sight as one is wheeling through the mountains.

No one was home when we arrived, so we decided to wait. While we were parked alongside the road, a car buff pulled in to talk with us and look over our trailer. He was considering a trailer purchase and was keenly interested in how well our unit was behaving on the road. Naturally, we gave the trailer high marks in every department. This hobbyist, an acquaintance of Ernie Peter's, said that Ernie had gone up the mountain to pick up some lumber for the new house he was constructing, and that he should return soon. About half an hour later, Peter arrived in a vehicle that caught us by surprise. His daily driver turned out to be a 1956 Ford Ranchero. That's right, a '56 Ranchero!

Now everyone knows that Ford didn't introduce the half car/half truck Ranchero until the 1957 model year, so this '56 Ranchero has to be a custom rig. And it is. Starting life as a sedan, the '56 Ford was converted by Peter into a Ranchero-type vehicle. It even carries Ranchero nameplates on its doors.

Photos by Bob Stevens and Ken New

1. *As the Cars & Parts team headed west, eagerly pursuing its car search mission, stops were kept to a minimum to help make up for some of the 20 or so hours lost in Bowling Green. At every stop we checked the trailer connection, safety chains, trailer lights (brake, turn, stop, etc.) and tightened the wheel lug nuts. The Trailer World unit was doing its job nicely.*

2. *Crossing the mighty Mississippi River into Missouri is normally an exhilarating experience, but this time, with a wide and lengthy trailer in tow, it was a bit disconcerting. Keeping the trailer on the home side of the yellow line was a task, but one managed with the proficiency of a skilled, experienced trucker. We were proud of ourselves. Still, there was little margin for error.*

3. *Keeping the right fender and tire away from the guard rail was a chore that demanded intense concentration for the full run across the wide*

Mississippi River. The trailer literally fills the roadway from line to line on such narrow passageways. The trailer, though, responded beautifully, snaking tightly behind the van and reacting with precision to every movement of the tow vehicle.

4. *The tight confines of a bridge provided a good test for man and machine (and trailer). All passed with nary a tarnish to physical being or reputation.*

5. *After a fast track thru Missouri, we arrived in the beautiful Ozark Mountains in southwestern Missouri. It was quite late, closing on midnight, when we checked into a motel in Branson, Mo. The next morning we drove the short distance to Ernie Peter's place in Lampe, Mo., just north of the Arkansas border. We were greeted by a collection of 1955-56 Fords scattered across the front yard. An exciting sight!*

6. *Ernie Peter (left) chats with Ken New, art director for Cars & Parts, and the*

conversation is all 1955-56 Ford. Peter has a number of restored and partially restored cars, and acres of parts cars — and virtually all are '55 and '56 Fords.

7. *Just after arriving at Peter's house, we again checked the lug nuts on the trailer wheels. They again required some tightening.*

8. *Ernie's daily driver is a 1956 Ford Ranchero. Since Ford didn't introduce its Ranchero car/truck pickup until 1957, Ernie's Ranchero is obviously a custom creation. Rather stylish, though.*

9. *During our visit to the Peter residence, our host was hauling in lumber and other materials for a house he had under construction. The '56 Ranchero was ideal for his hauling chores. The customized '56 Ford allows one to envision what a Ranchero might have looked like had it been introduced one season earlier than it was.*

Once we were over the novelty of Ernie Peter's little truck, and the customary greetings and introductions were out of the way, we began our inspection of his fleet of mid-fifties Fords. Peter is an Ohio transplant who moved to the Ozarks to enjoy his car hobby in the beautiful solitude of the Missouri mountains. Also, he says, the taxes are low and government doesn't intrude on one's space, as is often the case in more metropolitan areas. The lack of congestion (people and traffic) is, indeed, inviting.

Several of Peter's Crown Vics were intriguing machines, including a couple of glasstops. But they weren't for sale. The only Crown Victoria he had that fit our qualifications was a reasonably solid black and white car. We carefully examined it and found that it contained a fair amount of plastic body filler, but would definitely be restorable with just an average amount of body work. The interior was relatively complete and certainly restorable. This example was equipped with the 272-cid V-8, automatic transmission and a radio. Plus — best of all — it had the desirable glasstop, making it one of only 1,999 Crown Victorias to leave the factory with

10.

10. Ernie Peter is a real mid-fifties Ford fanatic, and he's a walking encyclopedia of 1955-56 Ford information. His pride and joy is this 1956 Crown Victoria painted a two-tone black and pink. It's neat!

11. The car is fitted with a continental kit, and a lot of other goodies. The car is not for sale, so Ernie

placed a sign in the car's side window offering the car at $60,000 cash, thereby gently but firmly advising browsers to move along and not ask any silly questions.

12. Ernie Peter (left) offers Ken New a peek under the hood of his special Crown Vic.

13. The pink and black '56 Ford hosts a multi-carb

Thunderbird V-8. The car really scoots, Ernie says.

14. The pink and black Crown Vic is one of only 603 glasstops made in '56. The glasstops are, indeed, the rarest of the rare.

15. The midly customized pink and black Crown Vic carries a 140-mph speedometer at the center of its instrumentation package. Impressive!

11

12

13

14

15

16

18

17

19

20

21

16. One car that was legitimately for sale and did qualify as a prospect was this black and white '55 glasstop.

17. The car showed a lot of use, wear and general deterioration, but it was not beyond the scope of our proposed project.

18. The interior needed a total refurbishment, but was fairly complete and not beyond repair. The car had an automatic transmission and a radio.

19. Ernie Peter, Lampe, Mo., surveys the underhood area of his black and white glasstop. He seemed to be quite attached to all of his cars.

20. The black and white glasstop was powered by a well rested 272-cid V-8.

21. The glasstop was in reasonably decent condition, considering that it was original. It showed

some deterioration, but not all that much. Ford made only 1,999 Crown Victoria glasstops in the '55 model year, making it the rarest of all '55 Fords.

22. New checks the rear quarter for filler. The car had a fair amount of plastic in it, but no more than we anticipated. It really wasn't a bad deal at $5,000, with the glasstop and all. Our biggest drawback was the color scheme — black and white simply don't photograph that well. We still needed something stronger color-wise.

23. The numbers on the black and white glasstop matched up perfectly. It was, indeed, an original '55 Crown Vic glasstop (64B), painted raven black and snowshoe white (AE) with white vinyl and black bodycloth (AT) for the interior. It was tempting.

22

23

an original half-glass roof in 1955. A rare car when new, let alone some 30-plus years later. Also, all numbers (body style, engine, paint and trim codes, etc.) checked out. His asking price of $5,000 seemed reasonable. Our biggest reservation was the color scheme: Black and white paint treatment with a black and white interior. We noted the car in our mission diary, but we would pass on this one, at least for the time being.

Peter's other cars included some 60 parts cars scattered across his acreage. Most of them still had a few good parts to surrender. In a large building on the property, Peter had hundreds of parts for 1955 and 1956 Fords, including many mechanical items, radios, etc. He sells his used parts primarily by mail, with minimal walk-in trade.

Peter has an interesting situation with cars, parts, and related memorabilia all over the place. Walking onto his property is almost like stepping back in time to the peaceful fifties. We saw nothing newer than a '57 Plymouth anywhere on his acreage during our walking tour.

We also benefited from the tips Peter gave us in buying a good Crown Victoria. He told us what to look for in examining a body for problems, and what to expect in restoring a 1955-56 Ford. A couple of his tips sounded good. He advised us to use moly piston rings, and also to replace the rope rear seal with a newer style neoprene seal to prevent those pesky oil leaks inherent to the older Y-block Ford engines.

He also suggested that we use a later 292 camshaft or have a groove ground into the center journal to improve upper engine oiling. The older cams have a hole which usually got clogged after 50,000 miles or so, he warned. Our engine rebuilders cautioned against this camshaft modification, however, claiming that it would weaken the cam.

After a round of farewells, we bid Lampe, Mo. good-bye and took highway 13 south toward Arkansas. In a short time we found ourselves in Fayetteville looking over the impressive collection of Crown Victorias amassed by Dennis Mullens, a local fire department official.

24

26

25

27

28

29

30

31

24. Another "keeper" for Ernie Peter was an orange and white glasstop, another super nice car. It carried a price "sticker" of $35,000, which avoids a lot of nuisance from non-enthusiasts.

25. The orange and white '56 Crown Vic carries a rear-mounted continental kit. We found that there are many variations on the continental kit theme as applied to 1955-56 Fords.

26. The road to Ernie Peter's "back 40" is lined with parts cars, including a couple of non-Ford vehicles.

27. One car Ernie was serious about selling was this rather solid looking '57 Plymouth two-door sedan, priced at a reasonable $750.

28. Alongside the Peter residence is a large building housing numerous Ford parts. He deals in all kinds of used 1955-56 Ford parts — body, mechanical, interior, etc.

29. This Crown Victoria was past the stage of salvation, but it may still yield a few parts.

30. With its trunk lid supporting its hood, this Crown Vic may never see the road again, but it might help some of its more fortunate cousins gain a second lease on life.

31. At the rear of the lot, some 60 parts cars are stored, and most of them are Victorias, including several Crown Vics.

Having corresponded and conversed by phone with Mullens, we knew beforehand what to expect, yet we were still amazed at the collection of Crown Victorias we viewed in the fenced-in lot to the rear of Mullen's building on the outskirts of Fayetteville. Among the cars stored there were 28 glasstops. Incredible, but true. He had 21 glasstops of '55 vintage and seven from the 1956 model year. It was worth the trip just to see what Mullens had. And, he had a lot.

About every color combination was represented, including white two-toned with red, pink, purple, turquoise, orange, black, etc. The cars covered the full range from junker to jewel, and so did the prices. Most of the Crown Vics we surveyed, though, were definitely restorable. Some had migrated from the salty midwest and showed evidence of corrosion damage. Others were native to the south, and looked it!

We found several decent candidates, but many were just a bit more of a challenge than we wanted to drag home. Two glasstops, a pink and white number and a red and white car, attracted our attention. They carried the proper numbers and were basically complete, but we rejected them on the basis of condition. One other deteriorated glasstop, but one with a bit more potential, was a purple and white glasstop that needed floors, trunk, rocker panels and new bottoms for the rear quarters. But the color was right, and the glass in the top was in very good condition. Best of all, it came with a super solid black

32. *Shortly after leaving Peter's place, heading south for Arkansas, we drove past a used car dealership on the south side of Lampe that showcased a number of vintage cars. Among them were (from left) a 1964 Thunderbird hardtop priced at $3,250, a 1957 Mercury four-door, and a 1951 Pontiac two-door hardtop. Who could resist the temptation? We stopped and looked them over.*

33. *We proceeded from Missouri into Arkansas, bound for Fayetteville where we were to rendevous with Dennis Mullens, a very likable and knowledgeable hobbyist, seen here surveying the storage yard holding most of his Crown Victorias. Mullens, an officer with the Fayetteville Fire Department, might be considered king of the glasstops, since he owns 28 of them.*

34. *In phone conversations and correspondence with Mullens, he had promised a yard full of Crown*

Victorias, and he didn't disappoint us.

35. *A pink and white glasstop crowds the barbed-wire-topped fence surrounding Mullen's lot in Fayetteville. The car was a bit too much for our purposes, although it did have an original interior zip-up liner for the transparent top.*

36. *Close-up shows the original glasstop liner, a rare sight today.*

37. *Most of the cars Mullens has for sale are restorable. Surprisingly, we found a few cars from the midwestern states of Indiana, Illinois and Michigan.*

38. *A few of the Crown Vics in Mullens' yard have been there for a while, judging by the growth around, in and thru some of them.*

39. *Mullens is having this 1956 Ford glasstop, an all-black number, restored. It's shown here in a shop in Fayetteville. The car is amazingly sound and straight.*

40. One car that really intrigued us was this purple and white '55 Crown Victoria. It had the glasstop but needed a lot of work.

41. The interior of the purple and white candidate appeared to be restorable, and fairly complete. Missing parts, such as the radio and dash emblems, would be simple to replace.

42. The glasstop on Mullens' purple and white '55 was in very good condition, and would merely be cleaned if we acquired this car. All the special Crown Vic trim was either on the car or included in the deal.

43. The engine was grimy, untouched in a long time and missing many items, including the air cleaner. Not beyond hope, though.

44. Mullens was willing to make a package deal with the purple and white '55 Crown Vic, throwing in an extremely solid all black parts car to make one really super restored automobile.

45. The parts car, a local item, was rust-free and really solid. Believe it or not, someone had cannibalized this super strong Crown Vic to build another car. It was virtually gone from the cowl forward.

46. The all-black parts car had a really beautiful floor pan — not a rust hole anywhere.

47. The trunk, the temporary resting spot for the gas tank, was as strong and solid as the rest of the parts car. Using this shell, it would be possible to produce one really sharp glasstop out of the purple and white car.

48. One look at the inside of the trunk lid is evidence enough that this Crown Vic was spared any exposure to salt. If one needed a parts car with a decent shell from the cowl rearward, he'd be hard pressed to top this little number.

parts car, a genuine southern car with a superb floor, trunk, cowl, etc. The two made a good pair, and would produce one super finished glasstop Crown Vic. The two cars were priced as a package deal at $4,000, which we considered very reasonable. But we wondered about the expense and feasibility of splicing together two bodies to cash in on the solid structure of the black parts car and the sharp color combination and glasstop of the purple and white car. Still, it was the most promising candidate we'd interviewed to date. But, with assurances from Mullens that he could deliver the two cars to Ohio at a later date, we decided to pass on the deal for the time being.

Before leaving Fayetteville, we had an opportunity to view one of Mullens' personal Crown Vics, an all-black '56 glasstop, in a local restoration shop. The super slick beauty was as solid a car as we'd seen in our six months of searching for a project car. It wasn't for sale, which was probably just as well since it was all black.

A truly fine collection of cars has been assembled by Mullens over the years. The cars are stored in a well secured building and are fully protected from weather, vandals and thieves. Among the cars in the collection are a 1949 Mercury convertible, an MG, a Boss Mustang, a '56 Crown Vic glasstop, a pair of magnificent 1966-67 Shelby Mustangs, and others. We left Mullens' place envious of his situation. We were also a bit deflated in that we hadn't found the right combination of year, make, model, condition, equipment, and color.

But our visit to Mullens' provided even more information. Also, he had a number of select NOS parts available that could prove useful once we'd found a car. We made note of several key items. Of special interest was his stock of reproduction glass panels for the glasstop models, all priced at $1,000 a whack. The tops were made several years ago and it's highly unlikely that another run will be made. If we acquired a Crown Vic with a transparent top, we knew where to go for replacement glass.

We had thoroughly enjoyed our afternoon with Dennis Mullens. The experience was worth the long trip, even if we were about to leave empty-handed. We departed Fayetteville bound for Joplin, Mo., where we would spend a quiet, restful night before heading home the next morning.

As we rolled onto the freeway near Joplin on Thursday morning, we were naturally disappointed that our trip hadn't produced solid results, as evidenced by our empty trailer tagging along behind. It had been an educational, enjoyable, safe and rewarding trip, but we still fell short of the big payoff.

As we motored across Missouri, we checked local newspapers and car trader type publications, but came up dry on every score. We stopped in Rolla to briefly check out the Memoryville U.S.A. Museum owned and operated by George L. Carney. It was a worthwhile stop.

The museum is housed in a large, rambling building with several levels. The top level contains the actual museum where some 60 cars are on display, including some very rare automobiles. There's also a gift shop on the main level. On the next level down, a small town street has been recreated from the turn of the century, complete with a pawn shop, an apothecary, a barber shop, an art gallery, a photographer's studio, a printer's shop, a bank, a hardware store and others. It was quite interesting viewing all the artifacts of pioneer America.

Moving to the bottom level, we found George Carney himself, where he was personally supervising operations in the restoration shop. The museum not only restores its own cars, but also restores cars on contract from private individuals. The restoration shop was filled with cars at the time of our visit and we saw workmen finishing metal, rubbing out paint, and so on. The shop is a purely professional operation. Carney said that his shop is usually restoring between 15 and 20 vehicles at any one time. His shop restored the 1917 Federal truck owned by the late actor, John Wayne.

In addition to his restoration business, and the museum, Carney sponsors the annual Ozark Extravaganza each September. The show and swap meet, now several years old, got off to a slow and very expensive start, Carney relates, but has now become very popular and successful.

During our visit we mentioned the main purpose of our trip, and how we had failed to connect with just the right car. Carney's daughter-in-law and a couple of men in his restoration shop kindly produced a few leads for us involving local car collectors, but we were unable to cash in on any of them. We did appreciate their generous assistance, though.

After a second quick trip through the museum and the row of old fashioned shops, we again pointed the van eastward and headed for home. We'd be in St. Louis by noon, and home in Sidney, Ohio by late that evening.

We never made it!

49

51

50

49. *We were really captivated by a couple of the cars found at Mullens' place, but we decided to pass on them, at least for the time being. We still hadn't quite found what we were looking for when we originally launched the project, so we turned east and headed for home. The trailer was working out beautifully, and actually drawing more attention than our fancy Cars & Parts van. We answered numerous questions about* the trailer. We were truly delighted with our experiences with our new hauler, so it was easy to brag about it. At this juncture, we're in a rest area just east of Joplin, Mo., parked alongside a pickup truck from California pulling a junior-size car hauler.

50. *In Rolla, Mo., we stopped for a brief visit with George L. Carney and his Autos of Yesteryear, the Memoryville, U.S.A.* Museum. We were impressed by Carney's courteous and competent staff, and his impressive restoration facilities. The 60-vehicle museum is well worth the price of admission.

51. *We discovered somewhere in western Missouri that we'd lost our temporary trailer license tag, but we decided, being out-of-staters, that our best bet would be to push on and take our chances. We were never stopped.*

1

STAR SEARCH

It had been an enjoyable but exhaustive trip, our little venture to Arkansas and Missouri in search of a restoration project car for *Cars & Parts*. We'd seen a lot, and we'd learned a lot. We'd also met some very nice hobbyists, toured one museum and visited two restoration shops. The *Cars & Parts* van and the Trailer World car hauler had performed flawlessly. The weather had cooperated, and the scenery had been very nice, even spectacular at times.

A Crowning Victory!

2

3   4

Yet there was one ingredient missing from an otherwise perfect trip. The trailer was still empty!

As we pulled into St. Louis shortly after noon on Thursday, the fourth day of our excursion, we were both anxious to get home that evening, while still a little disappointed that we didn't have more to show for our efforts. In downtown St. Louis, to the eastern side of the city, we departed the eastbound freeway to gas up at a Shell station. It's always dangerous pulling into a gas station with the *Cars & Parts* van, especially when you're in a hurry and not really interested in idle conversation with inquisitive attendants and motorists. Usually we face questions like: "What kind of parts do you sell?"

When we're on a schedule, we try to avoid prolonged conversations, and normally one question will lead to another, and so on. It's not that we're unfriendly, and certainly we'd spend time with genuine car hobbyists, but usually we get tangled with people who aren't even remotely interested in old cars. Since our name, *Cars & Parts*, is not all that identifiable,

5

6

we can often waste a lot of time explaining who we are and what we do. An introduction, of course, leads to additional questions and further discussion, wasting even more time.

Well, at this particular gas station, a well-intentioned but persistent individual was asking the usual series of questions. Being polite, I answered his questions as briefly and honestly as possible. Then he asked what we were doing hundreds of miles away from our home station. I explained, in part, that we were searching for a project car for our magazine, at which he quickly rattled off several cars he knew were for sale in St. Louis. None was appropriate, and I then explained that we were looking for a specific type of car, either a 1955-56 Ford Crown Victoria or a 1963-64 Chevy Impala Super Sport convertible. That stopped him cold. I paid for the gas and headed out the door. But he followed me.

My compatriot had already pulled the van away from the pumps to let cars waiting behind us pull into the self-serve island. As I walked slowly to the van, our new acquaintance suddenly recalled a nice old Crown Vic for sale on the other

1. The grand winner in our 10-month search for a solid, running, restorable and presentable project car is this pretty red and white 1955 Ford Crown Victoria. We stumbled onto this one quite by accident in St. Louis, Mo., on our way home to Ohio. It was a chance encounter that produced some real dividends; the subject of our lengthy search was at last in our possession.

2. Wearing its crown proudly, our new project car posed for many photos during its first few days with its new owners, like parents with a newborn child. It's always fun buying a vintage car, even if you're buying it for someone else. This example had received bits

and pieces of restoration work over the years, but it was still basically original, except for mirrors and a few other items. It was an original red and white Crown Victoria.

3. The interior, still pretty much in unrestored original condition, was a bright and refreshing red and white, complementing the exterior two-tone paint scheme. The car was equipped with only a few options, including an automatic transmission, a three-speed Fordomatic, and a radio.

4. From all appearances, the engine was an original item, a stock 272-cid V-8. It ran very well, impressing us with the way it started, idled, throttled up, etc. No evidence of major problems, either.

5. Loaded up and ready for the trip back east, the Crown Victoria looked good sitting on the Trailer World car hauler, which was still performing up to specs, and still drawing a crowd at every stop. The entire team — van, trailer and car — were nicely color coordinated.

6. We were excited about this little number from the moment the garage door swung open and we saw it resting comfortable in the corner of the owner's three-car garage. It was low on options, but received high marks for its overall condition. It actually looks sharper here than in real life, as photos can conceal many flaws.

7. *The 1955 Crown Victoria emerges from its winter haven; it had been tucked into the corner of the owner's garage for a few months of winter hibernation. We knew immediately that it was the car for us, if its credentials proved genuine.*

8. *The data plate was important to us, and one of the first items we checked in examining the car. It read properly, indicating that the car was indeed a real 1955 Crown Victoria hard top, body style 64A, and that it was factory finished in torch red and snowshoe white.*

7

side of town. He couldn't remember the owner's name, or where he lived, but he did recall that the guy worked at a barber shop in a motel on the far northwest side of St. Louis. No, he couldn't remember the name of the motel either, but he did give us directions to its approximate location.

It meant backtracking about 25 miles or so, but our well-meaning friend was sincere and we owed it to him, and to us, to check out this lead before giving up altogether. Our chance encounter with this likable individual, Jim Williamson, was about to send us in the wrong direction, temporarily, but it would be worth it.

Normally one might be a bit suspicious of a total stranger in such a situation. It would be a great prank to send two out-of-towners on a wild goose chase halfway through St. Louis. And, it would be just our luck to fall prey to such mischief. But Williamson seemed to take a genuine interest in our trip, our objective and our problems. And he knows cars. He's the owner of Jim's Auto Detailing, a private shop at 6201 Famous near the Hampton and I-44 interchange in St. Louis. His firm performs all types of auto detailing. He had stopped at the Shell station on his lunch break to have a soda with a friend of his who worked at the station. Again, it was a total coincidence, and our instincts told us to check it out before leaving Missouri. We pulled back onto the freeway, but this time heading west.

We followed Williamson's instructions and traveled west, then north, then south, arriving at the business strip of St. Ann, a small suburban community to the northwest side of St. Louis. We found ourselves in a nice area near the airport. We finally found the motel, or at least so we thought (it was the one across from the McDonald's restaurant — the only directions we had). We drove and then walked around the motel and couldn't find a barber shop, though, not even in the basement. A quick trip into the lobby and we were greeted with the information that a

8

barber shop was located about 100 yards behind the motel. We entered the barber shop with high expectations, and a lot of apprehension.

"Do either of you own a Crown Victoria?" I asked the two barbers, who were busily trimming a couple of customers. "Yes, I do," the younger of the two responded, very reluctantly. "Why?" he asked, almost indignantly.

His hesitation was understandable. Here's this total stranger standing there asking questions about his rare collector car. I introduced myself and briefly explained my mission. "Well, who told you about my car, and who said it was for sale," he inquired. I related our encounter with Jim Williamson. But our barber friend, Bill Cook, insisted he'd never heard of a Jim Williamson, or his auto detailing shop.

I refreshed his memory: "He said that he talked with you about your Crown Vic at a car show early last summer, and that you had indicated that you would sell the car for the right money." He suddenly remembered Williamson, and his conversation with the auto detail man. Then he informed us that he had been more or less kidding Williamson, and the car really wasn't for sale.

We were dismayed, having apparently wasted another hour or so. Noting our disappointment, Cook offered to let us view the car and hinted that he might consider

selling it in view of our special mission. As a former subscriber and occasional newsstand buyer of *Cars & Parts*, he professed an interest in our project. Great, we were in business!

As he cut hair, we listened to him describe the car. It sounded ideal for our purposes. There was only one problem. He was booked solid with appointments until the shop closed at 8:00 p.m. that evening. It was now only 3:00 p.m. Even though his house was only a few miles from the shop, he couldn't break away even for 15 minutes to show us the car; and his wife was working until 8:00 p.m. that evening also. In fact, he was to pick her up at a hair salon on the way home. After a brief conference, between the author and his companion, Ken New, art director, we decided to spend the night at the motel in front of the barber shop, and wait to see this Crown Vic later that evening. We checked into the motel, then visited a local restoration shop specializing in 1955-57 Chevys, and drove through a few car dealerships (we enjoy some of the new cars, too). Finally, quitting time at the barber shop arrived, and we followed Cook to his residence. It was worth the wait. As Cook opened the garage door, a gleaming red and white '55 Crown Victoria appeared almost magically before our eyes. At first look, we knew we'd found our car. As we approached the car, Ken and I looked at each other and knew instantly that we had lucked upon a car that appealed to both of us and satisfied our objectives, at least on the surface.

Bill started the car (it hadn't been run in weeks, yet it fired after a reasonable number of cranks). It seemed to run particularly strong. It was crammed into the corner of his three-car garage, so he pulled it out into the middle of the garage so we could get a little more light on it and really inspect it. The more we examined the car, and the closer we got, the better we liked it. It was sound, solid, and presentable. It was the kind of car that many peo-

ple wouldn't even think of restoring. Just drive it and enjoy it as is!

Yet we could readily see its weaknesses: Faded upholstery and carpet, torn headliner, inoperative radio, defunct washers, busted lenses, plenty of body putty, dented stainless, cracked steering wheel, undetailed engine compartment, incorrect shade of red paint (poor match between body and roof), pitted and scratched chrome, etc. It could use a little of everything, we determined, and lots of some things.

Since it was a little more car than we initially envisioned, and certainly more presentable than we had anticipated, we had to spend a little more than we expected, but were able to remain within our projected budget limitations.

One of our main concerns was the car's authenticity. We carefully examined the identification plate. It was genuine, alright, and had even been covered with paint during an earlier restoration effort. The ID plate, commonly known as the

9. *Aligning the car properly in front of the ramps, the driver proceeds slowly and surely onto the trailer. Loading was really much easier than we anticipated. The trailer, incidentally, hardly budged under the weight (about 3,400 pounds, even with lots of plastic body filler), and would actually perform better loaded than*

empty once on the highway.

10. *One very pleasant feature of the Trailer World unit is that a car's doors will clear the low profile fenders, facilitating easy exit (and access).*

11. *The self-storing ramps on the Trailer World trailer were a cinch to work. A cotter pin is popped free and the*

holding rod is removed; then the ramp is pulled out and the forward end placed over the lip.

12. *The rod is then inserted back thru its holes, aligning it with the end of the ramp so that the rod runs directly through a sleeve in the end of the ramp. The cotter pin is reinserted and it's ready for use. After the car is loaded, the process is reversed to secure the ramps for travel.*

13. *We balanced the load (from front to rear) as best as possible. The trailer remained stable and didn't seem to be adversely influenced by where the car was situated.*

14

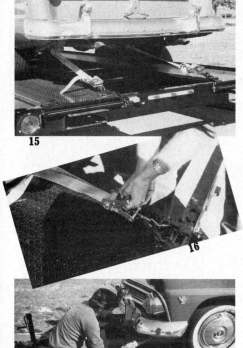

15

16

17

18

14. *The trailer is low enough to the ground to permit simple entry and exit from the car. We checked the wheel lug nuts for tightness before leaving St. Louis, and several times between there and Sidney, Ohio. The load put an extra strain on the trailer, obviously, as the wheels required tightening a couple of times. No real problem, of course, as the wheels remained secure at all times and never posed any problems.*

15. *The ratchet style tie-downs are the only type to use. They're easy to hook up and very easy to tighten down. They also require periodic inspection and possible adjustment while on an extended run, but they work very nicely.*

16. *Just a couple of snaps of the ratchet and the tie-down is pulled taut.*

17. *After the tie-down straps are tightened, excess webbing is gathered and wrapped around the taut lines and then tied in a knot so they won't flap in the breeze.*

18. *A few Cars & Parts readers spotted our van as we were loading up in St. Louis and stopped to chat, and investigate our presence hundreds of miles from home. We met a lot of nice "car people" on our trip.*

"patent plate", showed the serial number U5UW169656. This translates as follows: U = engine code for 272-cid V-8; 5 is the model year (1955); second U is the code for the assembly plant, Louisville, Ky.; W is the body style code for Crown Victoria; and the 169656 is the sequential production number.

The other code on the bottom of the plate reveals even more about this specific car. The first entry, 64A, tells us the car is a Fairlane Crown Victoria with the solid top (64B is the number for the Crown Victoria with the glasstop). The next code, RE, reveals the exterior paint scheme as a two-tone torch red and snowshoe white. The next item, L, stands for white and red vinyl trim scheme. The rest of the code, 9, G and 36169P, all relate to the car's production code.

Obviously, everything checked out. It was the right year, make, model, body style, color combination, trim scheme, etc. We huddled out of earshot and decided to make our move. It was the car for us. An offer, some friendly discussion, a counter-offer and some more friendly discussion and we had struck a bargain.

A CROWNING VICTORY! We finally had our project car.

We bid our friendly host good evening and returned to the motel, where we spent our first truly peaceful night since leaving home four days earlier. We were filled with the enthusiasm and satisfaction of our success.

The following morning, we were up early and off to the nearest bank. Some five hours later, the money wired from headquarters had arrived and been deposited in the seller's bank account. We loaded the car on the trailer with the ease and speed of experienced veterans. The self-storing ramps worked nicely and the car moved onto the trailer with absolutely no problem. We used the ratchet type tie-downs we bought at Trailer World, and were we glad we selected this type. The ratchet style hooks up cleanly and tightens easily. It's good advice to check the tie-downs at every stop and adjust them if necessary. They'll loosen a little, but not enough to cause problems. The rig looked good, all hooked up and ready for the road. After a full week of traveling, we were also ready for the road.

Our friendly and courteous barber friend gave his Crown Vic a final look and handed over the title. We had already examined this very important document and made sure that the VIN number on the title matched, digit-for-digit, with the number on the patent plate, and that the proper signatures and notations, including a notary stamp, had been made. We were in business.

Back on the road, we immediately noticed that the trailer tagged along behind with nary a whisper. We weren't sure how the unit would perform with a full load, but we were surprised to discover a load actually improved the trailer's tracking ability, straight line performance and even its braking capabilities. We did adjust the variable resistor before leaving St. Louis to compensate for the load on board. The suspension system proved more than adequate for our 3,400-pound load, showing no ill effects even on some rough roadway encountered east of the Missouri line in western Illinois.

The miles flashed by as we headed for home at maximum legal speed, and with only the very minimum number of stops

19. The loading exercise was completed without incident. All systems on the van and trailer were checked out (brakes, lights, etc.) and we were ready for the open road, once again. The rig looks sharp, all hooked up and buttoned down for the long ride home.

20. Before we left St. Louis, the car's former owner, Bill Cook, stopped by to take one final, lingering look at his Crown Victoria. It's tough separating a man from his car.

19

20

STAR SEARCH

Analyzing our prize!

1

dictated by the need for fuel or food. While we eagerly sped toward home, our thoughts were mixed between a homecoming after a week on the road, and the new acquisition following on the trailer behind us.

The car we had settled on, and found quite by chance, was a good one with a strong health record. The car was originally from Kansas, a normally dry section of the country and one noted for its low-corrosion cars. The Crown Vic then migrated to Jefferson City, Mo., with its second owner, and then to St. Louis with owner number three. Cook acquired the car from its third owner. We, then, were the car's fifth guardian.

We were really grateful for the trailer we had with us, since the car was suffering from a few problems, including a leaking rear brake line and a couple of hoses that were showing severe signs of cracking and deterioration. It's possible that the car could have been driven back to Ohio with a few minor repairs, but it was certainly a relief knowing that we didn't have to find out if it would make it or not. All it had to do was travel a few feet onto our waiting trailer.

The fifth and final day of our venture was coming to a close, and successfully. We crossed Illinois into Indiana and headed for home sweet home in southwestern Ohio. This time we'd make it!

1. Safe and sound back in Cars & Parts' hometown of Sidney, Ohio, the newly acquired project car is displayed in front of the magazine's headquarters. The Crown Vic drew a lot of attention.

2. The car was really rather presentable, and even looked near show quality from a distance. Up close, though, the faults were quite apparent.

2

26

3

3. It's easy to see why the Crown Victoria of 1955-56 is such a popular model with car collectors, both Ford and non-Ford enthusiasts. Its truly rakish appearance and sporty appointments qualify it as one of the most memorable Fords of the fabulous fifties. We were ready to get started on the restoration project, anxious to restore this aging gem to its former beauty.

4. The special Crown Victoria trim, including the tiara strip splitting the top, is in very good to excellent condition. A few pieces need some attention, but we are in generally good shape in this department.

4

Upon our arrival back home in Sidney, Ohio, we were greeted by an encouraging and excited staff. Everyone, including the publisher, was impressed by the project car we'd brought home. It really did look quite presentable. The novice, in fact, would be hard pressed to criticize the car in terms of its condition. It was, to be certain, a flashy fifties Ford that could be owned, driven and enjoyed as is.

But then we aren't novices, nor are we content to leave this 1955 Ford Crown Victoria "as is". That is not the purpose of our project. Instead, we're going to have this solid, complete and very desirable collector car disassembled, restored to near original specs and reassembled. Of course, we will follow the car through its various restoration phases and chart its progress, while at the same time presenting a series of restoration articles, including some interesting and valuable "how-to" pieces. With this criteria in mind, we were still comfortable with the car we'd found and hauled back from Missouri.

After the excitement of our new purchase wore off, we began to view it with more of a critical eye. The closer we looked, the more our car looked like a project car. The old '55 Ford, now code named Vicky, was full of surprises. No real problems, as we were scheduling a major restoration anyway, but as we examined the car we discovered that it indeed needed some major work, including panel replacement.

We took a couple of hours one afternoon and examined our project car in minute detail. We found loads of plastic body filler throughout the car, although the greatest concentration was in the rocker panels and the rear quarters. However, plastic was also found around the headlights, on the underside of the car, in the rear body section and around the wheel wells on the front fenders. There seemed to be a little plastic everywhere, and a lot of plastic in a half dozen or so spots. New panels, and some metal and lead work would cure these ills.

Naturally, we had planned on a fair amount of body work, and a complete stripping of the body, total paint removal, application of a primer coat and the spraying of a finish coat of new paint. We'd also make sure that all body panels are properly fitted and aligned, as well as doors, hood and trunk lid. The body and its major components would be adjusted and shimmed as necessary, and new mounting hardware would be used as needed.

All chrome and stainless trim will be removed. Bumpers, door handles and other chrome items will be polished, or replated if necessary. If not capable of being plated, they'll be replaced. Stainless pieces will be straightened, cleaned and buffed, except for a couple of items too dented or damaged to be repaired.

Most, if not all, of the nameplates and emblems will be replaced, preferably by new-old-stock pieces, although reproduction may be used where availability and price considerations favor the latter. All of the emblems were weathered and faded beyond hope, and their chrome housings were pitted and marred to the point of no return.

The glass is all in fairly good shape on Vicky, although it will probably be re-

moved and polished, and new weather-stripping installed. Also, a small bulls-eye in the windshield will be repaired.

The whitewall tires that were on the car when we bought it are in decent shape with lots of tread showing. We'll just give them a good cleaning once the major restoration phases are completed. The wheel covers are very clean and straight requiring only a good polishing. The wheel cover centers, however, are another story. They are faded and in need of replacement.

Moving inside, we find that the Crown Victoria requires a full refurbishment, including new door panels, new upholstery, new headliner, new carpeting, etc. The sun visors and rear shelf also need help. The Crown Victoria trim on the inside is in good condition for the most part — the same as those exterior trim pieces exclusive to the Crown Victoria. A few items need replating or replacement, and the seat side shields and select other parts will be refinished. The radio doesn't work, neither does the windshield washer system. They'll be fixed. The clock, also inoperative, will likely remain so. The heater control has a broken lever and will receive appropriate attention.

5. *The hood ornament is pitted and scratched, making it a good candidate for rechroming.*

6. *Emblems, such as the Fairlane script and the Ford insignia on the hood, will probably be replaced with new-old-stock parts, or reproduction, depending on availability and cost.*

7. *Fortunately, the hard-to-find and expensive trim pieces exclusive to the Crown Victoria are in good condition and usable with little or no work.*

8. *Metal areas around moldings and at the edges of panels, doors, etc.,* appear to be the worst in terms of rust, at least on the surface.

9. *One can easily determine the presence of body filler by viewing the rear quarters at an angle, and noting the waves — just like the ocean.*

10. *More evidence of unchecked corrosion.*

11. *Paint and metal are separated by plastic body filler in several spots. The wheel covers are solid and straight, and will merely be polished, although the emblems will be replaced by NOS or repro substitutes.*

12. *The headlight pods show evidence of terminal corrosion.*

13. *The most severe rust damage was easily spotted in the rear quarters, a common spot for early rust damage.*

14. *Plastic filler falls out of the rear quarters, with a little help from a probing screwdriver. The extent of the plastic repairs surprised us; there was considerably more repaired damage than we had at first thought. Since it was all going to be properly repaired, it really didn't matter. We had planned on putting in new panels anyway.*

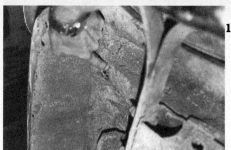

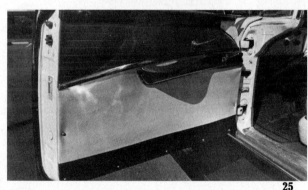

15. Paint is chipping off in sizable chunks. The bubbling on the door, of course, also indicates problems trying to work their way to the surface.

16. Although still basically a solid car, holes and other damage from rust and age were also discovered underneath. As we would find out later on in the project, there was even more damage underneath than we realized.

17. Some trim pieces are dented, scratched and otherwise damaged beyond repair. Most, though, will be straightened, buffed and reused.

18. We'll need a new Fordomatic script emblem for the trunk lid, although the trim piece across the bottom of the trunk lid is in excellent condition and may have been replaced at some time.

19. Ford crest on the trunk lid is due to be trashed, and the trunk lock is inoperative. Access to the luggage compartment is gained via a screwdriver rather than a key.

20. It appears that a former owner did some paint touchup right over rust and other damage. The license plate holder screams for help.

21. It isn't any better on the other side.

22. Close inspection of the car's trim moldings revealed the early signs of cancer. Early detection is still the best remedy, for cars as well as people.

23. Door handles are a toss-up as to whether they're replated or replaced with NOS or reproduction. Price will be the determining factor here.

24. New taillight housings and lenses are on the parts list. Nothing looks worse on a freshly painted car than cracked and dull lenses, and bad chrome.

25. Door panels have obviously been tampered with in an early restoration attempt. Replacement panels of original design will replace ones on the car.

26. Rockers show lots of damage, repair and more damage. We'll probably need new rocker panels.

27. Door sill moldings will have to go. Nothing could be done to save these, at any price.

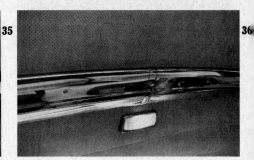

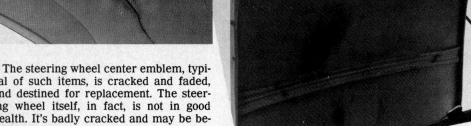

The steering wheel center emblem, typical of such items, is cracked and faded, and destined for replacement. The steering wheel itself, in fact, is not in good health. It's badly cracked and may be beyond repair.

The speedometer, odometer and gauges all work and seem to be in proper order, although they'll be fully checked out before we're through.

Moving along to the mechanical side of Vicky, we find that most major components — radiator, carburetor, fuel pump, water pump, oil pump, etc. — will require rebuilding or replacement. The engine, of course, will receive a complete overhaul, including conversion to lead-free fuel operation. The engine will be removed, torn down, rebuilt with new or reconditioned parts, balanced, reassembled and re-installed. The engine compartment will be detailed and new hoses, cables and belts will be installed. Wiring, too, will be upgraded with new items.

28. New emblem for the steering wheel is on the shopping list, and the wheel itself is badly cracked and may be beyond repair.

29. Dash is in pretty decent shape, but will receive a general cosmetic refurbishment. Transmission indicator reveals one of the Crown Vic's few options, the three-speed Fordomatic transmission.

30. Control knobs are intact and decent, needing only a good cleaning.

31. Cosmetic work across the dash will improve things dramatically. The radio needs work, and the heater control is busted. Clock doesn't work either, but we'll probably leave that as a "decoration only" accessory.

32. Ford script and V-8 emblems on the glove box lid could probably be reused, but minor pitting may encourage their replacement.

33. Seat side shields will be stripped, primed and repainted.

34. The little sewn-in panel on the driver's side is in amazingly good condition. Carpeting will be replaced, as will non-original floor mats.

35. Headliner is decent to the front. Sun visors will need reworking.

36. Most of the interior trim is in pretty good condition. The roof on a Crown Vic is simply gorgeous, on either side.

37. Headliner toward the rear of the car is separating. Several stains are also present. Since the badly faded upholstery, carpeting, door panels, sun visors and rear shelf require replacement, the headliner might as well go too.

38. Hood is clean and solid, but will be stripped, primed and repainted.

39. *New battery cables are needed, and an original style battery may displace this aftermarket unit. The car has been converted to 12-volt electrics, and we may allow that non-original feature to remain intact.*

40. *Hoses are cracked and generally deteriorated. All hoses and belts will be replaced with new ones.*

41. *Washer system is incomplete and inoperative.*

42. *The engine, complete and in good running condition, will be removed, totally rebuilt and re-installed. Major components, such as the radiator, fuel system (carburetor, fuel pump, etc.), oil pump, and so on, will be rebuilt or replaced. The engine will also be made compatible with lead-free gasoline.*

43. *The first step in our project, after the acquisition of the automobile, was the research involved in authenticating the car's restoration. We started by gathering all available factory shop manuals, owner's manual, sales literature, etc.*

The starting motor and generator will be rebuilt to original specs, and the gas tank will be removed, cleaned, sealed and re-mounted. All fuel and brake lines will be checked and replaced as necessary. Speaking of brakes, the entire system will be refurbished. The front end will also be rebuilt, and the suspension will be attended to as deemed necessary. The transmission and rear end, both of which are working fine but are leaking, will be merely inspected and resealed.

And then, after going to all that trouble and expense, we're going to give the car away!

PART TWO

The Restoration Begins

1. *Situated adjacent to U.S. 30, the three buildings of the Classic Car Centre in Warsaw, Ind., contain more than 27,000 sq. ft. of space, with the latest in restoration and repair equipment.*

2. *Vicky, the Cars & Parts project car, was afforded a warm and enthusiastic reception.*

For the true car hobbyist, entering the Classic Car Centre in Warsaw, Ind., is a little like Alice stumbling into Wonderland. It's the adult toy store that offers just about everything a hobbyist could want.

Right up front there's a spacious, well-appointed showroom where a dozen or so restored collector cars are showcased in carpeted, air conditioned comfort. Most, if not all, of its inventory is devoted to antique, classic, special interest and modern sports and luxury cars.

The showroom also houses an accessories department where numerous automotive-related items are offered. Adjacent to the showroom in the same building is a fully-equipped service department for routine maintenance and some special mechanical restoration projects.

Behind the showroom in a separate building are the Classic Car Centre's machine shop and body shop. Behind that facility in still another building is the restoration shop, which caters to the more involved, more complex restorations where a rare, exotic automobile, such as a 1910 Packard or 1932 Rolls-Royce, is being completely refurbished in painstaking detail.

The 27,000-square-foot facility offers collector car sales, service, parts and accessories, body work, engine rebuilding and complete restoration. It is a full-service facility, with the latest equipment.

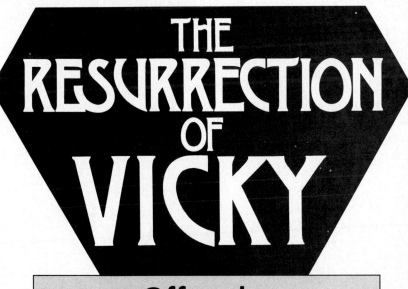

THE RESURRECTION OF VICKY

Off to the restoration shop!

3. *The service department handles all types of automotive repair work and accepts everything from Model A Fords needing a lube job to a modern Ferrari requiring some fine tuning. The service department is located in the main building, alongside the showroom.*

4. *The machine shop is impressive. It's very clean and extremely well organized ... and it's maintained that way on a continuing basis.*

5. *Very expensive and highly sophisticated equipment fills the machine shop. It's the best-equipped engine shop we've visited.*

6. *A special room within the machine shop is reserved for engine balancing. Special equipment enables trained technicians to thoroughly balance an engine way beyond factory specs, producing a stronger, more powerful and much more durable engine. Our Crown Vic's 272-cid V-8 will be treated to the full scope of balancing services.*

7. *To insure the best in paint application, the body shop sports a paint booth employing a European mist/vacuum downflow system in "an environment so pure that air particles are reduced to an incredible five microns," according to Classic Car Centre literature.*

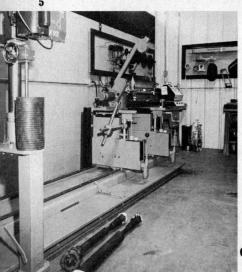

8

9

10

2

11

8. *A Camaro awaits final detailing in the body shop's holding area.*
9. *Terry Ritter (left), body shop manager, helps Tom Cripe rub out a fresh coat of paint on a 1963 Corvette.*
10. *A Model A coupe body towers over the body shop as its various components are worked on at ground level.*
11. *Ritter does some finishing work on a Porsche "whale tail".*
12. *Tom Cripe welds a patch into a Model A fender.*

Obviously, we were impressed by the Classic Car Centre and its various operations. We had decided to visit it when the local restorer in our hometown area who had agreed to handle our Crown Vic project sold his building, auctioned his equipment and car parts and moved to the Carolinas. Since he was the last professional restorer in the Sidney, Ohio, area who could and would handle such a project, we were forced to scout beyond our logical boundaries for someone else as capable and agreeable.

Our search was relatively brief as one primary consideration was logistics. We couldn't stray too far from home because we wanted frequent access to the car during its restoration for photographic and reporting purposes. The primary goal of our project from the very start was the development of a series of articles on restoring a vintage car, and that requires close and frequent contact with the car and the specialists handling the restoration. Warsaw is only about 2½ hours from Sidney, so we decided to choose it for Vicky's restoration after an extended visit during which we viewed the premises, the equipment, and talked with the people who would be doing the work.

It was the people who really convinced us our decision was right, beginning with owner Jerry Ferguson, who had started Classic Car Centre about a year earlier, in 1986. As we were introduced to the Centre's top people, we became certain our choice was a good one. After all, we would be hanging around, peeking over shoulders, taking pictures, asking questions, and otherwise generally being under foot for the next few months as the car was restored. We could tell that everyone we met really did want to have us around.

We also were pleased to see the latest in modern equipment and technology everywhere we went. Classic Car Centre certainly is equipped to handle anything that might be necessary in restoring Vicky.

After our tours and discussions, we were anxious to get our 1955 Crown Victoria to the Centre for a complete inspection, so we could get our restoration project underway. As our Vicky entered the body shop for dismantling, she joined a rather impressive array of motor cars entrusted to the Centre for restoration. Among them were a 1930 Chevy coupe, 1930 Ford Model A coupe, 1951 Packard convertible, 1938 Ford panel truck, 1938 Packard, 1954 Lincoln convertible, 1955 Thunderbird, 1972 Jaguar XKE convertible, etc.

We'd already learned quite a bit about our car and our project needs, but we still had a lot to learn about Crown Victorias, about our specific car, about body work, about engine rebuilding, about ....

And, as we're about to discover, we've got good teachers!

1. *Up on the hoist, the Crown Vic sheds its body parts as Gary Odiorne (left) and John St. Cin of the body shop drop the front bumper.*

2. *Away from the front sheet metal, the grille still looks good and straight.*

3. *Cars & Parts Editor Bob Stevens thumbs the dust away from the grille. It looked pretty good. We later decided a rechrome wasn't needed and a good polishing would suffice.*

THE RESURRECTION OF VICKY

Stripping the car and diagnosing its needs

The trip delivering Vicky to Warsaw was uneventful, as it should have been. We merely loaded her on the trailer and headed in a northwesterly direction. In less than three hours after departing Sidney, we had Vicky unloaded and in a bay of the body shop, where disassembly and inspection would take place.

Terry Ritter, the accommodating body shop manager, assigned John St. Cin and Gary Odiorne to the task of removing all exterior trim and the interior from our car. With two professionals wielding the tools, we were about to experience a real exercise in stripping a car.

Both Odiorne and St. Cin have been around cars most of their lives, and that was apparent when they started in on Vicky. The first items removed were the bumpers and side moldings, those thin stainless strips decorating the fenders, doors and rear quarters. No real problems here, except that care had to be exercised to save as many molding clips as possible. Some of the trim clips on the Crown Vic are nearly impossible to find, we had been warned, so we saved as many as we could. Even many of the badly rusted and bent clips will be cleaned, straightened and galvanized.

The bumpers are nice and straight, and very solid. In fact the rear bumper will only be cleaned, polished and buffed. The front bumper, although in nice general condition, will have to be rechromed, so we added that item to our list of parts to be plated.

Most of the exterior trim will merely be cleaned and buffed, professionally, although two or three pieces are extensively damaged and will probably require replacement. We will leave the final judgement on some of these parts to the pros. We may even attempt to repair and buff a few of the pieces ourselves.

Terry Ritter was closely monitoring our progress right from the start. Jerry Ferguson, owner of the Classic Car Centre, had assigned Ritter as our overall project coordinator, so in addition to directly supervising the body and paint work he was also serving as liaison with all the other departments involved in our project, including the machine shop.

A very well organized individual, Ritter approaches this and other assignments with a keen eye for potential problems, and a keen mind for devising solutions. He worked for two years in a general mechanical repair facility and body shop specializing in Mercedes and BMW, two nameplates which are a bit more complex than most automobiles in respect to engineering. He then owned his own body shop for five years before joining the Classic Car Centre when it opened in early 1986.

One quick examination and we determined that at least 10 of our trim clips were beyond salvage, so we added them to our shopping list. We hope to locate originals (these particular items are not and have not been reproduced), but may have to accept a workable substitute, using similar clips from another model or having some custom clips made.

The two body shop specialists assigned to the teardown phase of our project, Odiorne and St. Cin, seemed to be enjoying the task at hand. Odiorne, of Bremen, Ind., was very familiar with the Crown Vic and knew just what tools and procedures to employ for each dismantling job as we

4

5

4. *Hood needs only a new finish to restore showroom appearance.*

5. *Benefits of buying a relatively solid car are reflected in the trunk lid. No dents or rust here!*

6. *Pot metal on trunk represents one of the big buck '55 Ford items to restore. Replating could run into hundreds of dollars on a badly pitted piece. NOS pieces are no softer. We were lucky to have bought a car with a piece needing little more than chrome polish. The hood bird showed a few pits, though, and will require plating.*

7. *Experience told Gary and John to unbolt the bumper with caution. Support bars appeared to be sprung slightly. Injury could result.*

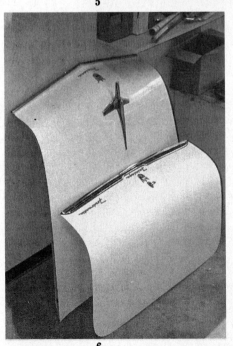

6

7

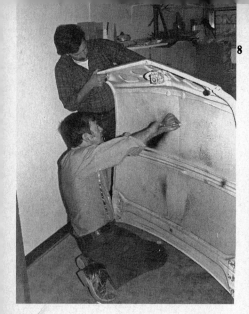

8

9

proceeded around and through the car, removing everything that wasn't welded in place.

The other half of the demolition team, John St. Cin, was also having fun, reducing Vicky to a pile of parts right before our eyes. St. Cin, who would be the central character in our story on the rejuvenation of the body, would have numerous opportunities in the weeks and months ahead to demonstrate his prowess in metal working, welding, paint stripping, priming, metal prep, etc. St. Cin is a recent transplant to Warsaw. When our project commenced, he was residing in Mishawaka, Ind., about 45 minutes away, but he has since relocated to Warsaw.

A former body shop owner and manager, St. Cin is exceptionally well versed in the body man's art. He's experienced in all phases of body repair and restoration, including metal work, welding, panel replacement, painting, etc. He's also very familiar with fiberglass body repair and painting, having restored a number of Corvettes over the years. In his 25 years in the body repair business he's rebuilt, reworked and restored many vehicles, including new, late model and collector types, but he says he's never gotten into as much fine detail as he has since joining the staff at the Classic Car Centre. Many of the cars he now works on are destined for point judging in some very serious show competition. He is, however, enjoying his participation in the refined art of show car quality restorations.

The more parts Odiorne and St. Cin removed, the worse the car looked, of course. But, at the same time, we were discovering that our car was as basically solid as we had initially determined. The consensus of opinion was that the car was indeed a Kansas car — not the best (such as California or Arizona) but certainly better than most areas of the country. Yet, time and the elements had taken their toll on Miss Vicky, and her previous owners had rendered a variety of repairs in hopes of restoring her original beauty and extending her mechanical service life. Some of these attempts were successful, others

10

11

8. *Cars & Parts staffer, Ken New, holds the hood as John St. Cin removes the hood ornament. The hood pad was probably removed a few years back when the hood was repainted.*

9. *Door sill plates were a sham. New repros will take their place.*

10. *Small painted body parts, such as the rear license plate mount, will be blasted, then primed and painted at the same time as the body.*

11. *Rear seat bolsters wear original fabric in decent condition. Front cushions were recovered sometime in the past. Although presentable, the old interior will be replaced.*

12. *Only a few bolts in the teardown were so rusty that they broke. That made front seat removal a snap.*

12

13. Worn, smelly old carpet will be trashed.

14. Solid condition of the trunk floor was impressive, especially the very solid bottom of the spare tire well, which is typically a haven for rust.

15. Closer examination of the trunk and some hammer pecking revealed rust-out around body mounts.

16. Once stainless body mouldings were removed, the original torch red and snowshoe white paint separation line was revealed. Repaint was a near match.

17. Crown Vic was loaded with shiny trim. Several pieces were attached with rusty, irreplaceable fasteners.

18. Solid appearance of floor was deceiving at this point. Sand blasting revealed minute holes in the areas directly ahead of the front seat, where driver and front seat passenger usually place their feet.

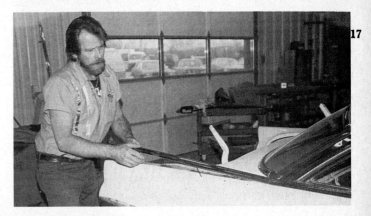

only highlighted a problem, or made it worse.

One such problem area was uncovered when the door sill plates were removed. The sill plates themselves are probably the worst items on the car, condition-wise, and are definite candidates for the junk pile. But underneath the sill plates we found that cheap replacement panels had been screwed and riveted over the original rocker panels. This repair panel is the type of unit that is merely bolted on over old rusted panels and then "melded in" with putty and covered by sill plates. It will all be ripped out and new, high quality replacement panels installed ... and properly.

As more and more items came off the car, we found additional body putty in some places we hadn't expected it. And it

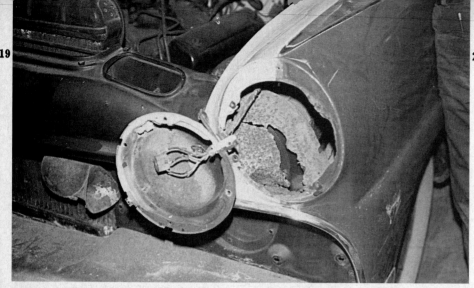

19

20

21

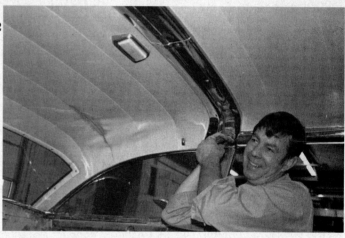

22

19. Behind a drooping headlight, a rust hole is found in the bucket. We'll patch it once the metal is cleaned.

20. Gary needed his trusty fire wrench to persuade a stubborn fender bolt to give up its 30-year hold.

21. The stainless parts that are unique to a Crown Vic were in remarkably fine shape.

22. Small pits and blemishes tarnished the special Crown Vic trim in the interior. All inside trim unique to a Crown Vic is chrome plated, while outside in stainless steel. John enjoyed this job, he said.

23. Backing off from our project car we captured this assemblage of what appears to be a car-like affair. That semblance soon faded as teardown progressed.

was a bit worse than we had imagined. But Vicky was still a good, solid Crown Victoria, and one definitely worthy of our restoration efforts. The experts at the Classic Car Centre all agreed that we had a reasonably solid and complete car, and one that hadn't been damaged by accidents or deteriorated by the elements beyond the point of cost-efficient restoration. It's critically important to start with an exceptionally solid car when one is not pursuing a total ground-up, frame-off restoration. Again, we didn't want a 98-point show car, and we wanted to avoid removing the body from the frame.

It's important, they added, to select a car with solid cowl and body seams. Frequently, they explained, the asphalt-type material used to coat the cowl and cowl area seams can often trap moisture and salt, which penetrate the porous asphalt-like coating. Our car, fortunately, was very strong in all the critical body seam areas.

As the tires and wheels came off the car, we gave them a good inspection. The wheels, including the spare, are all in decent shape and will be cleaned, stripped and repainted. The tires, wide whitewalls in G78x15 size, will be cleaned and re-mounted. The Grand Prix Premium 78 tires appear to be in excellent health and show only minimal tread wear. There's also no evidence of cupping, or uneven wear. They should provide thousands of miles of trouble-free service under normal

23

driving conditions and reasonable care.

As we ventured into the interior of the car, we found a number of interesting items hidden away in the dark recesses of this 33-year-old buggy. In the trunk, we found a 1969 Mustang emblem, and buried under the front seat was a Ford "Swift Sure" power brake pedal. We freed a coat hanger from untold years of captivity behind a side panel in the rear passenger compartment. Under the rear seat we discovered modern-style seat belts, as well as seat belt anchors driven into the floor.

Naturally, we also found an assortment of chewing gum wrappers, paper clips, rubber bands, bolts, nuts, screws, candy wrappers, a fast food burger carton, a penny, etc. It was all discarded along with the door sill plates and carpeting. Well, almost ... we pocketed the penny.

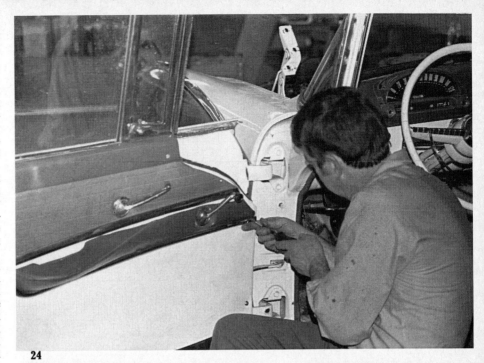

24

But one non-original item uncovered while extracting the interior did give us a bit of a jolt. We had thoroughly inspected the car and double-checked its data plate and numbers to authenticate the red and white paint scheme. But, all of a sudden, John St. Cin is holding a rear side panel that was pink in color. It was the metal side panel on the left or driver's side in the back seat area. After further inspection of the interior, we determined that the original panel had been replaced by a used panel at some point, possibly when the window regulator broke and a used one was installed. All of the old paint under the trim, including some identified as original, was either red or white. Later we would find even more proof that Vicky was an original red and white car as the windshield and rear glass were removed, etc. (Actually, pink and white would have been a super color combination, being very appropriate for mid-fifties Ford, very flashy and very nostalgic for many of us who "cruised" the fifties.)

We did find a couple of things that weren't quite right. The horns, for instance, were both incorrect. One was even a Delco unit. It's apparent that one of the car's earlier owners adopted new non-original horns when the car was converted to 12-volt electrics.

25

After an exhaustive examination, we concluded that the car's odometer reading of 69,900 miles is probably inaccurate and that in all likelihood, Miss Vicky has seen six digits at least once. Subsequent mechanical disassembly and inspection would further support this contention.

Despite its apparent, and not so apparent, problems, our '55 Crown Victoria was still a good investment, even though we probably paid more for it than we should have. The car was certainly worth the $6,000 we spent in its initial purchase, because it was a solid, presentable, and operable automobile with decent paint, interior and mechanics. The reason we acquired a car in this state was that we needed something above average to start with to suit our promotional, advertising and editorial purposes. We needed a car that looked good and could be driven, at least enough to satisfy our photographic requirements.

Since the car was to appear on the cover of the magazine and in advertisements

26

24. *Door panels were recovered in the past. It was an adequate job, but fell a bit short in fit and color match.*

25. *Window tracks and hardware were found to be in excellent condition.*

26. *Last remnants of the headliner were removed and saved for matching with new materials.*

43

before its restoration, we needed one that was photogenic and very strong in the areas of paint, chrome and interior. For our actual restoration project, one of the cheaper $2,000 to $4,000 cars we encountered would have been sufficient, since we were planning a restoration that would be just a few steps short of a total, frame-off rebuild. Still, this was the car that served all of our purposes.

Even with the project now barely underway, we had already gained a good measure of respect for the men in the body shop, and a good deal of admiration for the facilities, equipment and tools they had at their disposal.

It's truly amazing how quickly and cleanly a couple of professional body men can strip a car. It's fast and dirty, but effective. In fact, it's almost frightening to see how a relatively sharp looking car can be reduced to a pathetic metal hulk in just a few hours. When only a shell is left languishing before you — devoid of all chrome, trim, emblems, and other appointments — it's kind of sad. But our hopes were buoyed by the prospects of a professional refurbishment restoring Vicky to her former beauty and glory!

27

28

29

30

27. *Two of the last parts removed were the front fenders. A couple of the bolts were almost impossible to reach with normal size wrenches.*

28. *Front fenders showed much orange peel in the paint, which covered up sheet metal repairs performed sometime in the past. Radio antenna hole is incorrect and will be sealed up.*

29. *The ends of the bars that hold the headliner in place at*

the roof line are cradled in small cups, allowing easy removal.

30. *Almost hidden by an over zealous dabbing of undercoating, rusted out holes were found beneath fenders near the rear bumper.*

31. *"I could have torn it up like this without your help," quipped Ken New (center) to body shop foreman Terry Ritter (left). The actual restoration of Vicky to her former glory is about to begin.*

31

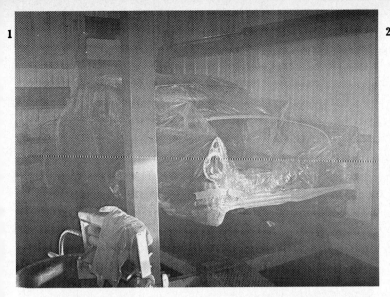

An outline of plans to restore Vicky appeared in the May, 1987 issue of *Cars & Parts.* Those plans, as envisioned by a group of car hobbyists/magazine types, were a step or two above a driver. It didn't turn out that way. In a short time a full-fledged, no holds barred, frame-off restoration was in full swing. You can probably recite a similar favorite story by heart — a close friend (maybe even you) started out to restore a driver for himself and then things got into a state of seriousness that car lovers find hard to describe; one thing leads to another. The wiring is yanked, the plumbing is pulled and in no time flat an all-out war on everything dilapidated and ugly is waged. The same thing happened to Vicky.

As originally planned, Vicky's body and the engine would be restored in a reasonable fashion by the experts at Classic Car Centre and a driver would be delivered to the *Cars & Parts* staff. Some slightly, unsightly deterioration would be overlooked. The body would not be taken off the frame, the clock and radio would not be fixed, a new hi-tech brake lining to improve stopping power would be used, yet the brake lines repaired only as needed for safety's sake. Those plans, and others,

THE RESURRECTION OF VICKY

The frame gets a bath and parts cleanup begins

1. *Completely gutted of upholstery, stripped of paint and wrapped in a giant baggy, Vicky was taken to Classic Car Centre's service area for a power wash of the chassis and underbody panels.*

2. *Kansas gumbo was bonded like cement in many places.*

3. *Alexas Maldenly attacks the build-up of mud and grease stuck to Vicky's frame with a power wash wand spraying a strong solution of soap and degreaser.*

4. After softening for some 20 minutes the build-up of oil and mud still refused to let go and Alexas chipped it away with a large screwdriver.

5. The cakes of mud and grease were so stubborn, it took a second washing to clean the frame.

6. Details of engine crossmember and steering bars were nearly lost in the build-up.

7. Passenger side railing shows signs of a previous repair to the front crossmember. Sloppy welding is evident.

8. Out behind the body shop, John St. Cin takes advantage of low humidity characteristic of sub-freezing temperatures to sandblast some inner body rust. Sandblasting snouts tend to plug when heavy humidity is present.

9. Perforated toe board will be replaced. Sandblasting has a tendency to open up perforation not easily seen otherwise.

10. Cowl and adjoining air tubes cleaned up beautifully without incident.

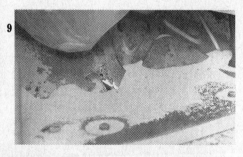

changed dramatically as the restoration proceeded.

The crew at Classic Car Centre became attached to Vicky and saw the project as an excellent opportunity to show its stuff. The rust holes in the quarter and rocker panels would be repaired in first rate fashion only after the rusty metal living in the inner structural panels was clipped away and replaced. Terry Ritter, Classic Car's body shop foreman, gave orders to master body man, John St. Cin, to leave nary a spec of rust, patch every hole with new metal and "do it right."

In the months ahead we'll follow along as Vicky is brought back to life. In-depth features will appear on the restoration chores performed. We'll go through the cylinder heads to wean Vicky of her taste for leaded gas and she'll learn to live on unleaded. The rusty, inner structural metal that many so-called restorers hide with a batch of bondo will be completely removed and replaced. Along with other improvements the frame will be unbolted, sandblasted, painted and worn parts replaced before it's slipped back under Vicky's body, which also will be given a top-shelf restoration.

This chapter in the series of articles on the restoration of Cars & Parts' Sweepstakes car involves cleaning of body and chassis parts by steam cleaning and blasting with sand and glass beads. The body, stripped of its last vestiges of paint as

11

12

13

14

11. *Paint and rust on headlight buckets, fender skirts, fastening brackets, hinges and a multitude of smaller parts were removed in a handy glass bead blasting cabinet. Convenience of cabinet and gentle nature of bead blasting makes it a natural for cleaning small and delicate parts.*

12., 13. & 14. *Small parts blasted chemically clean are ready for priming.*

15. *A few short minutes spent inside a bead blasting cabinet will produce results days of elbow grease cannot match.*

15

recorded in a previous article, was taken into a power wash pit where heavy layers of grease and sludge were removed from the engine support area and body undercarriage using a power washer that expells 750 psi pressure. After that assault, body shop personnel began an attack on rusty body parts and assorted hang-on parts that needed to be refurbished.

Next door to the body shop in the complex of buildings at the Classic Car Centre is an all-purpose service center. There, general service work from tune-ups to major engine overhauls are performed alongside an area devoted exclusively to cosmetic detailing. Heading up the detail crew is a lady who doesn't mind getting a little dirt under her fingernails. This lady, Alexas Maldenly, has over seven years of experience in paint and body shops around Warsaw — not counting the lab and classroom time spent in a local tech

school where she majored in automotive. The men at Classic Car Centre exhort a professional respect for Maldenly. "She knows what it takes to produce a quality finish and how to maintain it," offered a fellow serviceman.

Vicky's frame and undercarriage were caked with Kansas mud and crud that required a double-shot treatment of degreaser and soap. Maldenly fired up a power washer and proceeded to soak the build-up with a soap and degreaser solution of her own formula. Asked if she gets many jobs like this, Maldenly winced and said that normally the jobs aren't quite so dirty. A routine day's work, she said, will be a rubout and wax on a Ferrari or a vintage T-Bird or a power wash of the engine and rails of a venerable old Caddy. Maldenly says she enjoys the work while a fellow worker nodded to the truthfulness of her statement.

Back in the body shop, rinsed of all greasy grime, Vicky was given a quick once over by body man John St. Cin, the technician charged with revitalizing Vicky's body parts. St. Cin will spend many hours and days with Vicky in the months ahead.

He probably wouldn't admit it, but I believe St. Cin loved Vicky from the moment he saw her. A veteran of some 20 years in body shop work, St. Cin is one of the rare breed who has experienced practically every phase of auto body repair from Auburns to other Crown Vics like Vicky. It was a pleasure watching him delve into the project while quipping lightheartedly at fellow body shop personnel.

St. Cin says there's no better way to clean auto sheet metal than with a sandblaster. "It's chemically clean and ready for paint — but you've got to be careful to not warp the body panels." The same can be said for a glass bead blasted surface, with one exception: The warping tendency is lessened. Both sand and glass bead blasting equipment were available to St. Cin as he began to remove rust and failing paint from Vicky's chassis and body parts.

In restoring virtually any type of vehicle, the hobbyist at some point will have to decide which method of stripping he prefers in removing paint, rust, grime and various contaminants from his car's body, frame and other metal components. The *Cars & Parts* project car, the celebrated 1955 Ford Crown Victoria, dubbed "Miss Vicky", has received a multi-faceted treatment of steam cleaning, sandblasting, scraping, sanding, etc., to clean, strip and prep the various components for restoration.

It was determined that a number of parts were best stripped via the commercial chemical process. These parts, mostly under-hood items such as radiator shrouds, aprons, etc., were hauled to a special facility in Indianapolis, Ind. The operation, housed in a non-descript structure in an industrial section of Indy, is called Central Indiana Redi-Strip, Inc. (4020 Millersville Rd., Indianapolis, Ind. 46205), and it's run by two partners, Boyd Birchler and Joseph Ewing.

The Redi-Strip operation, billed as "America's Metal Laundry", is a franchise setup and there are outlets around the country, as well as a number of similar independent operations. The very nature of the business, though, makes it a difficult one to operate efficiently, economically and safely. Consequently, the survival rate is not the best and the number of such op-

THE RESURRECTION OF VICKY

Degreasing and derusting ... the professional way!

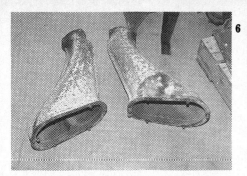

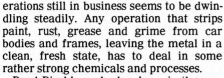

erations still in business seems to be dwindling steadily. Any operation that strips paint, rust, grease and grime from car bodies and frames, leaving the metal in a clean, fresh state, has to deal in some rather strong chemicals and processes.

Boyd Birchler, who has been in the professional paint stripping and derusting business for nearly three years, says that most car parts, including bodies and frames, are submerged in a special alkaline solution designed to strip away rust, grime, dirt, grease and other contaminants without ruining the metal.

Parts are placed in a large cradle and lowered into the tanks. Car bodies and frames are also lowered into the huge vats. The tanks are 20 feet long and about five feet deep. A periodic current reverse system is used, and at room temperature. Parts remain in a tank overnight. The following morning the parts are lifted out of the tank and moved to an open area of the plant and washed thoroughly with regular water. Power washing apparatus is used.

The same parts are then dipped in the alkaline solution again, and power washed again. This would normally satisfy the vast majority of car parts. Some particularly troublesome pieces, however, may require additional treatment. If so, the process is repeated until parts are in satisfactory condition.

The process is slower than an acid solution, but much kinder to the metal. Acid is very fast, Birchler admits, but it threatens metal. The alkaline formula is protective of the basic metal. In fact, he says, the solution is so effective that an engine block can sometimes be treated and then not require boring; it can then use standard size pistons. In other cases, Birchler continues, some engine blocks which have already been completely machined are brought in for treatment. That, he says, demonstrates confidence in the integrity of his derusting/degreasing procedures.

1. The parts from Miss Vicky selected for treatment at the chemical stripping plant are placed on the floor and on a skid for inspection and evaluation. Sizing up different parts for a fair quote is another tough aspect of the business.

2. Birchler carefully examines each part to accurately determine condition and metal content. Both are important factors in estimating charges. Some metals have to be separated from regular steel.

3. Boyd Birchler, a partner in Central Indiana Redi-Strip, Inc., of Indianapolis, Ind., explains the inner workings of the commercial stripping business from his in-plant office. Good

communication with customers is paramount to success or failure in this business, he says.

4. Parts at the commercial stripping operation are placed in large metal crates by job and by type of metal to await their baptism in the stripping tanks.

5. The front inner fenders from Miss Vicky were analyzed and deemed appropriate in terms of condition and content for regular chemical stripping. The piece will emerge from the process ready for restoration.

6. Vent tubes were also approved for treatment, as were all of our parts. Nothing was rejected, or tagged for special treatment.

7. Devoid of all grease, dirt, rust and grime, the parts for the '55 Crown

Victoria project car are readied for shipment back to Warsaw, Ind., where they'll be restored and re-installed. The rusted appendages or wings on the two radiator shrouds were badly deteriorated. The one on the right was patched with new metal, while the other one was fitted with a complete new wing fashioned from metal.

8. Birchler is so confident that critical machining surfaces aren't altered by his alkaline solutions, he frequently dips honed engine blocks. This block and heads came from an Indianapolis customer.

9. A Crown Victoria body — not Miss Vicky's — waits for its turn in the tank. The huge tanks easily accommodate a full-size auto body, or frame.

10. *Commercial stripping removes all paint, grime, undercoating, etc., and produces a really clean looking hunk of metal. But it also uncovers any former sins, and we soon learned that our Crown Vic was better than this "other" girl.*

11. *This car appeared pretty solid, even better than our Crown Vic. Layers of roofing pitch brushed on by a previous owner to hide some inferior floor pan welds withstood the first dunking in Redi-Strip's vats. Pete Hornbuckle hand scraped the goo prior to a second night in the vat which did the trick.*

12. *This Crown Vic (unlike our Vicky) has solid rear frame mounts holes (see arrows). Vicky's were rusted and wobbly.*

13. *Spare wheel well shows signs of rust out as well as a layer of plastic filler atop the rear fender.*

14. *Ready for restoration, the "other" Crown Victoria body sits on blocks awaiting delivery to the customer and, presumably, restoration. It was a fortunate coincidence that the Crown Victoria body shell was at the Redi-Strip facility, since we weren't going to have the body from our car totally stripped via the chemical method.*

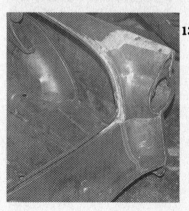

There are two metals which are not compatible with the standard process. Both zinc and aluminum do not react properly to the alkaline, which is a caustic solution. Central Indiana Redi-Strip can still effectively treat parts made of zinc and aluminum, even complete bodies, but a different procedure is employed, including separate tanks and a special treatment formulated specifically for aluminum and zinc parts.

Regular metal parts, once fully stripped and degreased, can be further treated with an optional iron phosphate treatment, which is a 2% solution applied in the final wash. It's injected or blown into all crevices, holes, etc., and it etches the metal for better paint adhesion. It runs about an extra 10% for the iron phosphate solution.

Our parts, consisting of inner fenders, heater and vent tubes, splash shields, radiator supports, heater ductwork, radiator fan and miscellaneous other metal pieces, were basically about average for old car parts, Birchler said. Most of our pieces had some deterioration with a layer of surface rust and grime. About 15% of all the work performed at Central Indiana is comprised of vintage car parts. The rest of the firm's business is concentrated in industrial work.

All types of metal car parts are welcome, including bodies, fenders, frames, wheels, engine blocks, dash panels, heads, etc.

The type of car body seen most frequently by Birchler is the 1955-57 Chevy, while the 1957-59 Ford retractable hardtops are the second most common. A typical car body will run about $420 for a complete treatment. The average '57 Chevy body will cost about $75 to $80 more because they're harder to strip, partially because of the undercoating on '57 Chevys.

Also, estimates can vary substantially on similar bodies, or other components, due to type of metal, condition, etc. For example, at one time in the fall of 1986, Birchler had seven 1957 Chevy bodies in his plant for stripping. The difference in quotes on the seven bodies was $165 from

the worst to the best in terms of condition. This is why Birchler insists on personally inspecting a body, or other piece, before quoting a firm price. In this particular instance, the cars were markedly different in condition; some had new floors, some had rusted floors, some had no floors at all, for example.

Birchler's operation does a lot of old car frames, and the most common frame brought in for stripping is a Corvette frame. The fiberglass Vette bodies may be immune to corrosion and rust, but those steel frames certainly aren't.

When parts are returned from Redi-Strip, they're generally ready for prepping and painting. Most of our parts came back from the "metal laundry" in excellent shape, ready for additional restoration. A couple of parts required some new metal, as the missing rust and decay created a swiss cheese effect. One of the larger parts had to have an entire new appendage made from new sheet metal.

Commercial services are often the best answer for removing paint, rust, and grease from metal car parts, and in some cases, there is no alternative!

PART THREE

Rebuilding the Engine

1

THE RESURRECTION OF VICKY

Yanking the engine and disassembling it

The heart of any vintage automobile, especially one out of the nifty fifties, is its engine. While styling, bright two-tone color schemes, wire wheel covers, rear-mounted antennas, pleated vinyl interiors and fender skirts were all the rage in the post-war era, car nuts first looked under the hood of a car before offering any serious comment. The horsepower race was in high gear and auto makers were not only loading their models with tons of chrome and trick power options, but also packing the best that modern engineering could afford under the hood.

A car without an engine, of course, is a bit useless. It's also rather pitiful, like a defenseless creature whose fangs have been removed. Well, after having all the exterior chrome stripped away and the interior removed, that's the next step for Vicky — engine removal and complete disassembly.

First, a brief description of the engine is in order. The *Cars & Parts* project car is a 1955 Ford Crown Victoria powered by the basic 272-cid V-8 engine, the small version of the famous Y-block Ford engine. This mill proved a decent performer back in the fifties and although it never achieved the popularity of the small block Chevy V-8 of the same era, it attracted a faithful following and still commands great loyalty among Ford buffs. Introduced as an all-new powerplant in 1953 in the Lincoln line and expanded to Ford and Mercury in 1954, the Ford Y-block gave birth to a variety of mills during its nearly decade-long service life before its discontinuance with the start of the 1963 new car season. In its various sizes and horsepower ratings, along with different carburetion setups and electrical systems, the Y-block Ford V-8 would become known as the Ford powerplant of the fifties.

The 272-cube engine in Vicky, our project car, had a horsepower rating of 162 at 4,400 rpm, and produced 258 lb./ft. of torque at 2,200 rpm. Its compression ratio was 7.6 to 1 and it had a bore and stroke of 3.62"x3.30". These are decent specs for a mid-fifties engine and one of the first of the new breed of ohv V-8 engines.

Removing and disassembling a modern V-8 engine is a routine procedure for the veterans in the machine shop at the Classic Car Centre in Warsaw, Ind. Engine rebuilding shops across the country, as well as major restoration shops, are also equipped and experienced to efficiently and safely handle the type of work being undertaken and chronicled here.

Vicky made her final moves under her own power in the short 50-foot run from the body shop to the restoration facility. The interior was already removed, so body shop employee Gary Odiorne sat on a makeshift seat to drive the *C&P* project car from one building to another in the Classic Car Centre complex. The restoration building is extremely well equipped for all types of mechanical and general

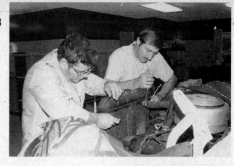

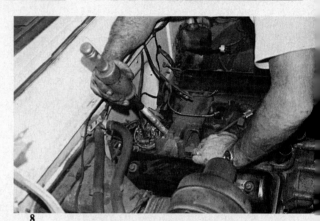

1. Stripped of all bright work and her interior, Vicky, the Cars & Parts 1955 Ford Crown Victoria project car, is moved to the restoration shop by Classic Car Centre's Gary Odiorne.

2. For safety's sake, Terry Hygema suggested the first order of business should be draining the fuel tank of gasoline. A fire extinguisher was kept handy throughout the teardown.

3. Hygema disconnected the fuel line, unstrapped the gas tank and dropped it away from Vicky.

4. Classic Car Centre's two resident engine builders extraordinaire, Terry Hygema and Gene McGuire, start the disassembly by removing the radiator hoses and core. The two former diesel mechanics have years and years of experience keeping semi trucks on the road.

5. Crankcase oil was drained and analyzed for metallic particles indicating worn components, a burnt odor suggesting bearing troubles and moisture indicating cracked heads, a fractured block or a leaky head gasket. Overall, Vicky got poor marks in the intake area and lower engine case.

6. Teardown was systematically approached. Each component was examined for telltale evidence of failure. Carbon tracks found inside the distributor cap caused misfiring and fouled spark plugs.

7. Vicky's electrics had been converted to 12 volt. Resistor block on the firewall was installed to lower voltage to six volts at the distributor. Amateurish wiring literally fell off in McGuire's hand.

8. Typical of Ford Y-block distributors, the one dispensing fire to Vicky's cylinders was frozen tight. Initial attempts at removal proved futile. McGuire will wait for unhampered access once the engine is out of the chassis. International Compound No. 2 or another anti-seize compound would have prevented this problem. Timing hasn't been set in years.

9. Extreme care should be taken when hooking a powerplant to an engine crane. Leveling bar keeps engine off tilt.

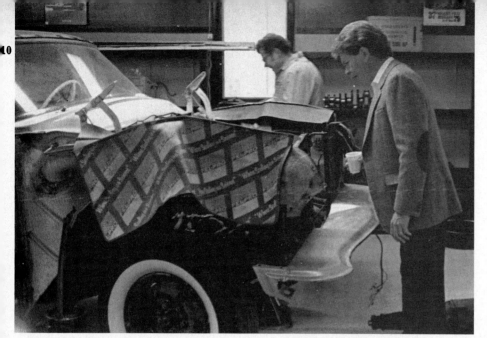

service work. Good tools and equipment are vital to efficient and safe repair and restoration work.

The first order of business, after disconnecting and removing the battery, was to elevate the car. Heavy duty hydraulic floor jacks were used to lift the 3,400-pound automobile, and then jack stands were positioned underneath to support Vicky. Remember to always use a jack or jacks of adequate capacity for the load being lifted, and *never* work on a vehicle or get under a vehicle supported only by a jack or jacks. Always support a vehicle with jack stands that are in good condition and of adequate capacity. Too many deaths and injuries have occured involving people working on improperly supported vehicles. It's not worth the risk!

With Vicky squared away on large, high-capacity jack stands, our teardown crew went to work, beginning with the fuel tank. Gasoline, from the standpoint of both vapors and flammability, should be removed

10. *Jerry Ferguson, owner of Classic Car Centre, inspects the empty cavity under the hood of the Cars & Parts Crown Vic project car. Ferguson regularly checks the status of all major restoration projects in his shop.*

11. *Cars & Parts' Ken New unbolts the driver's side inner fender, while Gene*

McGuire tackles the passenger side metal. Air tubes (solid as a jug) will be chemically dipped to remove a thick layer of undercoating, surface rust and paint.

12. *Lug at front motor support is broken and must be replaced.*

13. *Parting company, the body will be taken to the*

body shop for restoration. The engine will be disassembled, then taken to the machine shop. Both will meet again at a later date, fully refreshed and ready for a reunion.

14. *All hang-on metal, hoses, etc., will be cleaned and repainted or replaced as appropriate.*

from the premises early in the mechanical teardown. Our two experts, Gene McGuire and Terry Hygema, co-managers of the Classic Car Centre's machine shop, drained the tank of all fuel, transferring it outside to the tank of a vehicle in use. It would be many months before Vicky would be back in business, and it certainly didn't make sense to store gasoline for that length of time, especially such a small quantity. Once drained, the tank was removed. It will be cleaned and treated with a sealant before remounting.

Next in line were the car's other fluids. The engine crankcase was drained of oil, which was properly disposed of, and the radiator and engine block were drained of coolant. The fan blade and belts were then removed and the radiator itself yanked, also with attendant hoses.

While McGuire was busy under the hood with the radiator and the generator, Hygema was on a creeper under Vicky removing the fuel line, the starter motor and the exhaust system. The fuel line will probably be replaced, while the generator and starter will likely be rebuilt. Everything, so far, had come off the car with just a little persuasion, but things would get tougher as we proceeded.

A lot of the small hardware-type items, such as bolts, nuts, screws, mounts, shims, etc., will be gathered and sent out to a

14

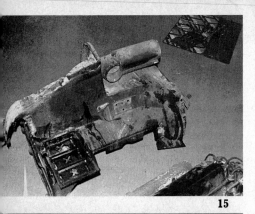

15

16

17

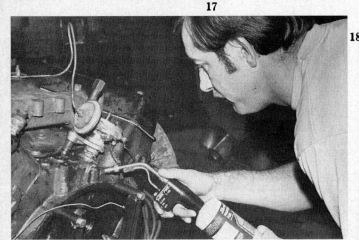

18

1

20

plating shop for a treatment of cadmium plating. Then later, when the parts come back from the plating shop, it'll be determined which parts are usable and which have to be replaced. Some pieces, such as the motor mounts, were deteriorated beyond the point of rescue. Some would simply crumble when the engine was pulled. When fresh rubber parts are installed in the rebuild-and-restore process, silicone spray will be used to help preserve them.

The radiator, which worked well and didn't leak in our pre-teardown tests, was visually inspected once out of the car and may be usable as is, with just a good flushing and some fresh paint. All the hoses and belts will be replaced with new items, of course, and it's likely that the thermostat will be pitched in favor of a new one. Hygema said that radiators are funny little items that can present lots of surprises.

15. *Battery box is fairly solid despite oozing battery acid, which usually settles in the bottom and causes rust out. A rubber pad will be used to isolate it from electrical ground.*

16. *Bumper splash apron is remarkably solid.*

17. *Vital fluids from the transmission and motor spill onto the floor. The Y-block V-8 shows signs of a previous cleaning, while the inaccessible top of the transmission housing is caked with greasy crud.*

18., 19. & 20. *Stubborn distributor is heated. Using a special Snap-On distributor removal tool, McGuire pried the distributor loose. Choose an engine boss or other heavy casting area to support the base of the tool, otherwise a cracked block could result. Note the oily crud on the shaft.*

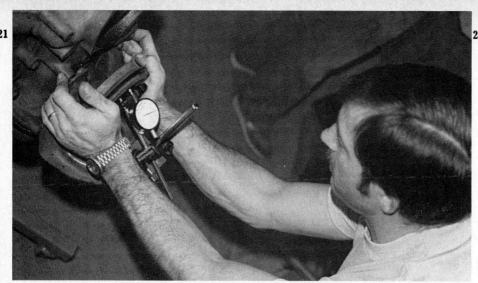

21

22

23

24

25

Usually, when the core becomes very flexible, almost crumbly, the radiator is shot and not rebuildable. Our radiator is within operational tolerances.

McGuire doesn't believe in many additives — oil, fuel or coolant — so we'll probably just refill the radiator with a 50-50 mix or other recommended blend of quality anti-freeze and distilled water. He loves to expound on the merits of non-mineraled water also. We'll get to that in a later chapter of Vicky's resurrection. In respect to other fluids, we'll probably use synthetic brake fluid and top quality chassis lube throughout. Also, in respect to the brakes, McGuire recommends that we use a non-asbestos-based brake lining material, which he says is outstanding and will out-perform conventional asbestos and similar lining materials. "There's no comparison," he says.

As McGuire and Hygema swiftly disassemble the car before our eyes and cameras, the normally quiet interludes between action photos and descriptions of precisely what's happening are filled with tales of exciting adventures and challenges relating to their experiences on the Great American Race. McGuire and Hygema both served as crew members aboard a 1912 American LaFrance fire truck in the first two editions of the transcontinental race for antique cars and trucks. The fire truck, owned by Dr. Bob Fuson of Warsaw, Ind., encountered more than its share of problems in those first two attempts and our dynamic duo related many of their more entertaining experiences, including many which can't be revealed

21. *Lateral movement of the crankshaft was checked with a dial indicator. At .009" to .010" there was a definite problem, McGuire assured us, explaining that end thrust play should have been between .003" and .006". Normally, an engine with a standard manual transmission will show more wear than one teamed with an automatic transmission. The thrust bearings and thrust surfaces on the crankshaft*

had obviously suffered serious damage.

22. *Crank pulley/harmonic balancer is yanked away from block with a gear puller. Never hammer on this type of combination. It could separate.*

23. *Fuel pump suction was within acceptable limits, despite the unit's poor condition and a suspect diaphragm. A rebuilt one will be substituted.*

24. *Original rubber spark plug wire holder is mushy and useless. Fortunately, repros are available.*

25. *Clogged crankcase breather screen may not have been replaced since new. Totally plugged condition caused excessive engine blow-by due to extreme pressure in crankcase.*

26. *Failing exhaust gasket was just shy of blowing prior to the teardown.*

27. *Ironically, valve cover insides showed signs of a recent cleaning and new gaskets. Valves were probably set not too long ago.*

26

27

here. The chatter, though, sure made the time pass quickly.

Before the engine was yanked, it was checked out on an oscilloscope and related test equipment. The test results were really somewhat encouraging, although they did indicate that our engine required a complete ignition tuneup, including plugs, points, distributor cap, etc. More detailed scope analysis would point toward a complete engine rebuild.

The plug wires — cheap, low-grade replacements — will give way to new silicone cables, which are more expensive than regular plug wires, but far superior in construction and performance, McGuire says.

The distributor cap showed signs of carbon tracking and sparks going wild inside. Naturally, it will be replaced when the engine is reassembled, as will the spark plugs, points, condenser, etc. The distributor itself proved troublesome. It wouldn't budge, despite the rather energetic use of a puller with two guys working it. It was decided to leave it alone until the engine was completely out of the car. It was also decided that when the distributor is re-installed, International Compound No. 2, or a comparable anti-seize product, will be used. McGuire says this will make it simpler to pull the distributor in the future. "If a guy puts a wrench on it 12 years from now, it will break loose and come out with just normal pressure," he says.

Top-side, McGuire was telling one of his Great Race stories — the one about the time they slowly and quietly rolled up behind a fellow competitor who was driving a small, open roadster and, once within a few feet of him, hit the sirens, literally blowing their competition into the weeds. In the meantime, on the bottom-side, Hygema was discovering that our gearshift lever was connected to the three-speed Fordomatic transmission with a strand of baling wire. (Good thing we hauled our prize from Missouri back to Ohio on a trailer.)

Not to be out-done by his erstwhile companion, Hygema matches McGuire's tale with a Great Race story of his own. This one involved the 1912 American LaFrance fire truck being driven through rush hour traffic in a major western city. With every-

ORIGINAL DRIVETRAIN SPECIFICATIONS
1955 FORD CROWN VICTORIA

Engine type: OHV, 90° V-8, Y-block
  Displacement: 272 cu. in.
  HP @ RPM: 162 @ 4,400
  Torque @ RPM: 258 lb./ft. @ 2,200
  Compression ratio: 7.6 to 1
  Bore x stroke: 3.62"x3.30"

Crankshaft: Precision-molded alloy-
  iron; 8 counterweights, cast integrally
  Main bearings: 5, replaceable insert,
  steel-backed babbitt
  Torsion damper type: Rubber-floated

Connecting rods: Forged I-beam
  Lower bearings: Steel-backed
  copper-lead
  Upper bushings: Bronze

Camshaft: Quiet-contoured, high-lift;
  precision-molded alloy-iron
  Bearings: 5, steel-backed babbitt
  Drive: Silent chain

Cooling system:
  Type: Series-Flow
  Pump: Centrifugal, one; 65 gal./min.
  @ 4,400 rpm
  Thermostat: 1 positive-action; opening
  temp range: 157-162 F
  Radiator: Tube and fin, cushioned
  Radiator cap: Vented pressure;
  nom. open. press. (lb./sq. in.) 13
  System capacity without heater: 19 qts.;
  with heater: 20 qts.
  Fan: 3 blade

Valves: Free-turning
  Intake: Chrome steel
  Exhaust: Precision-molded,
  high-alloy steel
  Valve guides and seats: Integral
  Valve clearance adjustment: At
  rocker arm

Block and heads:
  Special alloy-iron

Fuel system:
  Carburetor: Duplex downdraft
  Air cleaner: Oil bath
  Choke control: Manual
  Fuel pump: Inverted, diaphragm
  Manifold heat control: Butterfly valve
  Actuation: Bi-metal thermostat
  Exhaust muffler: 3-chamber,
  reverse-flow, triple-wrapped (dual on
  Fairlane and station wagon models)
  Fuel tank capacity: 17.5 gal. (station
  wagons: 19 gal.)

Pistons:
  Type: Autothermic, tin-plated aluminum
  alloy, w/steel struts
  Compression rings: 2; cast iron; upper,
  chrome-plated; lower, phosphate coated
  Oil rings: 1; expander-spacer
  w/chrome-plated steel rails

Lubrication system:
  Main bearings: Pressure
  Conn. rod lower brgs.: Pressure
  Conn. rod upper brgs.: Mist
  Cylinder walls: Pressure stream
  Camshaft brgs.: Pressure
  Camshaft drive: Directed gravity
  Tappets and push rods: Gravity
  Rocker arm brgs.: Reduced pressure
  Oil pump, type: Gear, with non-floating
  screened inlet
  Crankcase: 6 qt. oil w/filter
  Oil filter: Full-flow,
  replaceable cartridge
  Crankcase ventilation: Continuous,
  directed-flow

Engine Electrical:
  Distributor: Single breaker point
  Spark advance: Vacuum differential
  Firing order: 1-5-4-8-6-3-7-2
  Generator: 6-volt, low cut-in*
  Maximum rating: 35 amp.*
  Regulator: 3-unit type*
  Starter motor: High-torque
  Drive: Anti-kickout
  Control: Ignition-starter switch
  Spark plugs: 18-mm, anti-fouling
  Gap: 032"
  Battery: 6-volt*
  No cells and plates per cell: 3, 17
  Capacity, amp. hrs. @ 20 hr. rate: 90

Transmission:
  Type: Fordomatic 3-spd. automatic
  Gear ratios: Low, 2.40; second, 1.47;
  high, 1.00; reverse, 2.00
  Torque converter: Single-stage,
  3-element, hydraulic
  Controls: Full hydraulic valving
  Positions: P-parking; R-reverse;
  N-neutral, Dr-drive; Lo-low
  Fluid capacity: 10 qts.

Rear axle:
  Type: Semi-floating; banjo type steel
  housing; Hotchkiss drive;
  2-pinion differential
  Ratio: 3.30 (3.55 opt.)

* Project car upgraded to non-original 12-volt electrical system.

28. "Gunksville," quipped McGuire. Use of high-paraffin high-ash-content oil and operation on dusty roads are the makings of corrosive, abrasive gunk. "Not a pretty sight!"

29. Oil tubes feeding oil to the top of engine were roughly 30% clogged. Clogged passageways prevented adequate lubrication to top end areas.

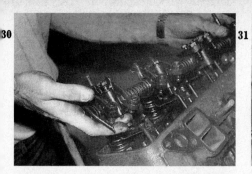

one, including several other Great Race competitors, ground to a halt, the fire truck crew simply hit the sirens and flashing lights on the old rig and watched with amusement as the crowded traffic lanes ahead opened a small passageway, like Moses parting the Red Sea. The fire truck slipped thru cleanly while traffic fell in tightly behind, snarling the truck's rally competitors in a sea of cars. One of those competitors would later file a grievance with Great Race authorities.

With the driveshaft unhooked, the crew moved in a large engine hoist with balancer and all the other right equipment. With everything hooked up, the engine was slowly lifted up and forward, an inch or two at a time. As it cleared the fenders and front frame pieces, the hoist was pushed away from the car and the engine and transmission combination slipped free as a single unit. The transmission was detached from the engine and placed on a skid on the floor. It'll be cleaned, drained, resealed and refilled with premium transmission fluid.

The motor was wheeled over to an engine stand, lowered onto the stand, bolted down and unchained from the hoist. The latter wouldn't be needed now for quite some time, not until Vicky is ready to receive her rebuilt engine. With the engine removed, we could plainly see that a fresh set of motor mounts would be required. The front mounts were half gone, and the others were only marginally better.

Break time! Another Great Race adventure. It seems this enterprising young television reporter was interviewing members of the 1912 American LaFrance crew, standing on the running board of the huge fire apparatus while he asked his questions. Great Race officials gave the crew its starting signal, yet the exuberant interviewer ignored urgent requests to dismount as it was critical that the rig start on time. After repeated warnings, McGuire dropped the big fire-fighter into

30. *Rocker arms and tappets looked good. They will be cleaned and reused. Note bottomed-out adjusting screws. Valves may have been ground once or twice in past or excess cam wear is showing up.*

31. *Rolling the push rods on a flat table top, McGuire demonstrates a proven technique of checking for straightness.*

Bent ones, naturally, should always be replaced, not straightened and reused.

32. *Impact driver set is really handy when tearing down older engines.*

33. *Bolts holding crankcase breather tube needed a bit of persuasion. Characteristic of high crankcase pressure is an oily film below crank end.*

34. *Inspection of cylinder heads and block surfaces indicated an uneven crush of cylinder gaskets. It's certain that a decking of the block is needed.*

35. *Carbon deposits cake the piston tops. Number three cylinder (third from left) shows excessive oil build up and soft carbon deposits from burnt oil. Next cylinder to the right is not quite as bad and the first cylinder is just starting to carbon up. Note heavy lip wear in cylinder three.*

36. *Burned exhaust valves in both heads reveal signs of improper valve seating. An uneven mixture of fuel to the various cylinders is evident as seen by the dark build up. The cause could have been a cracked manifold or incomplete scavenging of combustion chambers.*

37. *A close examination of head gasket impression between center bores revealed a gasket subject to blow at any time, and probably soon.*

38. *Sloppy, stretched timing chain is typical of medium to high mileage engines. Gears are worn. "It's almost unbelievable that it didn't jump time," McGuire said. The oil passages to the chain are plugged.*

39. *"A new chain won't droop like a limp banana,"* commented McGuire. *Droop shouldn't be more than ½".*

40. *Razor-sharp teeth indicate at least a .050-.060" wear of dry gears.*

41. *McGuire and Hygema concluded con rods were restorable. Ring lands and* wrist pins are worn. A scuffing of piston skirts and a distortion of bearing pattern in bearing saddles were also noted.

42. *Tangible evidence of the lateral movement of the crankshaft, as measured in an earlier photo, appears as a shiny side on the bearing caps.*

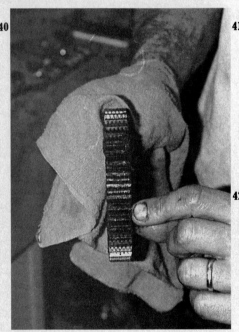

cork gaskets. The problem with sealants, he says, is that people tend to use too much and the material gums everything up. Some people will opt for gaskets with an aluminum finish, or even apply a coat of aluminum paint over cork gaskets. He prefers the new brand of aluminized gasket, which he feels seats better, seals more thoroughly and lasts longer.

With the valve covers off we were able to get our first close-up view of the engine's vital innards. Vicky's mill had obviously had some serious top end work at some point in her life, although we did find sludge build-up, which McGuire and Hygema credit to the use of oil with high sulphur and ash content. The ash buildup was in layers. Modern oils, they explain, have less than half a percent ash content, and do not present a sludge buildup problem like older oils.

Because of the ash buildup present in most original engines, McGuire and Hygema recommend that only non-detergent oil be used because detergent oil in an older, non-rebuilt engine will separate sludge from the engine's internals and this sludge can then move freely and plug oil lines, filter, pump, etc. Of course, they recommend using only a top grade of non-detergent oil. And, if the engine has been rebuilt, then detergent oil of a premium quality should be used.

As we continue to tear into the engine, McGuire reminds us of the importance of good manuals, including factory shop and owner's manuals and such aftermarket manuals as *Chilton's* service and repair manuals. They're indispensible to the at-home hobbyist, he says.

McGuire is opposed to using an air wrench on an engine. It's too easy to strip threads, bust the head off a bolt or even damage the block or casting into which the bolt is threaded.

The fuel pump came off easily, and it was evident immediately that a rebuild or replacement pump would be needed, al-

gear and blasted away from the starting line, with one TV reporter clinging to the side of the rig and watching his microphone cable snap. It's likely that the antics of the Fuson crew, at least in those first two races, generated a lot of extra publicity and even some notoriety for the Great American Race. Officials declined comment.

Getting back to the project at hand, we are now staring boldly and confidently at a 272-cid Ford V-8, which is poised atop its engine stand virtually daring us to dismantle her. Armed with the best that Snap-on has to offer, we oblige. First, of course, is that stubborn distributor. McGuire has sworn revenge. We all stepped back!

Keeping himself under control, and maintaining a clean, healthy mental attitude, McGuire selected a beefed-up engine boss and attacked the stubborn component

with a special distributor puller, Snap-on model CJ99, a $20 tool. It took a couple of shots and a little heat from a torch, but the puller worked nicely, extracting the distributor with the proficiency of a dentist yanking a tooth. Stuck distributors are common with old Ford Y-block engines, they said, and the only way to remove them without inflicting damage is via the proper tool. In some cases, though, nothing will work and the distributor will have to be destroyed while still in the block and removed a fragment at a time. Naturally, it becomes a "parts distributor" at that point, with the owner merely salvaging what pieces he can.

On the other hand, the valve covers came off easily, thanks to the cork gaskets used, and the lack of a gasket sealer. McGuire cautions against the use of any sealant, oil or other similar material with

43

43. *The crankshaft showed wear in its journals.*

44. *Worn cam gear rules out its reuse. Dwell and timing variations are obvious. If one checks number one and eight cylinders' timing and finds a variance of 2°, there is a problem with the timing gear train, camshaft or distributor drive gear. The culprit is usually the timing gears.*

45. *Flaking cam lobe is another bad sign. Once hardened cam surfaces are broken through, cam is trash. Another no-no, as those flakes are loose in the engine.*

46. *Shiny areas on the valve tappets were caused by incomplete contact of the tappets throughout the bores.*

44

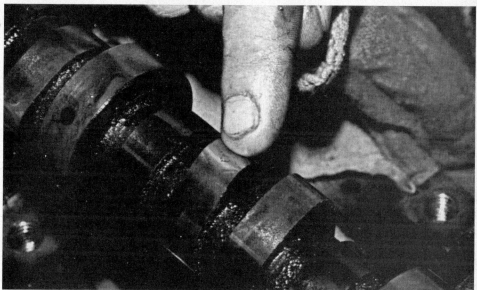

45

though its action seemed capable enough and it was certainly working alright when we drove Vicky into the shop. The crankcase breather was also working, we think, but we don't know how. It was atrocious. It obviously hadn't been serviced in a very long time, although McGuire said it is common to find really filthy, clogged crankcase breather filters in old cars of all kinds. A new unit will be installed.

McGuire used a gauge to measure crankshaft end play, and he discovered excessive thrust movement. Such lateral crankshaft thrust puts uneven pressure on rods and other internal components as the crank is moving from end to end while it spins. It's more noticeable and more prominent in a car with a standard shift transmission. Our engine showed .009" to .010" thrust play, and it should be in the area of .003" to .006" — quite a difference. That will be corrected in the overhaul, of course.

In removing the pulleys and front crankshaft vibration dampener, always use the correct type and size of puller. The dampener on this engine is quite worn and was about to spring a leak. It will be reconditioned using a Speedi-Sleeve, which will be tapped onto the dampener after gasket sealant is applied. Note: Never send parts like the crankshaft vibration dampener to be acid dipped as the chemicals will erode the part's rubber pieces.

The valve train itself appeared to be pretty clean with uniform wear and no abnormalities. The heads were then pulled, and it was discovered that we were about to blow a head gasket. If the car had been driven very far, McGuire predicted, the gasket would have blown and possibly damaged the head. The copper-coated head gasket found in this engine is not nearly as good as the Teflon-coated head gaskets now on the market, such as the Fel-Pro gaskets that will be used in the re-assembly of Vicky's engine. The Teflon-coated type of head gasket responds better

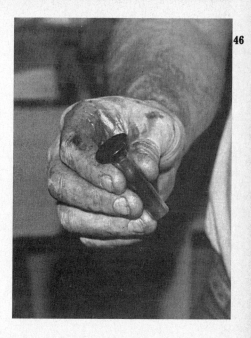

46

47

47. *As son Kevin steadies the block, Gene McGuire drives the cam bearings from their seats. Y-block Fords were notorious for spinning cam bearings. If a bearing comes out easily, it is probably spun and oil holes in the bearing and block are misaligned. Oiling has stopped. Remember the oil tubes old-time mechanics ran from the crankcase to the top of the valve covers?*

48. *Holes are punched into a freeze plug to aid removal. Care should be taken not to damage seats or penetrate cylinder walls.*

49. *A conglomeration of parts, some good, some bad. Vicky's engine will never be the same.*

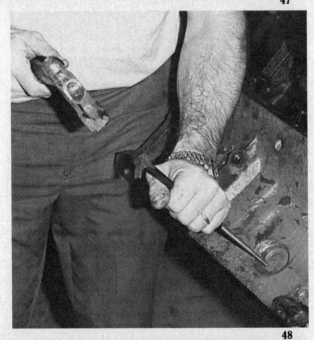

48

49

to the different head and block conditions caused by heat, cold, stress, etc.

Our teardown specialists next attacked the engine's bottom end, pulling the oil pan. The pan itself is nice and straight, and was reasonably clean. The oil pump also appears okay, but will be replaced. The timing chain, we discovered, was very loose, actually on the verge of jumping. It was so loose, in fact, that it could almost be removed by hand without loosening or removing any bolts. The timing chain should be firm and, when placed flat on a bench it should not droop in the middle, virtually standing up by itself. Naturally, this timing chain was not in the best of shape. It had even chewed up the timing gears, scoring them both badly. A new timing chain and gears are quickly added to the shopping list.

The main bearings are original design Clevite bearings, and could conceivably be original. The crankshaft, which appeared to be in excellent shape and has never been turned, will be magnafluxed to check for cracks before it's machined for reuse.

McGuire recommends that only a block of wood should be used to knock stubborn rods and pistons out of an engine. Handle all such parts with appropriate care, of course. The pistons in Vicky's engine are of the directional variety; they each have a notch at the top pointing to the front of the engine, a difference in piston orientation from one side to the other. Naturally, they must be properly installed with the notches in the right direction. The pistons and rings were original issue.

A hammer and chisel were used to knock freeze plugs out of the block. Again, exercise care to prevent damage to the engine and protect one's hands and eyes by wearing gloves and goggles, or safety glasses.

An expanding arbor was employed to drive out the cam bearings, one at a time straight thru the block until all five were removed. It was immediately ascertained that a new camshaft would be required. The cam gear, in this case an integral part, was well worn and pitted; nothing abnormal, just average wear and tear.

With the engine in pieces and virtually stripped to the bare block, it gave us a prime opportunity to inspect the various components, from the smallest parts to the block itself. Overall, the trusty old Ford Y-block V-8 had survived the years in very good shape. One could almost believe it was out of a very low mileage car. It did, though, appear that the engine had received not one but two top end rebuilds. It was certainly an engine worth rebuilding, with most major components proving reusable with proper machining.

The engine, or at least its many parts and pieces, would now be transferred to the machine shop for a variety of intriguing operations — from grinding, milling and decking to balancing and final assembly. Meanwhile, the body will be rolled back to the body shop for restoration, starting with paint removal.

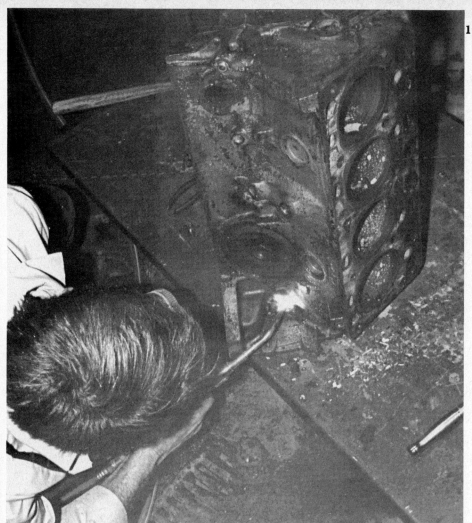

THE RESURRECTION OF VICKY

Hot tanking engine parts

When entering the well-equipped machine shop at Classic Car Centre, Warsaw, Ind., one sees an impressive array of machine tools used in engine rebuilding. One is a huge crank grinder. Then there is a spray welder and an engine balancing stand. Others include a giant boring bar, a mill, a valve grinder, overhead cranes, honing machine and other precision equipment used in renewing vintage and worn engine blocks. Flashy, heady stuff for any vintage or performance car owner who entertains thoughts of having an engine rebuilt.

Continuing the tour it would be easy, maybe even excusable, to pay little attention to the somber-colored tanks lined up back in the corner. Behind a half-wall adorned with hanging coats and shelves bulging with assorted boxes and bins of drill bits, carbide tips, etc., is a rather unglamorous area devoted to cleaning engine components. What appears to be of little importance in a cursory glance may well be one of the most vital areas of the machine shop. The far most area in the shop is actually the reception room where tired, sick and foul smelling engines enter an overhead door for their first treatment

Photos by the author

1. All oil and water galley plugs in the block were removed before hot tanking began. Stubborn ones were urged out with the fire wrench.

2. Greg Long, a technician at Classic Car Centre, scrapes built-up crud from Vicky's valley cover. Engine parts were hot tanked in a caustic solution prior to machine work.

3. This stuff, a combination of sludge and soft carbon, will make an engine run 10°-15° warmer.

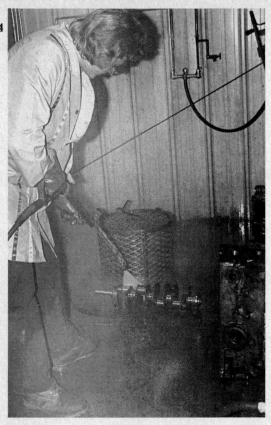

on the road to clinical recovery. There, dirty, smelly engines are torn down and chemically cleaned by Bill Brown and crew before any machining operations are performed. Brown, a mild-mannered sort, is impressive with his knowledge of trivial things like Crown Vics and afflictions and illnesses generally found in run-down, sick old engines.

Brown and his assistants tear down engines and run the parts through a gauntlet of hostile sprays and dips to rid them of crud, grease and other filthy build-up which has accumulated over the years

"out in the real world," as Brown calls it.

It's impractical to start machining work on engine components with crud build-up on them, Brown advised. "This stuff will scratch glass," remarked helper Greg Long as the pair delivered a long and detailed lecture on the merits of cleanliness. "Cleanliness is paramount in this machine shop," piped Brown. "It's gotta be."

The first step in cleaning engine parts is an exhaustive spraying with a mobile power-er washer which dispenses scalding water between 200°-210°. For many shops and shade tree mechanics such a cleaning

would be more than adequate, but serves only as a starter at Classic Car Centre.

The next prescription served up by the good doctor prior to admittance to the clinical sanctuaries of the machine shop is a hot tanking, a hot bath for some 30-40 minutes in a caustic solution of water and alkaline sodas followed by another thorough hosing with the power washer. "If we are to get it back as good as it was built originally, or even better, we must have things as clean as possible," Brown commented on Vicky's engine.

Sandblasting an engine block is not advised by engine rebuilders. Abrasive grit is bombarded into microscopic holes inside the block to be loosened once hot crankcase oil is sloshed over it. No amount of spray washing or hot tanking will expel it. Follow along with the accompanying photos as Vicky's engine is prepped for resuscitation.

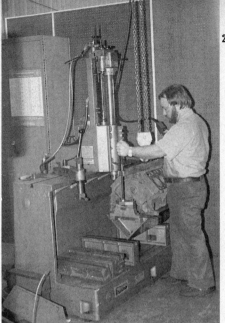

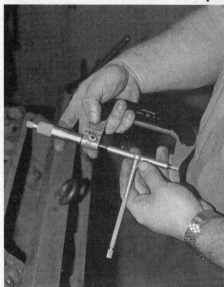

THE RESURRECTION OF VICKY

Reboring the cylinders

1. *Bob Frantz, Classic Car Centre machine shop technician, drops Vicky's 272-cid V-8 block into an angled cradle. Main caps will be torqued down during boring and honing operations to simulate the stress of an assembled engine.*

2. *Once the cradled block is set into position, one bank of cylinders will be oriented 90° to the boring bar.*

3. *Extremely accurate bubble gauge is used to parallel the crank centerline and deck surfaces. Decks will be trued later.*

4. *Locked snap gauge is miked to set the carbide cutting tool to the diameter necessary to clean the cylinders throughout the bore lengths.*

How come my newly rebuilt engine smokes like a freight train? That's a familiar question to which mechanics rattle off a batch of reasons, such as loose valves in the guides, etc.

Another candidate is improper cylinder sealing — a possible cause of the smoking engine problem which will be examined in this segment of the Resurrection of Vicky series. Cylinder sealing is perfect only when two critical measurements are absolutely on the money. The ring-to-bore contact must be flawless and the mating of the valves to seats must be absolute at all points.

You never seem to hear the guys at the local car club meetings talking about exotic cylinder bores, yet they'll talk all day about the benefits of pop-up pistons, flame travel characteristics and such. The truth is, though, that the functions of fancy pistons, rings, etc., are no more important in the scheme of a proper running internal combustion engine than the cylinders, even though cylinder design may be rather simple. The role of the cylinder is normally not given much thought by car enthusiasts. Ironically, many engineers devote considerable resources exploring the mysteries of those hollow voids, which are largely ignored by hobbyists.

Cylinders are the pathways of the pistons. Those pathways must be perfect as any interference or deviation can restrict natural piston travel and hinder performance. In addition, cylinder bores hold the ramming pistons in line to translate torque to the crank, act as the furnaces for thermal combustion and serve as an escape route for spent gases. The kinetic functions of cylinders are vitally important. They also add static strength and rigidity to the engine block.

A natural phenomenom of a piston-driven engine is the tendency of the piston to grind cylinders out of round. An engine that has pushed a car 100,000 miles is an engine that has measurably out-of-round cylinders, according to Bob Frantz, the Classic Car Centre technician assigned to prepping Vicky's tired block. During the

5

6

7

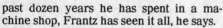

8

9

10

5. Dial bore gauge records out-of-roundness and taper of bore. Bottoms and tops of cylinders were measured to determine the amount of cylinder taper.

6. It took a .030" overbore to clean up all the cylinder wear ridges.

7. An interested observer, Cars & Parts Editor Bob Stevens, watches Frantz finish honing the cylinders. Roughing up cylinder walls with a cross-hatching pattern aids in setting new piston rings and in the retention of oil on cylinder walls.

8. Block is splashed liberally with lubricating fluid while cylinders are honed.

9. Post-honing operations include chamfering all bolt holes. Only a high performance engine shop would go to this extreme.

10. The tops of the cylinders were deburred and cleaned.

past dozen years he has spent in a machine shop, Frantz has seen it all, he says.

When pistons slam a few million times up and down the cylinders during an engine's lifetime, the bores will be worn oblong, out-of-round, and the job facing Frantz is to regrind those cylinders back to perfectly round. Often, as in the case of Vicky's V-8 block, an appreciable amount of overbore is required to clean the cylinders. Frantz explained that Vicky's engine is of the conventional mass produced design, which includes integrally cast cylinders. Many times, low production engines aren't built in that manner. Frantz cited exotic race engines and industrial engines as examples where designers often incorporate cylinder liners made of exotic metals deemed too expensive or inappropriate for use in casting the entire block.

There are two basic types of liners. Dry liners are sleeves which are driven inside the block cylinder for an interference fit. It's a dry fit. The other type is the wet liner. In this case a sleeve driven into the block makes contact with the coolant for a wet fit. When liners of the wet type are incorporated into the design, repairs are possible without disassembling the entire engine.

The specialists at CCC estimated that a .020" bore would be all that was necessary to clean up Vicky's cylinders. In actuality it took a .030" bore due to an eyebrow in one cylinder which wouldn't disappear at .020". Obviously, it would have been unwise to have purchased pistons prior to determining the overbore. For instance, there was an incident where an unfortunate enthusiast bought .020" pistons from an unknown vendor at a swap meet. There's no way he could properly fit .020" pistons into a .030" over bore or return the pistons for a refund. The clearance was far in excess of acceptable manufacturer's specs, so the unfortunate buyer was out the cost of the pistons.

The boring machine at Classic Car Centre is a top-of-the-line Peterson model. It's a precision piece of equipment which cradles the block and orients the boring bar 90° to the centerline of the crank. This type of boring machine is preferred for exacting high performance work in contrast to the other common type of boring machine, which mounts on the deck and incorporates a boring bar that twists down to cut the overbore.

Frantz took measurements inside the cylinders to register cylinder taper and any out-of-round condition. His initial judgement that .020" would clean up the cylinders proved to be partially correct. Seven of Vicky's cylinders cleaned up at

.020" while one was a fingernail shy. Frantz decided to uniformly bore all cylinders to .030". He says that bores in recent mass produced engines aren't always uniform. Often one or more cylinders may have to be overbored due to piston sealing problems in their appropriate cylinders. Thus the bore, piston, rings, etc., in one cylinder may not be of the same spec as its neighbors.

An expensive mistake commonly made by both pro and amateur rebuilders is failing to measure all bores and pistons when inspecting an engine for a pending rebuild. Another mistake is to assume that a set of new pistons will measure consistently. Measurements will vary slightly. For those who demand perfection, normal production tolerances aren't acceptable. He explained the method to determine the correct optimum bore size: The piston should be measured perpendicular to the pin and that measurement included with the piston-to-bore clearance.

Once Frantz finished boring the last cylinder of Vicky's engine, he latched onto the block and lifted it into a precision honing machine. Here the cylinders were finish honed to size using a cross-hatch pattern. Cross-hatching helps insure good piston ring seating and oil retention on the cylinder walls during initial start-ups.

1

2

Installing a sleeve

Vicky's block didn't need sleeves. What you see here is not a fix to the Crown Vic. During boring operations, Bob Frantz, the technician in charge of boring the cylinders, was asked what he would have done if a cylinder had been cracked? "I'd sleeve it," he said. The accompanying photos detail the installation of a dry sleeve. This is an appropriate companion to the cylinder boring article since many old car restorers encounter this type of problem when rebuilding vintage engines.

3

4

5

1. *This is not Vicky's engine. In the shop for a rebuild this block was suffering from a cracked cylinder.*

2. *Bore was cut oversize to a predetermined depth for insertion of the sleeve, leaving the light-colored lip ring at the bottom of the cylinder. The sleeve will set firm on that lip and below the cylinder head to prevent movement of the sleeve. Some shops don't leave the lip.*

3. *Interference fit of dry liner to block was .0005".*

4. *Frantz hammered sleeve into bore using a sleeve driver.*

5. *Sleeve reaching above bore will be trimmed to deck height.*

To get an old engine back up to snuff, normally the block decks should be resurfaced to achieve correct deck and piston clearance and to straighten out any misalignment of the decks and the crankshaft.

Over the past 30 years, Vicky's engine had been subjected to the normal rigors associated with a road car that manages, by a stroke of fate, to survive to a ripe old age and become a highly sought after collectible. Precision checks of the block indicated a slight warpage existed between the heads and block decks (possibly due to an overheating condition or compression leak that occurred sometime in Vicky's past). In addition, the head and block's mating surfaces should be trued to attain maximum gasket crush for a good seal.

The engine restoration team at Classic Car Centre, Warsaw, Ind., under the tutelage of engine restoration expert Gene McGuire, approached the task of decking Vicky's engine after an extensive and time consuming check to determine if the block had any unseen cracks. Using an Irontight Pressure Testing Machine, a device that seals all engine orifices with plates, stoppers, etc., the block was pressurized to 60 lbs. and soapy water was brushed over it to detect any bubbles created by escaping air.

Vicky's block was crack free. A second test at Classic Car normalized the casting. McGuire explained that "normalizing a casting" was a means of relieving hidden stress within a casting by heating the casting to 600°, cooling it to 300°, and shot peening it.

Earlier, the engine had been hot tanked to rid it of carbon buildup, etc., that could cause false readings when checking vital measurements — or foul up precision machining operations.

Machine shop employee Greg Long took

THE RESURRECTION OF VICKY

Decking the block

1. *The block was bubble-leveled to bring it into perfect alignment with the decking machine's grinding wheel.*

2. *Cranked down to within a whisker of touching, the grinding wheel is passed over the block on a trial run.*

a measurement from the main bearing saddle to the top of each deck. Using that measurement as a guideline, Long determined how much deck material to remove to make each deck surface parallel and an equal distance from the crank centerline.

A decking machine is a specialized milling machine which can be programmed to surface grind as little as .0005" off a deck surface. Under normal circumstances a block will never be milled more than .004". "You never take off any more than necessary to clean it up," McGuire says. Cutting beyond that point will adversely alter compression and the piston to valve clearance is reduced. If a deck is ground over .020", alignment of the intake manifold can be altered on V-type engines, such as the Y-block destined to be reinstalled in Vicky's chassis. That problem can be remedied by milling a compromising amount from the intake port surfaces of the heads.

Using an overhead crane, Long transferred Vicky's block to the deck grinding cradle, supported it and secured it in place. Next, he leveled the deck laterally and lengthwise with an extremely accurate bubble scale and programmed the mill to pass just a whisker above the deck surface. Then he gradually dropped the grinding wheels. After a few passes, the decks cleaned up. A minor divot was found near a center port on the passenger side. Long reasoned that since the divot was slight and located away from the cylinder bores, additional grinds to eliminate the divot were not worthwhile. "The head gasket will take care of that," he concluded.

The staff at Classic Car Centre had determined that the block was in respectable shape (if not top notch shape) after 30 years of use. Decking the block cleaned up a few minor sins and the block was as beautiful as ever. This concluded most of the major engine rebuilding chores; only the cylinder boring job remained.

3

EDITOR'S NOTE: In the pursuit of various editorial projects, *Cars & Parts* and its staff members occasionally employ certain types and brands of equipment, tools, vehicles, services and supplies. The use, display and description of these products or services do not constitute an endorsement of said products or services, or their manufacturers or suppliers. Nor does it imply any warranties or guarantees to the performance, durability, safety or suitability of those products or services by *Cars & Parts*, Amos Press, Inc., or its employees.

3. Classic Car technician, Greg Long, turns on the cutting lubricant spray and a sweep is taken across the deck surface.

4. Remaining head gasket stains will gradually disappear with each swipe of the grinding wheel. Each pass takes off half a thousandth (.0005") of metal.

5. Areas around cylinder bores cleaned up after only a few passes while the surfaces near the area where the exhaust ports exit were warped. Note the recessed area where the grinding wheel hasn't made contact (arrow).

1

1. When the engine was disassembled, spalling and roughness were found on the cam lobes. Cam was trashed and replaced with a new one.

2. Excessive wear on the integral distributor drive gear was another reason for discarding the old cam.

3. It isn't necessary to replace push rods unless they are bent or metal fatigue is found at wear points as illustrated by the rough end of this rod.

4. Non-perpendicular relationship of valve rocker arms to push rods was the result of a long-forgotten attempt by a marginal mechanic to smooth the rough surface with a hand file. Both rocker assemblies will be replaced.

2

3

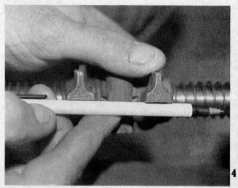

4

We weren't too far along in the disassembly of Vicky's engine when we realized that the old 272 was about as tired as an engine can be. We had one exhausted Y-block on our hands, although it may have stood up to the average old car lover's "nostalgic" driving for several years provided he didn't push Vicky too hard. The engine was full of sludge, all close tolerances weren't and practically every metal to metal contact point showed excessive wear due to a breakdown of the lubricating oil film.

One of the engine components facing almost certain death within a few thousand miles was the camshaft. If you've followed the Vicky series from the start, you may recall the chapter on engine analysis. We recorded the engine's tired condition as the staff at Classic Car Centre tore the engine apart piece by piece. The first two photos in this segment are repeated as a reminder of the problems discovered. Metal fatigue and spalling were found on the lobes and irregular wear was noted on every cam profile. Unlike crankshafts, cams aren't normally reground and polished by engine rebuilders but rather replaced with a new one.

Terry Hygema, machine shop supervisor at Classic Car Centre, says cams for some

THE RESURRECTION OF VICKY

Replacing the camshaft and cam bearings

5. New cam bearings were readily available at a local parts house in Warsaw, Ind., home to Classic Car Centre.

6. Gene McGuire checked the fit of the new bearings prior to setting them in place.

7. Visual inspection to check the alignment of the block and bearing oil holes is one step that can't be overlooked.

8. Components of cam bearing tool include various fittings and drivers to accomplish bearing replacement in almost any engine.

9. Bearing is placed on inserting tool.

10. McGuire carefully hammers the bearings, making sure the oil holes in the block and bearing are lined up.

5

6

7

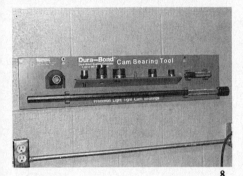

8

9

10

industrial uses are built up by spray-welding, then reground. "But it's a last resort, have-to situation and is not recommended under any other circumstances." Owners of older cars who cannot locate replacement cams can have a new cam ground from a blank. Hygema winced as he said, "That can be really expensive, but sometimes that's the only avenue available."

Vicky's original camshaft is of alloy-iron construction — a mass produced one-piece casting. Five steel-backed babbitt insert-type block-held bearings are used. There's one cam lobe for every intake valve and one for every exhaust valve. Bearing journals are larger in diameter than the cam lobes to permit removal of the shaft from the front end. End thrust is controlled by a thrust plate at the front of the engine.

At the front end of the engine, Vicky's cam is connected to the crankshaft by a drive gear sprocket and a timing chain. The arrangement of the cam sets the firing order of the cylinders and determines the exact time and length of each valve opening. Common features of Vicky's cam are its driving relationship to the distributor via a separate gear and the fuel pump via an extra lobe on the cam. The manner in which the oil pump is driven is some-

what uncommon as it is driven by an intermediate shaft which fits in the distributor driveshaft.

In a four-cycle engine, such as the one with which we're dealing, the camshaft spins half as many revolutions as the crankshaft. Each valve (both intake and exhaust) opens and closes once every two revs of the crank. When valve timing is correct, the exhaust valve will open a few degrees before the power stroke and close only after the exhaust stroke is complete. The corresponding intake valve will open before the end of the exhaust stroke and close only after the intake stroke is completed. Closing the exhaust valves after the end of the exhaust stroke promotes better scavenging of spent gases. Closing the intake valves after the end of the intake stroke takes advantage of the inertia of the flow to ram the air-fuel mix into the cylinders.

Between the cam and the valves are several other components which must also function perfectly to achieve maximum performance. Those components include the valve tappets, push rods and rocker arms. Normally the tappets are changed when a new cam is installed while the push rods and rocker arms are reused. Due to metal fatigue on the push rod ends

and unlevel surfaces on the rocker arms (see photos), it was necessary to replace both component groups when rebuilding Vicky's engine.

A new Sealed Power cam and bearings were purchased from a local Warsaw auto parts supplier. Replacing the bearings involved the use of a general service replacement cam bearing tool. All oil holes in the bearings were aligned with holes in the block. Number three cam bearing supplies oil to the rocker arms on Y-block Ford engines. It's not unusual to find tired old Y-blocks with this bearing spun or the hole plugged, thus the oil passage is closed up and the rockers are starved for oil. Years ago, a quick fit by shadetree mechanics to facilitate rocker arm oiling consisted of running a copper tube from the bottom of the engine to the top of the valve cover where a hole was drilled so the tubing could drip oil onto the rockers below.

Understanding the operation of a cam may seem rather simple. Recognizing what appears to be a rather funny-looking stick of iron with bumps is only a small portion of the cam story. In fact, it appears that cam science has yet to be fully explored and understood even by automotive engineers who continually spec out

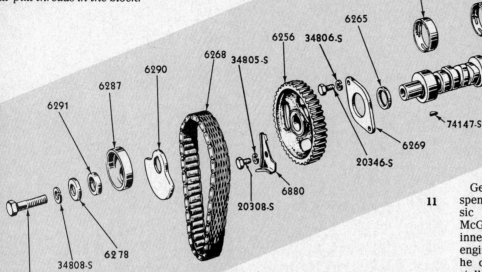

11. *Typical V-8 camshaft assembly is depicted in this illustration from a Ford chassis parts manual.*

12. *Snapping-head of Snap-On torque wrench alerts mechanic when torque spec is met. Camshaft bolts are hardened. McGuire warns that overtorquing then will pull threads in the block.*

different cam grinds for testing.

With Vicky or any other machine the cam grind should match the use of the vehicle. Vicky is essentially a glorified cruise machine and doesn't need a high rev cam as used in a drag machine. The geometry of her stock cam was computed some 30 years ago by engineers shuffling a raft of numbers compiled from the compression ratio, carb volume, cubic inch displacement, drivetrain figures, loaded car weight, as well as the intended use of our 1950's vintage grocery-getter.

The new Ford buyer in 1955 could not order an optional cam. There was only one grind available. The trick cams, etc., synonymous with the high performance engines of the late '50s and '60s existed only on racetracks and in the minds of innovative automotive engineers. Interestingly, the Ford parts book lists only one cam for both the 272 and 292 engines. The other components in the valve train, such as push rods, springs, tappets, rocker arms, etc., are also take-it-or-leave-it items in our book. The day when a potential customer could walk into a dealership and spec out his car was still on the horizon.

Gene McGuire, master engine rebuilder, spends most of his time coaching the Classic Car Centre's team of mechanics. McGuire is equally at home describing the inner workings of an internal combustion engine. As McGuire installed Vicky's cam, he described his recommended cam installation techniques. McGuire said, "I rebuild every engine as if it were my personal engine. The slam-bang type of workmanship always catches up with you. Old car hobbyists may find it interesting that some race engine shops spend 100 hours prepping an engine." The Classic Car Centre team will often also go to that extreme.

McGuire began the camshaft installation by peeping inside the block with a mini-flashlight, searching for oil delivery holes in the cam bearing seats. He pointed out that the oil holes in the cam bearings must register perfectly when installed. Otherwise the life of new cam bearings will be short, at best.

McGuire pressed the new cam bearings into place by carefully hammering on the head of the cam bearing tool. Bearing no. 1 was sunk .005-.025" below the front face of the bearing bore for clearance.

Next, the camshaft was prepared for insertion by coating the distributor gear and cam lobes with Sealed Power Cam Lube 55-400. Then it was slipped into place as per Sealed Power guidelines:

Extreme care must be taken not to damage the cam or bearings.

• To obtain optimum performance use new timing components. Tighten camshaft retaining bolts and thrust plate bolts to the proper torque specification and proper end play.

• Check assembly to make certain timing marks are in proper alignment.

• To help guard against excessive lobe wear, new lifters must be installed. Lubricate each lifter body and foot surface with Sealed Power Cam Lube 55-400 or any good camshaft lubricant before installing.

Once the engine assembly is completed and recorded in future segments of the Vicky series, McGuire will fill the crankcase with oil and run the engine at fast idle (roughly 1,500 rpm) for several minutes (15 at least) to insure a proper marriage of the cam and lifters.

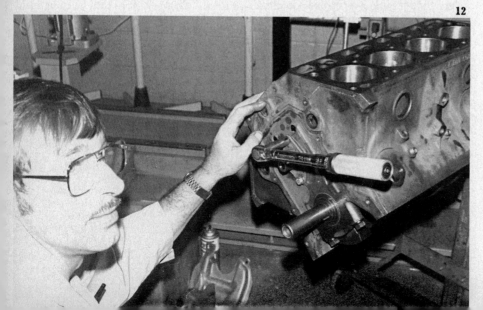

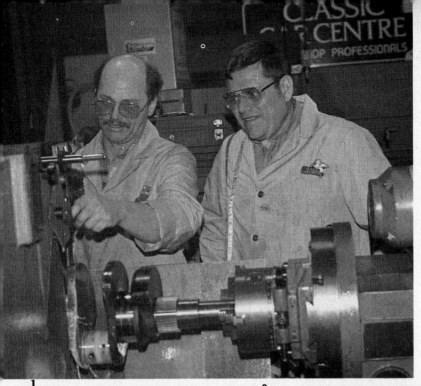

1

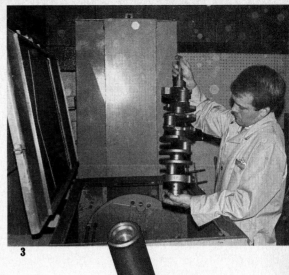

2

3

4

5

THE RESURRECTION OF VICKY

Reconditioning the crankshaft

When one fields a successful tug-of-war team, the heaviest, strongest and meanest-looking guy anchors the squad. The crankshaft in Vicky's engine is similar. It's a heavy, massive hunk of metal that anchors a team of eight connecting rods. It's asked to withstand a constant battering from eight aggressive pistons. No other chunk of metal in the engine is built stronger or designed to endure such punishment.

As the heart of an internal combustion engine, the crank collects all the reciprocating motion of pistons and connecting rods and transforms it into rotary motion. Each firing of every piston, as well as counter slams from backfiring, lagging, misfiring, etc., hammers the crankshaft.

The unglamorous but critically important crankshaft is a primary concern for Jim Roach, the masterful crank grinder at Classic Car Centre, Warsaw, Ind., where "Vicky," *Cars & Parts'* 1955 Ford Crown Victoria, is being restored.

Roach is typically surrounded by a crowd of cranks, some big, some little, and all patiently waiting for their turn in his grinding lathe. He sees this bunch of bruised and battered rowdies as a pretty good bunch of boys. They may need slight char-

1. *Jim Roach (left) and machine shop foreman Terry Hygema dial-in specs to zero-in the crank grinder lathe head. Crank grinding is an uncompromising job. "A little too much ground off and it's trash," says Jim, adding, "I'd rather grind it six times than trash it the first time."*

2. *Classic Car Centre routinely builds up rare and irreplaceable cranks by spray welding, as is the case with this 1940s-vintage Caterpillar crankshaft.*

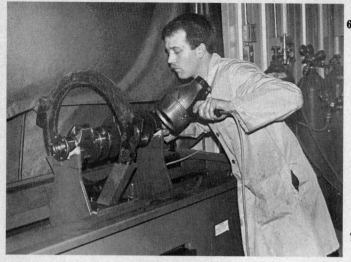

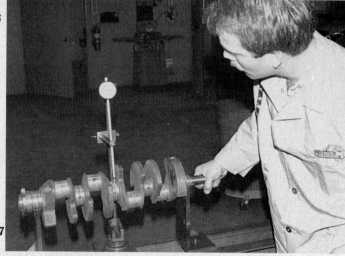

acter adjustment, he says, but there are certainly no problems here that a good scrubbing and a little machining can't cure. Once Roach scours and reshapes this bunch of ruffians, they'll look like new and spin with the best of them.

Roach has a solid mechanical background with more than 10 years as an aviation machinist at Bendix Corp. His qualifications are perfect for the unusual and varied demands of crankshaft grinding at Classic Car Centre. "It's not just 350 Chevy cranks day after day," Roach says. "When you grind cranks for vintage engines, each and everyone of these 'pups' is different — different metal compositions, different manufacturing methods, different histories."

Each used crank has its own set of problems that must be solved, he explained, pointing to the gang of cranks surrounding his grinding lathe. This particular group included cranks from a late 1930's Lincoln Zephyr, an '04 Olds, a Caterpillar out of the '40s, a 283 Chevy, and a Packard from the teens. Also, of course, there was the crank (coded EC for 272-cid V-8) from Vicky's engine.

"This crank doesn't look too bad," he said, revolving Vicky's crank slowly while closely inspecting it. "It should clean up nicely at around .020" or so. We'll put the micrometer on it and get started." Earlier he had cleaned the crank of all grease and debris, which would have fouled the readings.

Readers who have been following the series of articles on the reconstruction of *Cars & Parts'* project car will recall that the crank showed wear in the journals and that excessive lateral movement was discovered when the crew at Classic Car broke down the engine for analysis and inspection. Logged into the machine shop's work schedule, the Crown Vic's crank was tagged for a magnaflux test. "That's routine," according to Terry Hygema, machine shop foreman. "We'll inspect it for cracks, shotpeen it and check the straightness before we consider any grinding. There's no need to machine it if it's no good," Hygema said.

The crank's role in the scheme of an internal combustion engine is very important. It can affect balance, vibration, main bearing loads and the firing of the engine. If the crank is not straight, or if a journal profile or surface finish is fouled when the engine is reassembled, it can hinder good performance, and promote premature bearing failure.

Although our crank was out of the block, inspections can often be made while the crank is still in the engine. Dropping the oil pan and a rod cap or two will reveal the scratches, cracks, corrosion and discolorations that signal a defective crank. In addition, the connecting rods can be miked (measured with a micrometer) for taper and out-of-round conditions without dropping the crank. If bearing failure is found in an engine, the crank must be removed and thoroughly inspected and measured with precision instruments.

Should a crank fail the tests, a replacement should be found in the form of a new or remanufactured crank. Or, the old crank can be reconditioned by grinding, polishing and possibly straightening, if necessary and practical.

Inspection of a crank includes a check of taper, roundness and journal profile.

When a bearing has been spun, shutting off the oil supply, excessive heat is created at the journal. A hardness test with a sclerometer should preclude any machining operations. Next, a magnetic particle test is in order to insure that the crank is worthy of a regrind.

Magnafluxing Vicky's crank involved

3. Greg Long, a technician at Classic Car Centre, drops Vicky's crank into a shotpeening cabinet. EC code denoting Ford's 272 crank can be seen on the counterweight at the bottom.

4. Shot beads the size of small B-B's are bombarded at the crank inside the cabinet to relieve any stress within the shaft.

5. Out of the shotpeening cabinet, the crank is

marked to help employees identify Vicky's crank throughout the various machining operations. This is a cast crank; racing and industrial engines normally use stronger forged cranks.

6. Crank is magnafluxed to determine if cracks, nicks or imperfections exist on the surface of the casting.

7. Long checks straightness of crank in

V-blocks. Dial indicator will record deflection runout.

8. Casting flash on factory crank has survived in place for 30 years. But it might not last another 10 minutes, so it'll be ground off.

9. Hand-held die grinder is used to remove casting flash, burrs, etc., from counterweights.

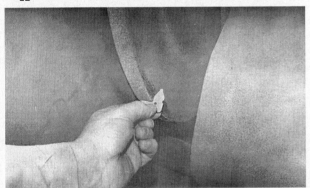

10. Technician points to journal fillet radius which will be matched when regrinding Vicky's crank.

11. The proper radius gauge — 5/32" — is pulled for checking the fillet radius.

12. A perfect match is seen as gauge is set in place at the fillet.

13. Grinding wheel was dress ground to 5/32" radius. Again, gauge is set in place to check radius.

14. All journals were measured at several points to determine the extent of out-of-round wear.

brushing an oily liquid containing magnetic particles onto the crank and placing it inside a magnetized coil. Under a tent in ultraviolet light, cracks not normally seen by the human eye were seen easily. No scars appeared, other than minute superficial marks and scratches, and it passed the test easily. Although there were none on this crank, larger cracks can usually be seen without the aid of magnafluxing equipment, and can also be felt by running a fingernail over the cracks. A trip to the shotpeening cabinet relieved surface tension and the crank was ready for grinding.

In the old days a mechanic carried a penny in his toolbox for testing the surface finish of bearing journals. If scars appeared on the penny after rubbing it across the face of the journal, the crank needed to be polished. That same technique is still in use at Classic Car, Gene McGuire, engine restoration expert at the

Center, says. "Those old guys knew what they were doing. It still works today."

A bent crankshaft should be replaced or restraightened, if possible. This was not a problem with the Crown Vic crank. To detect a bent condition the crank is supported in V-blocks and a dial indicator is set at the center or intermediate journals. The dial indicator will record the highest and lowest readings when the crank is spun 360°. Readings that indicate a variance of more than .0005" mean the crank is defective and should be replaced or reconditioned. An out-of-round, egg-shaped journal will reveal two high readings.

The procedure to straighten a crankshaft includes baking it for an hour in an oven at 350°-450°F and exerting pressure with a press ram at the bent journal. The amount of pressure is gradually increased until the crank deflection reads no more than .005" on the dial indicator.

When polishing a crank, either in a polishing lathe or crankshaft grinder, turning it in the same direction it will turn in an engine is the correct way to get started. All sharp edges around oil holes should be removed and the holes polished with a mandrel and drill. To avoid heat build-up, a crank should be polished only when it is revolving and never for more than a few seconds at any one point.

The specialists at Classic Car Centre decided to go the extra mile when grinding Vicky's crank by following a procedure known to race engine builders as indexing. Indexing is not normally performed on a regular car engine since it involves machining to extra close tolerances and requires at least twice as much grinding time. It also costs at least twice as much.

Terry Hygema explained indexing: "All journals (there are four on an eight-cylinder engine) are indexed on the degree

15

16

wheel on the lathe chuck to exactly 90° in relation to each other. That means the crank and centerline of the main bearings are 'dead nuts'. It's not uncommon for worn journals to be .020"-.030" off in relation to each other. Indexing will correct the errors. Keep in mind, indexing requires the removal of more metal than a normal grind. You've got to start out with a pretty good crank."

It took about eight hours to clean up the Crown Vic's crank journals.

Once the grinding operations were completed, Roach cleaned the crank, sprayed it with WD-40, retagged it, and placed it inside a plastic bag. The crank regrinding requirements of our Crown Vic project car were satisfied without incident by the capable staff at the Classic Car Centre. It had cleaned up at .030" and new bearings had been ordered.

Later, the reground crankshaft was polished, balanced and shelved to await the other engine components for final engine assembly.

17

18

15. *This journal, the worst of the lot, will need to be ground +22 thousands to true it up. Checking the bearing supplier's catalog, it was decided that it would be necessary to grind the crank to .030". The catalog listed .010", .020" and .030" bearings. The latter will be used and the crank ground accordingly.*

16. *Large grinding wheel at the rear kisses a rod journal as it is slowly advanced toward our .015" mark. Half off (.015") each side of the revolving diameter equals .030" taken off the crank.*

17. *Indexed crank is as good as new, maybe better.*

18. *Fitted with bobweights representing all hang-on components (con-rods, pistons, etc.), plus the harmonic balancer and torque plate, Vicky's crank was balanced on a Stewart-Warner Balancing Stand.*

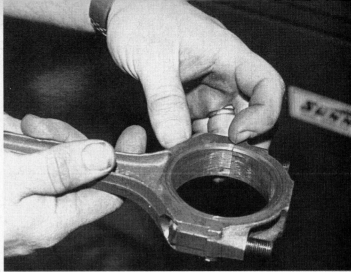

THE RESURRECTION OF VICKY

Resizing the connecting rods

To rebuild a tired old engine capable of delivering its second 100,000 miles of trouble free operation, one must attend to the smallest irregularities.

The 272-cid block residing under Vicky's hood seemed a bit more tired than the 69,000 miles displayed on the odometer. Opinions among the staffs at *Cars & Parts* and Classic Car Centre ranged from "Yes, it's actual miles," to suggestions that a rollback of the speedo may have taken place, or that it had rolled over one time. Everyone conceded that back in the days when "migrant mechanics" armed with electric drills routinely visited many used car lots in the country, rollbacks were commonplace. In fact, rollbacks were expected by the astute used car lot junky.

Regardless of any possible violations of Vicky's character prior to the day when Bob Stevens and Ken New, of the *Cars & Parts* staff, located her in St. Louis, the engine was dirty and tired and needed a rebuild. Plus, it's impractical to conceive of a frame-up restoration without going through the engine.

Connecting rods are an integral part of the piston-driven engine. The design and configurations of the rods may vary from engine to engine, but only slightly. The usual design consists of a beam shaft connecting two bores. At one end a small bore holds the pin inside the piston. At the other end is a larger bore (a clam-shell-bolted-

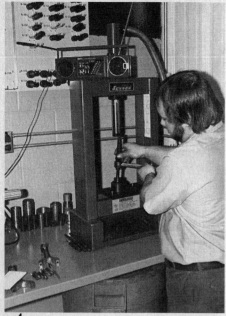

5

4

6

7

8

together-affair) that pins the rod bearings to the crankshaft. A rather elementary design, at best, but its importance can't be discounted.

Connecting rods are the vital links between the pistons and the crankshaft, and are responsible for converting reciprocating piston motion to rotary motion at the crank. Considering the fact that a set of rods is expected to endure the punishment exerted by combustion at the pistons and deliver power to the crank several thousand times every minute the engine is operating, the importance of the rods can't be over-emphasized.

This chapter in the series of articles detailing the restoration of Vicky, *Cars & Parts'* 1955 Ford Crown Victoria project car, describes the connecting rod rebuilding work of Bob Frantz, an employee of the machine shop at Classic Car Centre, Warsaw, Ind. These services are also available through many engine and machine shops across the country.

Frantz came to Classic Car Centre after spending several years running an engine rebuilding shop and working at a vocational education center where he taught machine trades. His knowledge and experience are invaluable. Frantz approaches rod sizing with a religious zeal and reverence not found in most people. "Rods are some of the most abused engine components," he said.

"Rods prepped incorrectly can be deadly," he said, adding that they can produce engine vibration, bearing failure, ignition and timing quirks, and engine breathing and burning problems. Used rods can suf-

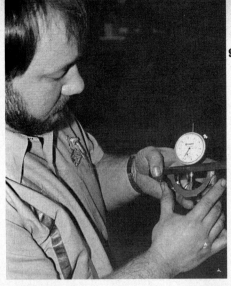

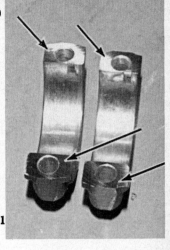

9. *Dial indicator is used to find exact bottom of arc. That's where 0° is set. That measurement will serve as a reference point throughout the operation — resizing the big end.*

10. *Rod cap is placed in Sunnen cap and rod grinder, where parting line surfaces are ground square to side bearing surfaces.*

11. *Parting surfaces (see arrows) were cleaned up with only a .001 grind. Sometimes it takes more.*

12. *Cleanliness is an absolute necessity when rebuilding con-rods at Classic Car Centre.*

13. *Studs were magnafluxed and found to be acceptable for reuse. Frantz reassembled correspondingly numbered rods and caps in rod box and torqued them to 40 ft./lbs.*

14. *Bearing manufacturers, such as CR Industries, publish specs for replacement bearings. Big end bore spec of 2.3120 to 2.3128 was recommended. Frantz says his policy is to aim for the middle, or 2.3124 in this case.*

15. *Honing machine has built-in dial gauge, which Frantz set to 2.3124.*

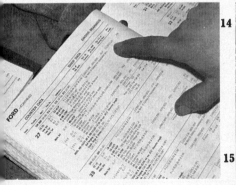

fer from twisted beams, stress cracks, out-of-round bores, plugged oil tubes and squirt holes or a combination of all these ailments. It takes an expert to pinpoint and correct problems of this nature since an engine will run with some degree of success with all of these problems.

During the rebuild, Frantz magnafluxed, x-rayed, shotpeened, resized and rebushed the small bores, and then fitted the rods with full-floating piston pins. The rods were balanced later, a precision process which will be explored in a later chapter.

At this point, it should be pointed out that the procedures described in this section are appropriate for almost any automotive gas engine, not just a Ford V-8.

Good rebuilding techniques cross most borders.

Resizing connecting rods is demanding, exacting work that must be checked and rechecked, then rechecked again using gauges that pick up discrepancies of no more than ten-thousandth of an inch. A hobbyist who rebuilds his own engine would be well advised to leave such tedious, precision jobs to the experts. Remember, these articles are not always exacting how-to stories on Vicky's restoration, but sometimes straight technical pieces to help educate the reader/hobbyist so that he knows what is entailed in a frame-up restoration, whether it be engine rebuilding, rust removal, etc. In the long run, he'll

spend his restoration money more wisely, or at least have a better understanding of the procedures and equipment involved.

The life of connecting rods can be extended if prep work is performed correctly. Excess flash at the parting lines should be removed, as well as any burrs and sharp edges along the beams. Cracks hidden by the flash and burrs will be easier to see when the rods are magnafluxed. It's not necessary to polish rods unless a racing mill is being built, which was not the case with Vicky's engine.

As Bob Frantz proceeded to address the rebuild of Vicky's rods, he commented on the insanity of resizing rods without magnafluxing them first. "Only a fool would spend time on rods suited for the trash barrel," he said, as he took the rods in hand and walked to the magnafluxing machine. Magnafluxing rods, or any other engine component, involves brushing a dye penetrant onto the rods, which are then placed in a magnetic field under ultraviolet light. Surface flaws and cracks not easily seen under normal light conditions are now readily detectable. When cracked rods are found, they should be replaced with ones that pass the mag test. Racing engine rebuilders x-ray rods in addition to magnafluxing, to detect any porosity within the casting. Magnafluxing will show surface nicks, flaws, cracks, etc., but it won't

16

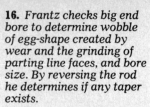

17

18

19

16. Frantz checks big end bore to determine wobble of egg-shape created by wear and the grinding of parting line faces, and bore size. By reversing the rod he determines if any taper exists.

17. Revolving honing bar has abrasive cutting stones mounted around its diameter.

18. Bronze bushings were pressed into the small ends of the rods. Note line up of oil holes in the bushing and rod. This is a must for proper oiling.

19. Micrometer reading on new piston pin indicated a diameter of .912". A set of piston pins won't vary one-half a gram in weight and within .0001" in diameter. They are made to exacting tolerances by manufacturers.

20. Maintaining center-to-center bore measurements from big end to small end is very critical. A dial indicator insures exactness to within a couple ten-thousandths of an inch.

21. Bore cutting tool is advanced to small end.

22. Pads at small ends are ground away as needed to balance small end weights from rod to rod. All eight of Vicky's rods were balanced within half a gram.

show cavities inside the rods. Usually, x-raying will! That's a good argument for having rods x-rayed.

Frantz recommends checking rod side clearances once an engine is assembled. Excessive side clearance can result in oil leakage past the rods and a demand for more oil. Consequently, it robs oil from other surfaces needing lubrication.

After the rods are magnafluxed to determine if cracks exist anywhere on the castings, they are baked at 600° to relieve any torsional twist (misalignment) that may exist between the ends. Both ends should be centered absolutely on the same axis. Any drift from that axis is known as twist. Many machine shops and most repair manuals recommend setting the rods in a jig and physically bending them back to a straight condition.

Gene McGuire, Classic Car Centre's machine shop foreman, prefers a heat treatment method. Baking at 600° seasons the rods to "normalize the castings", McGuire says. "It's a funny thing, but the twist you take out with a monkey wrench will come right back in a little while. The rod knows where it wants to be (in relation to the piston pin and crank) and it will return to that same place," he said. Baking allows the rod to set itself before machining operations begin.

Once out of the oven, the blistering 600° rods are cooled to 300° and shotpeened to relieve remaining stress, and to harden the surfaces. The resizing operations start now.

All eight of Vicky's rods were numbered according to the corresponding cylinder from which they came. Flash, nicks and imperfections were removed with a die grinder in a lengthwise direction to eliminate areas where stress could arise. The rods were shotpeened; then the small end bores were bronze bushed and honed to size. The big ends' parting surfaces were ground and the egg-shaped bores were resized after torquing down the rod caps.

Follow Bob Frantz at work in the accompanying photos as he reconditions the rods of the Crown Vic's V-8 engine.

20

21

22

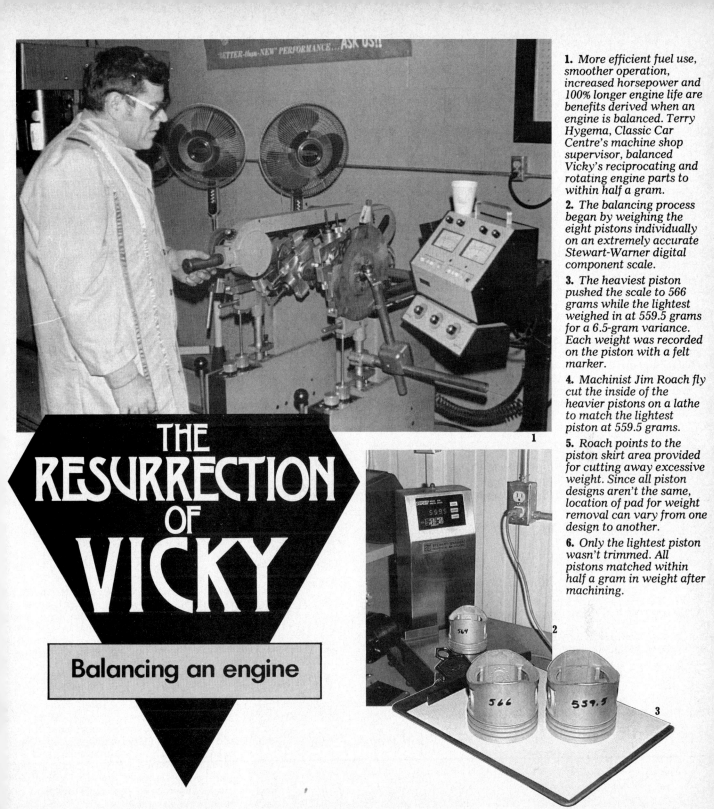

THE RESURRECTION OF VICKY

Balancing an engine

1. *More efficient fuel use, smoother operation, increased horsepower and 100% longer engine life are benefits derived when an engine is balanced. Terry Hygema, Classic Car Centre's machine shop supervisor, balanced Vicky's reciprocating and rotating engine parts to within half a gram.*

2. *The balancing process began by weighing the eight pistons individually on an extremely accurate Stewart-Warner digital component scale.*

3. *The heaviest piston pushed the scale to 566 grams while the lightest weighed in at 559.5 grams for a 6.5-gram variance. Each weight was recorded on the piston with a felt marker.*

4. *Machinist Jim Roach fly cut the inside of the heavier pistons on a lathe to match the lightest piston at 559.5 grams.*

5. *Roach points to the piston skirt area provided for cutting away excessive weight. Since all piston designs aren't the same, location of pad for weight removal can vary from one design to another.*

6. *Only the lightest piston wasn't trimmed. All pistons matched within half a gram in weight after machining.*

Engine balancing is not a do-it-yourself procedure. To install a balancing machine in the average collector car owner's garage is rather absurd. Not only does a balancer take up a lot of precious room and cost an arm and a leg, operating such a sophisticated piece of equipment is far beyond the knowledge or ability of the average old car owner who may never own more than a half-dozen collector cars in his lifetime. Balancing an engine is a big job which should be left to a trained professional using top quality equipment and state-of-the-art technology.

Since the series of articles on the restoration of *Cars & Parts'* project car, a gorgeous red and white 1955 Ford Crown Victoria, began in the fall of 1986, many readers of the magazine have written to express opinions on the project, offer helpful advice and to praise the staff's efforts. Most wrote to say that they liked the series and that many of their questions about restoration had been answered.

But one writer challenged *Cars & Parts* to keep the Vicky restoration series "in the backyard" — away from the likes of a modern well-equipped machine shop. He felt that we were promoting the argument that "backyard mechanics have been wasting their time and money." Nothing could be further from the truth. It was never our intention to suggest that hobbyists leave car restoration to the professionals. We have always believed that the individual car restorer is the heart of the hobby, yet there are certain jobs for which he is ill equipped. He may not have the skills required to do a satisfactory job, nor the tools. We felt that watching professionals at work would offer an excellent way of providing much needed information to the backyarder as well as making him aware of "good buys" such as the value of a precision balanced and blueprinted engine. For instance, the estimated $120 spent balancing a V-8 engine ($80 for a six; $70 for a four) is money well spent. Of course, we didn't expect the reader to slip out to his garage and balance his engine after dinner. However, we did consider it worthwhile to tell him about the better performance and fuel economy synonymous with engine balancing.

Balancing an engine is beneficial to longevity. And, it is extremely important to build durability into vintage engines during a rebuild. With replacement parts becoming scarcer every day, it makes

sense to take advantage of every available benefit.

Arguments in favor of balancing are pretty convincing. For instance, a one-quarter ounce of unbalance located four inches from the center of the crank creates a seven-pound force of unbalance at 2,000 rpm. That same force is multiplied nine times when the engine is revved to 6,000 rpm and up to 16 times at 8,000 rpm or the equivalent of 112 pounds. Our hypothetical example realistically could be one piston assembly one-quarter ounce out of balance. Imagine the destructive power of a full pound of unbalance, then translate that to the average hobbyist's wallet. Hundreds or even thousands of dollars can be wasted in no more time than it takes to open the garage door! Certainly, the average hobbyist can ill afford such a whirlwind of misfortune and should be advised of the pitfalls of assembling unbalanced engine components. The wise backyarder will perform the skills within his ability and means and use a competent engine rebuilder for tasks beyond his capabilities.

A basic understanding of engine imbalance will help him determine when the skills of a professional should be sought. Power impulses created by the engine set

up torsional vibrations in the spinning crankshaft. If that imbalance is left uncontrolled, crankshaft failure is almost always guaranteed when the crank is taxed under the stress of high speeds. To control the force of the pistons and connecting rods, balanced counterweights are placed opposite the rod bearing journals and normally a balanced flywheel and harmonic balancer are found at opposite ends of the crank to assist in stabilizing any irratic rotations of the crankshaft.

The machine shop at Classic Car Centre, Warsaw, Ind., is well endowed with skilled personnel and modern equipment. In previous segments of the "resurrection of Vicky" series, the CCC pros performed a precision rebuilding of all major engine components necessary to make Vicky's engine "hum a precision tune" for a second 100,000 miles, or more. Machine shop foreman Terry Hygema has been closely associated with the massaging of the Crown Vic's venerable Y-block from the start, directing the replacement and rebuilding of most engine components. Hygema was anxious to "get Vicky's engine on the balancer and blueprint it."

The balancing machine at Classic Car is the latest model from Stewart-Warner — a 2000-D Dual Digital balance machine capable of reading a tolerance of imbalance (weight x distance) in microscopic amounts. According to Stewart-Warner's amiable service engineer, Gary Hildreth, it will indicate the exact amount of weight (either grams or ounces) to be corrected in a crankshaft. An impressive piece of equipment, the unit is capable of accepting a shaft 10 feet long and features an rpm scale ranging from 0 to 600.

A banner on the wall of the machine shop at Classic Car boasts: "Precision Engine Balancing Service. Up to 100% longer engine life. Unbelievable engine smoothness. Greater horsepower. Better than new performance." Too good to be true? Not really, according to the folks at Stewart-Warner, who work with engine restoration shops throughout the country. Hildreth claims, "We have many shops doing old cars — V-12 Lincolns and many cars from the 1890s even! All have shown smoother running, less vibration and higher gas mileage."

There are two types of unbalance: static and dynamic. Static unbalance involves dead weight while dynamic unbalance occurs only with motion. To balance an engine, weight is taken off the pistons and connecting rods to equalize the weight of each piston assembly.

Another fact that most shadetree mechanics may have never considered is that most engines fall into two general categories. The in-line type, such as an in-line six or straight-eight, requires no bobweights to simulate the crank's hang-on parts. In-line engines have balanced crankshafts. Those cranks can be readily identified by the location of the counterweights on each end of the crank. They are in line and on the same side of the crank. The second classification concerns V-type engines, such as Vicky's Y-block Ford V-8. V-type engines have unbalanced crankshafts with large

4

5

6

7

8

counterweights on the ends which are not in line, but rather at opposite sides of the crank.

Since it is impractical to hang pistons, connecting rods, etc., on a crank and spin them outside an engine block, bobweights must be made up to simulate the exact weights as closely as possible.

Bobweights are two-piece affairs which when held onto a crank provide the engine balancing technician with a means to simulate 100% of the rotating weight and 50% of the reciprocating weight. To many the selection of bobweights may seem complicated. A Stewart-Warner brochure on

balancing manages to explain the selection in rather simple terms.

"On the standard V-8 engine, the bobweight total consists of 100% of the rotating weight and 50% of the reciprocating weight. You have two rod and piston assemblies per throw on the standard V-8. The rotating weight would be the crank end of both rods and the bearing insert. The reciprocating weight would be the weight of one piston, one piston end of a rod, one set of rings, pin and pin locks (if used). This gives you 50%, or half of the actual weight for the reciprocating part. Use of the following list will give you percentages and also ensure that you do not forget to weigh any of the parts."

To compute the rotating weight (100%) the following weights must be included: the weight of the two crank rod ends, two sets of bearing inserts, two sets of lock nuts (if separate), and the oil (estimate).

To compute the reciprocating weight (50%) these weights must be taken into account: the weight of piston, piston pin, piston pin lock (if used), one set of piston rings and piston end of connecting rod.

Balancing of Vicky's piston assemblies began by weighing the pistons.

Hygema determined the lightest piston by separately weighing all eight pistons on a precision Stewart-Warner #600175 digital electronic scale, which is accurate to within half a gram. As each weight was recorded on the piston castings with a felt marker, a 6.5-gram variance was found. The largest tipped the scale at 665 grams and the lightest at 559.5. Normally, piston manufacturers maintain relatively close weight tolerances when building production-run pistons, but for enthusiasts who demand absolute balance, those standards fall short and additional machining is required to produce equalized weights.

The other internal engine components

involved in balancing are the piston rings, pins (plus locks when used), connecting rods and connecting rod bearing inserts. Piston pins and rings, unlike pistons, are manufactured under extremely close tolerances and normally one pin or a set of rings won't vary more than half a gram from each other.

Machinist Jim Roach of the Classic Car Centre's staff carefully fly cut the insides of the seven heavier piston skirts on a lathe to match the 559.5 weight. Stewart-Warner warns that in extreme cases enough weight cannot be removed from the heaviest piston, thus either the lightest or the heaviest piston should be replaced with one which can be machined to the matching weight.

Pressing aluminum slugs into the piston pin of the lightest piston is another remedy yet it is not advised, under normal conditions, by Stewart-Warner. The balance equipment manufacturer also advises that the owner should be told when slugs are used since those two components (slugged pin and piston) should never be mixed with other piston assemblies or the engine will be out of balance.

Turning to the connecting rods, Hygema ground the balance pads on the big ends to matching weights on a belt sander. Then the small ends were equalized in a like manner using a rod weighing device in conjunction with the precision scale. Had pads not been cast into the rod design, all grinding would have been done along the length of the rods but not across the rods since grinding in that direction decreases rod strength and sets up focal points where internal stress can fracture rod castings.

Bobweights matching the piston assembly weight were assembled once all connecting rods were matchweighed. When bobweights spin they simulate the effect of the rod and piston assembly. Matchweights are small precision washer-like discs which permit one to add very small amounts of weight to the bobweights. Both bobweights and matchweights were stacked carefully in two equal stacks onto the digital scale until the exact piston assembly weights were matched. Four equal bobweights were required for Vicky's V-8 crank. The bobweights were then assembled onto the crank as it sat on trunnion bearing cradles and the balancing machine was actuated.

Within a short time Hygema was able to balance Vicky's crank assembly by taking metal from a couple of the crank counterweights, the torque converter plate, and the harmonic balancer. The crank spun smoothly at 6,000 rpm with the entire balancing procedure taking less than three hours total time, including a slight delay encountered when the rubber on the harmonic balancer was found to be loose from the metal. A quick trip to a local Ford dealer produced a new replacement part.

The V-8 engine is now fully and professionally balanced, and destined to run smoother, stronger and longer than even Ford would have thought possible.

9

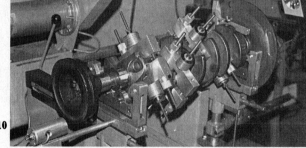

10

11

7. Connecting rods were balanced by trimming appropriate amounts of metal from pads at both ends of the connecting rods.

8. A belt sander is recommended for removing weight from rod pads.

9. Bobweights at 2,017 grams were made up to simulate the piston assembly weights.

10. Each bobweight was set up across from its opposing counterweight.

11. Drilling was required on a couple of counterweights to get things into kilter.

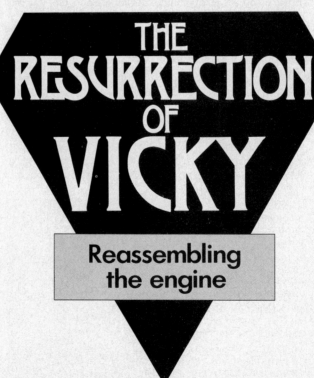

THE RESURRECTION OF VICKY

Reassembling the engine

It was quite a treat keeping company with the mechanics who rebuilt Vicky's tired 272 Y-block. The fixes made and comments heard are worthy of the attention of any restorer who may be contemplating having an engine rebuilt.

Several issues back in this series devoted to the restoration of *Cars & Parts'* Crown Victoria project car, we were there as Gene McGuire and Terry Hygema (members of the Classic Car Centre's staff) opened up the venerable V-8 that had pushed Vicky around Kansas and Missouri for some 30 years. We watched as each component was unbolted and analyzed. Parts found to be scratched, scarred, worn, etc., were carefully scrutinized and examined to detect the reason for excessive wear or failure. Among the ailments found were extreme lateral movement of the crank, cam lobes that had galled and pitted due to improper oiling, cylinder walls that were scored, and excessive wear between most moving parts. McGuire explained that all these marks were little biographical sketches that recorded the "history of Vicky".

The trained mechanic can "read these marks like a book," McGuire said, offering sympathy to old car owners who cannot

1. *All engine machine work was finished without incident and new replacement parts were readily available from a Sealed Power supplier. It was time to reassemble Vicky's engine. Gaskets are from Fel-Pro.*

2. *The freeze plug holes in the heads and block were measured with a digital readout caliper scale.*

3. *Correct size plugs were purchased after a check was made for eroded seats.*

4. *Joe Moon drives home a freeze plug. Driver should sit firmly in bottom of plug — not on the shoulders.*

5. *Bill Brown peeped inside the oil galleries to see if obstructions clogged passageways and restricted oil flow.*

6. *New plugs with plumber's Teflon tape were threaded into the holes. The Teflon seals in oil and aids plug removal at a later date. Years ago many mechanics tinned plugs to achieve the same results.*

7. *Bearing inserts .020" oversize were used to take up the slack created by the .020" taken from the crank during grinding operations.*

8. *Block was turned upside down on an engine stand for easy crank installation. Upper bearing caps fell easily into place.*

9. *Liberal use of engine bearing lube is good insurance against damage during initial engine start up.*

10. *Lube should be spread over all bearing shell surfaces.*

11. *Gene McGuire gently lowered the crank into place.*

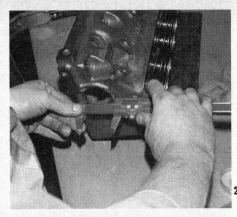

decipher the language written in a worn engine. When trained eyes examine an engine they see both the strengths and weaknesses, he added. It doesn't matter whether it's a recent-built engine that has suffered a systems failure or a tired and overly worn engine faltering on its last legs.

To properly rebuild either type, the mechanic must heed all unusual and excessive wear and restore clearances at critical wear points to acceptable factory specs. Otherwise he's playing a guessing game, according to McGuire.

McGuire warned that inept mechanics can be found almost anywhere and the careless old car owner who falls victim to these unprofessional practitioners can suffer dearly in the wallet. McGuire believes that potential customers should seek out rebuilders with bona fide credentials especially when selecting a shop to revitalize a vintage powerplant.

The fact that Vicky's engine had run without a major failure for an estimated 100,000 miles or more was a pretty good

indication that the factory did a respectable job of assembling the engine back in the fall of 1954. "The test", according to McGuire, "is to see if we can duplicate that good effort. Or better yet, improve or remedy problems inherent to the engine."

One such problem he mentioned was the chronic top engine oiling problem that he has seen in almost every Y-block Ford engine from the mid-1950s. It seems that the oil galleries to the lifter area clogged easily, preventing proper oil flow to the rocker arms and tappet areas. A properly cleaned block, a grooved cam from a later model Y-block and use of modern detergent oil should prevent a reoccurrence of this problem, McGuire said. The use of lighter weight aluminum pistons to lessen stress on the piston pins, rods and rod caps is an example of improvements to the '50s technology.

Follow along in the accompanying photos as the crew at Classic Car Centre, Warsaw, Ind., serves up fixes to Vicky's engine that should make her next 100,000 miles as rewarding as the first.

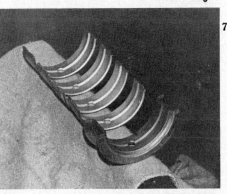

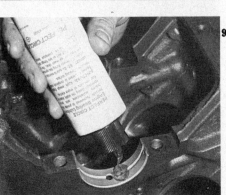

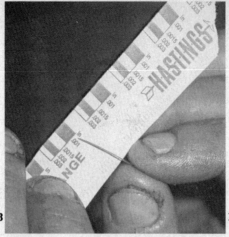

12 13 14

15

16

17

12. *There are five main bearing caps used in Vicky's 272 block. The center bearing (commonly called the thrust bearing) features side bearing surfaces to control lateral thrust movement.*

13. *Plastigaging material at .001" - .003" was used to check clearances.*

14. *Main caps were progressively torqued to 105 lbs. by starting at 80 lbs., then 95, then 105.*

15. *At this point McGuire checked the "rolling resistance". A resistance of 20 lbs. or less is required. Vicky's crank rotated freely with slight finger pressure.*

18 19

20 21 22

16. *Squeezed Plastigage at .0015" met Ford's recommendations exactly. All cap clearances were measured separately. Residue should be removed with carb cleaner.*

17. *Crankshaft end play came in at .0025", near the middle of McGuire's preferred range of .0015" - .0055".*

18. *Full-floating piston pin retainers are stock on a Ford Y-block.*

19. *Wrist pins and rod eyes were lubed, then the pins were inserted and worked back and forth to determine if they floated freely.*

20. *An inexpensive ring installer simplifies the job and lessens the risk of breaking rings.*

21. *When piston rings are assembled, the ring gaps should be oriented out of the skirt area "at least 10° - 15°", McGuire advised. Right index finger points to preferred 15° orientation of ring gap.*

22. *To insure that the rod cap bolts seated properly, Kim Durbin torqued them down before the rods were assembled to the crank.*

23. *A piston ring compressor snugly clamped the rings.*

24. *Each piston was gently pushed into the bore with a plastic mallet handle until the top of the piston fit flush with the top of the block. Never hammer on a piston. You've seen it a million times, but it's a no-no. You could break a ring.*

25. *Rubber hoses over threads protect crankshaft surfaces when inserting pistons into bores.*

26. *Many pistons are notched above the pin boss to indicate front of engine. Others are marked with an F on the flat surface near the pin.*

27. *Rod caps were deburred with an Arkansas stone, cleaned and lubed.*

28. *Arrow points to .001" - .003" Plastigage material.*

29. *Rod cap was torqued to 45-50 lbs. Snapping device on Snap-On torque wrench sounds off when spec is met.*

30. *Plastigage scale indicates that an excellent clearance of .001" exists between rod cap and crank journal.*

23

24

25

26

27

28

29

30

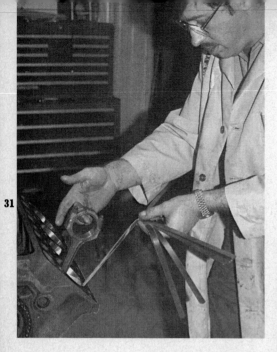

31

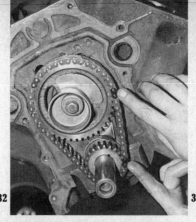

32

33

34

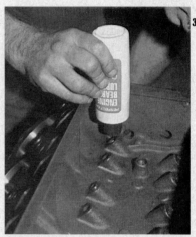

35

36

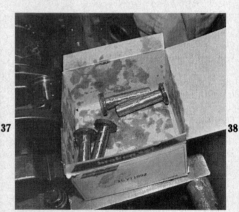

37

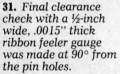

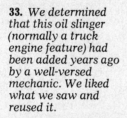

31. Final clearance check with a ½-inch wide, .0015" thick ribbon feeler gauge was made at 90° from the pin holes.

32. Always replace a sloppy timing chain that deflects more than a half-inch. Replace sprockets if the teeth are worn or damaged or if broken links are present. Dark links must be lined up with dots on sprockets for proper timing.

33. We determined that this oil slinger (normally a truck engine feature) had been added years ago by a well-versed mechanic. We liked what we saw and reused it.

34. Again a healthy dose of engine bearing lube was rubbed into the timing chain teeth.

35. Valve tappet bores were lubed as well.

36

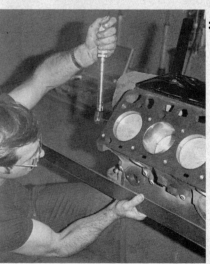

39

36. Valley cover was checked for flatness. Many times overzealous mechanics overwrench them into "bananas", said McGuire.

37. Feeler gauge was inserted at various points around the cover to verify good fit.

38. Solid lifters were well lubed prior to installation.

39. McGuire aligned the timing gear cover to the oil pan rail with a machined straight edge, then filed the surfaces for absolute level fit.

40

41

42

43

44

45

46

47

40. Wood block wrapped in a greased rag was used to hold crank while pulley nut was tightened to spec.

41. Head bolts were run through a die to true the threads, then the bolt heights were checked to guarantee that bolts wouldn't bottom out, thus preventing proper gasket crush.

42. Heads should be carefully guided into place to prevent scarring of surfaces. Alignment guide bolts add an extra bit of confidence, especially for heavier heads.

43. All engine makers prescribe a definite pattern for torquing head bolts. Charts are found in repair manuals.

44. Wiggling rocker arms were replaced. Note uneven wear on the tips of the original arms.

45. New rockers and precision workmanship make a beautiful sight.

46. Transmission was rebuilt by a local shop in Warsaw, Ind., then painted by the body shop at Classic Car Centre.

47. Good as new or better! Vicky's engine was dropped into place on new motor mounts from King & Wesley Obsolete Parts Co., Courthouse Square, Liberty, Ky. 42539. Spark plug wire holders are from the Ford Parts Store, 4925 Ford Road, Box 226, Bryan, Ohio 43506.

PART FOUR

Unleaded Gas Conversion, Fuel System Fixes

1

2

3

THE RESURRECTION OF VICKY

Converting to unleaded gas

The evils of running a vintage engine on unleaded fuel have received a justifiable amount of press in recent years. Vintage car owners, construction equipment operators, farm implement owners and others have expressed concern for the welfare of their engines, which require a fair amount of lead to cushion the contact of valves and valve seats. Without that cushion, valves and valve seats gradually erode and performance fails.

Born in the mid-'50s, Miss Vicky, the *Cars & Parts* 1955 Ford Crown Victoria project car, is fitted with an engine that falls within the ranks of those accustomed to a strict diet of leaded gasoline. When the *Cars & Parts* staff conceived the idea of a project car, one of the first restoration priorities targeted was conversion of the Ford V-8 to make it compatible with unleaded gas. The future health of vintage car engines had been an item of concern at *Cars & Parts* and among hobbyists for sometime.

Back in 1985, when misguided soothsayers forecast doom for the collector car hobby, the staff at *Cars & Parts* was a bit more optimistic and launched a campaign to investigate the situation and explore feasible solutions. In an article appearing

1. *Joe Mooney, Classic Car Centre's head and valve specialist, reams out the valve bores to accept. 030" oversize bronze spiral wall valve guides.*

2. *Two common types of insert valve guides are illustrated. Phosphor bronze sleeve (bottom) and screen-door spring-like bronze spiral wall guides offer essentially the same attributes; greater heat dissipation, reduced friction in the valve guide*

in the April, 1985 issue of *Cars & Parts*, Editor Bob Stevens searched for rays of hope among all the confusion. Stevens reported the state of affairs at the pumps at that time and warned of the ensuing demise of leaded gasoline, detailing the reasons vintage automobile owners should be concerned.

For a hands-on point of view, Stevens visited an engine rebuilder's shop, Comer & Culp, Sidney, Ohio, where he reported on fixes to the exhaust and intake valve areas which make a vintage engine compatible with unleaded fuel. Naturally, when the Crown Vic restoration project was conceived, the staff was anxious to test a converted engine and gain some additional first-hand experience. The engine specialists at Classic Car Centre, Warsaw, Ind., were also eager to wean Vicky of her propensity for leaded fuel. Gene McGuire, co-manager of CCC's machine shop, explained that applying current state of the art technology to Vicky's cylinder heads and valves would satisfy her habitual dependence on lead, plus garner such other benefits as keeping the engine cleaner internally and extending exhaust system life.

Classic Car Centre's expert machinist on

area, precision fit and superior wearing qualities over Vicky's stock integral cast guides. Solid bronze guides (not illustrated) are also available.

3. Classic Car's engine restoration specialist, Gene McGuire, recommended the screen-door variety due to its superior ability to retain oil in the bores when Vicky would be in long term storage: Note coils (arrow). Both sleeve and spiral guides come in standard lengths for oversize bores.

4. All 16 protruding valve guide ends are flush cut to a consistent height. Mooney set bottoms flush.

5. Vicky's integral cast valve seats were in respectable shape due to a diet of strictly leaded fuel. Yet it would have been foolish not to expect accelerated valve seat wear with unleaded gas.

6. Head is positioned on the deck of a TCM-25 machine and bubble leveled on every axis to insure precision cuts.

7. Carbide-tipped cutting tool spins and cuts to a predetermined depth. Use of cutting lube is not advised due to hardness of carbide tip.

8. Valve seats are cut away slightly smaller than diameter dimension of insert to facilitate an .005"-.006" interference fit, which will hold inserts in place when subjected to extreme combustion chamber temperatures. Oversized induction hardened valve seats of .005" were used.

9

10

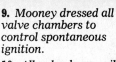

SEALED POWER

12

13

11

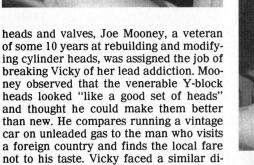

14

9. Mooney dressed all valve chambers to control spontaneous ignition.

10. All valve bores will be dressed (see arrows) to eliminate all casting burrs, etc., which could act as diesel glow plugs and foul up ignition timing.

11. Selecting new valves for use with Vicky's unleaded diet wasn't much of a problem. Currently most valves available from Sealed Power and other valve manufacturers are induction hardened. Twenty or more years ago they were not.

12. Every new valve was measured to insure precision size. Mooney says valves for newer cars carry very consistent measurements. "Older valves weren't always that way," he added.

13. Valve heights are measured with a precision dial indicator.

14. Valves found to be out of sync were ground to spec.

15. Valve stem to guide clearance gauge is used to insure stem bore specs are met.

16. All new valves were resurfaced to an exact angle of seat.

heads and valves, Joe Mooney, a veteran of some 10 years at rebuilding and modifying cylinder heads, was assigned the job of breaking Vicky of her lead addiction. Mooney observed that the venerable Y-block heads looked "like a good set of heads" and thought he could make them better than new. He compares running a vintage car on unleaded gas to the man who visits a foreign country and finds the local fare not to his taste. Vicky faced a similar dilemma.

Born, bred and raised in the 1950s, she had grown accustomed to a leaded diet. Up until a few years back, former owners had experienced no trouble finding Vicky's favorite fuel at most any crossroads in the country. Recent owners had been less fortunate. They had seen leaded gasoline (notably premium high octane varieties) almost banned, and lower octane numbers and reduced lead content appearing on pumps designated for leaded regular. Mooney noted that current lead content available in domestic regular gas rates less than .1 grams per gallon of gas (since Jan. 1, 1986), and that may disappear in the near future.

Like the child who was told that freeze-dried fruit tasted the same as fresh fruit on his morning cereal, Vicky expressed signs of dissatisfaction when asked to diet exclusively on unleaded. Her valves began to chatter, her carburetor sputtered and choked, and she wasn't happy.

15

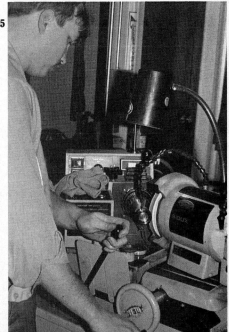

16

The staff knew it couldn't guarantee the availability of leaded gas in the future and voiced its concern to the good motor doctors at Classic Car Centre. "No problem", they said. The machine shop had all the necessary tools and expertise to put Vicky back in the pink. By using induction-hardened swirl-polished valves and installing hardened valve seat inserts, as those used in most U.S. engines built since 1971, Vicky could be weaned of her lead dependency. Gene McGuire says the shop normally charges between $400 and $600 for an unleaded conversion, depending on the number of cylinders, the complexity of the modifications, and the parts interchange in respect to stock currently available. In addition, he recommends three-angle grinding of the valve seats at 30°, 45° and 60°, respectively (a standard procedure at Classic Car Centre), to eliminate sharp edges which when heated act as glow plugs and cause infrequent and uncontrollable ignition misfires.

An added benefit is the chomping action of the added angle (middle) which sheers away carbon buildup and aids good breathing characteristics for added power. According to McGuire, the 1987 Buick Grand National gains 30-35 horsepower from three-angle seats. In addition, an idling engine will run smoother and remain cooler.

The heads had been hot tanked earlier to rid them of any contaminants and oil-buildup residue. Mooney magnafluxed and x-rayed the heads for unseen hairline cracks. Magnafluxing heads or any other engine component involves brushing a dye penetrant onto the heads, which are then placed in a magnetic field under an ultra-violet light. Surface flaws and cracks not easily seen under normal conditions are readily detectable. An x-ray picks up unseen porosity within the castings, which would deem them unworthy of rebuilding. Parts which fail either test should be replaced with parts that pass the tests.

Vicky's heads received high marks on both.

Mooney placed the heads in a 600° oven for an hour, removed and cooled them to 300°, and shot peened them to clean the castings and help relieve hidden stress. This procedure helps "normalize the castings". The phrase is used to describe a procedure in which the castings are heated to induce the inherent tendency of the castings to assume their natural shape, then the castings are shot peened to help permit the escape of stress contained within the castings.

Mooney then checked the heads for warpage. During long term operation a natural phenomenon occurs. Heads conform to match the contour of the block. That's normal, but heads can be warped when an engine overheats or suffers from a compression leak. Mooney took a precision straight edge and feeler gauge to check for warpage at the ends and between the cylinders and at several points lengthwise. An appreciable amount of warp was not noted on either of the two banks. Mooney turned his attention to the valves.

"Valves function like clockwork," he explained, "to take in a mixture of fuel and air and exhaust spent gases at exact intervals. A slight malfunction and you've got trouble."

Checking with engine part suppliers, Mooney learned that valves currently available for rebuilding Y-block Ford engines are already induction hardened, unlike those available for rebuilds only a few years ago. Gene McGuire advised that if one should purchase valves for an unleaded conversion, he is advised to "make sure the valves are of the newer (induction hardened) type and not old stock (unhardened)". The latter "may have spent the last 10 to 15 years on a shelf," he explained.

McGuire said that any valve over 20 years old is certainly "suspect". An alternative available to restorers who cannot

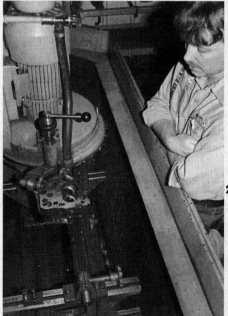

17. Wet seat-grinding bench includes rotary shaft supporting a honing stone, a flexible lubricating tube, stone dressing tool and an assortment of stones.

18. Pilot shaft extending through the valve guides assures perfect concentric contact of polishing stone to seat.

19. Heads were bolted onto deck grinder for resurfacing.

20. Leveling on lateral and horizontal axis is checked with a bubble gauge. Leveling screws were turned and the heads (ground separately) were ready for decking.

21. Initial passes took off approximately .002" per pass. Slight warpage was evident when grinding stone failed to make complete contact.

locate induction hardened valves is to "order stainless steel blanks and size them or have the (old valve) stems and faces hard chromed or spray welded with Stellite." This service is available at Classic Car Centre and many engine rebuilding shops throughout the *Cars & Parts* readership area.

Vicky's exhaust valve stem diameter measured .341" and the intakes miked to .342". That's about normal. Mooney noted an inconsistency in the distance between the valve spring seat and top of the valve stem. The new exhaust and intake valves miked at 2.003" and 1.996" while the old exhaust and intakes measured out at

1.9985" and 2.003", respectively. Mooney decided to machine all valves to 2.000" since new valve seat inserts would be installed.

Next, Mooney locked one of the heads into a TCM-25 Head Shop machine (a better description might be an extra accurate milling machine) and bubble leveled it on the bed. He then squared vertical inclination to the tapping pilot. Here the cuts would be made in the heads for inserting bronze spiral-wall valve guides, induction-hardened valve seats and the three-angle seat modifications performed.

Bronze spiral-wall valve guides were suggested by the experts at Classic Car Centre due to the design's superior oil retention capabilities in comparison with bronze sleeve guides. That's a real advantage, especially since Vicky will likely be subjected to long-term storage. Other benefits include greater heat dissipation, reduced friction, precision fit and superior wearing abilities beyond Vicky's stock guides.

Converting to bronze wall guides required that the heads (in particular the valve guide bores) be absolutely clean, dry and free from corrosion. A cutting lubricant was not necessary since Mooney

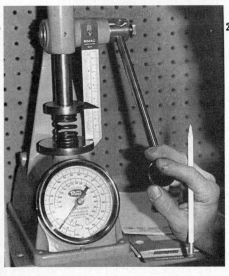

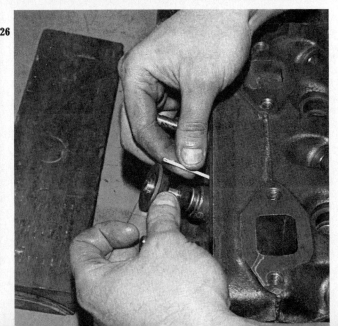

22. *With the valves in place, positive-type valve seals are installed. These seals, made of teflon, will meter oil into guide bores.*

23. *Positive and non-positive valve seals are shown. Mooney highly recommends the former because the latter permits inconsistent oiling of stems and bores.*

24. *Quality valve springs and keepers will assist in proper opening and closing of the intake and exhaust ports to the cylinders.*

25. *Valve spring tension indicator showed that the old springs were shot. Tension loss in excess of 10% of specified load was found. New springs figured in at 1.780 lift and over 90 lbs. closed and 161 lbs. open. The old lift was 1.390.*

26. *Once specified height was determined, Mooney cut a coat hanger to the correct length and used it as a gauge to shim-up spring height to proper installed height.*

remachined the bores with a carbide cutting tool. The tapping bit and bore inclinations were then squared to promote accurate machining of the guide bores.

The bores were recleaned and Mooney selected a bronze wall bushing and slid it onto the appropriate inserting tool with the protruding guide tail extending into the thimble and locked in place. He then wound up the bushing and carefully threaded it into the tapped valve guide bore. Protruding tails of the coils were cut with side cutters and plastic bushing retainers were installed over the guide inserts. This prevented the insert bushings from turning when the bores were honed .001" oversize. The plastic retainer was removed and the extending coil tails were dressed flush with the guide towers. If a guide insert of this type is ruined, it can be removed easily with needle-nose pliers by pulling it straight out.

Replacement with a new bushing follows these same procedures. Installing bronze valve guide sleeves is somewhat similar, except that the new bushings are driven into the guide bores.

Before counterboring the heads to accept hardened valve seat inserts, Mooney miked the inside and outside seat diameters and ordered appropriate standard blanks from his supplier. Once the inserts arrived, Mooney reached for his micrometer and double checked each one for precision manufacture. Mooney says, "You can't trust anything when rebuilding a quality engine," although current engine component manufacturers do a remarkable job maintaining close tolerances. Occasionally, a reject slips by inspectors.

Valve seat inserts are a god-send to vintage car owners. Made of extremely hard alloys, inserts reduce wear, prevent leakage, reduce valve grinding frequency and permit the burning of unleaded fuels. The inserts were pressed-fit into slightly undersize cast iron head counterbores for an interference fit of .005" to .006". Aluminum head interference fits normally range from .008"-.010".

The last procedure to finish up a high-tech set of heads was to mill the gasket surfaces in a deck grinding machine. Heads were placed in a decking mill, bubble leveled, and then ground with a stone, which gradually removes head material in .0005" increments. The operation provides a smooth gasket surface and squares up the heads in relation to the decks.

What did it cost to convert to unleaded? "Around $500 ... that includes everything done to Vicky's engine," says Classic Car Centre's Gene McGuire. "New valves, springs, head work, everything if heads are delivered here to Classic Car," he added. "Other charges should be expected by the customer who hires our shop to remove and replace the heads — and customers who have valve-in-block engines, such as flathead Fords."

27. Final valve assembly went smoothly. New machined heads glistened. Mooney says the cosmetics are important to customer satisfaction.

28. Each valve was pressure tested at 25 lbs. psi to see if valves were seating properly.

29. Sprayed with WD-40, heads were bagged to await the finishing work on other components and final assembly.

Modifications to Vicky's heads took the better part of a day. Mooney had taken a pair of heads destined to eventually fail from the lack of leaded fuels (even if rebuilt to bare-bone stock specs) and given them a new lease on life.

THE RESURRECTION OF VICKY

How to rebuild your carburetor

1. Carb rebuild kit, consisting of new paper gaskets, accelerator pump, power valve and assorted O-rings, gauges and fittings, is designed for a wide variety of Ford two-barrel carbs. Here are the tools that will be needed in disassembling the carb.

2. A carburetor should not be soaked in a carb cleaner solution unless it is extremely dirty. Even though dirt and grime build up was excessive, screws spun out with little effort. Old Ford script carb had probably never been rebuilt.

3. Neglected carb with dirt build up and partially clogged ports and passageway is probably less than 50% efficient.

4. Air horn also received a liberal spraying to remove any debris that may have survived the dousing in the cleaning tank.

If you suspect that this segment of the Crown Vic restoration series will involve just another boring rebuild of a rather uncomplicated Ford two-barrel, you're wrong! Carburetor rebuilding procedures are adequately outlined on installation sheets in practically every carb kit produced in the last 30 years, as well as factory shop manuals. These procedures describe the how-to's of installing new replacement parts and hardly need to be repeated here. This segment of the Vicky series will concentrate on the things those books don't tell you when restoring a Ford two-barrel or other carbs — the things an old line mechanic has learned over the years.

When Classic Car Centre's master mechanic Gene McGuire started squirting Cyclo carb cleaning fluid onto Vicky's carb, I fully expected that we would re-

trench some old ditches. Actually, I had underestimated McGuire's savvy with carburetors. He doesn't just replace parts according to detailed instructions and assume the attitude: "Well, if they give me new parts, then I'm going to use them. And, I don't need to know why I'm replacing them." That's not the way McGuire works. McGuire reads parts. Through the course of Vicky's restoration, I have watched him read Vicky's parts like I'd read a book. He sees things — tell-tale suggestions of wear, fatigue, build up of foreign matter, etc. — ailments which aren't normally covered in print.

When McGuire picked up Vicky's carb, it was obvious that before he would rebuild the old Holley-built two-barrel, he'd read it. There seems to be a world of difference between the rebuilder and a reader-rebuilder. Any rookie wrench can lay in

new carb gaskets, O-rings, etc., but it takes a seasoned mechanic to detect the maladies that waste away a carburetor. Within seconds, McGuire had discovered that the shaft holding the two throttle plates was wobbly. The tension spring had pulled and tugged the shaft to one side, which after a few million depressions of the accelerator pedal had worn the hole oblong and created a vacuum leak. "Mechanics call this condition the 'slobbering Holley'," McGuire joked.

"Any carb sucking air will run lean, producing a false idle," he added. You can check for this condition while the carb is on the car by placing a drop of motor oil over the shaft hole. If the revs slow down, a leak is present. Or you can try for reverse results — if the idle picks up when blowing propane through a tube onto the shaft opening, a leak is present.

5

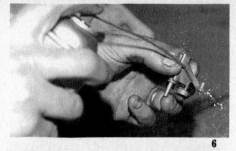

6

7

8

9

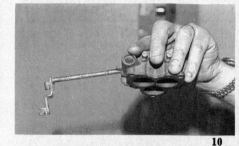

10

5. Gene McGuire, machine shop co-manager, began the rebuild by examining all used parts. The full length of the accelerator pump spring should touch when rolled over a flat surface. If it is warped, replace it.

6. Nozzle bars, right and left, tend to clog and should be sprayed liberally with carb cleaner. Goggles or protective glasses should be worn to prevent droplets from getting into your eyes.

7. The 1955 Ford service manual tells you not to remove the throttle plates and shaft from the throttle body if the plates are damaged. McGuire pointed to a vacuum leak at the lever side of the shaft due to excessive wear. He decided to ignore the warning and repair the vacuum leak. Small gasket has lost its resilience and no longer seals around throttle shaft (see point of knife blade).

8. McGuire used a die grinder and cut away the peened ends of the brass screws holding the plates.

9. Throttle plate is beveled on leading edge to insure good contact of plate and housing.

10. Screws were extracted and the shaft slid free from its bore.

11. A rubber O-ring with proper diameter hole was picked from an assortment pack and slipped onto the shaft.

12 & 13. McGuire then measured the O-ring and with the assistance of fellow machine shop employee, Jim Roach, a 1/32-inch deep overbore matching the O-ring dimension was drilled into the body. Shaft and throttle plates were carefully reassembled and screws repeened on open ends. Locktite was applied to the threads as a precautionary measure.

14. Brass cap seal at opposite end of shaft was still intact and working well after 30 years.

11

12

13

Tools and lube needed in carb rebuilding include various sizes of screwdrivers, a spray can of carb cleaner (McGuire's favorite is Cyclo), a spray can of white grease or Vasoline for lubricating moving parts, a rifle cleaning brush to clean oxidation from threaded areas and an air gun to blow away debris. Never use sandpaper under any circumstances, McGuire warned. Grit is likely to remain even after the carb is blown thoroughly with an air gun.

McGuire says he's not real fond of using an agitator to clean carb parts. It tends to remove the coating which restorers cherish and it may have sealed holes in the porous aluminum castings. Removing the coating could unplug the holes and produce a leak.

McGuire continued to read parts from the pile while delivering a sermon on the do's and don'ts of carb rebuilds.

"Nowadays, he says, chemicals in fuels are widely used in the old car hobby and the bottom of the float bowl seems to be a favorite hang out for stray chemicals. "Make sure you clean all parts," he warned, "especially the bottom of the bowl." Fuel tanks are also favorite hangouts — however not easily accessible for cleaning." The least you can do is install an in-line fuel filter near the carb, he advised. It should be easily accessible so sediment collected in the filter can be quickly removed.

"Don't ever drill out a jet." Holley warns against it, according to McGuire. If you notice that a jet has been drilled out, pitch it and get a new one. New jets for Vicky and most other domestic cars are readily available at most automotive parts outlets for a few dollars.

Other do's and don'ts include:
• Never set a needle with a screwdriver. Use your fingers if space permits. Seat the needles, then back them out 1½ turns.
• Never tighten carb bolts too much. You could bend the ears of the carb and prevent flush contact with the intake manifold. Once the carb is off the car, check for straightness of the throttle body's mating surface by running a straight edge across the surface in different directions.
• Restorers who attempt carb rebuilds

14

15. *McGuire drew on his vast experience with carburetor rebuilds and engineered a non-original two-stage power valve arrangement (left) to replace the replacement unit in the rebuild kit.*

16 & 17. *To clear the taller two-stage power valve, a* hole was milled in the throttle body and a brass engine freeze plug was pressed into the hole. Now when Vicky's vacuum falls to around 12.5 the fuel will start to flow. The original required a drop in vacuum to 6.5 before fuel started to flow. Originally designed to provide good fuel economy on recreational vehicles, the two-stage power valve (Napa-Echlin part number 2-4311) is expected to produce an estimated 10% increase in fuel economy in comparison with the stock factory assembly.

15

16

17

should be on the lookout for jets that have been changed. Several years ago when gas prices skyrocketed many car owners changed jets to lean the gas mixture. In conjunction with the switching of jets the practice of retarding the timing a few degrees just before pinging started was popular. Many service stations specialized in such fixes. Some even soldered jets and redrilled them. "Scrap such jets," McGuire advises. A better bet for those wishing better fuel economy is to install oversize jets (at least five numbers up or down), then test fuel economy against numbers established before installing the new jets. Once numbers are available for comparison, install jets two sizes over original specs and test for better or worse numbers, gradually working toward optimum economy. Granted, a bit of work is involved, but the results are honest and not hypothetical.

• Sag or acceleration hesitation is usually associated with the accelerator pump or its linkage. On occasion, it is caused by clogged air bleeds or fuel passages.

• Ignition problems can be diagnosed incorrectly as carburetor problems.

• Hard starting cold engine: Check choke system first. Could be a sticking choke plate or linkage. Below 75°, the choke plate should snap shut when the throttle opens on a cold engine.

• Never use motor oil, or similar oil, etc., to lube a choke linkage. It will attract dirt and grime later and will bind the mechanism in cold weather.

• Choke problems can involve either the bi-metal sensing unit or the linkage, or both. The bi-metal thermo spring can be deformed by excessive engine heat and lose its resilience. Replace the spring.

• A choke plate can become lodged by backfiring. The choke plate screw must be loosened to permit repositioning. Screws should be securely pegged to prevent vibration from shaking them loose. After loosening use care to prevent further damage.

• A stuck choke plate on a warm engine can cause hard starting problems. If choke is stuck in a partially closed position, the

fuel mix will be too rich. The linkage is probably out of adjustment.

• An out-of-sync fuel bowl vent can also cause hard start problems. Vapors must be vented properly to prevent them from loading up the intake manifold during hot soak when a warm engine is turned off for a short period. Normally this condition isn't noticed if engine is allowed to cool down to the point when the vapors escape or condense.

• Percolating fuel caused by engine heat. Fuel boils out of fuel bowl and into carb resulting in a too-rich condition. Fuel bowl float level is too high. Check float level specs found on sheets inside carb rebuild kits. Some carbs have sight plugs and ex-

ternal screws which permit adjustment of the float level without removing the air horn or float bowl. Proper fuel level is reached when fuel is at the bottom of the sight plug hole.

• Flooding can be caused by dirt that has settled between the float needle and seat. A possible quick cure (without disassembling carb) is to disconnect fuel line and run a long hose into a can, etc., to catch fuel. Run engine until fuel is burned and engine dies. Reconnect fuel line and restart engine. Sudden surge past needle and seat will sometimes dislodge debris. If it doesn't, the fuel filter inlet and needle and seat should be cleaned or replaced. Check for foreign material (usually rust in older cars) which has been dislodged in the fuel tank. A fuel filter helps, but tank should be flushed, cleaned and sealed.

• Stalling after start up can be caused by flooding or it can also be caused by a lack of fuel. Fast idle cam screw may need adjustment to increase air flow.

• Rough idle accompanied by black exhaust smoke can be caused by a leaky power valve rubber diaphragm.

• Manifold vacuum leak can cause rough idle. Open seals or cracked hoses can be the culprits.

• A stressed or weakened throttle return spring can cause inconsistent idle. Replace with new one.

• Dirty air cleaner or filter will restrict air flow.

• Sticking power valve in up position will cause a too-lean fuel condition. Opposite occurs when power valve is stuck in down position — too rich a mix and fuel economy suffers. Replace or repair power valve.

• Dirty fuel filter can restrict fuel flow. Weak fuel pump produces same symptoms.

• Dieseling after shut down: Because spark is retarded, the throttle plate must be opened wider to have sufficient power to idle engine. Retarded spark makes engine run hotter. Due to wider opening of throttle, extra fuel and air in the hot spots of the combustion chambers ignite. Some carbs in newer cars have a built-in anti-dieseling device.

As McGuire finished up the rebuild of Vicky's carb, he continued to read the parts. "This power valve is very inefficient," he said. "A two-stage power valve would eliminate stumbling at traffic lights and produce better fuel economy," he added. A visit with a local NAPA outlet counterman produced some interesting ideas. The original single-stage power valve opens when the vacuum drops to 6.5. A two-stage power valve (NAPA-Echlin part no. 2-4312) operates in a vacuum range from 5.5 to 12.7. Thus by leaning out the carb jets and installing a two-stage power valve, Vicky should expect a mpg gain around 10 percent.

Jury-rigging the throttle body to accept the taller non-original valve required milling out a hole and pressing in a brass freeze plug ... and the job was finished!

At this point, McGuire was satisfied with the carb, which read as sweet as a letter from home.

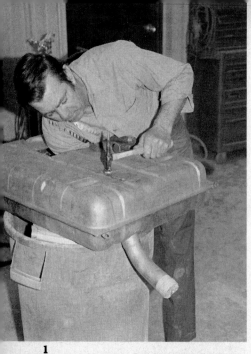

1

2

3

4

5

This segment of the Resurrection of Vicky series addresses a problem that every old car owner faces at one time or another: a leaky gas tank.

A couple of months back, Vicky's diet was changed from leaded to unleaded gas by the machine shop staff at Classic Car Centre, Warsaw, Ind. By cutting hardened valve seats into the heads and installing induction hardened valves, Vicky's dependency on leaded fuel was cured forever.

At the other end of the fuel system, another problem was being addressed by John St. Cin of the Classic Car Centre's body shop. The gas tank was a real mess as rust had eaten away the sending unit pickup screen and a section of the tank right underneath. St. Cin examined the tank and suggested a replacement as the easiest approach, but our hopeless expression probably told him a tank might be difficult to locate on short notice.

At that point, he figured he could patch the tank once the layers of undercoating and rust were removed from the outside. Since tanks for '55 Fords, as well as most vintage cars, are scarce, we appreciated St. Cin's willingness to take the latter approach. We didn't want to slow down the

THE RESURRECTION OF VICKY

Plugging holes in the fuel tank

1. *Hot tanking removed varnish buildup and internal rust while external sandblasting removed corrosion and revealed pinholes around the area where the pickup tube and screen reside. John St. Cin cut the perforated section away.*

2. *Like any good body man, St. Cin used the opportunity to straighten a few dents in the bottom of the upside-down tank.*

3., 4. & 5. *Inside the tank St. Cin had discovered the pickup screen was rusted away. He bead blasted the remaining pieces and fashioned a new screen held in place by a used piston ring.*

Crown Vic project by taking time to locate a usable tank. In addition, prior experience had taught us that most used tanks would probably be no better than what we had.

St. Cin began the repair by hot tanking Vicky's gas tank in a caustic solution to remove corrosion, etc. All rust came off readily but the rubbery undercoating refused to budge even after a third dousing, and fourth, leaving St. Cin no alternative but to hand scrape the remaining residue. With that completed, the tank was taken to the sandblasting pit where it was blasted with approximately 70 lbs. of pressure. All undercoating and corrosion hiding underneath quickly disappeared.

Next, St. Cin pushed the tips of a pair of shears through one of the larger rust holes to cut away a 5x7-inch chunk of rusty metal. Having gained access to the tank's interior, St. Cin discovered the sending unit screen had seen better days, having evaporated into rust heaven. St. Cin, like any good body man, took advantage of the gaping hole to hammer and dolly out a few unsightly dents.

With the dents removed, St. Cin turned his attention to the problem with the pick-up screen. He made a screen from a piece of non-soluble fiberglass screen to be held in place by a discarded piston ring. It did the trick. Within 30 minutes the sending unit was repaired and hidden away under a new patch panel cut from a scrap piece of sheet metal and MIG-welded in place. A word of caution to anyone who might follow St. Cin's lead and weld a gas tank. Unless you have washed the tank with gallons of soapy water or hot tanked it (as in Vicky's case), don't go near a gas tank with an open flame with the intention of welding it, even if it hasn't held gas in years. An explosion and possible injury would likely follow. Be safe, not sorry!

St. Cin finished the sheet metal with a hand grinder, slapped on a layer of plastic filler for aesthetics, leveled it, then primed and sprayed the tank with a heavy coat of roofer's aluminum paint. Duplicating the original galvanized finish was ruled out due to an urgency to proceed with the project. If time had permitted, we could have taken the tank to a galv-plating shop for a new coat of galvanizing. Or it could have been spray welded with aluminum to achieve a near-original look. Our last step was to seal the tank to prevent corrosion in the future.

Bill Hirsch (396 Littleton Ave., Newark, N.J. 07103, phone 201-642-2404) recently introduced a new formula gas tank sealer that is resistant to alcohol. One quart was enough to seal Vicky's tank. That's true for most tanks. The new formula is specifically aimed at the car owner who may use fuel that contains additives. Hirsch advises customers that the sealer will "immediately stop all rust corrosion and leaks forever. No etching or boiling out of the tank is needed." Just remove the tank, pour in the sealer and slosh it around to cover all inside surfaces. The sending unit should be removed before using sealer. Once out of the tank, it may need attention similar to that which Vicky's unit received.

The tank looks great back under Vicky's trunk area. And it's comforting to know that now there's not much chance of wasting even one drop of unleaded nourishment through a leak in the tank.

6

6. New ears were welded onto the lid and then onto the tank to hold the repaired strainer in place.

7. Repair patch was trimmed to size and MIG welded.

8. A few trips across the welds to straighten the metal with a hand grinder and the repair was completed.

9. St. Cin sealed the tank with a quart of Bill Hirsch's gas tank sealer. Hirsch recently introduced a new alcohol-resistant formula for car owners who use gasoline charged with octane boosters, alcohol, etc. A quart is adequate for sealing a 25-gal. tank. Vicky's tank was then painted and installed.

7

8

9

Upgrading the Electrical and Exhaust Systems

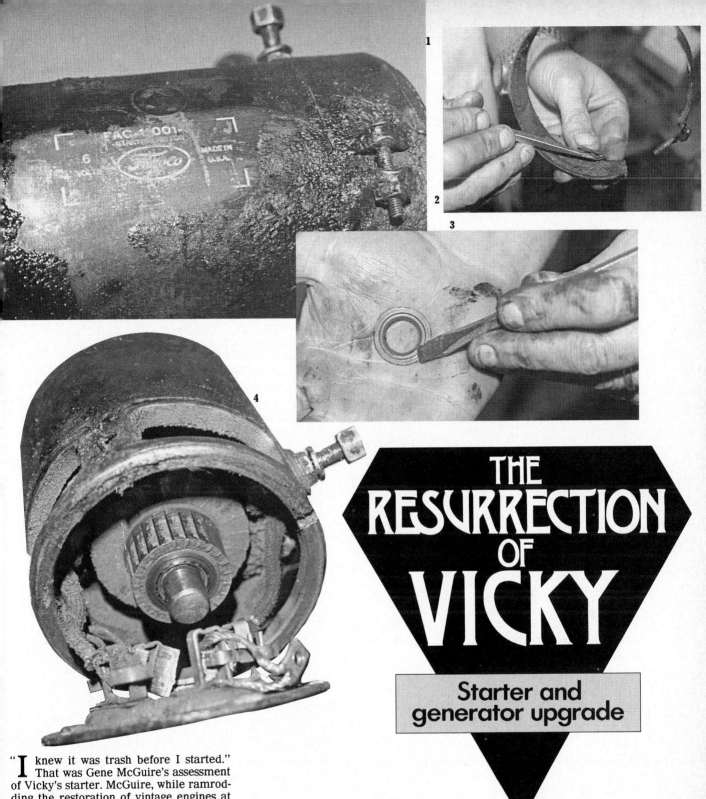

THE RESURRECTION OF VICKY

Starter and generator upgrade

"I knew it was trash before I started." That was Gene McGuire's assessment of Vicky's starter. McGuire, while ramrodding the restoration of vintage engines at the Classic Car Centre, Warsaw, Ind., has rebuilt many starters of different types. The afflictions can fill a book. "After a few thousand miles, most starters have .008-.010 thousands of an inch of lateral movement. And brushes won't stand up to lateral movement," McGuire says. Vicky's starter was no different. "It would have lived for a little while longer before it died," he added.

The above investigation was purely academic.

We wanted to know how Vicky's electrics had held up for 30 years — yet we had no intention of repairing the starter. The fix would never take place. From the beginning we had decided to retain the 12 volt conversion already in place. Old car buffs will tell you that 1955 was the last year for six-volt positive ground electrics in Ford cars and trucks. Following the lead of others from Detroit, Ford decided their 1956 vehicles would be cranked and fired by the superior 12-volt system. It was a good decision.

The switch included, among other things, a new 12-volt starter, coil and ballast resistor, generator, regulator, dash gauges, horns, heater motor, light bulbs, and, of course, a 12-volt battery. Also, the battery tray took on a long slender design rather than the more squarish one used in earlier years. Interestingly, all engine hang-on parts bolted right up, the new

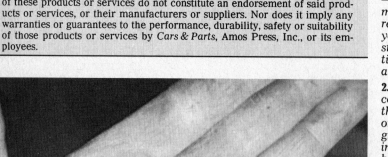

1. *Under a layer of crud, the original factory legend — FAC-11001-A starter motor, 6 volts, etc., — was readable after some 30 years. Vicky's gummed up starter spun erratically at times, necessitating a look at its innards.*

2. *Gene McGuire quickly confirmed his suspicions that the starter was a bit on the tired side. Brush grit and oil covered the inside of the starter cover band. The buildup conducts electricity and is counter productive to a strong starter system.*

3. *Fiber thrust bushing showed excessive wear. Lubrication with a synthetic chassis gear would have prevented this.*

4. *Grubby condition existed throughout the inside of the starter housing.*

5. *Brushes were mere nubbles measuring less than a quarter of an inch in length. New brushes are usually ½" to ⅝" long. (Actually .454-inch in 1955 and .66-inch in '56.)*

6. *By testing the starter on an ohmmeter, McGuire determined to his amazement that the commutator wasn't shorted out.*

7. *McGuire illustrates the procedure for holding a stubborn generator pulley while removing the bolt.*

8. *It took heat to separate the two once the bolt was removed.*

9. *McGuire found the same type of grime inside the generator that he had found in the starter.*

5

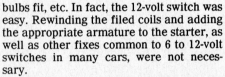

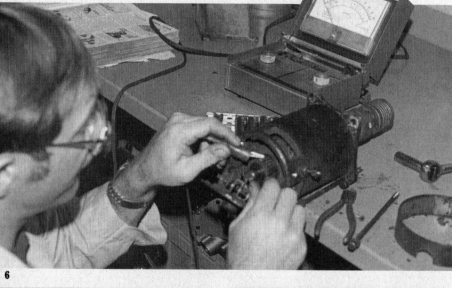

bulbs fit, etc. In fact, the 12-volt switch was easy. Rewinding the filed coils and adding the appropriate armature to the starter, as well as other fixes common to 6 to 12-volt switches in many cars, were not necessary.

Admittedly, we had second thoughts about the conversion to 12-volt. Some purists had openly voiced their disapproval of the decision to stay with the 12-volt setup. We didn't entirely disagree, at least not in principal, with their contentions that the car should be restored to original specs, including six-volt electrics. But we didn't want to lose sight of the fact that we were building a driver, a street-show car that could be driven from coast to coast, without concern that mechanical problems or

6

7

8

9

a lack of leaded fuel would prevent the driver from maximizing his enjoyment while cruising in this vintage machine. Anyone who has ventured forth in a six-volt car on a subzero morning or a sun-drenched 100° afternoon knows first hand the aggravation of a slow-cranking six-volt system.

For the sake of dependability and efficiency, it was decided to retain the 12-volt system. In this particular case, it just didn't make sense to undo a good deed!

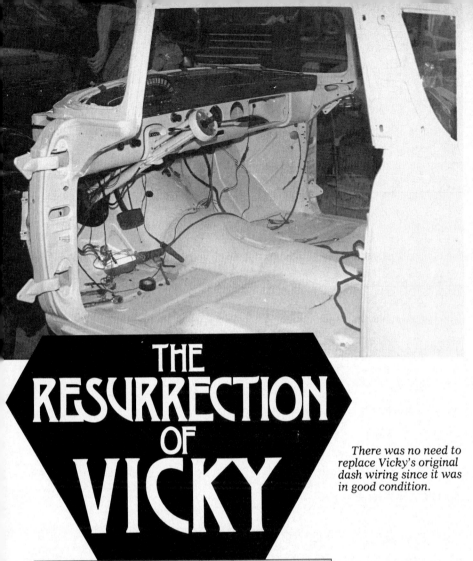

THE RESURRECTION OF VICKY

Six to 12-volt conversion

There was no need to replace Vicky's original dash wiring since it was in good condition.

Sometime in the past, probably when Vicky's engine became tired and required an extra surge of juice to crank it to life, a previous owner had switched the original '55 Ford six-volt electrical system to 12 volts.

Before we turned the first bolt in Vicky's restoration, we weighed the pros and cons of restoring the electrical system to its factory-original six-volt status. Although the staff of *Cars & Parts* are basically purists, not one of us had strong convictions about undoing a modification we thought made a lot of sense. All members of the staff could cite at least a half-dozen instances where a six-volt system had let them down. These ranged from a growling, slow-cranking old six-volt beast that refused to fire on a cold winter morning to a postwar V-8 rod that gave us anxious moments on a summer af-

ternoon with a hot-start problem. We all agreed that Vicky's conversion from six to 12 volts had been a good fix for a car that was meant to be driven rather than shown.

So we decided to rebuild Vicky's non-original 12-volt electrics and leave the conversion in place. We braced ourselves for the wrath of purists who, we were convinced, would hammer us unmercifully since *Cars & Parts'* publication policy generally favors factory-specification cars over those that have been modified, altered or otherwise customized.

Interestingly, the purists seemed to agree with us. Though not one voiced vehement objections to our decision, their ranks seemed to be split between those who felt it was "sorta OK" to those who wanted to know in specific detail just exactly how to perform the upgrade to 12 volts. Surprisingly, most six-volt car owners who contacted the magazine said they had considered upgrading to 12 volts when they were restoring their cars. A few who had converted to 12 volts wrote lengthy letters describing their conversions, offering their experiences to other readers as

encouragement. Some of these letters are part of this article.

The main objection readers had to converting their cars to 12 volts was a fear of "frying" their cars. They also had a desire for an "original look" in their engine compartments. These purists balked at having an array of hang-on brackets, devices, etc. under the hood.

To a large degree, we were able to satisfy even the purists when we left Vicky's non-original electrics in place. We retained the factory look and the benefits of quicker starting as well as the ability to handle greater electric requirements. The only telltale items in Vicky's engine compartment are the 12-volt negative ground battery, the 12-volt horns, and the ignition resistor, which is partially hidden on the intake manifold under the air cleaner. Otherwise, it's very hard to tell Vicky's no longer a six-volt car.

There have been many conversions of six-volt cars to 12 volts over the years. When owners describe how it was done, each one sounds completely unlike the others. Yet when these conversions are mapped out in wiring diagrams, all follow a basic pattern.

Despite this commonality in all conversions, most hobbyists seem to be more baffled or afraid of electrics than anything else about their cars. Though most can be walked slowly through a detailed explanation of Vicky's electrics, many simply freeze up and cannot imagine Vicky's electrics working on a car with another name, such as Cadillac, Chevrolet, etc. Despite the fact the principles are the same, most hobbyists simply cannot translate them from one car to another.

The goal of this article, then, is to describe the setup used on Vicky, as well as those used by other hobbyists, as a means of demystifying the six to 12-volt conversion and how it works.

The best advice we can offer to anyone considering a switch to 12 volts is to have a pretty good idea of the existing electrical system. This can be done simply by studying the shop manual of the car in question. That done, simply follow the most appealing version of the several conversion methods discussed below. A careful reader will note little differences in philosophy and use of equipment, but basically it's all the same.

First, let's take a look at what we did to Vicky:

• To switch to 12 volts, we started with a 12-volt battery with negative ground. Vicky originally had a six-volt positive ground setup.

• The generator was replaced by a '56 Ford 12-volt unit (Ford converted to 12 volts that year). Another option would have been to put field coils from '56-'63 Fords into the '55 casing. That's also true of many earlier Fords, even those in the '30s. An easier method would be to use the 12-volt generator with the '55 end frame.

• A 12-volt voltage regulator from a '56 Ford was used.

• We used a 12-volt coil.

• The distributor, points and condensor required no changes.

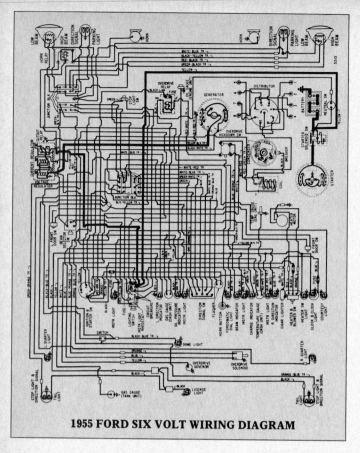

1955 FORD SIX VOLT WIRING DIAGRAM

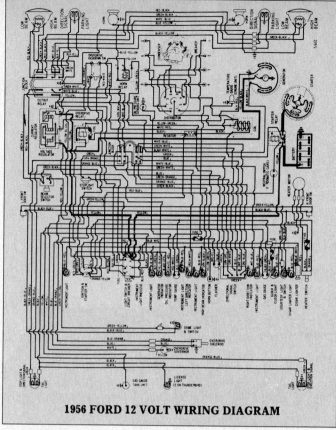

1956 FORD 12 VOLT WIRING DIAGRAM

• All light bulbs, headlamps, parking light bulbs, dash bulbs, etc., were replaced with 12-volt units. The sockets required no modification, by the way.

• A 12-volt turn signal flasher was substituted for the original.

• A ballast resistor was installed in-line between the ignition switch and the coil. We used a factory '56 unit and bracket to keep the Ford look. Generic ballast resistors, however, are available at any auto parts outlet for cowl or similar mounting.

• We didn't do anything with the starter since the larger six-volt field coils are more than adequate to handle the load. Usually, six-volt units will outlast 12-volt field coils.

• All original wiring was retained. A 12-volt wiring diagram from a '56 Ford showed where the wires were to be rerouted. A wire for the ballast resistor was added.

• A voltage resistor (voltage drop unit) was installed in-line between Vicky's feed (hot) line and all dash gauges and the radio. The heater motor was upgraded to a 12-volt unit. The ammeter wire was wired in the opposite direction through the loop on the back of the meter.

Since all of Vicky's dash units are six-volt, the resistor had to be installed to lower the line voltage to the gauges. Although we didn't pursue this plan, here's what Ford did in the late '50s when all Ford cars and trucks were switched to 12 volts: A constant voltage regulator was inserted in-line between the ignition switch ("A" terminal) and the gauges so that six-volt gauges could be used. Two types of "instrument cluster voltage regulators" (Ford's current catalog name), parts B7A-10804-B or B9MZ-10804-C, still can be pur-

chased through Ford dealers for about $10. Either unit will work, though the second unit is a bit larger. Notice the 1960-62 Ford Falcon wiring diagram shown here for location of the unit. Also, note that six-volt heaters and such accessories won't work if the Ford units are used. A voltage-drop device is the answer and can be used for both instrument gauges and accessories. These units can be purchased at speed shops.

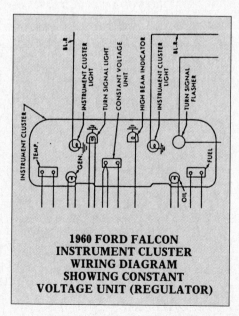

1960 FORD FALCON INSTRUMENT CLUSTER WIRING DIAGRAM SHOWING CONSTANT VOLTAGE UNIT (REGULATOR)

Following are methods employed by other old car hobbyists who have taken advantage of 12 volts in their originally six-volt cars. Their comments were sent to

Cars & Parts in response to articles and reader letters about six to 12-volt conversions, and were written to be shared with other hobbyists.

• **Walt Szeezil, Wildwood, Ill:** I converted my 1947 Cadillac to 12-volt operation and it is the best improvement I feel that can be made in an older car. The car is now a modern everyday drivable auto. It can be serviced on the road in any good repair shop and driven anywhere in the country.

These are the basic steps:

1. Get a wiring diagram for your car. You will need it, particularly for work under the dash. You can use your existing wiring harness; the conversion does not require rewiring the car.

2. Buy a copy of Peterson's *Basic Ignition and Electrical Systems*, approximate cost $6.50.

3. You are going to convert to a 12-volt negative ground system, regardless of what your six-volt is.

4. Have your present generator rewound to 12-volt negative ground and have the rewinder or a good repair shop match up a proper 12-volt regulator that is compatible with the output of the rewound generator.

5. This is the most difficult part of the conversion, as you cannot put any capacity regulator on the generator. You could replace both generator and regulator with an alternator, but this would not maintain original appearance and there are mounting problems.

6. Leave the starter alone. Simply clean it up and rebuild with new brushes and bearings if you wish. No rewind is neces-

sary if you keep your car in tune. It should last indefinitely.

7. Replace the coil with a matched 12-volt coil and ballast resistor, which can be obtained from a parts store. If the parts store people are confused, go to a speed shop; this is old stuff to them.

8. The ignition system is now converted; only the coil change is required. Most 12-volt cars run on six-volt ignition systems, so you can keep your present points, condenser and spark plugs.

9. Buy a good 12-volt battery. The ignition switch, starter button and solenoid do not have to be touched.

10. All the light bulbs must be replaced with 12-volt bulbs, including the dash bulbs. If you want to be able to dim the dash lights, you must replace the headlight switch. The rheostat will overheat if you dim the dash lights; if you leave them on bright, you can use your existing headlamp switch. The high beam switch for your headlamps does not have to be replaced. Existing fuses also are fine and do not need replacing.

11. Heater motors must be replaced with 12-volt motors. I replaced the defroster motor, but avoided replacing the heater motors in my Cadillac. There were two heater motors under the front seat wired in parallel; I rewired the two six-volt motors in series and they run on 12 volts.

12. The dash gauges can be operated on six volts by wiring a voltage limit switch in series with the gauges. This will provide six volts to the gauges. This was used by auto manufacturers in the early days of 12-volt systems.

13. The ammeter is just an electrical flow meter and operates on either six or 12 volts. The oil pressure gauge is mechanical and is not involved in the conversion.

14. If the car has turn signals, replace the flasher with a 12-volt unit. You may have to rewire the unit if it was downstream of the newly-installed voltage limit switch.

15. The radio cannot be used. I replaced mine with an AM/FM stereo. I also installed a driving computer with cruise control.

16. Do not connect up the battery until the conversion is complete. First, remove all the fuses. Then connect the battery, polarize the regulator by momentarily bridging the "armature" and "battery" terminals and put in the fuses, checking the ammeter as you do. Start it up and drive a car that looks like an old one, but starts and runs like a new one.

• Richard Startz, Jr., Karnes City, Tex.: I have an interesting method to whip the voltage drop problems with dash gauges. I use a special resistor wire. This wire is used only in the ignition circuit of 1963-74 GM cars and trucks. It is white and is approximately 48 inches long. Its purpose is to reduce 12 volts to the 6.6-8.8 volts required for proper ignition point life as a full 12 volts to the ignition will burn points quickly.

Desired voltage to any circuit is achieved by adding or subtracting from the wire's length. Adding another wire by using a crimp-type connector for the splice will reduce voltage further. If more voltage is required, just cut off enough until the desired voltage is reached. Add this wire only from battery source to feed terminal of the desired circuit and never use it as a ground, or, for instance, as a splice from a gauge to a sending unit. Beware that while reducing voltage, this wire gets quite hot and should be kept away from combustible material like upholstery or plastic.

Using these wires in place of things like voltage drop resistors or two six-volt batteries and other Mickey Mouse gimmicks may sound like a lot of extra work. But while these other devices wear out or become weak, these GM resistor wires never wear out unless grounded. They will last as long as anyone owns the car. They are worth the extra time.

These wires are not available over the counter at GM dealerships, but they are available at any wrecking yard. They are easily removed by splitting the wiring harness open from the firewall connector to the ignition coil and them cutting them out. Most yards give them away or charge a dollar or so apiece. How many are needed depends on how many circuits are involved. One for the ignition and fuel gauge are the minimum. If other accessories such as radio, heater or power accessories are used, then naturally other wires are needed.

Incidentally, I've always retained the standard six-volt coil and used enough wire to reduce the voltage to six volts, and I haven't had any trouble with short point life or hard starting. I've even used these resistor wires on bulb-type headlights so I could retain a car's authenticity. I had a '35 Chevy wired that way. I don't know if these wires would work for things such as the power windows used on early Packards or Cadillacs and I've been a little curious to try them out on one. I've used these wires many times for gauges, heaters and accessory radios, and I've never experienced any troubles there either.

Compared to other methods, I've found these resistor wires to be simple, cheap and readily available, just as Henry Ford would have wanted it. They are easily installed and totally trouble-free if properly installed. These wires work on positive or negative-ground systems without adversely affecting circuit operation. On Fords, I convert to negative ground. For Ford gauge regulation, I retain the stock voltage regulator and use a resistor wire to reduce current to six volts at the feed terminal for the regulator. These wires do not hurt radio operation or reception, either.

My efforts have been confined to Chevys, Fords and Plymouths, but I don't see why it wouldn't work on other cars, except for reasons of total authenticity. Authenticity is great until you're stranded in five o'clock rush hour traffic in the middle of July with temperatures and tempers over 100 and your vintage beauty is holding up traffic for miles. Then, authenticity doesn't mean much, purists aside. I recommend this mostly for people like me who consider their old car a driver, not a showpiece.

Thanks to these *Cars & Parts* readers, and the six to 12-volt conversion on Vicky described earlier, the mystery and fear about making old cars electrically modern should be dispelled. If not, it should be clear that it's not as hard or as dangerous as might have been thought.

When it comes to driving old cars with original six-volt electrical systems, it simply makes sense to update to 12-volt operation. We're sure Vicky's new owner will agree.

SWITCHING FROM GENERATOR TO ALTERNATOR

An alternator spins at twice the revolutions per minute of a generator, charges at idle — unlike a generator, and is considerably more efficient. All of these make it more attractive to those who desire an increased-capacity electrical system for the addition of CB radios, tape players, air conditioners, etc. To complete a generator to alternator switch, a compatible external voltage regulator with breaker point-type contacts must be used. Or, better yet, use a late-model GM (post-1973) alternator with internal regulator. It requires no charging adjustments, nor are they possible. With the internal regulator, caution should be exercised when jump starting a stalled vehicle. Before the jumper cables are taken off the positive and negative terminals, turn off accessories, radio, defroster and so forth to avoid an excessive surge of electricity which can burn up a regulator. Make sure you get as much of the alternator's wiring harness, particularly the connectors, from the donor car as possible in order to make your conversion simpler, by the way. Don Stickler, Berlin Center, Ohio, sent the accompanying wiring diagrams for the use of an alternator, either the internal or external regulator GM-Delco type.

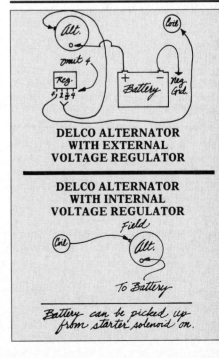

DELCO ALTERNATOR WITH EXTERNAL VOLTAGE REGULATOR

DELCO ALTERNATOR WITH INTERNAL VOLTAGE REGULATOR

THE RESURRECTION OF VICKY

Aluminizing the exhaust system

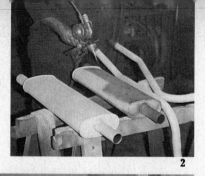

1. *All our advance work to fit the various pieces of the quickly-rusted exhaust system wasn't in vain. Spra-Met recommends that the pieces be properly fitted before the aluminizing process begins.*

2. *Tailpipe sections that slip inside the mufflers were taped off and not blasted or aluminized since metal buildup creates tight fit problems. The back and forth hand movements to apply the metal coating are similar to spray painting techniques.*

3. *"Almost any surface can be sprayed," Jim Everhart said. While metallizing this cast iron exhaust manifold, he proved the point by spraying a piece of wood. To insure even longer life, the entire system was coated with a clear sealer.*

4. *Bruce Everhart (standing) and sons Dave (left) and Jim reinstalled the exhaust system and posed for this quick shot before we trailered Vicky back to the restoration shop, Classic Car Centre.*

Vicky's exhaust system was restored in the usual fashion: new pipes, mufflers, clamps and brackets. The time was early spring and since Vicky hadn't been outside we didn't think about the effect of spring rains on all that bare steel. That soon changed.

When early April rolled around, our '55 Crown Victoria was semi-restored. But we had announced that our project car would be on display at the annual '87 Spring Carlisle swap meet sponsored by the Flea Marketeers in Carlisle, Pa. So even though restoration progress was far ahead of the monthly articles in *Cars & Parts*, we hauled a toothless Vicky without much trim and with no upholstery out of the restoration shop at Classic Car Centre, Warsaw, Ind.

As much as we hated to do it, Vicky was trailered uncovered and unprotected to Carlisle. Those readers who made the same trip will remember how wet it was that week.

Once set up in our Carlisle swap spots, we soon found many interested onlookers gathered around Vicky. Topside comments ranged from, "When should I pick up my prize?" to "Nice paint!" to "When will the grille go back in?" Down under, comments were similar, except for one jarring, reoccurring quip: "Can't you do something about those rusty pipes?"

All the foul weather had turned Vicky's brand new exhaust system to a bright autumn leaf shade of rust. "We're not done, you know, that comes later," was our rather embarrassed reply.

We thought about painting the pipes, but short of going to stainless steel, we were a little lost as to what to do. However, shortly after we returned Vicky to Classic Car Centre, the answer came. Bruce Everhart, Spra-Met Enterprises, 330 North Hampton Road, Box 156, Tremont City, Ohio 45372, 513-882-1384, contacted us to say that he'd like to flame spray the exhaust system.

We weren't too sure what he was talking about. But as he explained the benefits of aluminizing, we got excited about yet another way to upgrade Vicky's restoration. Everhart, formerly associated with Metco, Inc., a Westbury, N.Y., maker of flame spray equipment and supplies, was starting a metal coating business. Naturally, he was anxious to introduce metallizing to the old car restoration crowd.

Flame spraying, explained Everhart, involves coating thoroughly cleaned and sandblasted metals with the same or a different metal. The process involves drawing metal wire through a hand-held gun where the wire is continually melted in an oxygen-fuel-gas flame and is atomized by a compressed air blast which carries the metal particles to the previously prepared surface. Any metal that can be drawn into wire form (or powdered in more sophisticated operations also involving ceramics and carbides) can be used.

Applications for old car restoration obviously come to mind. They include adding corrosion resistance by aluminizing the exterior of the exhaust system (as in Vicky's case), building up worn bearing surfaces, increasing abrasion resistance of water

pump vanes, applying hardened surfaces to valves, and restoring previously unrestorable items, such as camshafts and crankshafts.

We trailered Vicky to the Spra-Met shop, where the exhaust system — from manifolds to tailpipes — was removed, sandblasted to white metal, then aluminized. Then the entire system was coated with a clear sealer. Ends of pipes that fit inside the mufflers weren't aluminized because the process builds up thickness that would have caused reassembly problems. When completed, Vicky had a pretty exhaust system that Everhart guaranteed would look like new on the exterior for a dozen years of more.

The flame spraying of metals has been used for years in the space, military, shipping and bridge maintenance industries, as well as in industrial equipment maintenance and restoration. It's exciting to know that the technology now is available to old car restorers.

PART SIX

Renewing the Suspension, Steering, Brakes

Paul Sanborn, a technician with Trailer World, Bowling Green, Ky., pulls a wheel off the Cars & Parts car hauler. The trailer was returned to the manufacturer for the installation of brakes on the rear axle and a routine checkup.

TRAILER UPGRADE —
TWO-AXLE BRAKING

For the duration of our Crown Victoria restoration project, starting with our western trip in search of a car, a trailer has been an integral part of our overall plan. We needed a reliable unit to haul our prize back from Missouri, and we've used it repeatedly to transport our restoration project from our headquarters to the restoration shop in Indiana and to and from car shows around the country.

The *Cars & Parts* trailer, a tandem axle steel unit with an overall length of 22 feet and a bed length of 18 feet, suited our purposes perfectly. It was large enough to handle our project car, a 1955 Ford Crown Victoria, without pushing it to capacity, yet it wasn't so big that it presented a towing or storage problem.

The trailer features a full complement of lighting, safety chains, tie-down rings, fenders, automotive-style wheels, electric brakes and self-storing ramps — all the equipment one needs to haul a vintage car safely and efficiently. Well, almost everything!

Shortly after our project got underway and several reports on our car search, trailer acquisition and western trip had appeared in the magazine, several readers told us that we were in violation of the law when hauling a load as heavy as the Crown Vic on a twin-axle trailer fitted with brakes on only one axle. We received several different interpretations of various state and federal laws and were a bit confused by the whole thing until a state trooper sent a copy of the federal statute governing trailer braking. We were, in-

deed, in violation of federal law every time we hit the road with our loaded trailer.

The Commercial Motor Vehicle Safety Act of 1986, which took effect on Feb. 16, 1987, provided a number of changes in trailer braking requirements, while restating and reinforcing the provision governing our situation. Our trailer has a GVW (gross vehicle weight) of 6,800 pounds, and the regulation requiring brakes on all wheels applies to trailers with a GVW of 3,000 pounds or more. We were clearly in violation of the law ... but only when hauling the Crown Victoria. When running empty, we were not in violation of the law, at least according to our interpretation.

The statute stipulates that the braking regulation applies only if the weight of the load being transported combined with the weight of the trailer exceeds 40% of the overall weight of the tow vehicle. In our individual situation, with a Ford stretch van weighing about 6,000 pounds, we could tow no more than 2,400 pounds ... legally. And that included the trailer's 1,560 pounds, leaving us a payload of just 840 pounds. But, since our project car was not a Crosley or Bantam, we were running afoul of the law. The '55 Ford Vicky weighs at least 3,500 pounds, and probably more.

Although we had covered thousands of miles with the trailer in tow and Vicky on board without noticing any braking problems with either the van or the trailer, we certainly didn't want to knowingly violate any laws — federal, state or otherwise.

The solution to our dilemma was, of course, the installation of brakes on the one axle not having any built-in stopping power. In our case, that happened to be the rear axle of our two-axle rig. So we promptly scheduled a return trip to Trailer World in Bowling Green, Ky.

The good folks at Trailer World advised us that they were going to replace the rear axle, a so-called "idler" axle, with one equipped with brakes compatible with our electric brake system. The brakes are engineered to activate automatically with the application of the tow vehicle's braking system ... all at the touch of a pedal. The trailer brake system, via a hand-operated control lever mounted on a panel under the dash, can be operated exclusive of the host vehicle's brake system.

The new axle was installed without incident by Trailer World technician Paul Sanborn, working under the direction of Don Owen. Sanborn took advantage of the opportunity to inspect the entire trailer, checking out all its vital functions. He greased the wheel bearings on the front axle, checked the performance of the brakes, lights, etc., and gave us a clean bill of health.

The new two-axle braking setup is working fine, although we frankly haven't noticed any improvement in braking efficiency. But then the former one-axle brake system seemed to perform admirably under all circumstances. The brakes worked well both before the fix and after. The only difference is ... now we're legal!

1

2

When the 1955 model year came around, Ford was as modern as its competitors in the suspension department. With independent coil springs and ball joints up front and laterally supported leaf springs in the rear, the *Cars & Parts* project car, Vicky, could easily deliver a comfortable 500-mile trip with the best of them.

That was saying something for Ford, which didn't introduce independent front suspension and dual longitudinal rear leaf springs until the 1949 model year. Ford even had waited until 1954 before finally getting rid of its outdated kingpin-style front suspension.

It all came together for Ford in 1955 when modern suspension, new styling, spiffy vinyl interiors and advanced tire technology made Vicky a comfortable ride no matter what the road might be.

But time and miles had taken their toll on Vicky's suspension. Up front, the ball joints were loose, which contributed to

THE RESURRECTION OF VICKY

Rebuilding the suspension

3

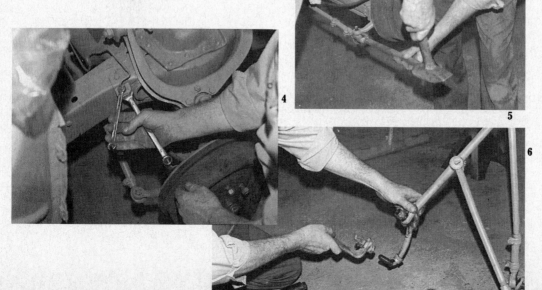

4

5

6

1. The frame and A-frame areas had been steam cleaned, partially sandblasted and coated with a water-repellant epoxy primer earlier. All components will be individually cleaned of remaining rust and grease before being repainted.

2. John St. Cin, a member of Classic Car Centre's body shop staff, began the teardown by removing the mushy old shocks, which will be replaced.

3. Fresh rubber stabilizer bar bushings will be used to replace the originals which have lost their resilience.

road wander and premature tire wear. The shocks were worn, and we suspected loose tie rod ends as well. In the rear, the leaf springs had sagged, and the shocks were just about shot.

In addition, we had serious reservations about suspension bushings, stabilizer links, and the idler arm. Intent on doing a proper ground-up restoration, we decided to completely dismantle the front and rear suspensions and replace just about everything but the front springs. Surprisingly, they hadn't sagged below proper ride height.

A front end rebuild kit was ordered from Kanter Auto Products, 76 Monroe St., Boonton, N.J. 07005, 201-334-9575. A new idler arm was purchased from Ed McMullen, New Ford Goodies, 18008 St. Clair Ave., Cleveland, Ohio 44110, 216-531-8685. New leaf springs were obtained from National Spring Co., 63 Grand Ave., Spring

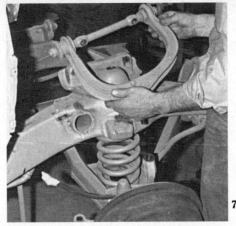

7

8

9

10

11

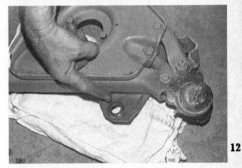

12

13

14

8. Both upper and lower ball joints had been subjected to abrasive dirt and sand thanks to leaking grease seals.

9. Releasing a coil spring under tension can be deadly. Securing the coil to the frame with a log chain before the tension was released would have been a good idea.

10. The A-frame to front engine cradle mount bolts were gently driven out with a brass drift to prevent damage to threads.

11. St. Cin had to wrestle the coil springs out of their cradles once the A-frames hung limp.

12. Badly worn stabilizer hole in lower A-frame will be welded and redrilled.

13. Build-up of grease around hubs had kept ball joint bolts well lubed and free of rust. The bolts came out without difficulty.

14. Ball joints act as pivotal points for the tires and wheels. Even a slight amount of wear permits a pounding action that soon destroys the unit.

4. Brake lines were removed and stored for patterns. At a later date new lines will be custom-made to original specs.

5. A pickle fork and hammer were used to remove the tie rod ends which were found to be loose due to worn internal parts. When inspecting tie rod ends also look for damaged, ruptured or missing rubber boots — a dead giveaway that dirt and grit have invaded the joints. Install new ends.

6. The idler arm showed marginal wear when worked up and down and will be replaced by a new unit. Slight looseness in an idler arm will cause toe change in the steering while driving. In turn, excessive toe change will result in premature tire wear.

7. When upper arm bushings are as worn as Vicky's were, spending money on a wheel alignment job is wasteful. It wouldn't last very long.

15. *All front suspension and brake components to be reused were sandblasted to remove rust and prepare the surfaces for painting.*

16-19. *Front end rebuild kit supplied by Kanter Auto Products included fresh ball joints, tie rod ends, upper and lower arm bushings and stabilizer links, plus all attaching hardware.*

20. *All sandblasted chassis suspension components and brake drums were painted before the reassembly was begun.*

21. *Eldon Nickel installed new tie rod ends onto refurbished tie rods. New zerk grease fittings were installed as well.*

22. *The best time to do chassis work is when the body is off the frame. There's good access from all angles. Vicky's frame was sandblasted and painted.*

23. *Primer and black acrylic enamel were applied by Classic Car Centre. New shackle bolts were used to attach the new leaf springs.*

24. *Nickel laid out the parts in order of disassembly then proceeded with reassembly.*

25. *Nickel and Tom Cripe visited the machine shop to press new bushings into the upper arms.*

15

16

17

18

19

20

Valley, Calif. 92077, 619-697-3544. New shocks, grease seals and hardware completed our shopping list.

As occasionally has been the case elsewhere during Vicky's restoration, we opted for the advantages of modern design and materials. We chose not to keep Vicky factory stock when it came to shock absorbers. We decided to install double-action Gas-a-just monotube units instead of original equipment single-action shocks. Of course, if our goal had been to make Vicky a 100-point show car rather than a car to be driven and enjoyed, we would have installed original-style shocks.

John St. Cin, the body man at Classic Car Centre, Warsaw, Ind., who was assigned to freshen up Vicky's body, gave the suspension rebuilders a head start when he cleaned up the front end and primed it while doing the body. His preliminary cleaning and painting after the engine had been pulled made the work go easier than it would have, considering the three-decade build-up of rust, dirt, grit and grease.

Once the body was off the frame, the front and rear suspensions were totally dismantled and removed. Then the frame and all suspension pieces that were to be reused got a good sandblasting, primer and a finish coat of black acrylic enamel.

Many restorations aren't as thorough as Vicky's, concentrating more on show than go. But we wanted Vicky to be as safe and sound underneath as she was when she came off the factory line back in 1955. The accompanying pictures show how relatively easy it was to restore Vicky's underpinnings.

21

26. Reattaching the A-frame components progressed at a steady rate until it was time to squeeze the coil springs in place.

27. Beefy casting of the new replacement idler arm adds a measure of safety to a critical area of control.

28. Professional coil spring compressing tool draws the coils down and makes safe work of an "accident about ready to happen."

29. Pretty, even though it's a bit dusty, Vicky's front end is as sound as factory original.

30. Rear end and axles received new grease seals. Gears were found to be within spec and didn't need attention.

31. New leaf springs corrected the rear end sag caused by Vicky's tired originals. The front springs were still all right after more than three decades!

32. We elected to upgrade the front shocks. Gas-a-just monotube units originally built for a Volvo matched up perfectly. Unit at bottom is a double-action replacement unit that was a few steps upscale from the single-action originals.

33. Almost ready to roll chassis should soon receive her spruced up body.

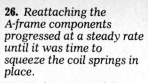
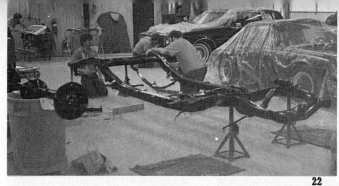

22

23

24

25

26

27

28

29

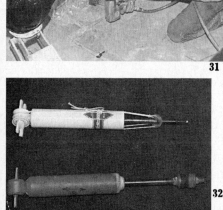

30

31

32

33

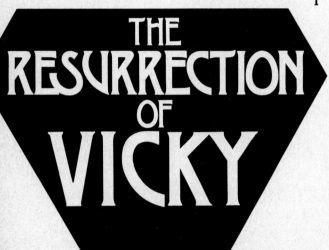

1

2

3

4

5

6

THE RESURRECTION OF VICKY

Rebuilding the steering box

1. *Vicky's steering box was disassembled to discover the cause of rough spots while turning and looseness at the center point of travel. The sector shaft and worm assembly needle bearings were destroyed during disassembly. The needle bearings might have been bad, but definite signs of wear were found on the steering shaft worm.*

2. *The pointer shows the worst part of the deterioration of the steering shaft worm assembly. Pitting, galling, chipping and wear had destroyed the precision of Vicky's steering.*

3. *Compare the chewed-up original with the NOS shaft and worm assembly (Ford #B5A 3524 B) on the right.*

4. *The faces of the sector shaft worm showed little if any wear, indicating the metal was much harder than that of the steering shaft worm.*

5. *A new shaft and worm assembly and a rebuild kit were all it took to return Vicky's steering box to like-new performance.*

6. *A new upper needle bearing for the sector shaft has been started into place. The tube on the right acts as a pilot for the steering shaft as well as a conduit for the horn switch wiring, which extends the length of the shaft.*

We'd like to have readers believe that every step in Vicky's restoration went smoothly and according to plan. Most of it, in fact, did. But every once in a while we'd uncover an unexpected missing part. Or a repair would take longer than expected, which caused something else to get snafued. Or we would take something for granted. In other words, Vicky's restoration progressed about like everyone else's.

One of those items we took for granted is the subject of this part in Vicky's restoration series: rebuilding the steering box. It wasn't until Vicky had been dismantled and stripped, mechanically and cosmetically, then rebuilt, refinished and reassembled that the steering box decided to let us in on its little secret. It waited until a pre-delivery test drive by the staff at Classic Car Centre, Warsaw, Ind. During the test drive, it was apparent something was wrong inside the steering box. Vicky's movements on the road were majestic, but a bit scary when the driver had to muscle the wheel through some rough spots.

Vicky had seemed to steer all right when we bought her. But then, everything in the front end was so worn and loose it was hard to tell exactly what was right and what was wrong. Stiff shocks and booster springs on the rear end also helped to mask any problems up front. Thus our original judgement was that the box seemed to operate smoothly when the shaft was turned lock to lock, and we decided to leave it alone. It was cleaned, lubed, adjusted, and painted, then set aside until reassembly time. We had made the same decision with the rear axle, the transmission and other components.

But once it was reinstalled in the car, which by then had a completely rebuilt front suspension and steering linkage, the steering box let us know the awful truth. There was a slightly rough feel when turning the wheel. In the words of service manager Roy Fannin, there was "a looseness, a rough spot at the center point, as if there was a notch out of the gear. The gear had a catchiness in it." The

Cars & Parts staff, receiving this information via telephone only days before we were to pick her up at final delivery, was disheartened. Remove the box and disassemble it, we said, fearing the worst.

Our fears were confirmed after the teardown. The worm assembly, an integral part of the steering shaft, was badly galled, chipped and worn. We had only a few days to find either a good used box (good luck!) or we could buy an NOS shaft and worm assembly. We didn't begrudge anyone the steep price being asked for such a slow-moving and hard-to-find item. Instead, we were thankful that one was available and gratefully bought it, as well as a rebuild kit which contained gaskets, seals and bearings.

Usually, a rebuild kit is all that's needed to return a steering box to like-new performance. What puzzled us about Vicky's steering shaft and worm assembly was why it should be so beat up. The sector shaft and worm assembly seemed almost perfect, even though it mated with the

120

7. Classic Car Centre mechanic Scott Parks continues his rebuild. In this operation he's installing the lower sector shaft needle bearing.

8. The needle bearing was recessed enough to accommodate a seal.

9. The lower sector shaft seal is about to be tapped into place.

10. After packing the lower tapered roller bearing with grease, Parks dropped it onto the built-in race. A thorough cleaning and inspection of the housing earlier had shown the race to be in good condition.

11. The steering shaft and worm assembly was installed, and a grease-packed upper bearing and race assembly was slid down over the shaft. Photo 3 shows the tapered ends of the worm assembly that pilot the shaft in the bearings and provide bearing surfaces.

12. Correct steering shaft and worm end play is determined by the number of gaskets stacked between the housing and the cap. The Ford factory used three when the box was built, but Parks discovered that the new shaft changed things a bit, and used five of the nine gaskets included in the rebuild kit.

13. A missing gasket on the steering shaft between the cap and steering column tube evidently was the reason foreign matter had entered the box and helped deteriorate the original worm gear. Parks obtained some corrosion-resistant felt battery post washers, cut a few to size, and fitted them to the shaft inside the cap. Vicky's new worm gear should be safe from her original gear's fate.

14. Parks gently installed the sector shaft and worm assembly through the needle bearings and end oil seal.

7 8 9

10 11

12 13 14

badly deteriorated worm assembly. The sector shaft and worm must be made of much harder steel, we reasoned. That meant the steering shaft worm must be softer. Somehow, foreign matter must have gotten into the box.

During reassembly, Assistant Editor Jim Scott was examining an exploded view of a Ford steering gear in a shop manual when he noted the factory used a seal on the shaft to prevent entry of contaminants into the cap. A seal had not been removed during disassembly, nor was a new one included with the rebuild kit. Since a missing seal at that point would allow dirt, moisture and anything else to enter the steering box just above the worm, we assumed the obvious, that we had found the cause for deterioration of the worm.

Scott Parks, Classic Car Centre's self-described "do-it-all man" who was rebuilding the steering box, patiently waited while we diagnosed the cause of failure. Then he disappeared for a while, returning with a can of corrosion-resistant felt battery terminal protector washers. He cut several to size, then installed them, thereby sealing the cap and steering tube junction and preventing anything from getting into the box in the future.

15 **16** **17**

18 **19**

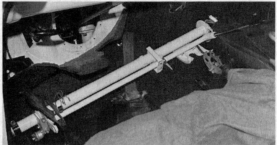

20 **21**

22 **23**

15. *A new gasket will seal out the elements and keep the grease inside.*

16. *The housing cover with thrust washer and adjusting screw then was installed. The squarish thrust washer is a slip fit between the fingers at the end of the sector shaft.*

17. *The cover was bolted in place, grease was injected into the housing through the filler plug hole (below the adjusting screw), the lock nut was threaded onto the adjusting screw, and the initial worm and sector roller mesh was obtained by adjusting the screw clockwise until all backlash was removed. Final backlash should be determined after installing the box in the car, but leaving the pitman off. Using a spring scale attached to the steering wheel to determine pulling tension through the high point, adjust the screw until specifications spelled out in the shop manual are achieved.*

18. *The pitman arm's splines are keyed to aid in fitting it correctly onto the sector shaft.*

19. *After installing the steering box, Parks crawled underneath to attach the Pitman arm to the steering linkage. Make sure the front wheels are pointed straight ahead when doing this.*

20. *The reinstalled box is ready for years of additional service. The cap and shaft will be covered by the steering shaft tube.*

21. *The steering shaft extends into the passenger compartment through a large access hole, which permits the whole assembly to be removed from inside the car.*

22. *Parks quickly installed the tube, steering wheel and assorted trim and other items that had to be removed to replace the steering shaft and worm gear.*

23. *Classic Car Centre service manager Roy Fannin turned the steering wheel through the center high point while repairman Scott Parks watched for correct wheel movement. After a minor adjustment, Vicky's steering passed a road test all looseness and "notchy" feeling gone.*

Hindsight is wonderful, but now we wish we had rebuilt the steering box when it was first removed. At least then we would have had time to find an acceptable used shaft and worm. But then we wouldn't have been able to provide as dramatic a learning experience for our readers.

The new parts now let Vicky steer as good as she did in 1955. Follow along in the photographs as Vicky's steering box is rebuilt and installed.

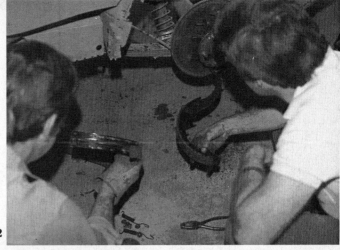

THE RESURRECTION OF VICKY

Brake system rebuild and upgrade

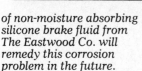

1. Cars & Parts *Art Director Ken New begins Vicky's brake rebuild by removing the shoe retaining springs. Both front and rear brake drum assemblies are of the single anchor (at top) self-energizing type.*

2. *Although the brake linings don't show excessive wear, they will be replaced with a non-asbestos DuPont Kevlar-based material to eliminate potential environmental and health hazards associated with asbestos, as well as to increase stopping power and lining life.*

3. *The grossly corroded condition of the brake cylinders was frightening. The cups in the rear cylinders were frozen solid. There probably hasn't been any braking at the rear in years. The use*

of non-moisture absorbing silicone brake fluid from The Eastwood Co. will remedy this corrosion problem in the future.

4. *A hammer and punch were needed to remove the pistons. They were scarred and will be trashed, along with the wheel cylinders.*

5. *Classic Car Centre's Gene McGuire demonstrates a method to determine if a brake drum is cracked. Firm taps around the circumference of the drum (this one is from a late model GM car) will displace rust and debris from cracks.*

We were surprised to find Vicky's brake system in a rather frightening condition. The brakes we thought were at least serviceable when we bought her turned out to be unsafe once we opened up the system. Naturally, we breathed a sigh of relief that we had decided to trailer Vicky the 500 or so miles from where we bought her in St. Louis to *Cars & Parts'* headquarters in Ohio.

How bad were Vicky's brakes? The metal brake lines, heavily rusted inside and out, fell apart when we removed them. The front wheel cylinders were badly corroded, but the rear wheel cylinders were so corroded and filled with junk the pistons had seized. The hoses were original. They showed dry rot, deep cracks and the effects of 32 years of use. The deeper we went into the disassembly process, the worse things looked.

What really surprised — and absolutely scared — us was the acceptable marks we initially had given a brake system that on closer examination was near total failure yet still operated the front brakes. Needless to say, our experience with Vicky's brakes has re-taught us a lesson: Never,

6. McGuire really didn't expect to find anything, but there was a three-inch crack along the inside edge. Obviously, a cracked drum is unsafe and should be replaced, which we had to do with one of Vicky's drums.

7. Vicky's drums were in pretty good shape. Only a slight .006-.008" cut was required to level the surfaces.

8. Dick Bruner from Classic Car Centre's service department sets up the Ammco brake lathe to make the first cut, which Bruner described as a rough cut.

9. Before sandblasting and painting the drums, a thick layer of tape was stuck to the braking surface. This prevents the brake lathe cutter from being gummed up by the paint.

10. Bruner ground the drums according to the manufacturer's recommendations for Kevlar-based linings. A service technician at EIS Brake Parts described the correct finish grind as considerably smoother than a 78-rpm record.

11. Classic Car Centre technician Jeff Nies opened the rear axles to check the bearings (they were within spec) and to reseal the wheel bearing retainers.

6

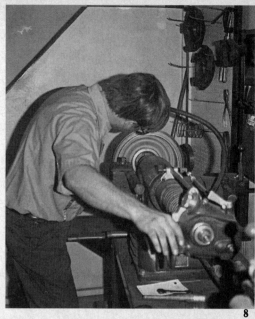
8

7

9

10

11

but never, take brakes for granted when buying an old car.

The only way to restore Vicky's brakes, and we suggest this is true for any brake system more than 10 years old, was to completely replace all lines, hoses, cylinders, hardware and power brake booster with new ones. The only major items that we reused were the brake drums, and we even replaced one of those because it had a crack in it. The parking brake cables also were fine, and we left that system as we found it.

The accompanying photos detail the various disassembly and restoration work that the Classic Car Centre, Warsaw, Ind., performed on our '55 Ford Crown Victoria project car's brakes. Though a number of the procedures are standard for self-energizing postwar hydraulic brake systems, we recommend following service manual procedures for your specific car, once new metal lines and flexible hoses have been installed. Additional do's and don'ts worth remembering are in the accompanying sidebar.

Once we realized Vicky's brakes needed a total rehabilitation, we decided to up-

BRAKE OVERHAUL TIPS

- When switching to silicone brake fluid, purge the system of all old fluid.
- The best time to purge a brake system of old fluid is during a complete overhaul.
- Never use solvents to clean brake parts. Use one of the special commercial brake cleaners, alcohol or new brake fluid. Keep brake cleaning fluid away from all rubber parts such as cylinder cups and hoses.
- Most commercial brake cleaners should be used in a well-ventilated area.
- Never reuse brake fluid purged from a brake system.
- Drum brake shoes should be arced when the friction surface of the drum is ground oversize.
- Most brake adjusters are either right or left-hand threaded; make sure they are installed on the correct side.
- There is no one perfect brake lining that satisfies all requirements.

- Brake shoes or pads purchased for vintage automobiles will not necessarily match the material composition of your old linings, thus affecting performance and causing adoption of different driving techniques.
- Riveted shoes may crack around rivets when the material gets hot; glued or bonded shoes avoid this problem.
- Drums should not be ground unless they are grooved or out-of-round.
- Drums and rotors should be ground in pairs (right and left side of car), or an unsafe pulling condition may result.
- Don't breathe brake dust. Never use an air hose to remove brake dust. Instead, wash the brake assemblies with water or cleaner and blow them dry.
- Drums ground oversize more than .60-.65 inches should be replaced; check manufacturer's specs to be safe.

grade to more modern materials in two key areas: fluid and lining material. The first was easy. To forestall future internal corrosion we installed silicone brake fluid. There have been reports of problems with silicone in systems with dual master cylinders and/or disc brakes, or in systems that have not been completely rebuilt with new parts and purged of glycol-based fluid. But none of these applied to Vicky's case. Her system was all-new, had a single master cylinder, and had no contamination from standard, water-absorbing brake fluid. In the future, Vicky's hoses may rot, the lines may corrode, and the wheel cylinders may rust, but it will be from without, not from within.

The second upgrade, brake linings, wasn't quite as easy to do. Gene McGuire and Terry Hygema of the Classic Car Centre staff recommended an aramid fiber-based lining material known as Kevlar, a DuPont brand name. Kevlar is used as a replacement for asbestos in linings, and provides better braking and longer wear life. It is used in many European and some Japanese passenger car applications, as well as heavy duty bus and truck fleets in North America. An additional advantage is that it eliminates the environmental and health hazards associated with asbestos.

The advantages of Kevlar-based linings seemed to be worth the effort to obtain some for Vicky, even though McGuire and Hygema warned us they weren't readily available. As with silicone brake fluid, the Kevlar linings would increase reliability and performance but not deviate from the original appearance or function — high priority items in the restoration of Vicky.

We had difficulty finding Kevlar linings through our usual vendor channels, as we had been warned. Most vendors had never heard of Kevlar. We were about to give up on what seemed like a good idea when we happened to talk to Richard Kondracky, the chief mechanic at EIS Brake Parts, in Berlin, Conn., and a former restorer of Rolls-Royces. Kondracky has extensive knowledge of how Kevlar performs since EIS manufactures Kevlar-reinforced replacement shoes and pads for a wide range of modern automotive applications. When Kondracky told us that no one "to his knowledge" had written about adapting Kevlar linings to a vintage car, we knew we were on the cutting edge of upgrade technology with Vicky's brakes.

Kondracky cautioned us to have the brake drums ground to a finish somewhat smoother than a 78-rpm record, to aid both in shoe break-in and in obtaining the highest coefficient of friction between drum and linings. He warned us to do some trial braking tests. As also is the case with metallic linings, which perform differently during braking than asbestos, Kevlar linings require driver familiarization. They have more stopping power and tend not to fade, among other characteristics. In other words, we were told, proceed with caution when using non-asbestos or non-asbestos-equivalent lining material that's different from the original equipment. This advice holds true even for late-model cars.

12. *A Midland-Ross power brake booster, which is correct for a '55 Ford, was found at a swap meet and fitted to Vicky's brake system, along with a new master cylinder and new lines. The vacuum tank*

bracket is a 1954 unit bent to conform to the '55's inner fenders. Ernst Truck Equipment, 2727 McDonald, Ft. Wayne, Ind. 46803, rebuilt the unit.

13. *New wheel cylinders were fitted on all four*

corners. Gene McGuire warned that honing old cylinders past manufacturer's specs will invite failure. Consult a brake manual for the correct procedure and measurements.

12

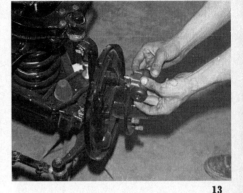

13

Finally, we consulted the maker of Kevlar, DuPont. Dr. David E. Hoiness of the Kevlar Special Products office in DuPont's Textile Fibers Dept. in Wilmington, Del., confirmed what we already had learned about Kevlar aramid fiber and provided a report he and co-worker Arnold Frances presented a year ago to the Society for the Advancement of Material and Process Engineering.

"Brake manufacturers and users report that brake materials reinforced with aramid in combination with other materials provide several advantages over brakes reinforced with other fibers. These include: longer brake wear with less vehicle maintenance, better friction properties, no rust-bonding performance problems and high reinforcement strength." Continued Hoiness and Frances, "Recent on-truck field test results show that brakes with aramid also exhibit less wear on brake drums."

Whatever Kevlar's other advantages might be, lengthening brake drum life is a key advantage in old car applications. Vicky's Kevlar shoes should make her drums last "forever," said the experts.

Once we were satisfied that Kevlar linings were a good choice, we redoubled our efforts to find Vicky some new shoes. Following up on a hint from Classic Car's staff, we talked to some trucking industry people familiar with the use of Kevlar linings. They directed us to a brake shop in Fort Wayne, Ind., where Vicky's brake shoes were stripped of the old linings and new Kevlar-based linings were bonded in place.

The owner of the brake shop was intrigued by the Vicky project and offered some tips to *Cars & Parts* readers. First, he advised, be prepared to pay two to three times the normal price for Kevlar.

Part of the reason is that it is a patented material. Second, though Kevlar linings are available for most modern vehicles, retrofits to older cars will require extra effort. It will help, once a brake shop that will install Kevlar linings is found, to provide the old shoes to use as patterns.

Another point to consider, the brake shop owner said, is that quality name brand non-asbestos linings are available that are not Kevlar-based yet offer increased braking power for vintage automobiles. "Keep in mind that there is no single lining material that works best in all situations," he said, echoing advice we had received from the EIS experts.

Though asbestos-based linings may be available for old cars for years to come, say brake industry officials, the trend is toward other materials since new car applications invariably determine what will happen in the aftermarket. As more and more vendors find it unprofitable to provide asbestos linings for an increasingly smaller market, the day will come when asbestos linings will be almost impossible to obtain, say these industry sources.

We could have stayed with asbestos linings for Vicky, but felt it appropriate to investigate the changing technology of brake linings since our intent was to make Vicky a car to be driven and enjoyed. Also, despite some reports from brake industry sources that asbestos fibers have their lung-grabbing hooks ground off when braking occurs, thereby rendering brake dust non-carcinogenic, there still remains the fact that brake lining factory workers have to deal with the hostile raw materials.

Follow along in the photos as Vicky gets new brake shoes and a better overall system than technology could provide in the fifties.

Wheels tend to be neglected during the restoration of a car. Thousands of hours and many, many dollars are poured into the renewal of the engine, body, chrome trim and interior, not to mention the various hidden components. The wheels, particularly modern pressed steel disc types, often are lucky if they get more attention than a fresh coat of paint. But wheels are critical to safety and handling, and deserve the same careful treatment as the rest of the car, if not more.

Vicky's wheels appeared to be in good shape, but they were subjected to the same scrutiny everything else received during the restoration.

Once the *Cars & Parts* '55 Ford Crown Victoria project car had been disassembled at Classic Car Centre, Warsaw, Ind., we removed the tires from the wheels.

The rims were inspected for damage. Luckily, no dents, major rust damage, bent centers, reamed-out stud holes or other problems were found. The bead sealing surfaces were not rusted. And the rims were within runout tolerances. Vicky had good wheels, so after a thorough cleaning and sandblasting, they were primed and then painted in the correct red body color Centari enamel.

Wheel cover restoration was equally simple. Vicky's stainless steel hubcaps needed nothing more than a good cleaning and buffing to bring them back to showroom condition. Reproduction plastic inserts replaced the deteriorated originals. The finished covers look brand new.

We replaced the over-size whitewall tires that came on Vicky with a set of brand new reproduction four-ply whitewalls in the correct 6.70 x 15 size, although Vicky's V-8 and Fordomatic options originally called for the optional 7.10 x 15 tires. The new tires' correct-width whitewalls are slightly narrower than the old tires that appear in all but the last article in the series. The finished wheel-cover-tire assemblies added that "right" look to Vicky that only the original equipment and appearance can give.

We were lucky with Vicky's wheels. Not all wheel restorations go so easily. Often, rim dents, severely rusted backsides, badly pitted bead sealing surfaces and other problems send restorers on a search for one or more new wheels, if not a whole set. All kinds of aftermarket wheels are available, if a non-original appearance is not important. But finding new original equipment wheels gets more difficult the older a car gets. If original equipment wheels can not be obtained from the manufacturer or from hobby vendors, often the only resources left are used wheels purchased at salvage yards and flea markets.

Used pressed steel disc wheels can be tricky buys. Bent centers, usually caused by sliding into a curb or into a ditch, or by clipping a corner too tightly, are the most difficult problem to spot. The only sure method of finding a bent center is to mount the rim on an axle or wheel balancer and spin it while measuring lateral runout at various points. Any lateral runout over 1/32-inch usually is unacceptable. Out-of-round conditions caused by impact damage or manufacturing problems also can be discovered the same way, but by measuring radial runout.

Other conditions are more obvious. While looking for a replacement rim for Vicky's spare at Dan Helman's Auto Parts salvage yard in Sidney, Ohio, we came across a number of good examples of those conditions. Though Vicky's spare wheel was perfectly good, no one noticed until very late in the restoration that it was a Chrysler wheel. It fit and worked fine, but we thought an original wheel would be more appropriate.

After first obtaining Helman's permission to look for wheels, we found all kinds in a huge pile, but no '55 Ford wheels. Returning to the main office, we asked him if there might be another place to look. "Oh, yes, I think there are some I took off a later-model Ford — they'll fit. They're in one of those busses stuff is stored in. What color bus? The rust-colored one!"

So off we went, looking through all the rust-colored busses. Finally, we found the right one, and the right wheels, except they were 16-inch rims and Vicky had 15-inchers.

We didn't find a correct rim for Vicky that day, but we found out a lot of other things about used wheels that will help other restorers facing the same situation. Follow along in the photos as we restore Vicky's wheels and wheel covers, and look for a good '55 Ford 15-inch wheel.

THE RESURRECTION OF VICKY

Restoring the wheels and hubcaps

1. *Vicky's wheels, after passing a thorough examination for problems, were deemed perfect. Following a sandblasting, they were primed and painted in the correct body color Centari enamel. Scott Cruthers of Classic Car Centre checks the primed wheels for thorough paint coverage.*

2. *Vicky's stainless steel wheel covers needed only a light buffing and new plastic medallion centers to be returned to good-as-new condition.*

3. *The new plastic medallions were secured in position by bending over tabs on the inside of the covers.*

4

5

6

7

8

9

10

11

12

13

14

15

4 & 5. The slightly over-size tires that came on Vicky (front wheel picture) were acceptable, but were not crisp enough in appearance. They also had a non-original whitewall width. The 6.70 x 15 reproduction whitewalls were correct, and add that "right" touch a thorough ground-up restoration requires, even when peeking out from behind fender skirts.

6. While looking for a Ford-built spare tire rim, we came across a number of problems used wheel buyers should know about. Corrosion on the bead sealing surface on this rim needs to be removed to avoid air leaks. This one probably will clean up acceptably, but might be

trouble later if corrosion reappears.

7 & 8. Lug nuts that have been overtightened will distort stud holes, upsetting the metal. It's only a matter of time before the holes become too enlarged for proper seating of the lug nuts and proper tightening torque. Watch out for metal distortion on both sides of stud holes, as is clearly the case with this wheel.

9. Loose lug nuts will destroy a wheel's usefulness forever.

10. Sometimes a rim lip can be bent enough to slip a credit card between it and a flat surface. All used wheels should be tested for lateral runout and out-of-round by spinning on a axle or wheel

balancer while measuring for deviations from specifications with a dial indicator or other device.

11. Some salvage yards mark used rims with part numbers. Learn a yard's numbering system and find out the correct number or numbers for the wheels you need before venturing into the yard, if the yard will let you find your own.

12. Most wheel manufacturers and car makers stamp wheel size codes somewhere on the rim. This wheel, a 14 x 5 JJ, is stamped inside the bead sealing surface on the outer ring.

13. Sometimes, a manufacturer stamps the

corporate logo on a prominent wheel surface. It's a big help to know this is a "Ford" wheel. Unfortunately, it wasn't the correct wheel for Vicky.

14. After searching all over Dan Helman's Auto Parts salvage yard in Sidney, Ohio, assistant editor Jim Scott finally uncovered two NOS but dirty '49-'56 Ford wheels, complete with factory shipping tags.

15. Unfortunately, the "A" suffix after the correct Hollander part number, 580, meant the rims were 16", and the yard marked them as such to make sure. Instead of fitting Vicky, they probably will nestle under the fenders of a Ford truck some day.

PART SEVEN

Body Restoration and Painting

Poor Vicky! First, we thoroughly dissected her being, removing all mechanical components, exterior trim pieces and the complete interior. Now we were about to strip her of her last vestige of dignity — her paint!

This is not what one might describe as a pleasant task. Naturally, any substance strong enough to turn hardened enamel paint into gooey putty in a matter of minutes is strong enough to smell obnoxious, burn the skin and otherwise offend the user. There are many quality products formulated specifically for stripping paint from metal. The one used by the guys in the body shop at Classic Car Centre, Warsaw, Ind., is Mar-Hyde Tal-Strip II, an aircraft coating remover made by Talsol Corp., 4677 Devitt Dr., Cincinnati, Ohio 45246.

It's strong stuff, and it works. Paint bubbles up quickly, separating from the metal with astonishing speed. In just a few minutes, professional body man John St. Cin is peeling the paint off the car with a stripping knife. He employs the kind of stripping knife that uses a regular razor blade in the working end. This type of knife, he says, works well on metal, and also fiberglass. In stripping the latter, he cautions, one should be a bit more careful as the blade can disfigure the fiberglass. St. Cin has a putty knife he prefers to use on such fiberglass-bodied cars as Corvettes; it's less threatening to the glass.

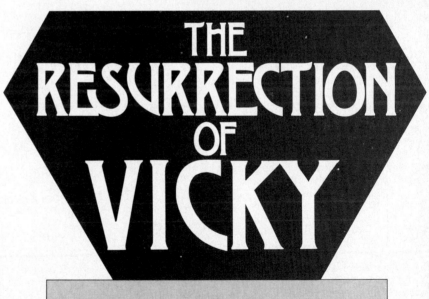

THE RESURRECTION OF VICKY

Stripping the paint

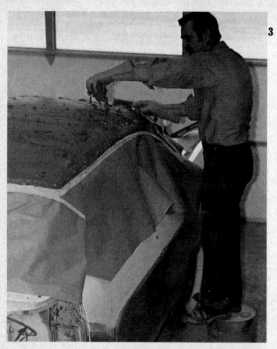

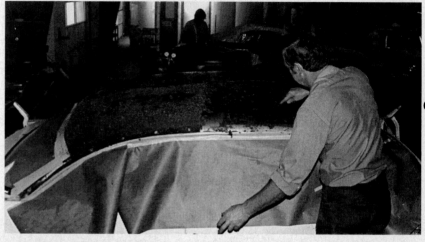

When stripping paint, it's easier and more effective to work in one direction on each individual component or body section, such as a fender, the roof, etc. It takes an average of about eight hours to completely strip a typical automobile once all the trim pieces are removed, St. Cin estimates. Of course, it can vary from piece to piece, depending on the type of paint, how many coats of paint and primer are encountered and the effectiveness of the stripping agent being applied.

Lacquer, for instance, is generally easier to remove than enamel. Paint stripping agents like Mar-Hyde can clear away lacquer almost like water running off a freshly waxed automobile. It's not quite a wipe and clean operation, but it's close, with the paint peeling off easily. This was the case with the trunk lid on the Cars & Parts '55 Ford Crown Victoria, which was painted in lacquer. On the other hand, those portions of the C&P project car painted in red are enamel, and they proved a bit more difficult to strip.

As the paint flowed off the car, a number of old sins surfaced. The front fenders, for example, had been subjected to numerous repairs. Some were quality metal repairs, while others were quick patch-ups using body putty. In the right front fender, St. Cin discovered a fair amount of plastic body filler and, at one spot, some aluminum foil had been tucked in behind the

1. With the roof stainless removed, body man John St. Cin commences to undress Vicky.

2. In just a few minutes, blistering paint starts to raise. After 15 minutes, St. Cin hand scrapes away the nasty residue.

3. Slick, shiny enamel is reduced to gobs fit only for the trash can.

4. Industrial strength paint remover is brushed on with overlapping straight strokes.

5. Paint scraper to left of pail is a folding affair that uses common drug store type single edge razor blades. Scraping edge can be renewed in a jiffy.

6. Second application of remover made short work of stubborn remnants of original torch red paint.

7. Ken New attacks the paint on the Crown Vic's hood. There were two layers of paint over the factory coat.

8

9

10

11

12

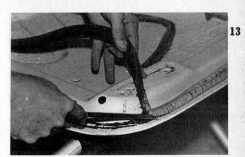
13

14

filler. Naturally, all improper work will be extracted and correct repairs rendered.

At one point in her lifetime, Vicky had a black top, we discovered as the red top coat was peeled off. The black paint had been applied over the original coat of red paint, which was revealed as the black paint was removed. Under the third layer of paint, the original red coat, we found the initial primer coat that had been sprayed on at the factory back in 1955.

The hood and trunk lid were both removed and the paint stripped using the commercial paint stripper. The old undercoating on the trunk lid was torn out and pitched. It was cracking and had been patched in several spots. Also, it had been painted white and should have been left in its natural black state.

Once the layers of paint were stripped off the car, paint residue was then removed using a lacquer thinner. It did the job!

Care was exercised in handling all of the various products used, particularly the paint stripping materials. Anything strong enough to remove paint from metal should be handled with caution. This applies to storing, handling, dispensing and applying such products, as well as disposing of them. Always wear protective clothing, especially a good pair of gloves. We found that the rubber gloves we used were virtually eaten away by the paint stripping

8. *For best results don't skimp on the paint remover, the manufacturer claims. It proved to be good advice.*

9. *Rubber gloves were worn to protect hands from toxic materials. It almost worked.*

10. *Paint remover soon broke down the rubber gloves and lit-up our restorers' hands.*

11. *While St. Cin and New continue the battle, Vicky sits quietly in the background.*

12. *Paint on trunk must have been inferior in quality. It literally flowed from the trunk lid as seen at the lower right edge.*

13. *All weatherstripping was dry rotted and although several pieces were restorable, all will be replaced with quality reproduction rubber from Dennis Carpenter Ford Reproductions, Charlotte, N.C.*

14. *Lower body wore additional coats of red, which quickly filled the trash can.*

15

16

17

19

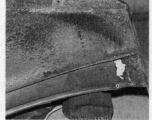

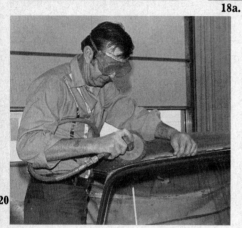

18a.

18b.

20

21

chemical. The product we used did have one advantage over comparable products in that it didn't have an offensive odor; most have a strong, punishing stink!

It's also recommended that a mask be worn, preferably a charcoal-filtered mask, and that eye protection is used at all times. Remember to follow the manufacturer's recommendations as listed on the label whenever a toxic or hostile product is being used. Always use common sense and put safety first in any restoration work.

22

15. *The farther down St. Cin scraped on the front fenders, the more the signs of deterioration became evident.*

16. *Plastic filler had been used to hide a parking lot dent along the door line of the front fender.*

17. *A patch panel was found on the lower end of the fender well. Since it was attached by spot welding (a relatively new method of welding in use now for some 10-15 years), we assumed the latest tidying up of the Crown Vic took place within the last five to seven years.*

18a & b. *Patch shown in previous photo revealed fairly nice work outside yet no insurance against future rust out had been taken on the inside of the fender.*

19. *A generous dousing with lacquer thinner on the fenders, hood and trunk lid cleaned the metal, prepping it for a light sanding, another cleaning and an epoxy primer coat.*

20. *Air-driven sander was used to remove some surface rust found along the rain gutter above the windshield.*

21. *It's amazing how a shiny, presentable coat of paint can be turned into such an ugly sight in such short order by paint remover.*

22. *Stripped to the bone, the old Crown Vic looks like any other hulk in the shop awaiting help!*

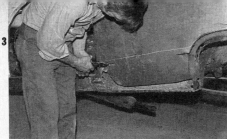

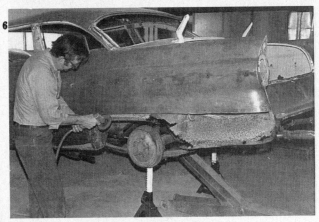

THE RESURRECTION OF VICKY

Restoring inner structural metal

A hobbyist generally wouldn't regard the restoration process as being one of destruction as well as reconstruction. If you've ever taken a fairly presentable car to a restoration shop for a ground-up restoration, you remember vividly your second visit to the shop. The car that you had been driving with pride only a few weeks earlier now resembled one of the disjointed heaps at the local junkyard.

Vicky, *Cars & Parts*' restoration project car, was a pretty sharp old car when she was found stored away for the winter in a garage in St. Louis. The guys and gals at *Cars & Parts* thought she was a great find and applauded her fine appearance, yet they were cautiously warned that one shouldn't be taken in by all that shiny red and white paint. Vicky's engine was a bit tired and there was a hideous cancer residing inside her body. The cure would entail a lot of work and considerable expense.

If you've been following the resurrection of Miss Vicky, you have watched as her

1. *"Used car lot quality" might describe previous body work to Vicky's lower quarter panels. In fact, prior to paint removal, the lower body looked pretty decent. A dose of paint remover and the uglies took over.*

2. *When John St. Cin, Classic Car Centre's expert body man, sliced the quarter, he laid open a wounded flap full of undercoating.*

3. Rusty inner panels are typical of mass production cars 10 to 30 years old. Inner metal is lucky to have survived this long without a dab of rust prevention.

4. Vibrating air gun released a deluge of sand deposited there many years ago. It had remained there, holding moisture and assisting nasty old Mr. Rust in his shenanigans.

5. Exploratory surgery taken a step at a time unveiled the crux of the cancer dwelling in Vicky's body.

6. Testing the extent of the rust damage and rigidty of the metal, St. Cin strapped on his safety goggles and ground off some surface rust.

7. Reconstructive surgery began after noting the relationship of the inner structural panels. St. Cin referenced all metal cutting to the point where inner panels met.

8. Patterns were cut from painter's masking paper. St. Cin prefers it to stiffer paper since it conforms easily to bent shapes.

9. The chunk of 20-gauge metal selected for the new panel was trimmed carefully before removing the reference point alluded to in photo 7. Leather gloves are a must to protect hands from nasty cuts.

10. A huge commercial size metal brake was used to match the bends needed to reproduce the old part.

11. A few minor cuts and nibs and it fit like a glove. Clamps were inserted through the trunk opening to grip the new patch and hold it in position.

12. You'd better have patches that match precisely before you cut away the old metal, St. Cin warns, or you'll be doing a lot of guessing.

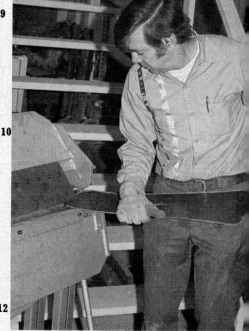

sins and shortcomings have been revealed. She had some rustout and a few dents, and she was a little tired and clogged in the engine compartment. Realistically, her physical condition was only a few steps up from a typical midwestern car that receives a frame-up restoration.

At the outset of the restoration project, the *Cars & Parts* staff had decided that a dry, rust-free western car would be a worthy candidate for a restoration. However, the staff conceded that refurbishing a western car that needed only a cursory restoration would, in fact, dilute the value of the series of how-to restoration articles planned for *Cars & Parts*. It was decided to take the more difficult path and find a car needing "everything".

In a previous segment of this series, Vicky was stripped of her paint and given a physical exam to determine how much damage she had suffered at the hands of "father time" and "mother nature".

In this segment, body man John St. Cin, a member of the body shop team at Clas-

sic Car Centre, Warsaw, Ind., assumes the roll of a demolition specialist and cuts deep inside Vicky's body to extract cancerous corrosion. Later, St. Cin hammered out sheet metal panels to begin the long arduous patching job required to resurrect Vicky's body to its former grace. St. Cin jokingly quipped that this was the fun part of the job — where he could get rid of his frustration by hammering, slamming and ripping away Vicky's fouled body parts.

As he moved around Vicky, making the rapping, clanking music that only body men make, he may have appeared to be playing games while cutting away body sheet metal at will. Yet, to the trained eye this was far from the truth. In fact, each nip of St. Cin's shears and every tap of his hammer was carefully calculated to help produce a revitalized, fresh Crown Victoria body reminiscent of the day Vicky was born back in 1955.

St. Cin began his assault by carefully cutting away small sections of the rear quarter panels to expose the rusty, perforated

inner structural metal residing underneath. His findings are recorded in the accompanying photos.

Vicky is typical of cars he has restored over the years, he says. He explained that cars from the 1950s were built with little regard for preservation of inner structural metal. Undercoating and sound deadener, which could have aided in the preservation of the bodies, were rarely applied to far reaching pockets deep inside rocker and quarter panels. Consequently, uncontrolled rust inside those areas ate its way through to the outside.

Following a familiar pattern, St. Cin fabricated patch panels from 20-gauge sheet metal he had salvaged from previous jobs. These patch panels were not available commercially, so the skilled hands of a craftsman like St. Cin are truly invaluable when performing a ground-up restoration.

In the next step in the body restoration St. Cin will complete Vicky's quarter panel repairs. Commercial quarter panel skins will be hung and readied for final paint.

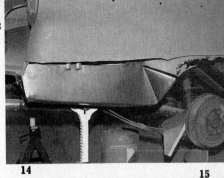

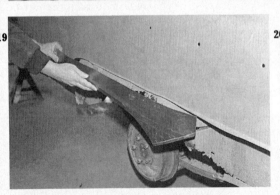

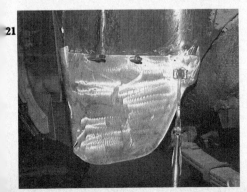

13. "You have got to have guts or be crazy to cut away metal like this," St. Cin quipped. The proficient body man must be a demolition expert before he is a reconstruction engineer. In this shot a flange has been made for fitting of quarter panel skin (see arrow).

14. Neatness of fabrication is evident in this shot.

15. Reproducing this simple box-lid panel was a snap for the adept St. Cin.

16. & 17. Inner fender lips were fabricated from raw stock using time-tested blacksmith techniques and tools.

18. Reproduction quarter panel was placed on its side and used as a go/no-go gauge to check the fit of St. Cin's handmade piece and the machine stamped quarter.

19. Beauty of hand-crafted fender lip will be lost once St. Cin buttons up the quarter panel.

20. Large mouth hand clamps were used to hold lip in place for welding.

21. Tip of fender tub was replaced with another St. Cin creation. Strange looking probes at top are clecos, small and efficient temporary fasteners popular with sheet metal fabricators.

Installing quarters

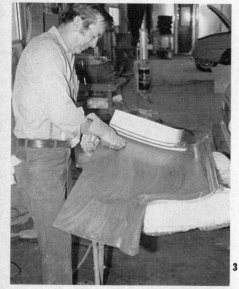

THE
RESURRECTION
OF
VICKY

Installing new quarters and rockers

1. Terry Ritter, body shop foreman at Classic Car Centre, examines the new quarters and rockers purchased from Made-Rite Automotive, Cleveland, Ohio. Ritter is sold on the fit of Made-Rite panels.

2. If you noticed that several photos seem to regress to a date earlier than last month's segment when John St. Cin repaired the inner structural metal, you're very observant. St. Cin fitted all quarters and rockers prior to repairing the inner metal. In this photo St. Cin blow dries the metal-prepped body.

3. He also metal-prepped the quarters, etc., and primed them before fitting started.

4. All patch panels were metal-prepped and primed. Charcoal-filtered breathing mask is imperative when spraying catalyst-based primers.

5. The repair panels were made to service four-door sedans as well. Two door repairs entail welding the pieces together. St. Cin hammers a lip made for the edge of a rear door.

6

7

8

9

10

11

12

L ast month when we tore into Vicky's rear quarters, we probably shocked a few faint-hearted readers who cringe at the sight of a body under the knife. Indeed, extensive surgery was undertaken as part of Vicky's body restoration.

John St. Cin, the expert body man at Classic Car Centre, Warsaw, Ind., sliced gaping holes into our Crown Vic's quarters to gain access to the eroded structural metal underneath. Literally, we were at a point of baring Vicky's soul to the whole world. All of Vicky's ailments were exposed and the crisis in her illness reached. It would be all uphill from this point as we forged ahead. Otherwise, the Crown Vic would be in failing health forever.

It would have been easier and less expensive to cover up some of the nasty mess. But that wasn't our goal, nor was it acceptable to the folks at Classic Car Centre. From the onset of the project we wanted to end up with as good a restoration as possible within our budget.

Vicky was quite a looker when she was brought back to *Cars & Parts* headquarters late last year. Fairly well preserved, she had inched into middle age gracefully. Yet, she was no cover girl. It was only under close examination that her true health was revealed. She was a little tired in the drivetrain, but not terribly so. Her primary failing was cancerous rust which had eaten away at the lower sections of her once beautiful body.

6. *Preliminary fit is checked.*

7. *St. Cin indicates the point where he'll lay open Vicky's sides for the new quarters.*

8. *Panels were held in place with wide-mouthed c-clamps for a quick check of overall fit.*

9. *Using the contour line just above the wheel cutout as a guide, St. Cin decided to trim the panels five inches above.*

10. *Electric shears made quick work of a hand-blistering job.*

11. *Overlapping pieces of quarters will be cut and joined above the wheel wells.*

12. *Wraparound section at the front of the quarters was cut away since it wasn't needed. Integrity of bends of replacement panels usually isn't as sharp and crisp as factory panels.*

This segment of the Resurrection of Vicky deals with replacement of quarter and rocker panels. More than any part of the series, it reveals her problems and bares all. John St. Cin, the jovial member of the body shop team at Classic Car Centre, performed major corrective surgery to eradicate the cancer residing in Vicky's inner body parts. That required skin grafts in the form of new replacement rear quarter and rocker panels.

Made-Rite Automotive (869 East 140 St., Cleveland, Ohio 44110, 216-681-2535) has a vast inventory of replacement sheet metal for vintage automobiles, including quarters and rockers for our Crown Vic. St. Cin was pleased with the quality of the panels.

St. Cin began the repairs by establishing points of reference at the cowl pillar, door posts and rear fenders, as well as contour lines along the rear quarters. St. Cin says you've got to work within those limitations to restructure the panels correctly. "If you don't, the doors will never fit right. And the car will leak like a sieve." He warned that misaligned doors never seem to work correctly. You've got to slam them shut and the added stress usually results in broken door glass sooner or later.

He also advises anyone who gets into heavy body work, such as quarter panel replacement, to take the time to establish correct alignment at the outset. It's too late and too expensive to make corrections after the finish paint is applied. Follow accepted body shop repair practices and when doubts arise don't hesitate to ask questions of professional friends in the business. Good planning and foresight are as important to a satisfactory conclusion as using the right hand tools.

The accompanying photos follow St. Cin as he grafts new skins onto Vicky.

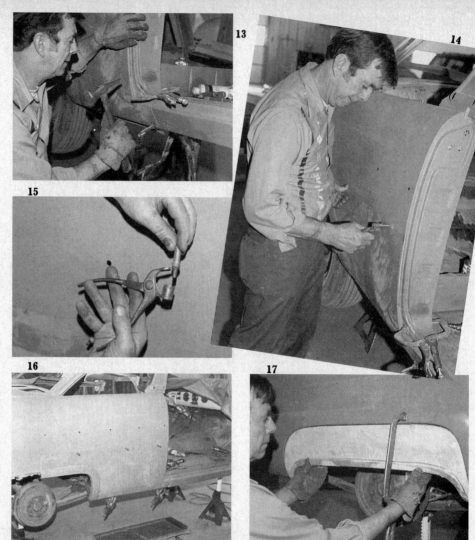

13. "You never seem to have enough c-clamps," says St. Cin. Even so, a little hammer persuasion is usually necessary.

14. Used extensively in aircraft construction, clecos are excellent temporary fasteners for holding sheet metal in position during all phases of panel replacement from fitting to welding.

15. Special pliers compress the protruding spring loaded end of the clecos to permit entrance into a standard ⅛-inch drill hole. Releasing the pliers pulls the sheet metal layers together.

16. Clecos are systematically plugged through the butting panels. A snug fit for welding is appreciated. The neat thing about clecos is that they permit removal and refastening of panels in exactly the same position. There's no wobble to worry about.

17. Fit of fender skirts must be resolved before the two panels are welded together.

18. The lower section of original was cut away for access to the inner structural metal which needed attention.

19. Air gun attachment makes a flange for overlap of replacement quarter over the original top half.

20. St. Cin stopped progress to fix the inner metal before finishing the quarters. Here he used a batch of clecos to firmly hold the panel.

21. The answer to why so many clecos were needed became apparent as the heat from St. Cin's welding torch tended to separate the butting panels. Hand-held welding shield is convenient.

22. Welds were gradually scattered across the lap joint until every hole was sealed shut.

23. A grinder was used to flatten the weld beads.

24. A thin layer of body filler will conceal the joint forever. The average onlooker will not realize the extent of Vicky's surgery unless he looks closely inside the trunk area.

19  **20**   **21**

22    **23**    **24**

Installing rockers

1. Even though typical rust out was found in Vicky's rocker panels, we were encouraged to find solid inner panels showing nothing more than surface rust, except for spots where body struts reached from the frame. (See arrow)

2. John St. Cin, a member of the Classic Car Centre's body shop staff, chisels the lower spot welds that held the original rocker. The hole you see is the remains of the shale rust pointed out in photo 1. It deteriorated from the vibration of the air chisel.

3. Lead was used at the factory to fill the body seam where the rockers and quarters meet. It melted and dropped to the floor quickly under St. Cin's torch.

4. Lower body metal was sandblasted. A patch made of new metal sealed the rust hole and the unit regained the body to frame stability that had been lost to rust.

5. The torch heat warped the metal slightly, requiring a bit of persuasive straightening with a dolly and hammer.

6. Sparks flew as a die grinder was used to cut away a lip of the old rocker. St. Cin wore safety goggles.

7. New replacement rocker slides under the cowl post.

8. With the fit at the front all set, St. Cin will begin to fit the rear end section.

9. Fitting the rocker at the rear required shaping a tucked-in fit.

10. One of St. Cin's most used tools is a section of I-beam that serves as an anvil. Here he straightens a lip on one of the rockers.

11. The door was hung to check for proper fit. St. Cin wedged open a tight fitting door and rocker with his favorite chisel-nosed body hammer. No welding took place until the quarter and rocker panels were properly fitted.

12. Things were looking good by the time St. Cin was ready to tackle the quarter panels.

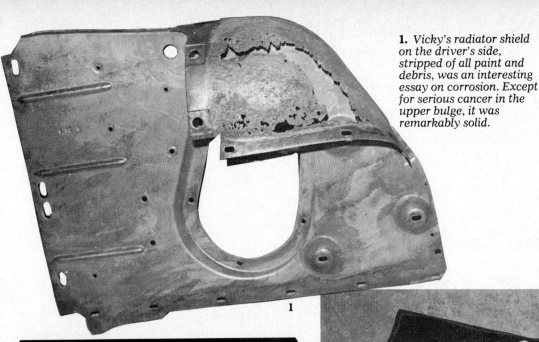

1. Vicky's radiator shield on the driver's side, stripped of all paint and debris, was an interesting essay on corrosion. Except for serious cancer in the upper bulge, it was remarkably solid.

2. The usual assortment of panel beating tools includes a sand bag, metal shears, panel beater's mallet, vise-type pliers, clamps, rawhide and body pick hammers.

3. St. Cin demonstrates panel beating by bellying out an oversized piece of flat sheet metal. The hammer and sand bag are available from The Eastwood Co., Malvern, Pa.

4. It took approximately an hour of careful tapping to match the shape of the rusted piece. As the piece took shape, St. Cin would

THE RESURRECTION OF VICKY

Panel Beating … how a pro does it!

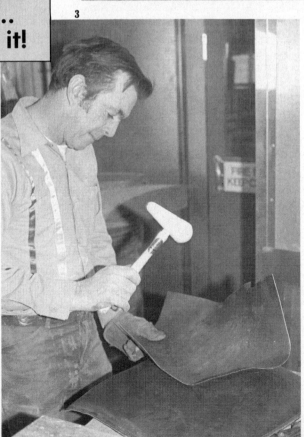

lay the beaten panel over the old cancerous piece and eye its lines and bulge carefully. Trimming was the last operation. St. Cin says, "It's tough to anticipate how the beating will pull in the edges."

5. After the thousands of pimples were smoothed out with a rawhide hammer and sand bag, hand shears were used to make the final trims.

6. An exact copy of the old panel (minus the rust out), the new panel will require no patching at all. No welds, and no patches.

7. St. Cin ground the edges to remove sharp spurs and lightly sanded the surface to accept a coat of epoxy primer.

Panel beating and '55 Crown Victorias are unrelated topics in the minds of most restorers. The thought of beating a panel for any Ford, Chevy or similar mass-produced car may seem absurd since replacement parts, either NOS or good used, can usually be located without a great deal of difficulty, provided one is willing to spend the money and has the time to spare.

When Vicky's front fenders were unbolted during body disassembly, some serious rust-out was uncovered in the bulging panels spot welded atop the air deflector panels adjacent to the radiator. Ironically, the flat sections of the two-piece parts were solid and needed only minor surface rust removed to restore them to brand new

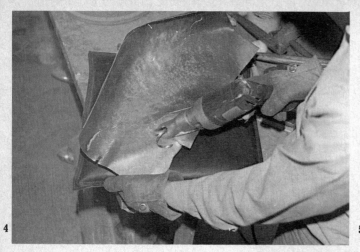

4

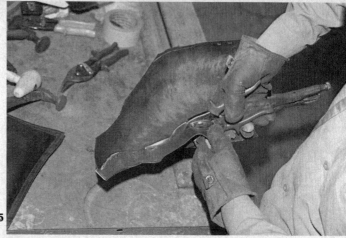

5

6

7

condition. Our options were clear. We could scrounge some replacement parts, weld patches to the remaining metal to close up the gaping holes, or shape new panels from raw sheet metal to match the old panels. We elected to pursue the former since repairing the panels was an excellent opportunity for John St. Cin, Classic Car Centre's expert body man, to display yet another one of his masterful skills.

Of interest to readers who are keeping tabs on the repair cost, the hour or so St. Cin spent beating the new panel into shape was less than half as expensive as the estimated $100 or $110 for an NOS panel. And, there was no appreciable delay in the project. In addition, the fix suggests an alternative for many restorers who feel their backs are to the wall when faced with locating obsolete sheet metal parts. Acceptable panels can often be made if one is willing to give it a try.

The basic tools of panel beating are a mallet and a sand bag. The shape and design of those tools can be as varied as the final intent of the panel beater. Some beaters use commercially available steel or wood hammers, hard rubber mallets, etc. At other times, commercial tools don't seem to fit the job and special tools are fashioned for special needs. The universal fixture that almost all panel beaters use is some sort of bag (usually leather) filled with grain sand or, on rare occasion, steel shot.

Another alternative used by some restorers is a wooden box filled with sifted clay or sand to absorb the concussion of pounding panels. Either device also works well

in leveling dents in hub cap skins, etc.

St. Cin used a two-inch moulded polyethylene bossing hammer with a pear-shaped head and a panel beater's sand bag available from The Eastwood Co., 580 Lancaster Ave., Malvern, Pa. 19355. If the rusted out section of Vicky's air deflector panel had required a gentle curve, St. Cin would have used a leather covered wooden slapping mallet custom shaped to fit the contour of the panel. Other tools included a tired old rawhide mallet with its face shaped on a grinder to match the concave surface of the air deflector panel. St. Cin used this hammer to smooth out the irregular, pimply surface left by the roughing out strokes of the bossing hammer. Conventional tin snips and clamps rounded out the selection of the tools St. Cin used.

There are two basic exercises in panel beating — shrinking and stretching. Shaping the deep clam-shaped part for Vicky required a generous portion of stretching blows with minor shrinking techniques used along the edges where the bolt holes were located. Stretching involves displac-

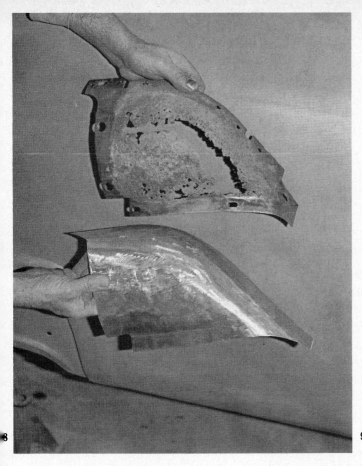

ing the metal to assume more surface. Shrinking metal does the opposite.

St. Cin selected a piece of 20-gauge sheet metal from his cache of scrap, cut it a couple of inches oversize, laid it on the sand bag and started beating the panel repeatedly on one side. Working in a circular pattern, he gradually worked his blows back and forth across the beaten section while increasing the bulge he was creating. It doesn't take one long to realize that panel beating is an unforgiving art that requires persistence and patience.

"You just can't stop halfway and expect the part to fit," St. Cin says. There always seems to be a point, he says, where "you wonder if the panel will ever fit — then you look things over carefully and start hammering some more." Watching the operation, one can see what he means. Several times he would hold the beaten metal up and eye it closely. Its resemblance to the old rusted panel was indeed questionable. Then St. Cin would lay the metal back on the sand and commence beating again. A little over an hour after St. Cin began working on the panel, the metal took on a shape that matched the rusted out panel like a carbon copy.

"It's not a real tough piece to make," he said. Small in size, it's manageable and is a structural piece which would seldom be seen once the car was reassembled, he added. It wouldn't have to match exactly, he reasoned, although it's obvious he wouldn't settle for anything less.

Had the job required duplicates, such as two headlight eyebrows, St. Cin would have cut cardboard templates to match

the contours at various points. These would be used as gauges when making duplicates. He added that templates would have been a good idea even for one panel, except today his confidence was soaring high and he had forgone templates. You will probably be somewhat arrested by St. Cin's panel beating skills.

Follow along in the accompanying photos as the replacement panel takes shape. It's amazing that the panel required absolutely no welding. Once primed, spot welded in place and painted, it looked like it had always graced Vicky's radiator air deflector.

8. *A clone? Well, almost, except for the lack of drill holes and rust out.*

9. *The new panel was primed before it was spot welded in place. The passenger side radiator shield is shown in this picture.*

10. *Passenger side shield required a small 2x4-inch welded patch panel using conventional repair techniques. Parts were primed and readied for a coat of black enamel.*

1. *Body man John St. Cin cut around the edge (arrow) so that the entire bottom plate could be extracted and replaced. The inside of the door looked pretty solid.*

2. *New metal has been welded into the hole, the welds smoothed and the whole door cleaned and primed.*

3. *Terry Ritter, body shop foreman, sets the controls on the shop MIG welder.*

4. *Unprotected inner lower edge of trunk lid caught run-off condensation and rust out resulted.*

THE RESURRECTION OF VICKY

Door lip and trunk lid repair

Vicky's doors were straight, didn't sag and at a casual glance appeared to be in pretty good overall condition. Unfortunately, that wasn't an accurate analysis.

On the lower edges, rust out in the form of scattered perforations hid beneath the rubber weatherstrips. Once the doors were unbolted from the door posts and laid across padded workhorses, the damage could be easily surveyed by John St. Cin of the body shop staff at the Classic Car Centre, Warsaw, Ind. After St. Cin had completely ripped away the weatherstripping, he poked around the rust with an old screwdriver and concluded that the doors were "really pretty good" and making repairs would not present any unusual problems.

He began by snipping away the rusty metal to remove a long rectangular shape that included the majority of the bottom edges. St. Cin figured rust protection measures had never been taken too seriously years ago. In addition the drain holes had been sealed shut by leaves and other debris. Once the bad metal was removed, the doors were lightly and carefully sandblasted to remove rust along the edges and also to etch the door skins for paint adhesion. Earlier, all paint had been chemically stripped from the body.

St. Cin cut a patch from a scrap of 20-gauge sheet metal left over from a quarter panel repair. Using a MIG welder, he lap welded the patch over the hole, exercising extreme care to sink the lap weld below the original metal line. Otherwise, the lower door edge would have had clearance problems after Vicky's doors were refitted to the door posts and the carpet and sill plates installed.

During the course of the Vicky resurrection series, several restoration techniques and products have been mentioned. One such piece of equipment is the MIG welder used at Classic Car. Several vendors to the old car hobby sell MIG welders designed for use by do-it-yourselfers. Among them are Eastwood and Daytona MIG. Do-it-yourselfers can order a copy of HTP America's, "Guide to MIG Welding" by phoning 1-800-USA-WELD. There is a $2 charge. Information on MIG welders, plasma cutters, metal working tools, welding wire and consumables, safety equipment and related accessories is featured.

Rust repair to the trunk lid followed a different route. The outer skin is crimped to an inner structure which adds strength to the overall assembly. At the lower points where the crimped metals meet, rust damage was also found. Like the damage to the doors, it was only somewhat unsightly and routine repair methods sufficed. Yet in this case the perforated metal was not removed. St. Cin decided that

sandblasting the outside lip and scratching away inner shale rust via the access holes (there weren't many) would cure the problem. He applied a rust prevention treatment, POR-15, to chemically stop the spread of existing rust.

Presanding or rust removal is not necessary, according to the supplier. Available in 8 oz. quart and gallon containers, this rust prevention treatment is a product of POR-15, Inc., Box 1235, Morristown, N.J. 07960. POR-15 can be safely used on auto body parts, gas tanks, and bumpers, as well as other non-automotive metallic parts. St. Cin feels that this type of rust prevention system is nearly perfect for halting the type of rust found in Vicky's trunk lid, where access is extremely limited. The only alternatives would have been to search for a rust-free trunk lid or reskin it. Both would have been impractical from a budget point of view.

1. *While some outriggers appeared fairly solid, others were in pretty ragged condition.*

2. *Undercoating had effectively kept road chemicals off the outside surfaces; however, rust had eaten through from the inside.*

3. *John St. Cin slips under the Cars & Parts' 1955 Crown Victoria project car and tests the rigidity of the body outriggers. He found them to be frail and in need of repair.*

THE RESURRECTION OF VICKY

Rebuilding the floorpan outriggers

3

The underbelly of an unrestored vintage car normally is not a very pretty sight. The topside of the car can sport bright, shiny paint and outwardly the car may appear to be "fully restored," while the underside remains as grubby as a rusty nail. The term "fully restored" can encompass many things and is often abused. It's a matter of interpretation. In this context, though, "fully restored" means just that: Totally, completely, 100-percent rebuilt.

The staff at Classic Car Centre in Warsaw, Ind., started at ground level and won't stop until every shard of metal and every component is brought back to like-new condition. The *Cars & Parts* 1955 Ford Crown Victoria project car is being fully restored literally from the ground up.

And it's not really a ground-up restoration unless the underside sheet metal is given the same attention as the topside.

A thick layer of black undercoating had been sprayed on the underbody of the 1955 Ford Crown Victoria project car. In fact, it seems that several zealous former owners had seen fit to coat the car's underbelly with a protective layer of undercoating. At some points the black stuff was half-an-inch thick. Yet, it still didn't solve the problem completely, as rust came through from the inside. A screwdriver could be pushed through the structural metal bracing the floorpans. It was readily obvious that some repair would be needed, as is normal with Fords some 30 years old. However, the extent of rust damage didn't

become fully apparent until the undercoating was scraped away. Suffering most from mother nature's dust-to-dust guarantee were the body braces (outriggers). These ragged shells had rusted out completely.

John St. Cin, the body restoration specialist assigned to revitalize our project car, Vicky, quickly surveyed the damage by picking around the underbody and testing the rigidity of the metal with a screwdriver and a pair of pump pliers. The outriggers nearest the front tires were rusted out more than the others to the rear. Extra servings of road salt had possibly quickened their demise.

St. Cin occasionally salts away bits and pieces of automotive sheet metal repair

4

panels for use on future projects. A chunk
from a replacement quarter panel, a door
skin, etc., can be used to repair a future
project. "It's the scrounger in me," St. Cin
says. "I just can't throw away parts that I
can use later. My garage at home is full of
this stuff. I can't believe how much I've
accumulated," he adds.

Tape measure in hand, St. Cin scooted
underneath Vicky to record the measurements of the rusted outriggers. Of the four
to be replaced, two would be almost useless for patterns.

Surveying the underbelly of an older car
is not the most pleasant job, especially
when dirt, rust, etc., fall into your hair and
face and onto your clothes. Worse yet is
the debris that gets into the eyes. There's
probably no hobbyist or body man alive
who hasn't made a run or two to a local
clinic to be treated by an ophthalmologist.
After a few painful experiences, St. Cin
has become a real believer in sound safety
practices and is quick to don his safety
goggles, especially when sailing under a
car with a grinder in hand.

Scanning Vicky's floorpan area from underneath, one could see thick, lumpy layers of undercoat. Several previous owners
had apparently added layer on top of layer to the black mess. They probably had
good intentions. Unfortunately, the sheet
metal pockets that were inaccessible from
either top or bottom had gone unprotected
for Vicky's entire life, and consequently
had rusted through. In addition, the heavy
undercoat plugged drain holes, which
caused welling of water inside the

5

6

4. Wearing protective
goggles, St. Cin cuts away
the rusty shells that
remain. They'll be used for
patterns to reconstruct
new ones from fresh
sheetmetal.

5. A conventional set of
sheetmetal shears includes
three basic shears. One
shear cuts right, one left
and one straight.

6. Each pair of shears is
stamped with its
appropriate application, as
seen in this Matco TS3 for
straight cuts.

outriggers. This introduced the three key ingredients of rust — bare steel, air and water.

St. Cin clipped and ground away the remaining fragments holding the outriggers to the floorpan. Two of them were sufficiently intact for use as patterns. The others were not, as illustrated in the accompanying photos.

St. Cin selected a flat chunk of sheet metal from his cache stored behind a work table. He says the excess cuts from quarter panels, etc., are suitable for making patches and constructing repair pieces not available commercially. Next, St. Cin pulled on a pair of thick leather gloves to protect his hands from sharp edges. He then reached for a trio of hand shears — one cuts left, one right and one straight. The snips are stamped for appropriate use and the handles are color coded green, yellow and red, respectively.

Transferring measurements from his notes St. Cin laid out the raw patterns with a permanent yellow marker and punched vital points with an awl to insure accuracy. Although Vicky's outriggers would not nor-

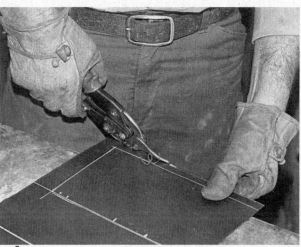

7. *The layout for new outriggers was scribed onto new sheetmetal with a paint marker while critical points were pinpointed with a hammer and awl.*

8. *Some trimming was required to fabricate an edge which will be used to anchor-weld the boxes in place.*

9. *Raw shape is cut out. Protective gloves are a must to avoid nasty cuts.*

10. *Sheetmetal brake aided St. Cin in bending the outrigger boxes to the correct shapes.*

7

8

9

10

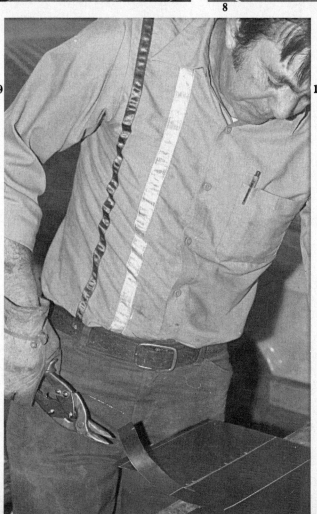

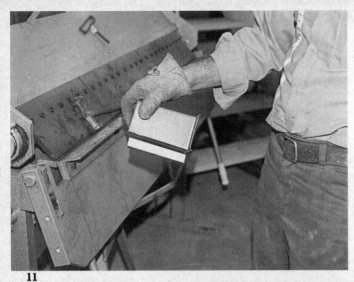

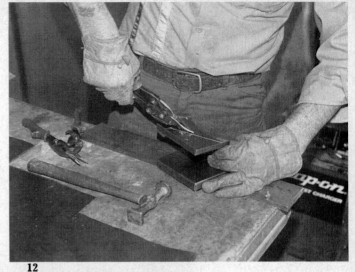

11

12

13

11. *A few bends and the basic shape appears. It's much easier and cheaper to make new pieces than to repair the rusty ones.*

12. *Oblique cuts were made to complete the triangular sides of the boxes.*

13. *A few taps with a body hammer were needed to dull some sharp edges.*

14. *Surrounding floorpan metal will be cleaned by sandblasting to prepare it for welding new outriggers into place.*

15. *Raw edges will be ground away once the new piece is welded to the floor and rocker panel.*

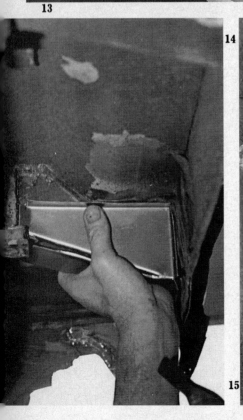

14

15

mally be seen, St. Cin insisted on exact fits. He says it's a lot easier to weld good fitting parts than "trying to fudge-in wide gaps with lots of welding rod." It looks better and reflects the meticulous care taken by a skilled craftsman. In short order, St. Cin flipped and clipped away the selvage. Occasionally he'd hold it at arm's length to size up the cuts and study the raw shape to see if it would match the one he'd already formed in his mind.

Once the patterns were free of phage, St. Cin commenced bending angles with a sheet metal brake. Oblique cuts were made by hand and St. Cin's handiwork assumed the shape of outriggers, which slipped effortlessly into position underneath the floorpan.

Hauled outside to the sandblasting pit, Vicky's underbelly was sandblasted in the spots where the outriggers would be welded. The welding was performed and Vicky's wounded underbelly was healed. The outriggers were as good as new, both structurally and cosmetically. The scars left by more than 25 years of neglect had been smoothed over by the specialists at Classic Car Centre. Later in the restoration program, the entire floorpan (inside and out) will be sandblasted, laundering it for a fresh new coat of paint.

1. Body man John St. Cin TIG-welded new braces into position. Note the hand-held spark shield, which has a see-through protective dark glass fitted to its shield.

2. Cocked in an overhead door glass frame, this chunk of one of Vicky's perforated floorpans tells a pretty convincing story. The old gal wasn't really that rusty, but rather than patch it, the Classic Car Centre body shop decided to replace it.

3. Like the body outriggers covered in an earlier piece, the subfloor structural braces were rusted away. Body man John St. Cin fashioned this replacement brace from scrap sheet metal.

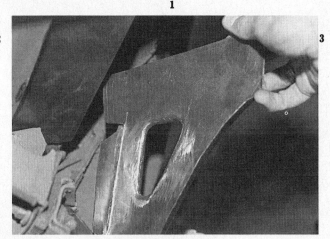

With any frame-off restoration there are tough, dirty jobs, such as replacing floorpans, that are less than glamorous. Such jobs require a vast amount of savvy and skill. Yet the guy who spends countless hours expertly hammering and shaping repair panels from raw sheet metal is rarely showered with praise, while the guy who shoots the paint often gets more than his share of credit. Proficient painting skills are admirable and certainly can't be discounted. But metal work is equally important.

The fact that the painter gets most of the praise is "just one of those things", says John St. Cin, Classic Car Centre's expert body man. He says that any painter worth his salt will tell you point blank that "the final paint will never be any better than the prep work." Those long hours spent shaping patch panels and tack welding are vitally important to the total restoration.

Classic Car Centre's body shop foreman, Terry Ritter, and body man John St. Cin are two professionals who have tremendous pride in their craftsmanship. That element of pride was an added benefit when

THE RESURRECTION OF VICKY

Replacing the floorpans

4. The driver's side floorpan was cut away and a replacement brace clamped into place (arrow).

5. Small brace patch will firm up the new floorpans. There won't be any oil can popping noises coming from Vicky's reconstructed floors!

6. Reproduction floorpan patch panels were purchased from the Ford Parts Store, Bryan, Ohio. A few clips with a pair of shears and it fell

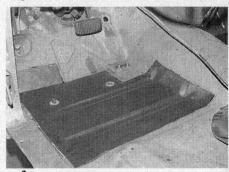

4

5

6

7

8

effortlessly into its new home. Patch at top right was cut from scrap stock.

7. *Body shop foreman Terry Ritter, die grinder in hand, joined St. Cin to assist in repairing Vicky's bellypans.*

8. *Going the extra mile, the specialists at Classic Car Centre clipped away all traces of corrosion. Nice clean edge cuts make repair welds effortless and don't fray the welder's nerves.*

the pair teamed to repair the floorpans of *Cars & Parts'* 1955 Ford Crown Victoria project car, affectionately known as Vicky.

When Vicky was taken to Classic Car Centre, Warsaw, Ind., for a complete restoration of body and engine, obvious exterior flaws in her makeup were known to exist. Yet there were some unseen glitches that only the trained eye of a professional could perceive. From the start, Ritter and St. Cin seemed to know how much rust-out lay beneath Vicky's rather presentable floorpans and how much time it would take to remove it and make repairs. Both men had traveled that road before.

St. Cin explained it very well. "After opening several hundred cans of worms, you know what to expect," he said. "Every car is different and will require special fixes," he added, explaining that there are general rules of thumb that give credence to an old body man's ESP. Ritter commented that every customer seems to know that the sheet metal closest to the road will probably be suffering the most from rust-out. But, he probably doesn't know that restoration of lower body panels usually takes at least 60% to 70% of the overall restoration time and money.

A pair of reproduction floorpans for the Crown Vic was available for around $100 from the Ford Parts Store, 4925 Ford Rd., Box 226, Bryan, Ohio 43506, (419) 636-2475. Floorpans can also be purchased from several other vendors who advertise regularly in *Cars & Parts.* Owners of the Ford Parts Store, Toby and Sandy Gorny, are prime movers in the Crown Victoria Assn. and have lent their support to our Crown Vic project from the start by supplying hard-to-get-parts, valued technical advice and encouragement.

The reproduced floorpan patches sold by the Ford Parts Store duplicate the area of Vicky's floor where rider's feet had tracked-in road salt, moisture and other fouling chemicals, which contributed immensely to the rusting of the floorpans.

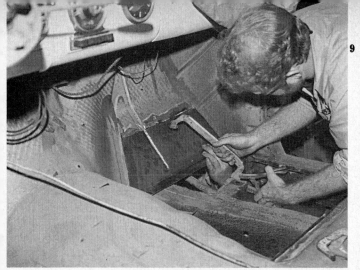

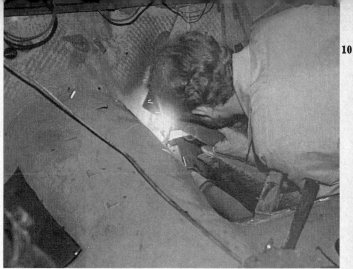

EDITOR'S NOTE: In the pursuit of various editorial projects, *Cars & Parts* and its staff members occasionally employ certain types and brands of equipment, tools, vehicles, services and supplies. The use, display and description of these products or services do not constitute an endorsement of said products or services, or their manufacturers or suppliers. Nor does it imply any warranties or guarantees to the performance, durability, safety or suitability of those products or services by *Cars & Parts*, Amos Press, Inc., or its employees.

9. *Good fits and giant hand clamps greatly simplify butt welding patch panels to existing floor.*

10. *Ritter spot-welded patch at two-inch intervals.*

11. *Final welding was performed in a hit-and-skip procedure to minimize sheet metal warpage.*

12. *Welds were ground off flush for aesthetics. Excessive high frequency shrill caused Ritter to don sound-deadening ear muffs.*

13. *Once initial fit of the repro pans was checked and body bolt holes drilled, St. Cin bolted the pans into place. This will eliminate any movement once welding starts. This section will be lap welded to the old floorpan.*

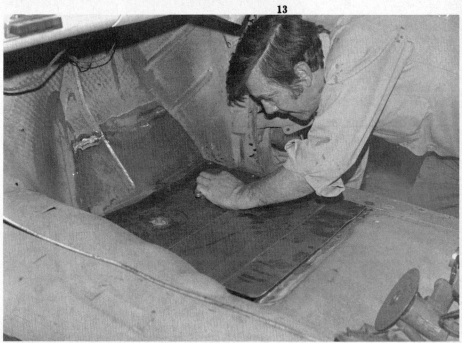

It took Ritter and St. Cin only a few minutes to cut away the perforated floorpans with a small air-driven hand-held grinder. The section shown in the accompanying photo is from the driver's side (normally the rustier of the two pans). You can see that rust-through is marginal and this pan probably would not be replaced by many restoration shops. Many shops would prefer to launder the metal and braze the holes shut — certainly a respectable repair by any standard.

However, the Ritter and St. Cin team elected to cut away the offending metal to gain top-side access to the floor braces underneath. Like the body outriggers, which received a full refurbishment (covered in a previous chapter in the Resurrection of Vicky series), the floorpan braces were either rusted away or rusted to the point of being functionally unstable. A major rebuild was needed to make them structurally sound again.

In a previous segment, we alluded to the scrounging nature of St. Cin, who constantly stows bits and pieces of sheet metal which he believes can be used to make repair patches. As usual, St. Cin turned to his cache of scrap sheet metal where he found a chunk of 20-gauge sheet metal stock from which to fashion repair braces not available commercially. Using his favorite blunt-nosed body hammer, a section of I-beam he uses as an anvil for metal forming, hand shears and a sand bag, St. Cin artfully pounded the raw sheet metal into shape.

Rough fitting of both homemade braces and commercial repro sheet metal floor-

14. *Next step was unbolting pan and drilling holes along the edges for spot welding of the lapping metal.*

15. *Slight warping occurred while TIG welding the pan into place. Ritter tapped it out quickly with a body hammer and flat dolly.*

16. *Leaning on a heavy screwdriver, St. Cin holds the pan in contact with the existing floorpan as Ritter welds it solid.*

17. *A corner or two to turn and welding will be completed. Good fit and craftsmanship brought the rough assembly to a semi-finished state.*

18. *After final welding, rough welds were dressed, holes for the original rubber drain hole plugs were drilled, and both pans were sandblasted, readying them for epoxy primer.*

14

15

pans was carefully executed. Some clipping of the repro pans with hand shears was required to suit the restorer's tastes. Ritter said that "clipping to fit" is a common practice since all cars tend to settle-in over the years, making each floorpan slightly different. St. Cin and Ritter chose to tack weld the braces and floorpans with a TIG welder since the metal warping tendency of heat created by a TIG welder is less than that produced by a conventional acetylene welder.

Two body bolts were located in each of the floorpan sections. To aid in fitting the patch panels and holding them in place for welding, holes were drilled and the pans were bolted to the supports underneath. Giant Vise-Grip C-clamps were utilized to secure the patches. Tack welds were laid at two-inch intervals. Jumping from side to side to avoid heat buildup and subsequent sheet metal warpage, the welding proceeded efficiently and safely. The floor area would be weather tight!

Since TIG welding creates a minimum of flying sparks, unlike stick welding, a novel hand-held shield was pressed into use by the team. Conventional shields are large affairs that many welders find cumbersome. Both butt welds and lap welds were employed in Vicky's floorpan repairs.

The repair of Vicky's floorpans was completed in approximately eight hours. Later the entire area was sandblasted (top and bottom) and coated with epoxy primer. Final finishing and paint will come later and the repairs will be out of sight. Inside the car, pile carpet will extend across the floorpans while the floor welds and grind marks underneath will be forever lost in a coat of colonial white Centari enamel. Out of sight — but not out of mind to those who have watched Vicky being brought back to life.

17

18

THE RESURRECTION OF VICKY

Sandblasting and priming the floorboard

1

2

3

4

Ask old Swag if his contribution to Vicky's restoration was all fun and games and he'll probably grin and tell you it wasn't too bad. But Tim Swagerle is not telling you the whole story. He is the one who handled the rather unpleasant job of sandblasting and priming Vicky's floorboard.

We must explain that Swagerle is a newcomer to the restoration game. After spending some 20 years on the railroad, he faced the option of moving to Chicago to keep his job or take severance pay and seek other employment nearer his home in Peru, Ind. Swagerle chose the latter route as it gave him the opportunity to pursue an old dream. Many restless hours had been spent riding the rails and wishing he were back home restoring old cars.

Although Swagerle had turned a few wrenches and straightened out a few dents in his life, he didn't consider himself a top-notch metal man when he approached Classic Car Centre and asked for a job in body restoration. At the time, Terry Ritter, body shop foreman, needed a rookie for some entry level chores. He liked Swagerle's eagerness and offered him a job

plus a stern warning that the opportunity would not be a bed of roses. But, it would place Swagerle within arm's reach of the body shop's professionals, from whom he could pick up tricks of the trade while he paid his dues.

While lying flat on his back underneath Vicky's carcass, freshening up the underbelly, Swagerle faced the reality of Ritter's so-called opportunity. The first 8-hour shift under Vicky's surly undersides scraping off undercoat, road tar and shale rust drove home just how much fun restoring cars can really be. He had anticipated the need for eye protection but had failed to consider that falling debris can get into your hair, inside your clothes and even into your ears.

Follow along in our photographs as the amiable Swagerle makes his contribution to the Vicky project. Somehow we can't help but believe that it seems unfair that the quality of Swagerle's labors will go unappreciated by most folks who stop and gaze at the restored Vicky. Few will peep underneath to check out the beauty of his work, but they should.

EDITOR'S NOTE: In the pursuit of various editorial projects, *Cars & Parts* and its staff members occasionally employ certain types and brands of equipment, tools, vehicles, services and supplies. The use, display and description of these products or services do not constitute an endorsement of said products or services, or their manufacturers or suppliers. Nor does it imply any warranties or guarantees to the performance, durability, safety or suitability of those products or services by *Cars & Parts*, Amos Press, Inc., or its employees.

5

7

8

6

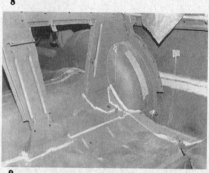

9

1. Tim Swagerle had his hands full (eyes, too — almost) when scraping the heavy undercoating and road tar from Vicky's underbelly.

2. Sandblasting doesn't remove heavy undercoating and road crud very well. Hand scraping is the only way "to do it right."

3. Scraping revealed loose body mounts in the trunk area which required new metal patches.

4. This photo, taken at an earlier point in Vicky's restoration, illustrates the mess Swagerle was up against.

5. With the floor jacks sitting on rollers, the crew moved the car outside to sandblast the underbody.

6. After the jacks were locked in place and the stability of the set-up checked, Swagerle cautiously ventured under the body to start blasting.

7. Once the body was back inside the shop, small holes were welded shut and ground flat. His stylish shop rag hat is for safety's sake only, Swagerle says.

8. Priming was also an "on-your-back" job. Proper air filter is an absolute necessity when spraying paint.

9. Seam sealer insures the blockage of moisture from the inner body recesses.

10. Look closely and you'll appreciate the potential danger for bodily injury from a sandblaster. The rock-hard ceramic tip was eaten away and had to be changed.

11. Swagerle's work resulted in an underbelly that was hospital clean and ready for finish paint.

12. Rolling jacks supporting Vicky's body gave almost unrestricted access to all areas.

10

11

12

When it came time to paint Vicky's body, we faced the same dilemma every car restorer faces: Which paint to use? There are nitrocellulose lacquers, acrylic lacquers, alkyd enamels, acrylic enamels, and urethanes. All have been or are being used extensively in automobile manufacture and restoration.

We first looked at the new space-age urethanes, which offer five-year sheen retention and a tough, flexible coating. We agreed with all the arguments in favor of urethanes as the best long-term paint. But we found it difficult to match the original Ford torch red with current urethane paint stocks.

We also looked carefully at acrylic lacquers. Lacquer's particularly easy to match, apply and retouch. Since Vicky is intended to be used as a car to drive and enjoy, we appreciated the fact lacquer would be the best bet in case of a scraped fender in the future.

But we picked a paint somewhere in between lacquer and urethane. We chose Centari, a DuPont acrylic enamel which offers durability, good gloss, and a wide range of colors. The Centari 1024-AH perfectly matches our '55 Ford Crown Victoria project car's original red. The 58352-A white is exactly like Ford's snowshoe white.

The Centari paint looks wonderful on Vicky today, and will for some time to come. It is close to the original enamel, but takes advantage of the improvements acrylic enamel represents. With reasonable care, the Centari should last longer than lacquers and be much less expensive to repair than urethanes.

As with so many other restoration decisions, paint selection is complex. We chose what we felt was the best paint for Vicky. The choice for a different car might not be the same. But a complete explanation of different paints and their advantages and disadvantages is beyond the scope of this article. However, in an accompanying sidebar we have listed some of the more basic information that anyone who anticipates having their collector car painted should know.

For detailed, step-by-step information, we advise consultations with painters and paint suppliers in your vicinity. Additionally, major paint manufacturers — DuPont, PPG (Ditzler), Rinshed-Mason, etc. — market detailed how-to-paint manuals through local paint stores.

These manuals are excellent sources of painting tips for professionals as well as do-it-yourselfers. The manuals explain the manufacturer's paint systems and prod-

THE RESURRECTION OF VICKY

Painting: Body prep and application

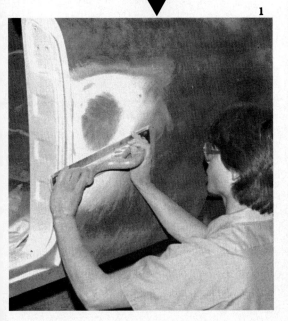

1. Tom Cripe found a low spot on the driver's side rear quarter panel. It will be leveled and reprepped before final paint.

2. Gary Odiorne pored over Vicky, circling small pits in the paint which needed to be filled.

3. To aid in final sanding, John St. Cin dusted the surface with a thin guide coat of red oxide primer over the Europrime primer. Block sanding a different color makes low spots and imperfections easier to locate. A protective breathing mask would have been a good idea. Very fine grit sandpapers (400-600 grit) are recommended for this step.

4. Uroprime 1130S primer-filler, an acrylic enamel primer by DuPont, was sprayed over DuPont's Variprime 15S, a self-etching primer. Reportedly widely used in Europe, this priming system offers the advantages of high build properties, easy sanding, durability and minimal shrinking.

5. *After the reprep work was finished, Cripe wiped the panel with enamel reducer to aid in spotting wavy surfaces.*

6. *Dane Ronk dusted the front fenders for a final sanding.*

7. *Eldon Nickel and St. Cin sighted down the DX330 enamel thinner-wiped passenger side quarter and looked for waves. This practice simulates the high sheen of a finished surface. No traces of the major body surgery that took place earlier could be seen. That's success!*

8. *Body shop foreman Terry Ritter (left) oversaw all paint prep during Vicky's restoration. After the long ordeal to get Vicky back to new-like condition, the straight lines and smooth surfaces were encouraging.*

9. *Jim Vetor (right) used an oscillating sander to smooth the inside of the hood while Nelson Lin (left) and Scott Crothers wet-sanded the door sill and striker panels with 500 grit paper.*

10. *Crothers displayed good form as he sponged off the sanding block to remove residue.*

5

7

8

6

9

ucts, so it pays to compare at least two before making a decision. Whatever paint is chosen, though, it will be far superior to the paint the manufacturer originally applied to your vintage car. Staggering competition among paint manufacturers in the last two decades has resulted in remarkable gains across the board where automotive paints are concerned.

But no paint job will be satisfactory if the body work has not been done correctly. There were several spots where additional preparation of Vicky's body had to be done before the topcoat could be applied. This alone made us glad we hadn't chosen the "don't look back" urethane paint route.

Almost as important as body preparation is the person who sprays the paint. The painter at Classic Car Centre, Warsaw, Ind., who sprayed Vicky was Charley Mann. An analytical person, Mann carefully studied Vicky's body inside and out as the metal restoration was nearing completion. It wasn't apparent at the time, but when he started painting Vicky it became clear that he had been planning the best order in which to spray the various parts of the car. His method gave superior results.

Follow along in the photographs as we detail the steps necessary to give Vicky a show-winning finish.

GENERAL RULES AND HINTS

- Follow manufacturer's recommendations religiously.
- Excessively thick coats of any type paint are not recommended.
- Don't mix brands — use paints, solvents, etc., made by one manufacturer.
- Health and safety tips on containers must be followed.
- Lacquer dries quickly and solely by release of solvents.
- Enamel dries slowly by evaporation of solvents and by oxidation. Oxygen molecules invade the paint to combine with the resin and act as a catalyst to chemically harden paint.
- Sandblasted surfaces are chemically clean but should be primed and coated immediately to cover raw steel which can rust overnight if left uncoated.
- Sandblasting can warp thin-gauge metal.
- Hot caustic paint stripping is quite economical for all-steel vehicle bodies, but should not be used on bodies with wood construction, and should not be used on aluminum or zinc panels or moldings.

10

11

16

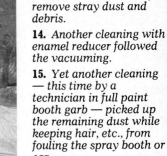

17

12

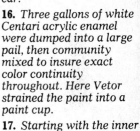

18

13

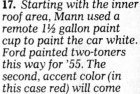

14

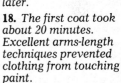

19

15

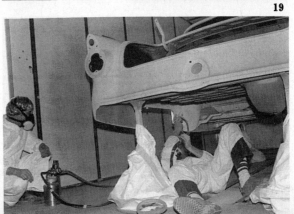

20

11. Parts to be painted black were wired to a metal frame, wiped with enamel reducer to remove all traces of fingerprints, dust, etc., then force-air dried and hustled into the paint booth for a coat of black enamel.

12. Master painter Charley Mann manned the spray gun for all finish coats including this inner front fender shield.

13. Once inside the spray booth all surfaces were vacuumed methodically to remove stray dust and debris.

14. Another cleaning with enamel reducer followed the vacuuming.

15. Yet another cleaning — this time by a technician in full paint booth garb — picked up the remaining dust while keeping hair, etc., from fouling the spray booth or car.

16. Three gallons of white Centari acrylic enamel were dumped into a large pail, then community mixed to insure exact color continuity throughout. Here Vetor strained the paint into a paint cup.

17. Starting with the inner roof area, Mann used a remote 1½ gallon paint cup to paint the car white. Ford painted two-toners this way for '55. The second, accent color (in this case red) will come later.

18. The first coat took about 20 minutes. Excellent arms-length techniques prevented clothing from touching paint.

19. With a helper to carry the remote paint cup, the sprayer glided around Vicky with ease. Full-cover garments and charcoal-filtered spray masks are a must to prevent breathing toxic fumes.

20. Vicky's body was supported at the corners by jack stands. The underside of the car received a topside-quality finish.

21. *A drying period of 15 to 20 minutes elapsed between coats. Once the second coat was applied, the oven was set to 140 degrees and timed to bake the enamel for one full hour.*

22. *The next morning, fresh out of the oven, a thorough search for flaws in Vicky's finish was undertaken. The doors, hood, trunk lid and miscellaneous white parts received similar treatment.*

23. *Mann checked the color break line on the door by holding a piece of side trim in place. This practice is good insurance against foul-ups, which at this point are usually major in scope. Spell that expensive and heartbreaking.*

24. *Bands of red acrylic enamel were sprayed across the door. The masked section at top remained white.*

25. *The engine, the black chassis and body surfaces which were to remain white were covered. Only areas to receive red remained exposed.*

26. *Still not satisfied with the driver's side quarter, Mann ordered a second surface prep session. Once that section was in primer, the paint crew prepared Vicky for a red coat by tediously masking all surfaces which were to remain white.*

27. *The finished chassis was rolled from the storage area and the body was carefully dropped into place. Plastic remained between the body and frame until the red coat was sprayed.*

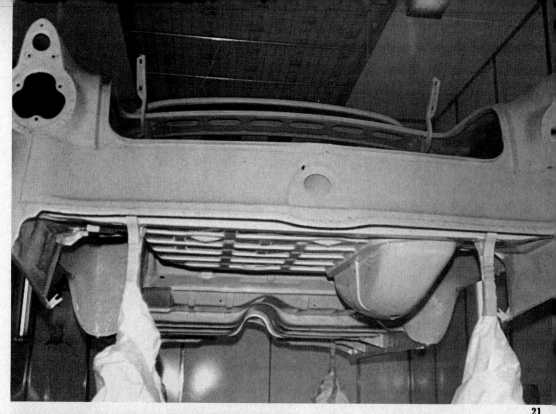

21

22

25

23

26

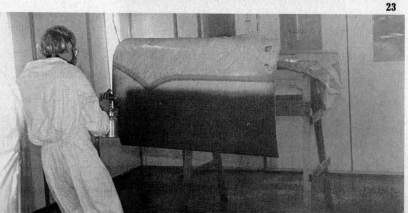

24

27

28. *Once the red paint had dried and cured for a few days, body shop personnel started the painstaking yet satisfying task of mounting trim and the hang-on components — doors, trunk lid, hood, etc. Vicky now would advance through her mid-life crisis with grace and beauty.*

28

AUTOMOTIVE PAINT POINTERS

Nitrocellulose Lacquer
- DuPont introduced nitrocellulose lacquer in 1924 for use on Oakland vehicles.
- It is named for cellulose (cotton derivative) treated with nitric acid.
- The first time a spray gun was used to apply auto finish was in 1924 to apply this paint.
- It is no longer manufactured by major suppliers in colors other than black and white.
- Disadvantages include poor ultraviolet resistance, very limited availability from independent custom mixers and low surface density.
- The Ditz Lac, Rinshed-Mason and Duco nitrocellulose lacquer currently available is old stock.

Acrylic Lacquer
- DuPont introduced acrylic lacquer in 1954.
- It is named for plasticizers in a chemically produced petroleum derivative.
- Advantages: Dries harder than nitrocellulose, improved ultraviolet radiation resistance, available in many colors, best choice of amateur painters and those with less than ideal painting facilities.

Acrylic Lacquer Primer-Surfacer
- Currently enjoys wide popularity.
- It has superior adhesion qualities.
- Effectively seals base material and/or existing painted surfaces, preventing interaction between incompatible materials.
- It is high in solid content for high build up of surfaces, thus enabling filling of minor surface pits and imperfections.

Enamel
- DuPont introduced it in 1928.

- It usually is referred to as synthetic alkyd, or straight enamel.
- Storage of enamels is a problem, since enamel combines with air in containers and hardens.
- Water-borne enamels currently are used by major automakers.

Conventional Acrylic Enamel
- Development was pioneered by Sherwin-Williams in 1963.
- It goes on thicker and wetter than lacquer.
- Dust control is essential during painting.
- It has enhanced coverage and filling properties, thus fewer coats are required.
- It has good resistance to ultraviolet rays.
- It is available in a wide range of colors.
- It has increased surface density over alkyd enamel.
- It is not conducive to custom color mixing since resin content of toners can cause adhesion failure.
- It needs no buffing and should not be polished for 30-90 days to permit adequate drying.
- Automakers use infrared ovens to speed up drying process.
- It is not recommended for amateur use since mixing, technique and timing factors are critical.
- Hardeners are available to eliminate recoat cycle, improve gloss and improve resistance to chemical damage and abrasion.
- Severe paint wrinkling can result if partially hardened acrylic enamel is top-coated.

Urethane
- Urethanes are enamels by molecular definition, but do not oxidize like enamel.

- They incorporate two parts and dry by evaporation of volatiles and by chemical reaction of isocyanates and hydroxyls which cross-link chemically to harden the finish. No oxygen is needed to dry the paint.
- Originally, they were developed for aircraft use.
- The most commonly-known brands are DuPont's Imron and Ditzler's Durathane (both are polyurethanes) and Deltron (acrylic urethane).
- Without a doubt, it is the most durable finish available today.
- Expensive!
- It's great for chassis parts, etc., that are subjected to harsh road chemicals and abrasion by sand, rocks, etc.
- Color selection is limited, but that's improving; Ditzler sells toners for acrylic urethane.

Original Finishes
- General Motors changed from nitrocellulose lacquer to acrylic lacquer in the late 1950s.
- Ford, AMC, Chrysler and GM trucks switched from alkyd enamel to "super enamel" (alkyd enamel with melamine modifiers) in the late 1950s.
- GM switched to acrylic lacquer by 1960.
- Super enamel users began converting to acrylic enamel in the early 1960s.
- GM and Chevy truck converted to acrylic enamel in the 1970s.
- Two-component finishes were introduced in 1970.
- Flexible paint additives were introduced in the 1970s.
- GM started use of water-borne enamel in 1973.
- The first basecoat/clearcoat system was used on Lincoln Versailles, Ford Granada and Mercury Monarch in the 1970s.

PART EIGHT

Interior Restoration and Refurbishment

1

2

THE RESURRECTION OF VICKY

Visiting the upholstery shop

3

4

1. On arrival at ABC Auto Upholstery, in Philadelphia, Pa., Vicky was moved inside and work began. Fords of the '50s are an ABC specialty.

2. Upholstery patterns for mid-'50s Fords line the walls at ABC. Along this wall we found rear quarter and door panel cutouts for '56 Crown Vics and convertibles.

3. Ron Murray, owner of ABC, shows a sample of his roll goods — specially reproduced material which duplicates original Ford yardage.

4. Murray calls Sonja Haywood his "sewing angel." Haywood cuts and sews every Ford kit built at ABC. She has over 20 years of experience.

Most car interiors that have been used begin to wilt after a decade. Few make it to Vicky's age without needing repair or total replacement, and her 32-year-old interior was no exception. Though it was presentable when we bought Vicky, the new paint and chrome the interior needed would have made the original seat and other fabrics look shabby. So we decided early on to replace the upholstery, headliner, door panels, carpet, and other "soft" trim items.

During the early stages of Vicky's body restoration, we began to look for a trim and upholstery shop to refurbish the interior of Cars & Parts' '55 Ford Crown Victoria project car. After contacting a number of shops, it became clear that one source was the choice for quality upholstery kits for most mid-'50s Fords. Every inquiry had pointed us toward ABC Auto Uphol-

stery, 4289 Paul St., Philadelphia, Pa. 19124 (phone 215-289-0555).

After discussing Vicky's body restoration schedule with Ron Murray, ABC Auto Upholstery's owner, it was decided that the best time to re-do the interior would be the last week of August 1987. Murray suggested that since both Cars & Parts and ABC would be at Spring Carlisle, we could deliver the seats, door panels, etc., to him then, which we did. So while Vicky's body was being finished, ABC was assessing the condition of the old interior, ordering any trim materials not in stock, and bead-blasting and painting the seat frames and springs.

The plan was for Cars & Parts to trailer Vicky to Philadelphia, then document ABC's fabrication and installation of all-new red and white interior pieces.

It was late Sunday afternoon as Vicky

neared the outskirts of Philadelphia via I-70. After taking some wrong turns, a phone call brought Ron Murray to the rescue. He led the way to his shop, where Vicky found herself in good company. Cars in for trim restoration at the time included a 1938 Cadillac town sedan, a Ford Model A coupe, a '42 DeSoto convertible, an early Corvette, an MG, and a host of others. We were a bit surprised to find such a wide variety of makes, having assumed ABC was strictly a Ford shop.

"Not so," said Murray, "we do them all. However, the Ford kits have really taken off. About 70 percent of our mail order business is Ford-related. The other 30 percent is roll goods for various makes. Ever since a man from Reading, Pa., asked us to do his '56 Ford convertible, word has gotten around and we have shipped more than 1,000 mid-'50s Ford kits."

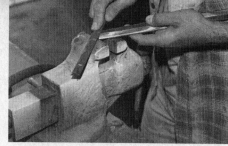

5 **6** **7**

8 **9** **10**

5 - 7. *Stainless trim in the rear seat area needed straightening. Tommy Hough tapped, filed and buffed the pieces using conventional body shop techniques. Note his Crown Victoria t-shirt.*

8. *Ford provided fold-over tabs to hold the windlace in place.*

9. *ABC's rear window shelf cardboards are custom-cut. The fronts are colored to match original boards while the backs are "cleared with lacquer" to provide a vapor seal.*

10. *Don Greenwood cut out new sunvisor boards, using an original as a pattern.*

11. *Tommy Hough is Murray's specialty man. Here he lends his artistic touch to the installation of garnish molding window felt.*

12. *Better than original quality is obvious in this comparison of a ragged used visor (from another car, not Vicky) and a new one by ABC.*

13. *A commercial-grade Pfaff machine sewed through the layers of vinyl and cardboard with ease.*

14. *Mel Frisby has worked as an upholsterer since his junior high days at Palmarantz School in Philadelphia. Frisby modified store-bought windlace with a plastic bead to insure a tight fit.*

15. *Ron Murray laced the springs with burlap webbing to "make a team of the springs."*

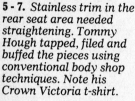
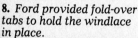

11

12

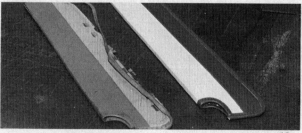

13

14 **15**

Despite the fact ABC sells a lot of kits, Murray doesn't like to see them installed by amateurs. "Whenever possible, we strongly recommend a professional shop in the buyer's area," he said. Though amateurs can do a good job, Murray's experience has been that nonprofessional installations "make our kits look bad."

Murray has owned ABC for 20 years and is proud of the services his shop offers, whether it is routine upholstery work, tracking down electrical shorts in power windows before installing new door panels, or finding just the right vintage upholstery fabric. "If we can't find a replacement, we can arrange to have the fabrics reproduced," he said. His suppliers require a 200-yard minimum order, which means Murray must be sure of the demand for the material before buying it. He had an order in for 1955 Dodge material

166

16

17

18

19

20

21

22

23

24

25

16. A piece of muslin was laid over the webbing. For long wear life, "the less hog rings and muslin along the edge, the better," Murray said.

17. Two layers of foam rubber padding were added to base materials. Gluing padding together prevents it from "getting lumpy later on."

18. New materials throughout combined with excellent craftsmanship have resulted in the sale of over 1,000 mid-'50s Ford trim kits by ABC.

19. The dramatic appearance of the sanitary white vinyl against the bright red inserts is so reminiscent of the fifties.

20. Murray says he is puzzled about why many restorers are hesitant to steam covers. According to Murray, some steaming should take place before any hog rings are used.

21. Mike Murray cut a new board from plywood on which to mount the rear armrest springs. ABC recommends making this board a bit undersize as most originals have bound and been broken over the years.

22. Hog rings are installed, starting at the middle and working outward to help eliminate wrinkles.

23. Greenwood and Murray stretch an upholstery "sock" over the padded armrest.

24. Mel Frisby mounts the armrest before the rear seat back is set in place.

25. The restored rear passenger compartment is breathtakingly beautiful.

at the time.

Specializing in one make or era, such as mid-'50s Fords, has its advantages, according to Murray. "We have become familiar with the strengths and weaknesses of the Ford designs. For instance, when talking to Ford owners we have found that the original boards used in the door panels and rear window shelves took on moisture. So we lacquer all cardboards to create a vapor barrier and that prevents warping."

Murray also said he has noted patterns and similarities in comments made by his Ford customers. One he finds especially amusing is the remark by many first-time customers that, "My car is perfect except for one door panel." Murray knows from experience that if he sells that one door panel, he soon will get an order for the rest of the interior once the new piece has been installed next to the original 30-year-old materials.

That was exactly what had gone through our minds as we assessed Vicky's interior initially. We could have cleaned and dyed the rear seat, which otherwise was in excellent condition. Unfortunately, the front seat wasn't. Then we looked at the less-than-perfect door panels, which had been recovered at some point by a previous owner, the carpet, the sun visors, and the headliner. Though the original interior was serviceable and fairly presentable, the repainted dash, the new chrome, the restored steering wheel and other interior refurbishments would have made anything less than all-new fabrics look shabby, if not plain old.

The accompanying photos show ABC's experts giving Vicky new upholstery that perhaps is even better than that installed by the factory in 1955. Next month we will show how ABC restored the headliner, door panels, and carpet.

THE RESURRECTION OF VICKY

Installing the headliner, door panels and carpet

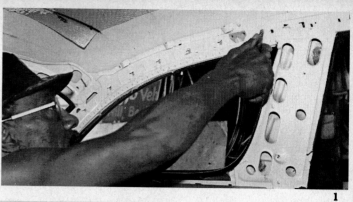

1. *ABC's Mel Frisby began the headliner installation by opening up the "cat claw" tabs that hold the tacking strips.*

2. *The seven 1955 Ford headliner bows came in different lengths. ABC removed and numbered them to insure that a mix-up didn't take place during installation.*

Producing a classy, show-winning interior for an old car doesn't happen by accident. It's possible for almost anyone to remove an original interior, disassemble it and painstakingly recreate it with new materials. But there's a world of difference in the finished product, depending on who does the work and the quality of the materials.

That's why we took Vicky to ABC Auto Upholstery, 4289 Paul St., Philadelphia, Pa. 19124, where mid-fifties Ford interiors are the specialty of the house. Owner Ron Murray says it has taken him years to

gather the knowledge and material required to satisfy discriminating Ford collectors. As was evident in last month's article, which described how ABC restored Vicky's seats, sun visors and interior stainless steel trim to like-new condition, Murray's shop indeed turns out high-quality work.

In this segment of the series about the restoration of *Cars & Parts'* 1955 Ford Crown Victoria, we continue with ABC's refurbishment of the passenger compartment. Though progress seemed slow as the ABC staff cut, sewed and installed the

headliner, built new door and interior rear quarter panels from scratch, created new carpeting, and performed a number of other tasks, it all came together rather quickly. The finished interior definitely is the work of professionals.

But professionals are human, too. Installing a new headliner "puts some nasty cricks in your neck," says Mel Frisby. He's the specialist who craned and twisted his neck while installing Vicky's new headliner. The tedious job also is rough on the knees, but Frisby finds his enjoyment of upholstery work far outweighs the aches

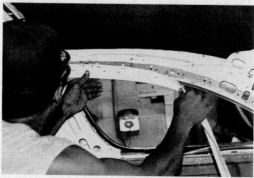

3. *The next step was to attach new tacking strips. Since the Crown has a large piece of interior chrome trim which splits the headliner in half, "the job is two jobs in one," according to Frisby.*

4. *Frisby cut a sheet of water-resistant jute for padding the headliner, then sprayed it with contact cement.*

5. *Makers of contact cement recommend coating both surfaces (in this case the jute pad and the inside of Vicky's top) with cement. That done, Frisby quickly stuck the pads into place.*

6. *The original extruded vinyl headliner piping was reusable after a cleaning with lacquer thinner. There's no need to use reproductions since the originals weather well and can be dyed to color match if necessary.*

7. *ABC maintains a number of mid-'50s Ford headliner patterns. It takes about two hours to cut and sew a new headliner and a full day to install one.*

8. *After the headliner bows were passed through the loops sewn into the headliner, Frisby hung the bows in the roof retainers and began to carefully stretch and staple the edges to produce a wrinkle-free installation.*

9. *An example of the fiberglass reproduction armrest available from one of ABC's suppliers is shown below a broken original.*

10. *Tommy Hough ground the edges of the new armrests to remove sharp points that might cut the vinyl after installation.*

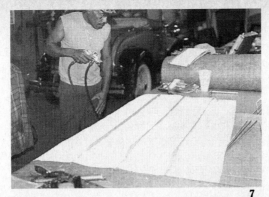

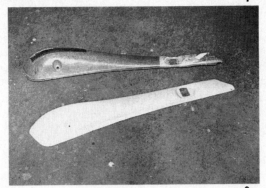

7

8

9

10

and pains. In fact, he's been around auto upholstery shops since the days when Vicky was new.

Despite a few wrinkles around the dome lamp and some stress tears near the windshield, the original headliner was in reasonably good shape. Like the rest of the interior's white vinyl, the material had yellowed. It could have been cleaned, repaired and re-dyed. But we simply couldn't visualize doing a patchwork job on the interior when the body had received a thorough restoration to flawless condition.

As Frisby removed the old headliner, the metal bows were numbered and poked through holes in a piece of cardboard so they could be reinstalled in the same order. While out of the car, he said, headliner bows should be derusted, cleaned and painted to rule out potential rust problems in the future. Moisture causes unpainted bows to rust and stain fabrics, even vinyl. Headliners made of mohair and other organic materials are especially vulnerable to rust stains.

Snipping out material for a new headliner was relatively easy since ABC has mid-

11

12

13

14

15

11. *Fiberglass doesn't accept staples very well. To facilitate stapling the vinyl covering to the armrest, Murray copies the "Thunderbird style" and fashions a tacking strip from door panel cardboard, then glues it to the back.*

12. *The finished armrest not only looks new, but it's also of better construction and*

should last longer than the original.

13. *During a previous owner's attempt to repair the armrests, the stainless steel trim that skirts the lower edge of the armrests was discarded. Since we didn't have the pieces, we asked Murray to give it a "1956 Crown look" — no trim. This*

gave us time to find replacements. Murray proudly pointed out that his door panels feature a heat-sealed ribbed section just like the originals. The touch of authenticity separates ABC's panels from other maker's wares, Murray claims.

14. *New cardboards were made to close up the door*

mechanism access holes (see arrows).

15. *One of the many mid-'50s Ford patterns at ABC includes this one for laying out the trunk liner board that fits on the back of the rear seat. ABC used water-resistant boards to replace all originals.*

16

17

18

19

20

21

16. *Original rear seat back liners rarely escape damage through the years.*

17. *Kick boards are installed, then covered with vinyl.*

18. *Murray related an amusing story about many owners of basket-case cars who have called ABC to describe "strange-looking things that look like oversize sun visors. They're really talking about rear seat kick boards," Murray quipped.*

19. *Each interior rear quarter panel trim piece on a Crown Vic is an elaborate affair that requires six to seven hours to restore.*

20. *To prevent panel warping and water stains, ABC covers interior rear quarters and doors with plastic sheets to seal out moisture.*

21. *Since the repro armrest is thicker than the original, ABC recommends adding an extension (see arrow) to window and door opening cranks.*

fifties Ford patterns handy as a result of specializing in FoMoCo interiors. A headliner can be constructed without a pattern, but it is an exhausting exercise involving measuring, sewing and drawing on years of experience to smooth the many problems that can arise during fabrication and installation.

As it was, it took Frisby a full day to install the new headliner that required only a couple of hours to cut out and stitch together.

Once the headliner was in place, the ABC crew restored the door panels and interior rear quarter panels. Again, cardboard patterns were hanging nearby and appropriate vinyl roll goods were in stock. Owner Murray is justifiably proud of the

vinyl materials ABC uses to reproduce Ford interiors. While many trim shops attempt to duplicate the rolls and pleats on the top of mid-fifties Ford side panels by sewing, ABC uses material that has been dielectrically embossed to exactly duplicate the original factory appearance.

It took about two hours to cut, sew, assemble and install each door panel. It took an additional six to seven hours to reproduce each interior rear quarter panel.

One aspect of ABC's restoration work that is impressive is the quality of the materials used. The quality almost always exceeds OEM specifications. Examples include the water-resistant (not to be confused with waterproof) boards used to back up the side panels, and the jute used

behind the headliner.

ABC also pays attention to details. Full-time mechanic/electrician Mike Kagan troubleshoots and repairs problems that affect interior restorations. At the time of Vicky's visit, ABC was restoring the interior of a loaded 1957 Cadillac. The right front power window mechanism did not function. So, before the restored door panel was installed, Kagan pinpointed and fixed an electrical short.

Quality materials, skilled craftsmen, and the many unique tricks of the trade garnered only through years of experience point to one inevitable conclusion: upholstery work is best left to the professionals, such as the team Vicky encountered at ABC.

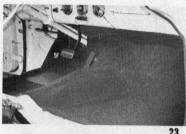

22

23

24

25

26

22. *John McLaughlin cuts carpet padding for the rear passenger compartment.*

23. *The perfect fit and inviting look of fresh carpet almost makes you want to take off your shoes and relax.*

24. *The ABC owner's son, Mike Murray, pointed out the quality touches built into an ABC carpet. In 1955 loop pile carpeting was used by Ford and T-Bird while Mercury and Lincoln used smooth cut pile.*

25. *Mike Kagan is the resident mechanic and*

electrician at ABC. His skills bring relief to customers whose cars have electrical problems, such as this '57 Cadillac with power windows on the blink. A short was found and fixed before the door panels were reinstalled.

26. *Just before Vicky left ABC's facility, the main shop crew posed for this photo. ABC owner Ron Murray (at left) is joined by (from left) Vicky, Mike Murray, Mike Kagan, John McLaughlin, Mel Frisby and Tommy Hough.*

Vicky's steering wheel was not exactly unsafe. It's highly unlikely the driver would have put the car into a ditch due to the wheel breaking, for instance. In fact, structurally it was sound and only after sliding onto the driver's seat and grasping the wheel did one notice the cracks in the plastic that enclosed the hub.

Over the years, the strain to keep Vicky right of center had been more than the plastic hub surround could endure. One could have assumed that the cracks were the result of the weak two-spoke design. Had the wheel been of the stronger opposed three-spoke design as the one used on the companion F100 truck of '55, the plastic probably would never have let loose. However, regardless of the reasons why the plastic had failed, the cracks were unsightly and the restoration of the steering wheel was added to the "Resurrection of Vicky" project list.

Jack Turpin (Steering Wheel Restoration, Peaceful Valley, Box 2474, Waterfall Drive, Rt. 2, Cleveland, Ga. 30528, 404-865-2242) was contacted about the project. As the ailments found on Vicky's steering wheel were described, Turpin jokingly broke in to finish up the description. It soon became clear that Turpin is a

THE RESURRECTION OF VICKY

The steering wheel is restored

1. A pretty nice wheel by most standards, but gaping cracks at the ends of the spokes near the hub are unsightly.

2. John St. Cin used a conventional steering wheel puller to remove Vicky's wheel.

3. The wheel was stubborn and didn't want to budge, requiring an extra dose of St. Cin's patience to bust her loose.

4. Plastic is completely loose from the metal hub. A screwdriver could be inserted with ease.

knowledgeable craftsman who has become "very familiar with steering wheels".

Turpin says that after restoring hundreds of steering wheels, he can recite the most common failings by heart. The '55 Ford wheel is no exception. He described the cracks in Vicky's wheel in vivid detail. He even knew of a commercially available white paint (Ford's Wimbleton white, a pickup color) that exactly matches Ford's colonial white of '55.

Turpin runs a one man mail order service where he restores many steering wheels each year. Turnaround time is two weeks under normal circumstances.

Several years ago, Turpin published the *Steering Wheel Restoration Handbook, from Antique to Milestone*, for fun and profit. The only how-to guide for restorers considering steering wheel restoration. At $10.95 postpaid, the well illustrated manual walks the restorer through all the steps involved in refurbishing a wheel. Included are chapters on the restoration of hard rubber and bakelite materials, rim transplant on brittle plastics and the techniques and materials used. A related chapter deals with dash and gearshift knob restoration. Interestingly enough, Turpin's book deals with restoring steering wheels in far worse condition than Vicky's. Restoring Vicky's wheel was a snap for Turpin's expert hands.

To restore the cracked hub on Vicky's wheel, Turpin employed a crack filling technique that he has developed over the years. Visible cracks (including hairline cracks) are sawed out and the raw edges beveled with a hand file or power grinder. The beveled edges are cleaned and a knife or spatula is used to spread PC7 epoxy into the cracks. Turpin recommends PC7 because it has "workable stiffness" characteristics and is slow to harden. PC7 is available from The Eastwood Co., Malvern, Pa.

Repaired surfaces are built up beyond the original contours, then gradually worked down to achieve a smooth surface ready for priming. An automotive grade sandpaper of 220 grit is suggested for final smoothing. Any low spots, imperfections, air bubbles and pin holes, etc., must be dug out with a knife and filled with more epoxy, then resanded.

Turpin uses Mortons Eliminator or Feather Fill polyester/catalyst hardened primers. Both are known for their high-build characteristics. They can be wet sanded. Until recently Feather-Fill was a dry-sand only product. Turpin noted that both primers require a 70° or above application temperature. Among the many advantages of these products are: perfect bonding to clean surfaces, non-penetration by other paints and solvents, and non-shrinkage. Conventional commercial grade color finish coats from R.M., DuPont and Ditzler are recommended by Turpin. (Note: Always exercise extreme care when handling or using any automotive paints, body fillers, primers or other chemical products; always read and follow the manufacturer's instructions.)

Color sanding with 500 grit sandpaper and compounding with 606-S DuPont rubbing compound complete the job. The wheel is then ready to be installed. The wheel should not be waxed for 60 days.

Vicky's wheel came back looking brand new. In the meantime, an order had been placed for a repro horn button. Several weeks later, once the dash had been repainted, the wheel and horn button were reinstalled.

After months and months of watching parts being ripped from Vicky's body and chassis, it's refreshing to see beautifully restored pieces being bolted back into place. The installation of the restored steering wheel is a particularly satisfying accomplishment.

Photos 5 thru 8 taken from Jack Turpin's "Steering Wheel Restoration Handbook."

5. *Cracks are opened to accept an epoxy filler.*

6. *Cracks are cleaned and filled with PC7 epoxy. "You have one or more hours to work the epoxy before it sets up," Turpin says.*

7. *An overdose of filler is built up to permit grinding of the surface down to the original contours.*

8. *Flatter surfaces are rough filed down, using a Nicholson coarse flat No. 12 Mill file while a rat-tailed file is used to level round contours.*

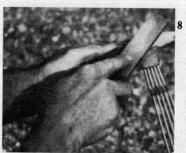

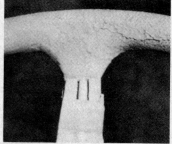

9. *Polyester primer buildup fills small pinholes and doesn't shrink like conventional lacquer primers.*

10. *The addition of a repro horn button from MacDonald's Ford Parts, Rockport, Ind., completed the steering wheel restoration.*

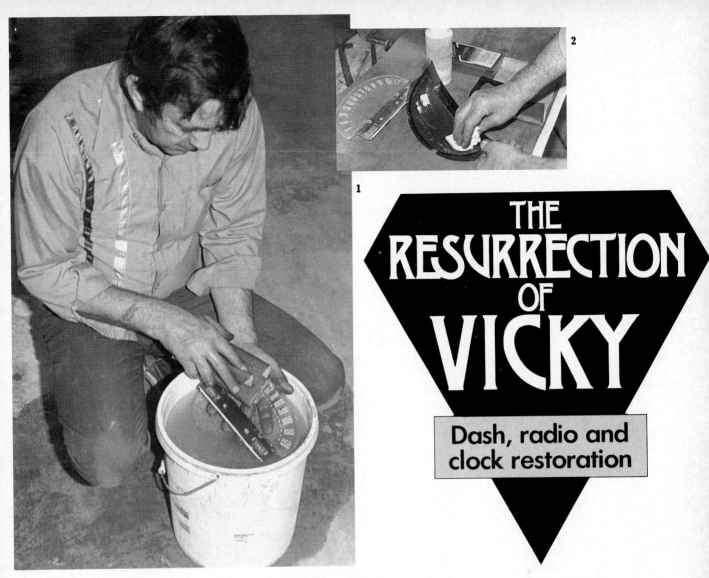

THE RESURRECTION OF VICKY

Dash, radio and clock restoration

Years ago when I was tackling my first full-fledged old car restoration, I learned firsthand how difficult it can be to keep up enthusiasm. It didn't take me long to appreciate what a back-breaker it was to be patient when attending to all the "little things." From the moment the chrome comes off till it's time to wash away the body shop dust, a restorer's enthusiasm usually climbs and drops in yo-yo fashion.

We are at a point in the Vicky series when completion of the restoration is not far away. One segment that came together quickly once all the repair work was finished was the dash area.

In a previous segment the steering wheel was restored. Earlier still, we had reported that the clock was out of order and the radio didn't play. Craig Lindsey, known to restorers as Ole "Doc" Clock, wrote to offer health care for the clock if we'd send it to him. When the clock arrived at his shop (P.O. Box 2234, Salisbury, N.C. 28144, phone 704-279-6019), he found it to be of George Borg manufacture. Borg was one of two makers who built clocks for Ford in 1955. The other, Westclox, has the distinction of being the maker of "the last wind-up model Ford ever offered," according to "Doc".

Once the bezel was removed, a special clock hand puller was used to extract the minute hand without damaging it. Next, out came the movement. Peering inside, "Doc" found it was very dirty and apparently had run for quite a while in a decrepit condition.

The pivot holes in the top plate were egg-shaped in two places. Under normal circumstances the fix for this malady would be to "tighten or reshape these holes using a staking set and special punch," said "Doc". However, Vicky's clock had received this fix somewhere earlier in its life. "Doc" doesn't prescribe a second such fix. Instead he elected to install a new top plate from stock. That done, he gave the clock a 10-minute cleaning in an ultrasonic bath, rinsed it thoroughly, dried it with a hair dryer and sparingly oiled specific points.

The winding mechanism was inspected, the contact points were cleaned and adjusted, the lens was buffed with a special compound to remove scratches, and the hands were repainted. Next, the dial face was sprayed with a clear satin gloss paint to restore the original appearance. Reassembled in new-like condition, Vicky's clock was allowed to run for a few days on

1. *A 12,000 grit (yes, 12,000) sheet for ultrafine wet sanding of plastic and painted parts was used to brighten up the speedo bezel and face. A kit including rubber block and sheets of 4,000, 6,000, 8,000 and 12,000 grit sandpaper is available from Micro-Surface Finishing Products, Inc., Box 818, Wilton, Iowa 52778.*

2. *Ultrafine liquid rubbing compound added just the right touch to make the speedo face look brand new.*

the bench while final adjustments were made.

"Doc" Clock repairs many car clocks. The problems with Vicky's clock are common ailments in pre-'57 clocks, he says. Another common suffering is burnt winding mechanism points and coils, usually caused by a weak car battery that welds the points together. In some instances, fires have resulted when the fuse refused to blow.

By the late '50s clock manufacturers were using movements of lighter and simpler design. They were "cheaper too," says "Doc", which is why most '58-'79 clocks wear out quickly. A satisfactory fix for many restorers is a quartz movement

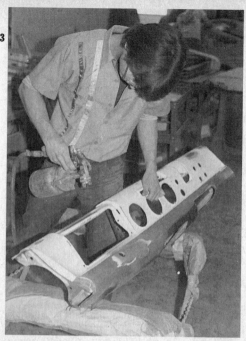

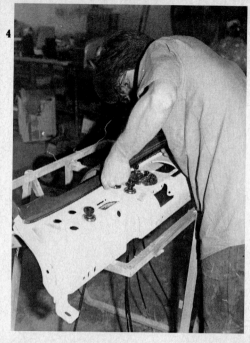

3. *Tom Cripe freshened up the paint on the dash.*

4. *Installation of most instruments and dash wiring was handled while the dash was outside the car.*

5. *Dash gauge needles were brightened with Day-Glo orange paint.*

6. *All rubber parts (exterior and interior) and dash pocket liner are quality reproductions by Dennis Carpenter Ford Reproductions, Box 26398, Charlotte, N.C. 28221.*

7. *Restored clock, courtesy of Ole "Doc" Clock, ticked away quietly as St. Cin installed the radio.*

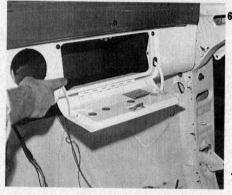

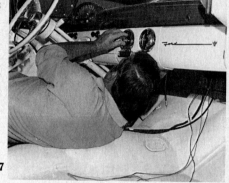

conversion which, although a bit more expensive initially, does away with 99 percent of routine service problems while appearing factory original. Perfect time is another nice benefit. "Doc's" turnaround time is normally two to six weeks depending on the complexity of repairs needed and "Doc's" busy schedule of car shows where he offers on-the-spot repairs when feasible. He also accepts sick clocks to be taken back to the shop.

Coming to the aid of Vicky's dead radio was retired electrician Leo Dangler, 2143 Blanchard Ave., Rt. 3, Findlay, Ohio 45840.

Dangler wrote to say that if we would ship the radio to him, he'd "repair it at no charge for the fun of having a small part in the restoration." Also, if it were unrepairable, he'd "send us a good one," he added, along with his doubts that the 6-12 volt conversion we had decided to retain was practical.

An error occurred when we reported earlier that Vicky's radio was dead. Actually, it wasn't dead at all although it was quite dormant due to a cracked speaker. We had been in such a hurry to get the project under way, we had jumped to conclusions. After a few weeks into the project, one of the staff at Classic Car Centre, Warsaw, Ind., was working with the dash and discovered the shattered speaker. A makeshift speaker was wired and the radio played beautifully.

"The offer is still open," Dangler said when we reported our mistake. We shipped the speaker to him for repair. On examination, Dangler opted to replace the speaker from stock rather than fix it.

Dangler is semi-retired and spends his winters in Florida. Ironically, he also is restoring a '55 Crown Vic. Radio repairs are performed from April till fall in his Ohio shop. Dangler prefers prior contact before a radio is shipped to his shop. He routinely examines the radio and advises

the customer of cost before repairs are begun.

During a phone conversation, Dangler said that the '55 Ford radios were almost bulletproof and few ever suffered major failures. Usually "the vibrator must be replaced and the buffer condenser goes, and sometimes the coupling condenser that connects the detector stage and output stage needs attention," he advised. The "majority of '55 radios were Motorola-built and a lesser number came from Bendix," according to Dangler. "They always worked very well. I have lots of them."

The staff at Classic Car handled the brightening up chores to restore the dash paint colors to the factory original colonial white and torch red. All chromed bezels, etc., were acceptable originals that needed little more than a good cleaning. Several products not widely known to the old car crowd were used to restore luster to the plastic components. Those are explained in the captions.

Once the steering column and wheel were back in place and the holes in the dash were filled with knobs, radio and clock faces, badges, trim etc., the look was breathtakingly nostalgic '50s. It's been a long haul since we started the restoration project, but now our enthusiasm is growing as Vicky's "little things" are renewed.

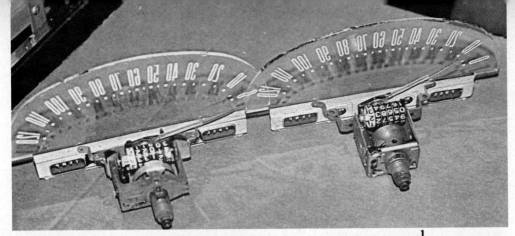

1. *Two types of speedometers were used on '55 Fords: the "somewhat repairable" cast pot metal housing King-Seeley on the left, and the "almost unrepairable" stamped steel housing Stewart-Warner type on the right.*

2. *Bill Heidemann of Bill's Speedometer Shop removes the face on the King-Seeley speedo he volunteered to rebuild as a replacement for Vicky's working but high-mileage unit.*

3. *A clip is pulled to allow removal of the odometer assembly, which Heidemann routinely replaces unless customers want the old one reused.*

4. *New odometers have nice, clean numbers; old ones generally have faded or soiled paint and numbers that are cracked, broken or peeling. Heidemann may be the only repairman who offers cosmetic restoration of odometer numbers.*

THE RESURRECTION OF VICKY

Speedometer restoration

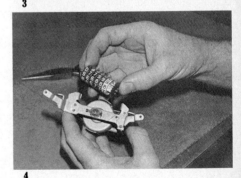

Almost everyone in the old car hobby has heard or used the expression, "If it isn't broken, don't fix it." Even though we were determined to do a thorough frame-off restoration of Vicky, we occasionally abided by that wise saying. For example, the transmission and rear axle operated just fine, so we simply cleaned, resealed, relubricated, and painted them. Nothing more was needed.

When it came to Vicky's speedometer, we had to polish and spruce up the plastic face. The speedometer and odometer assembly worked just fine, and we decided to leave it alone. Past experience had taught us that these assemblies rarely failed, and that any attempts on our part to clean, lubricate or otherwise "improve" it likely would foul up what appeared to be a perfectly good unit.

On the other hand, we were fairly certain our *Cars & Parts* project car's odometer had turned over 100,000 miles at least once, and appeared to be well on its way to 200,000. Though everything worked smoothly now, we weren't certain how many more miles were left in the assembly, nor did we know if the speedometer

still gave accurate miles per hour readings.

Fortunately, we weren't the only ones with those concerns. Bill Heidemann, an old car hobbyist who runs Bill's Speedometer Shop, 3353 Tawny Leaf Ct., Sidney, Ohio 45365, telephone 513-492-7800, had been following Vicky's progress in the magazine. When we wrote about restoring the dash, including the clock and other items, but not the speedometer, he offered his services.

Heidemann has been running his shop from a well-equipped and stocked room in his home for the past six years. He restores, repairs and recalibrates all types of mechanical speedometers and tachometers, makes speedometer cables to order, and refurbishes speedometer and gauge faces, as well as odometer numbers. Most of his business is in American car instruments. "I always have '30s-'50s stuff to work on. It's still the bulk of my business, but I expect that to change. I get a lot of GTO and Camaro speedometers now. I do only a little foreign work simply because I don't have the parts. Other people specialize in foreign cars, and those of us in this business often refer customers to each other."

Though Bill's Speedometer Shop is a spare-time hobby business, Heidemann repairs and restores an average of one speedometer or tachometer a day, year-round. It's all done by mail order or UPS,

except for the occasional local job, such as Vicky's. Turn-around time "is about three weeks; cosmetic restoration takes longer," he says. A typical order involves disassembly and cleaning, replacement of all bushings, a new odometer, lubrication, and recalibration, for which he charges $50, including shipping. If the odometer still looks and works okay, and the customer doesn't want it replaced, the charge is $12 less.

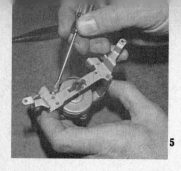
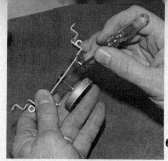

5

6

7

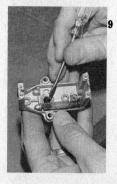

9

10

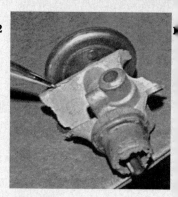

12

Hobbyists are fortunate that speedometer shops like Heidemann's exist. Many years ago, most towns of any size had their own speedometer shops. There were only a few manufacturers of speedometers who supplied car manufacturers. They and local car dealers relied on the local repair shops to service the instruments. Both Stewart-Warner and King-Seeley, for example, supplied complete speedometer assemblies, including faces and pointers, to Ford in 1955. Vicky's original instrument was made by King-Seeley. Then in the late '60s and '70s car makers started making their own speedometer assemblies, most of which cannot be repaired because replacement parts are not stocked. General Motors instruments, though, still can be repaired because replacement parts are available.

The result of this "replace, don't repair" trend was that small-town speedometer shops have disappeared. Now, old car enthusiasts have to rely on other hobbyists like Heidemann to get their speedometers repaired. Heidemann says he drifted into the business because a lack of local speedometer repairmen forced him to work on his own cars' speedometers. Then he began to collect equipment at flea markets, started buying parts inventories, other hobbyists started asking him to fix their speedometers, and, well, it's a familiar old car business story.

Except for the recent new-car trend to electronic speedometers, speedometer technology has changed little over the years, says Heidemann. Better metallurgy after the '20s and '30s produced pot metal housings that no longer "grew" and cracked, and lots of postwar cars have plastic parts that can be difficult to repair. But one mechanical speedometer is much like another, Heidemann says, the main differences being the materials used.

Follow along in the pictures as Heidemann performs his magic on a King-Seeley speedometer he rebuilt to replace Vicky's original unit.

5. *The screwdriver tip points to staking material that must be removed before the bridge can be removed from the main housing.*

6. *Usually the speed cup needs no attention, but the screwdriver is pointing to a potential wear point where the shaft transitions to small from big size. This must be checked and the speed cup with shaft must be replaced if needed.*

7. *The cross worm gear pulls up and out easily. A check is made for damaged teeth.*

8. *The brass bushing in the center of the magnet often is worn. The puller tool shown threads onto the end of the housing, making the removal of the magnet and bushing an easy task. A special magnet press is used to reinstall the magnet and new bushing.*

9. *The worm gear is inspected for chipped or worn teeth, which would cause the odometer to cease functioning properly.*

10. *In restoring a speedometer, "The most important thing to do, if you don't do anything else," says Heidemann, "is to pull out the plug and wick (lower pointer) and lubricate the main bearing (upper pointer) here." He lubricates this point and others with sewing machine oil: "Dryness is the biggest enemy of a speedometer. However, too much grease on the cable eventually will work its way back into the speedo housing and gum up things to the point where the cup rubs on the magnet."*

11. *The colored plastic lenses behind the "oil" and "gen" light openings always fall off, so Heidemann pays special attention to securing them in place.*

12. *Heidemann checks calibration of the speedo with a Sun Speedometer Tester he picked up at a flea market. At 1,000 rpm on the machine the speedometer showed 65*

mph, when it should show 60 mph. Usually, if magnetism is bad, a speedometer will run slower than actual vehicle speed, he says. He properly recalibrated the speedo by demagnetizing it and remagnetizing it, then fine tuning it to 60 mph at 1,000 rpm. However, Stewart-Warner magnets were "seasoned" until the '60s, which meant they couldn't be recalibrated this way. Instead, the repairman had to adjust the hairspring, a much more ticklish procedure.

13. *Not all speedometer restorations are as easy as Vicky's. The speedometer housing pointed out here is from a '28 Dodge, and is just as cracked, broken and destroyed as it looks. This one has suffered irreparable deterioration, thanks to bad metallurgy, but Heidemann says he's successfully restored others using modern bonding materials.*

PART NINE

Final Assembly, the Renewal Is Complete

THE RESURRECTION OF VICKY

Chrome plating

The flash and gleam of fresh chrome adds the quintessential finishing touch to most restorations. Not even the world's best paint job — say 30 coats of hand-rubbed lacquer that look five feet deep — can make up for tired, dull brightwork. Putting old chrome on a fresh body is like painting a house but not the trim, or taking a shower and donning dirty clothes.

Cars & Parts' project car, a '55 Ford Crown Victoria, has lots of brightwork. Much of it is stainless steel on the exterior, which was restored fairly easily, as we described in last month's issue. Now it's time to show how we did the chrome, a good deal of which dresses up Vicky's interior. And, since it looks uncouth to have shiny chrome above a rusting tailpipe, we aluminized the exhaust system, as detailed in an accompanying article.

At the start of the restoration of Vicky, we salt-belt midwesterners had to marvel at the overall good condition of Vicky's chrome trim. Granted, there were some weak points such as the front bumper, which needed to be rechromed. But the grille and rear bumper definitely didn't need any more than a good cleaning and polishing.

The hood ornament and chromed interior appointments were in somewhat respectable condition after more than three decades, but it was apparent that they would stand out like sore thumbs against new paint, upholstery, and the new repro emblems, badges and door handles.

The steps to refurbish Vicky's chrome began when the slightly pitted pot metal hood ornament was padded carefully, boxed in protective cardboard, and shipped to Pot Metal Restorations, 4794C Woodlane Circle, Tallahassee, Fla. 32303, 904-562-3847.

Unlike many plating shop operators who shy away from pot metal restoration,

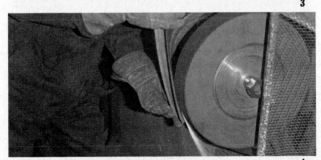

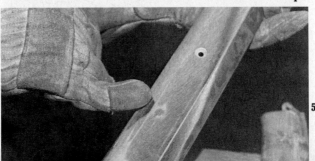

1. *J&P Custom Plating polisher Randy Smith buffs a piece of Vicky's window molding on a commercial-size arbor with a 320 grit sandpaper belt to ready it for chrome plating. The next step is a light run over the part with a 600 grit belt.*

2. *Most pieces like this inside window trim upright contained minor pits, but were straight and required only minor buffing. The old chrome had been removed previously in an acid bath.*

3. *A hand-held die grinder with radial abrasive tabs was used to remove small pits in the arc of this interior tiara strip.*

4. *The sparks flew, yet Smith was dressed for the occasion from head to toe, otherwise polishing compounds "permeate everything," Smith says.*

5. *Grind marks reveal a low spot in the inner windshield molding. Smith raised it from the inside with a small body hammer, then wheeled it again.*

6

7

8

6. *Small pockmarks (not deep, yet unsightly) dotted the long decorative pot metal strip that mounts above the rear seat. Smith elected to remove the blemishes by grinding a thin layer of surface metal from the entire piece.*

7. *Block sanding by hand to finish out the piece innsured that this rare part would not be damaged. Replacing it probably would have cost a bundle.*

8. *Smith doctors a buffing wheel with an abrasive compound. The open, unguarded wheel invites an accident.*

9. *A deep dent was found on this pot metal piece that mates to other trim pieces at the rear seat corners. Slight heat was applied before the dent was raised from the reverse side and removed.*

10. *The speed of the camera's shutter caught the flat clipped edges of this abrasive wheel in stop-action. The wheel is used to grind sharp inside corners.*

11. *Crown Vic trim will receive a copper plating, then it'll return to the polishing department for final buffing.*

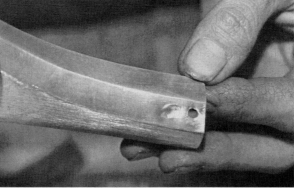

9

10

owner Bill Tatro makes it his primary business. Tatro's shop offers a pot metal restoration process which "fills the pits rather than grinds them out," he says. Fine details, such as those common to feathered mascots, are retained. In less than a month the hood ornament was restored and returned. The craftsmanship seemed well worth the cost, a little less than $100.

Chrome plating is not a do-it-yourself operation. The procedures, chemicals, and equipment are foreign to most vintage car owners. These elements of the unknown appear to be fertile ground for breeding anxiety and frustration, particularly where replating pot metal is concerned.

John Goodrich, president of J&P Custom Plating, 807 N. Meridian St., Box 16, Portland, Ind. 47371, describes the problem: "Practically every car owner has heard that rechroming pot metal is difficult and tells me about going into a shop and being told that the shop won't touch pot metal. So, we talk more about pot metal than anything else."

Understanding the basic operations of plating and having some idea what the plater's problems are will help you discuss your needs with a chrome shop, Goodrich says.

The chrome plating process places a base metal and plating material into a tank of electrically-charged (DC) liquid. The elements for plating include a bar of plating material (the anode which acts as a positive pole) and the pieces or parts to be plated (the cathode which acts as a negative pole). When the liquid is charged, current flows to the cathode delivering small portions of the plating material and depositing it onto the pieces to be plated. The skill of the plater is appreciated when one fully understands the idiosyncrasies associated with varying temperatures,

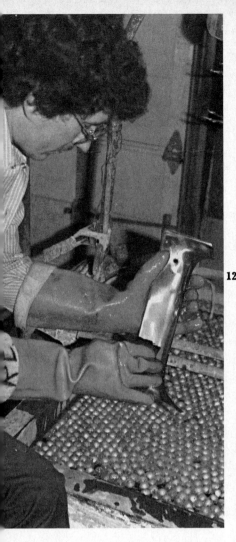

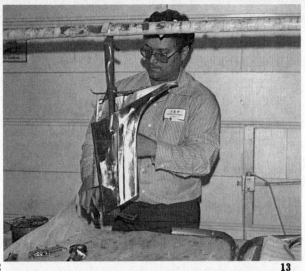

12

13

14

amperage, metals and time which can take years to comprehend and master.

Interestingly, what you see (the chrome) is not the biggest expense item. Preceding the last operation which deposits a micro-thin layer of chromium onto parts is a sequence of time-consuming hand operations. For example, parts for restoration must be hand sorted, numbered and catalogued before being entered into the shop's schedule. Some shops even photograph parts since verbal descriptions are inadequate.

The parts must be carefully watched as they are chemically stripped to the base metal with either muriatic acid for stamped parts and fabricated parts, or sulfuric acid if the parts are castings. At that point, repair work such as the welding of broken parts, etc., takes place.

A trip to the polishing department is next. There the parts are scrutinized to determine the steps necessary to produce a smooth finish that will accept a flawless chrome coating. Oftentimes, this direct routing is sidetracked when restoring vintage car parts. Automotive trim parts, especially castings (commonly known as pot metal), usually are weathered and pitted from many years of exposure to the elements. Grinding away the pits is a specialized art. In fact, in many cases removing the pits is unacceptable if fit and texture

details are altered from original.

Pot metal is a term given to die-cast metal parts containing the three zinc alloys — aluminum, magnesium and copper — which make up the base metal. Pot metal likely got its name because portions of the three metals can be melted at a temperature a little over 700° in an iron pot and then poured (cast) with virtually no effort.

Auto makers like the extraordinary ability of pot metal to reproduce the shape of an intricate die with amazing results. It also has a smooth surface that requires only minor polishing, plus it is easily plated.

The problem for restorers appears years later since old pot metal parts are difficult to replate. That's the reason many shops don't want to handle pot metal. A weathered piece is usually heavily pitted and has absorbed airborne chemicals and whatever else that came its way, thus it's not uncommon for a piece to refuse to accept new chrome. The alternative (sometimes) is to see if the plater is willing to lay on additional layers of copper to fill the pits and buff them smooth. However, this is expensive.

This brings up the subject of triple chrome plating. When platers refer to triple chrome they really aren't talking about three layers of chrome. The first

15

16

16. *Rubber tips put on threaded studs prevent an objectionable buildup of chrome.*

17. *J&P's tanks were barely big enough to take this grille for a 1968 GMC half-ton.*

18. *Rear bumper chrome didn't need replating. Classic Car Centre staffer Eldon Nickel sandblasted the backside and sprayed coats of primer and aluminum paint to protect it from rust.*

19. *Tim Swagerle, another CCC employee, brought back a new-like luster to Vicky's grille with chrome polish and elbow grease. It needed nothing more.*

20. *Measures to insure that employees are protected from polishing department dust (both internally and externally) are illustrated in this interesting photo of Randy Smith taking a break.*

17

18

19

20

layer actually is copper, which acts as a filler to build up the pits, etc., so the polisher can produce a mirror-like surface. Parts such as radiator shrouds for older cars often require several extended trips to the copper tank before a super-smooth surface can be obtained. Customers, although hesitant, are usually willing to pay the extra costs since a minor flaw will show up as a major flaw. Quality plating usually lies in the execution of the copper plating and buffing operation.

The next layer in triple plating is nickel. Nickel adds a silvery patina and acts as a barrier against corrosion of the copper and base metal. Many older cars had nickel-plated brightwork due to the carryover of practices from the horse-drawn era. Nickel has a yellowish tint.

The final layer is chromium, which usually is very thin. It adds a bluish tint while protecting the nickel, copper and base metal because of its strong resistance to oxidation. While it is possible to chrome plate directly on most metals, nickel and copper add the high luster and keep down the cost since a thickness of chromium equal to the thickness of the metals of triple plating would be cost-prohibitive. Of the three metals, chromium is the most expensive and rare. In fact, most chromium used in the U.S. must be imported.

Selecting a chrome shop for Vicky's

parts was difficult. Most plating shops were not within a day's drive of *Cars & Parts'* headquarters and in several cases the owners weren't receptive to a visit by one of the *Cars & Parts* staffers armed with a camera. But John Goodrich of J&P Custom Plating welcomed us to his shop.

Goodrich firmly believes that the best overall chrome plater in the world is Detroit. "There's better chrome on an Aspen than on a Mercedes," he says. "The difference is the guy who owns the Aspen doesn't think he has anything special and doesn't take care of it while the Mercedes owner keeps his car's chrome cleaned and waxed. Four to five years later the Mercedes chrome looks great and the Aspen's is trash."

Customers who contact J&P Custom Plating for prices are given a sheet describing the shop's procedure for receiving incoming work, the five levels of quality offered — from a quick plate to total restoration — and quotes based on a 100-point show judging plus appropriate delivery dates. Goodrich places only one restriction on his shop's capabilities. "We cannot do anything the laws of nature will not allow."

The accompanying photos detail how J&P put the showroom shine back into Vicky's chrome trim.

THE RESURRECTION OF VICKY

Straightening and buffing stainless steel trim

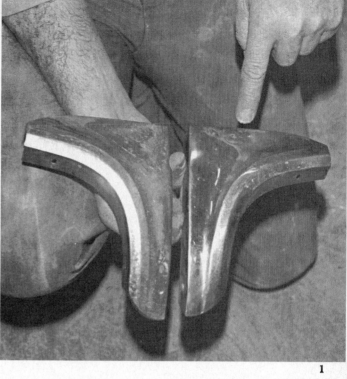

1

Vicky, *Cars & Parts'* project car, is well endowed with bright trim work. The long spears that grace the sides, the tiara strip that crowns the roof, the window trim and even the rain gutters — all were fashioned from stainless steel, the wonderful material that seemingly lasts forever.

Typical of a relatively well-preserved car, Vicky's upper stainless was in decent shape and needed only a routine buffing to spruce it up. However, the long spears behind the doors were marred with deep dents at the crowns and couldn't be straightened. They were replaced by reproductions available from the Ford Parts Store, 4925 Ford Rd., Bryan, Ohio 43506.

Other pieces such as the fender skirt ac-

cents, although available in repro form, showed minor dings and abrasion. They were restored using conventional metal straightening techniques and a stainless steel restoration kit available from The Eastwood Co., 580 Lancaster Ave., Box 296, Malvern, Pa. 19355.

The Eastwood kit includes six-inch buffs of sisal, spiral-sewn and loose-section cot-

2

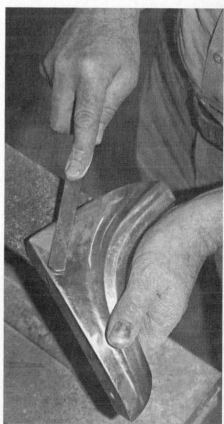

3

4

5

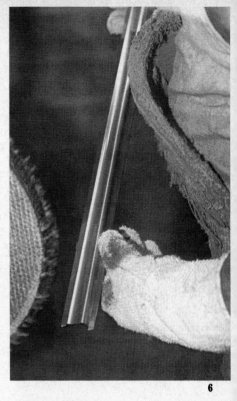

6

ton, as well as appropriate compounds — emery and stainless and white rouge — to bring out a mirror-like finish. A sheet of instructions completes the kit, which is designed for use by the amateur.

Jim McCrary, of McCrary Metal Finishing, Pasco-Montra Rd., Port Jefferson, Ohio 45360, handled the buffing chores on the trim that didn't need any metal re-

pairs. John St. Cin of the staff at Classic Car Centre, Warsaw, Ind., tapped, filed and buffed the fender skirt accent pieces to like-new condition.

Due to the amazingly good condition of most of Vicky's stainless, quick swipes across a sisal wheel dressed with a mild emery compound and a second trip over a loose cotton wheel doctored with white

rouge restored the stainless to assembly line brilliance.

The reason Vicky's stainless steel trim cleaned up so quickly has to do with the material itself. There are more than 30 different types of stainless steel available for commercial use. All contain iron and a percentage of chromium. The amount of chromium is related to the corrosive re-

7

8

9

1. Original fender skirt stone guards suffered a few minor dents over the years yet they were restorable. John St. Cin of Classic Car Centre points to the worst dent.

2. Dents were raised with the pick end of a body hammer. It was necessary to fold the inner lip over to gain access to the dents along the end of the guard.

3. Flat file was used to find the low spots at first, then later it and a rat-tail file were used to remove unwanted metal around deep scratches. The buffing steps came next.

4. John Kenton of McCrary Metal Finishing dresses a sisal rope buff with a gray stainless steel compound stick. Careful not to waste material, Kenton caught fly-away material on the piece of stainless.

5. Remember that any compound is abrasive. Wearing safety goggles is a must. Applying somewhere around 30 lbs. of pressure, Kenton passes the stainless trim across the buffing wheel. His objective is to avoid heat buildup and to remove only enough material to break through the thin

layer of dull surface oxidation.

6. After each pass, Kenton checked for any defects remaining in the surface. Strokes were made along roughly half the length of the trim then it was flipped end for end and the other end buffed.

7. Once all stainless was buffed to Kenton's satisfaction, he removed the sisal buff and fitted a soft cotton "color" wheel used to "brighten the material and wipe the surface clean." Slits in buff serve two purposes: better heat dissipation and

reduction of the crusty buildup of metal and compound.

8. There are literally dozens of different compound bars available for polishing different metals. Commercial bars tend to be larger than those generally available to hobbyists. This gray color bar is recommended for stainless steel.

9. Caught in stop action by the camera's flash, the color buff is actually rotating at several thousand rpm. Brightness is achieved in this process.

10

10. *Jim McCrary, president of McCrary Metal Finishing, inspects Kenton's work. Kenton has more than 20 years of polishing experience.*

The only piece of equipment you'll need to supplement the Eastwood stainless kit is an arbor and an electric motor capable of running at 3,400-plus rpm.

Begin by applying emery compound to the spinning sisal wheel. The correct amount will become obvious after you've allowed the emery to cut the surface. It will be necessary to replenish the emery compound as progress continues. This operation will wipe away most sandpaper marks.

Step two entails applying stainless compound to the spiral-sewn buff to remove the emery compound scratches. As polishing progresses, it may be necessary to back up to the filing or sandpaper stage to render a perfect job. Again, be patient.

Allow the part to cool before moving to the "color" wheel — this final operation brings out the high shine.

A word of caution: Heat buildup is a constant problem. Always allow pieces to cool between operations. If you should burn it, sanding the discolored spot with 400 grit sandpaper and repeating the buffing steps will usually solve the problem.

If you're the type of old car enthusiast who is adept with your hands and enjoys a rewarding challenge, with a little practice you should be able to restore stainless like the pros who restored Vicky's brightwork.

sistance desired while the addition of nickel will improve that resistance even more.

The varieties of stainless steel can be grouped into three basic classes. Ferritic stainless contains no nickel, 12 to 28 percent chromium and very low carbon content. The second class, martensitic stainless, is stronger and contains 12 to 17 percent chromium and a higher carbon content than ferritic types. Austenitic, the third class, contains 16 to 26 percent chromium and seven to 20 percent nickel for extremely corrosive environment applications.

Most automotive trim on U.S. cars built over the last 30 years is in the ferritic class. Normally, after decades of exposure to the elements, automotive stainless corrosion amounts to no more than a semi-dull finish on the surface that is easily removed.

Though professionals restored Vicky's trim, the job wasn't beyond the typical hobbyist's abilities. Tools needed for the amateur to effectively remove deep scratches and dents include a small ball peen hammer or similar striking instrument, a body dolly or similar chunk of metal, sharp fine tooth flat and rat-tail files, and several sheets of sandpaper ranging from coarse 220 grit to very fine 400 grit.

But perhaps the most important tool is the one Eastwood's instructions list as patience. You can't obtain satisfactory results with minimal effort.

To level dents or deep scratches, start leveling them from the back side. A dolly

should be held behind the dent on the good side. In the case of the fender skirt accent shields, St. Cin used a special sandbag instead of a dolly, also purchased from Eastwood. The flexible yet firm surface of the sandbag gradually matched the shields as beating began, yet did not mar the finish.

After a few carefully placed taps, examine your progress by *lightly* running a file over the surface. High spots will show file marks, the low spots will not. Don't be too heavy-handed with the file or you'll cut through the part and produce a piece destined for the scrap pile. Raise the low spots until the file marks touch across the surface in several directions. Also keep in mind that over-zealous hammering will stretch the metal, causing it to bulge and possibly not match the original contours.

The difference between metal finishing a fender dent and a stainless dent is that there is no filler available for stainless steel. It's that simple. If you are impatient with stainless, the work will not be satisfactory.

To give an idea of how much patience is required, each of Vicky's fender shields required two hours of careful tapping, filing and sanding to prepare them for polishing.

Hand sanding was carried out by working the surfaces using coarse to very fine sandpaper. At some point in the sanding process you will decide you have done all you can do to level the surface. Then it's time to begin buffing operations. Don safety glasses and mask at this point.

THE RESURRECTION OF VICKY

Glass replacement

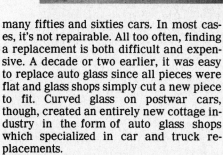

1. Mark Sand, a service technician from Quality Glass of Northern Indiana, removed Vicky's glass early in the restoration.

2. Since the original windshield and back glass weatherstrip gaskets were to be replaced with quality repros from Dennis Carpenter Ford Reproductions (P.O. Box 26398, Charlotte, N.C. 28221), Sand removed them the easy way. He cut them out.

3. Backglass side trim was removed separately.

4. Upscale Fords in 1955 featured grooved rubber weatherstrips which held stainless trim moldings in place. Extreme care is advised when removing them. If the rubber weatherstrips are to be reused, usually it's best to soak the rubber with a release agent, then remove the glass, moldings and rubber gasket as a unit.

5. Quality Glass installer Jerry Egolf removed excess rubber and sealer from glass edges to insure a weatherproof installation.

There's a saying which goes something like, "If it isn't broken, don't fix it." Unfortunately, that doesn't always hold true if you're restoring a car. A case in point is Vicky's windows. Though in fine shape, they needed to be removed so the deteriorated original weatherstripping and gaskets could be replaced. The danger, of course, was that we might break the glass.

The glass in our '55 Ford Crown Victoria was in excellent shape despite Vicky's age. Most cars her age aren't so lucky, having suffered some form of glass damage over the years, such as fogging, cracks, stone chips, sand storm pitting, wiper scratches, acid etching from industrial fallout, etc.

The design of Vicky's wraparound windshield and rear glass is typical of many fifties and sixties cars. In most cases, it's not repairable. All too often, finding a replacement is both difficult and expensive. A decade or two earlier, it was easy to replace auto glass since all pieces were flat and glass shops simply cut a new piece to fit. Curved glass on postwar cars, though, created an entirely new cottage industry in the form of auto glass shops which specialized in car and truck replacements.

Removing and reinstalling any collector car's glass is a job for professionals. Even though all we had to do was renew Vicky's weatherstrips and rubber gaskets, we didn't want to chance either breaking the glass or doing the installation incorrectly and winding up with water leaks and wind

drafts. We called in the professionals from Quality Glass, an automotive glass company in northwestern Indiana close to our restoration shop, Classic Car Centre, Warsaw, Ind.

We earlier had obtained all the necessary rubber weatherstripping and gaskets from Dennis Carpenter Ford Reproductions, P.O. Box 26398, Charlotte, N.C. 28221; 704-786-8139. Though most of Vicky's were in serviceable condition, deterioration was clearly evident. Since we had to remove the glass anyway to do a proper repair and repaint of the body, it made no sense from either a cosmetic or a functional point of view to reinstall the glass with the old gaskets and weatherstripping.

6. *To prevent scratches, Egolf put the back glass on a foam rubber-padded horse. The glass will be forced into the grooved slots in the rubber.*

7. *Silicone spray squirted onto the 't' edge of the trim and into the groove in the rubber (see arrows) expedites the installation of trim around the glass.*

8. *Strips of masking tape will hold the trim and rubber in place until Egolf installs the glass in its opening on the body.*

9. *A rope (see arrow) was inserted into a groove which will hold the glass to the body.*

10. *Egolf positioned the glass single-handedly. Usually this is a two-man operation.*

11. *By slowly drawing the rope from the groove (starting at top center), Egolf was able to pull the rubber gasket edge over the pinchweld flange and lock the glass in place.*

12. *Egolf coaxes the windshield in place by slapping it sharply with the palm of his hand.*

5

6

7

8

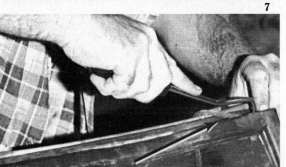
9

10

11

12

All auto glass falls into two categories: fixed or movable. Gaskets and weather-stripping is used to seal out noise and the elements in both cases. Vicky's side glass and vent windows follow fairly common postwar automotive sealing practices for movable glass. The pivoting vent windows have a compression seal rubber gasket, while the side glass is "sealed" by what sometimes are called "fuzzies". Some manufacturers use rubber strips that have a "flocked" surface that wipes the glass while others use the carpet-like "fuzzy" strips that keep out leaves and other debris but more freely admit water.

Two general methods for installing fixed glass are used: channeled rubber gaskets and butyl rubber ribbon gaskets. Vicky's windshield and back glass are held in place with the older gasket, the channeled rubber style. In the channeled rubber style, the gasket is molded to receive the edge of the glass in one channel, bright trim in another channel (if any is used), and the pinchweld flange of the window opening in yet another channel. The object is to keep the glass from touching the body by "floating" it in the rubber gasket.

Newer cars quite often use the butyl rubber ribbon gasket. This method of isolating the glass from the body makes for somewhat quicker and easier installations, though removals can be messy and time-consuming. The thin ribbon of sticky material is applied either in roll form or in caulking gun fashion to either the inside edge of the glass or the window frame itself. The glass is then positioned precisely — by machine at the factory, or by two installers. Then a caulking compound is applied to cover the edge of the glass, the sealant and the edge of the frame opening before trim is installed to cover the gap.

Both methods have their drawbacks and advantages, with styling often being the reason for selection in recent years. Bonding techniques hadn't come into vogue when Vicky was produced, so her rubber gasket replacement is quite typical of most cars made in the fifties and early sixties.

Quality Glass technicians Mark Sand and Jerry Egolf, pictured here removing and installing the front and rear glass, have mastered all techniques involved in

13

14

15

13. *These rubber weatherstrips from Vicky's vent windows are typical of the condition of all the original strips — brittle, cracked, worn and in need of replacement. The new reproduction weatherstrip from Carpenter's (left) is a duplicate of the original (right) in fit and quality.*

14. *John St. Cin tightened the frame rivets with the aid of a small pry bar which served as a mini-anvil.*

15. *Imperfections and scuff marks in the frame were buffed away to produce a smooth unscarred finish.*

16. *Gary Ordione bolted the vent window assembly to Vicky's doors. Adjustments to seal out entry of moisture, noise and dust around the windows will begin here.*

17. *Crown Victoria rear quarter glass assemblies are complex affairs, as is illustrated by this photo.*

18. *David Mihalko of Restoration Specialties & Supply (P.O. Box 328, RD 2, Windher, Pa. 15963, 814-269-3304) restored Vicky's window felts. Old dilapidated felts were replaced using new staples. Here the old felts from a roof rail have been removed.*

19. *Cleaning and lubrication took care of any problems that might prevent smooth movement of the window cranking mechanism.*

20. *To properly install Vicky's quarter glass, John St. Cin found it necessary to adjust the down-stop brackets, then wrestle the window and regulator mechanism assembly into place.*

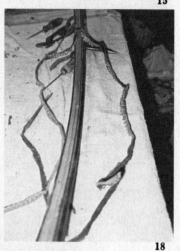

16

17

18

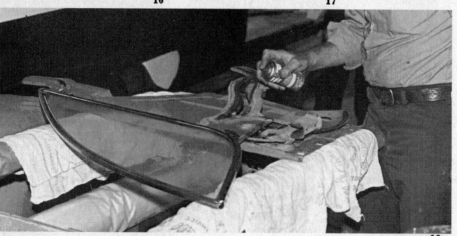

19

glass work, most particularly the magician's sleight-of-hand trick that delivers just the right amount of slap to "seat" glass when a rubber gasket is used. The difference between a professional and an amateur, of course, is whether or not the glass breaks while everything's being persuaded into position.

Side and vent window removal and installation is less critical, and most body repairmen routinely do a competent job. Amateurs, after studying a body manual and proceeding with care, can do it just as well. Usually, the most touchy part is prop-

20

21 & 22. *Roof rails are made of stainless and required only a buffing. New felt strips were stapled to the roof rail exactly as the original strips had been installed.*

23 & 24. *General hand tools and replacement felts and staples are illustrated alongside pieces of Vicky's outside tiara strip.*

25. *Mihalko demonstrates his method for replacing staples. Staples should hold felts tightly to prevent the up and down motion of the glass from bunching up the felts.*

26. *Quality restored pieces depict Mihalko's attention to detail. Replacing felts, stainless beading and rivets costs around $200 for an average car.*

27 & 28. *These two photos illustrate the method used to remove the rust from the fasteners which attach the stainless steel trim that runs along the outside of the rear quarter windows. The fasteners were bead blasted, then painted with roofer's aluminum.*

Photos 18, 21-26 by David Mihalko

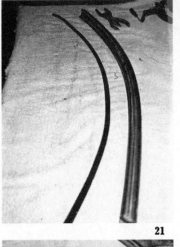

21

22

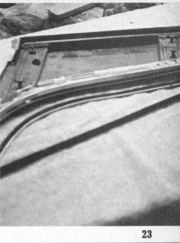

23

24

25

26

erly fastening the glass to the movable carrier bracket — too loose or too tight, the glass eventually breaks. The next most critical task is to align the glass to the frame and the opening so mechanical interference and potential breakage is prevented.

Follow along in the pictures as Vicky's perfectly good glass is removed and reinstalled with all new gaskets, weatherstripping and "fuzzies".

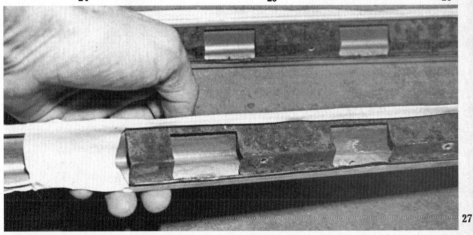

27

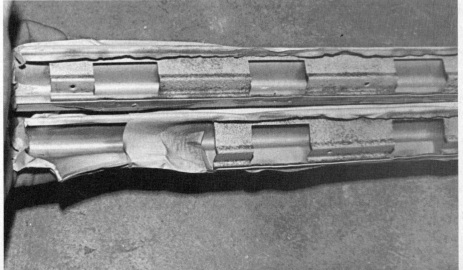

28

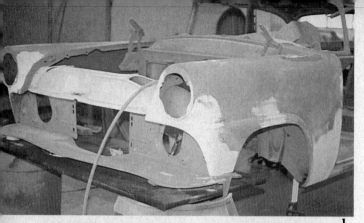

1

THE RESURRECTION OF VICKY

Body alignment, weatherstripping and final assembly

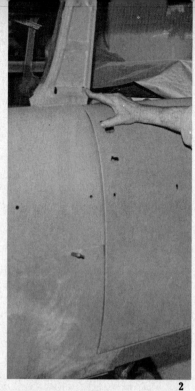

2

3

1. *Proper body alignment never can be achieved unless the frame is square and matches the manufacturer's specs. A pre-paint assembly of major body components will reveal misalignments. Correction of misalignments after final painting usually costs twice as much since the paint work will have to be redone.*

2. *John St. Cin had proper alignment in the back of his mind from the start of the body restoration. Here he checks door alignment before the replacement quarter panels were welded in position.*

3. *The door sagged a half-inch at the rear. Since rear fenders cannot be moved, alignment starts at the rear of the car. The doors are aligned to the rear quarters, then the front fenders are aligned to the doors. Hardtop model windows are adjusted from the vent glasses to fit the weatherstripping. Door hinges can be moved forward and backward, up and down, and even in and out to correct alignment.*

Alignment. Just mentioning the word to an experienced body man conjures up mixed emotions and memories of past accomplishments and frustrating encounters he would just as soon forget.

There's probably not a body man alive who hasn't had to rework a job because a fender or door alignment didn't satisfy a customer. The pain of all that extra metal work, new paint and no extra money on payday likely is still fresh in his memory. Once learned, though, the importance of proper body and panel alignment is a lesson a good body man never forgets.

This article about the restoration of *Cars & Parts'* project car, a '55 Ford Crown Victoria, will explore some of the problems associated with body and panel alignment. At this point, the basic body shell and all panels, doors and lids that were removed have been restored and painted. Now it's time to reassemble them and install weatherstripping and all badges and chrome trim. We also will be installing a reproduction rear-mount radio antenna. It will replace the original antenna on the right front fender simply because we think Vicky will look snappier with a rear-mount antenna.

First, let's talk about alignment. It has been said that the potential value of a car can be halved if the body components are not aligned properly. Not even the best paint work and chrome trim can hide eyesores such as uneven gaps around doors, deck lids that aren't flush, fenders that scrape paint off the edge of the hood, and trim that doesn't line up as it progresses from one panel to the next.

In short, improper alignment will foul up even the better-executed phases of a restoration. It is correct to assume that alignment stands alone as the one cosmetic and mechanical feature of a restoration that must receive high marks or a satisfactory restoration never will be fully achieved. No matter what an owner of a collector car may feel about his or her car, if it has even one improperly aligned panel, it impairs the owner's pleasure in and enjoyment of the vehicle. It's a sore spot that everyone else knows about, too.

Alignment begins with the frame. A frame that is out of square more than a tiny fraction of an inch will cause added work when the body panels are assembled onto the main body. This holds true for body-on-frame older cars as well as more

modern unit construction cars. If the frame is not square, many times the adjustment factors built into fenders, doors and other parts in the form of oversize and oblong holes, shims, tabs and brackets will not be enough to permit proper alignment.

If you are restoring a car, take time to measure across the frame in an "x" fashion with a tape measure to determine if there ever has been frame damage or distortion that was either repaired incorrectly or not at all. Body manuals which show how to find frame reference points and determine measurements are available for most cars and are very helpful at this critical initial stage. This is particularly important with unit body vehicles since body and frame can't be separated. However, if you can separate them, it is useful to put the frame on a flat surface such as a garage floor to visually check for warps and bends not readily discerned by measurements. If you can find a situation akin to a chair with one short leg at this point, it will save untold frustration and gray hairs later on.

Since Vicky required replacement of rocker panels as well as portions of the

190

4. *Ill-fitting fender skirts can be a nightmare since little adjustment is possible. Sometimes the skirts or the fender openings must be altered slightly.*

5. *The restored frame with engine in place was draped with plastic to await the restored body.*

6. *The crew at Classic Car Centre dropped the painted body onto the frame, leaving the plastic in place. The body was bolted to the frame later, after the red paint had been sprayed and the plastic had been removed.*

7. *The doors were refitted and the weatherstripping was glued in place. If the weatherstripping is oversize, proper alignment is impossible. Terry Ritter (in car), Tom Cripe (middle) and Eldon Nickel found these weatherstrip reproductions from Dennis Carpenter's Ford Reproductions (P.O. Box 26398, Charlotte, N.C. 28221) to be perfect fits.*

8. *Eldon Nickel (on floor) and Gary Ordione align the fenders on the leading door edges and the hood. Alignment is a chore that should be left to professionals.*

9. *Adjustments to the hood are possible due to the design of the hinges.*

rear quarter panels, alignment of doors and other panels that had been removed was critical.

Body alignment, assuming the frame is square, begins at the rear, where the door meets the rear quarter panel on each side. The body man at Classic Car Centre, Warsaw, Ind., who replaced those panels, John St. Cin, was concerned with how the rear of the doors lined up even before he welded the new quarter panels into place. Past experience had taught him to look ahead and test-assemble the new pieces before welding, as at least one picture shows.

Vicky's doors are typical of those on most cars. The hinges are designed so that adjustments in all directions are possible. If you ever encounter a bent hinge, though, it's a good idea to try and determine whether the hinge was bent in a collision or purposely bent by a repairman to align the door. Just because a hinge is slightly askew doesn't mean it won't work properly.

On the other hand, a hinge taken from a salvage yard car may have inherent problems that can add to the alignment problem you already have. So be careful when replacing a hinge. Sometimes a worn

hinge pin is all that needs to be replaced. Or it may be a case of missing or out-of-adjustment striker plates.

One trick body men use when removing a perfectly aligned door to do a thorough repainting job is worth knowing. It's even better than scribing a line on the body around the hinges. Simply drill a hole about the size of a 6d finishing nail straight through each hinge into the body. Then, when it comes time to rehang the door, use the holes and 6d nails as alignment devices. The result is a perfectly rehung and aligned door without all the hassles and chipped paint. A dab of body putty and a touch-up with paint will make the holes all but undetectable.

Once the doors are aligned to the rear quarter panels, the front fenders and hood can be installed and aligned to the doors and the cowl. Shims, oblong holes, floating or cage nut plates, etc., facilitate perfect alignment.

Trunk lids present their own alignment problems. Correct-fitting lids seal out moisture, dust and the like. A weatherstrip that's too thick or too thin can prevent correct fit. Assuming the weatherstrip is the right one, though, trunk lid adjustment fol-

lows standard procedures involving moving the lid back and forth and sideways to take advantage of slotted holes and floating threaded plates. Often, though, shims have to be used to raise or lower the edge nearest the back window. That point, in fact, is where eye-pleasing alignment begins on most cars.

Obtaining the correct weatherstripping often is the single most important aspect of insuring an easy alignment. For that reason, Dennis Carpenter Ford Reproductions, P.O. Box 26398, Charlotte, N.C. 28221, 704-786-8139, was the sole source of every piece of reproduction rubber used

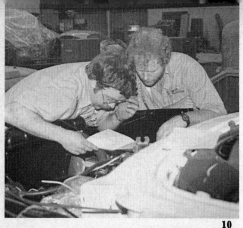

10

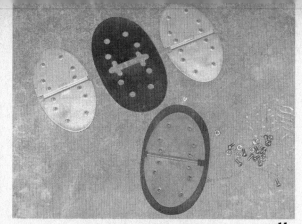

11

12

13

14

15

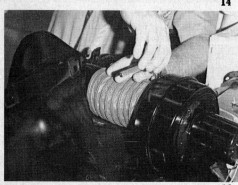

16

17

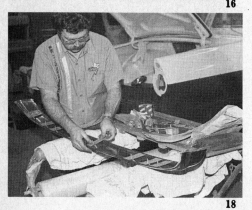

18

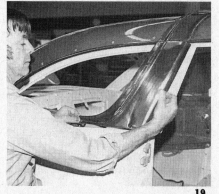

19

10. *Nickel and Ritter checked out all electrical connections in the engine compartment. A complete set of engine compartment decals from The Ford Parts Store (4925 Ford Rd., Bryan, Ohio 43506) will be added.*

11. *Replacing the weathered heater duct rubber seals (using a Dennis Carpenter product) required drilling out the factory rivets and sandwiching the new rubbers between the metal damper plates.*

12. *We riveted the plates rather than use the nuts and bolts provided in the repair kit.*

13. *The restored heater duct damper now seals like a new one.*

14. *Vicky's pitted and dulled chrome door handles surrendered their stainless steel pushbuttons to the new units from The Ford Parts Store.*

15. *A new rubber hood seal from Dennis Carpenter was fastened securely to the cowl.*

16. *Heater motor hoses are reproduction units available from a number of sources.*

17. *Organized table? Yes it is, believe it or not. The time spent to lay everything out in plain view took a few minutes but saved hours once the assembly of small items began.*

18. *The original tiara strip trim clips were derusted and galvanized by Galv-Plating, 933 Oak, Sidney, Ohio 45365.*

19. *Vicky started looking like a Crown Vic again when John St. Cin added the stainless center pillar covers.*

in Vicky's restoration. From hood bumpers to door weatherstripping, we found the Carpenter pieces to be quality products.

As is the case with a number of old car suppliers, Carpenter's business began when he reproduced a 1940 Ford plastic dash knob at home for a car he was restoring. Once other forties Ford enthusiasts saw his work, they asked him to mold knobs for them. From that humble beginning, Carpenter's business now services a worldwide group of Ford collectors ranging from early V-8 Ford enthusiasts to mid-sixties car and mid-seventies pickup fans.

20. *Tim Swagerle prepares to install new parking lamp lenses and gaskets from New Ford Goodies, 18008 St. Clair, Cleveland, Ohio 44110.*

21. *New Crown Victoria trim pieces courtesy of New Ford Goodies are quality reproductions that look as good as new originals.*

22 & 23. *The trick Tom Cripe used to quickly install the side trim could be used in countless other applications. Cripe put a piece of masking tape on the front fender trim and marked the location of the holes in the fenders. Then, he lined up the new trim clips and effortlessly snapped the piece into place.*

24. *New tail lamp lenses were housed in new chrome bezels courtesy of New Ford Goodies.*

25. *New back up lenses, trim and gaskets brought back the freshness of 1955.*

26. *Moulded rubber weatherstrips from Dennis Carpenter are exact duplicates of the originals. The weatherstripping came with a sheet of detailed instructions.*

27. *Masking tape holds weatherstrip until the adhesive dries.*

28. *Using a quality adhesive will insure that weatherstrip stays in place for many years.*

29. *A reproduction accessory antenna courtesy of Dennis Carpenter will grace Vicky's back fender.*

20

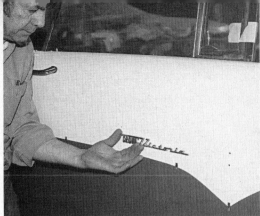

21

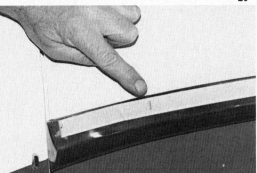

22

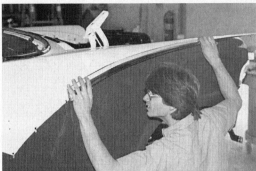

23

24

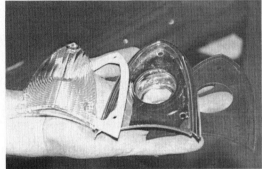

25

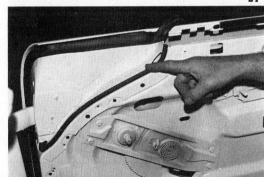

26

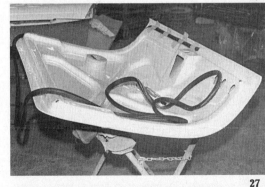

27

In addition to playing a role in body alignment, the weatherstrips used on Vicky's doors, trunk, window frames and in underhood applications are necessary to prevent the entry of noise, air and moisture. They are typical of practically every car built in this country from the late thirties to current models.

Properly made and properly installed weatherstrips insure long life of interiors, body integrity in closed compartments, and proper enjoyment of the car. Follow along in the pictures as Vicky's body is aligned and new weatherstripping is installed.

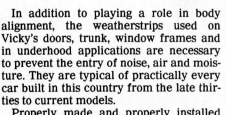
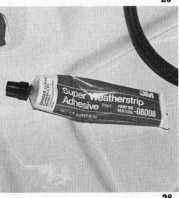

28

29

1. *The Fusons offer buyers a choice of two faceplates — the "toilet seat" type which holds a hubcap as illustrated, or a flat steel disc as shown in an accompanying photo. Both styles are factory-correct.*

2. *Mick and Jerri Fuson of F.W. Mfg. & Fabrication pose beside their driver, a black and pink '55 Ford Crown Victoria which sports one of their reproduction continentals.*

3. *Dale Sotzing (left) and Dave Myers, D & D Classic Auto Restoration, 4640 Orbison Rd., Troy, Ohio 45373, handled the installation of the continental kit. "No need to jack her up," Myers said. "We'll mount the kit with Vicky on the trailer."*

4. *Dale Sotzing took a quick look at the instruction sheets supplied by Fuson.*

5. *As supplied, the sheet metal components are primed with red oxide. The raw edges which run along the trunk line were taped to prevent scratches to Vicky's fresh paint.*

THE RESURRECTION OF VICKY

Installing a continental kit

Some people never seem to find enough words to describe the beauty and excitement that a continental kit adds to the backside of a '50s cruiser. Other people find them to be a bit tacky, even gaudy.

Both points of view are worthy of respect. However, as far as Vicky is concerned, we believe that adding a continental kit was the right thing to do. She was beautiful without it, but now she's gorgeous!

In this segment of the series on Vicky, *Cars & Parts'* '55 Ford Crown Victoria project car, we'll look beyond the pros and cons of continental kits to tell the story of the people who reproduced Vicky's kit and

the pair of bodymen who painted and mounted it.

People who have faced up to challenges and mastered them are always cause for wonder. The *Cars & Parts* staff has met quite a few of them while pursuing the exhausting restoration of Vicky. Yet no team has left a more lasting impression than Mick and Jerri Fuson. The couple is the driving force behind many quality reproduction continental kits adorning class-winning cars at the national Crown Victoria Assn. conventions the past few years.

The Fusons create reproduction continental kits that match factory originals in exacting detail at their company, F.W. Mfg. & Fabrication, P.O. Box 587, Farmersburg, Ind. 47850.

Interestingly, the replacement floorpans used to patch Vicky's rusty originals, as reported in an earlier Vicky article, originated at the Fuson plant, although they were purchased from another source. In

fact, it was reproduction floorpans that led to their continental kits.

It all began in 1985 when Mick Fuson brought home a shabby '55 Ford that had "five layers of floormats covering the rusted-out floors. It was so bad, my wife was afraid to let the kids ride in it," Fuson says. At the time, rust-free floorpans from western cars were selling for $750. That alone was enough incentive for Fuson to take his problems to his dad's metal fabrication shop, where he fashioned a set of pans for his '55.

"The rest is history," says Fuson. "One thing led to another and soon I was shipping 'necessary items' to '54-'60 Ford restorers as far away as Newfoundland and the Philippines."

Not too long after the floorpans went into production, Lyle Hutchins of Salem, Mo., brought a factory-original Ford continental kit to Fuson with a plan for reproducing them. Patterns were made from the Ford kit, and production began, continuing to the present time. Hutchins supplies the ring around the wheel cover either in a primered version to be painted body color or in a flat buffed stainless steel. Two different disc types are available. The "toilet seat" type hosts a hubcap. The flat disc type is the one we chose for Vicky. Both are factory-correct. Fuson stamps out the remaining parts on a 10-ton press. His wife, Jerri, cuts out and primes all Indi-

3

4

6. *The taped edges plus the use of sheets of paper along the body proved worthwhile when the fitting chores took place.*

7. *Myers carefully coordinated the measurements between the tail lamps and bumper. Otherwise the swing of the continental kit for trunk access would be difficult.*

8. *Jack stands were used to level the bumper while the bumper bracket bolts were tightened. Any type of jack can be used in this manner.*

5

6

ana-produced parts and handles shipping chores.

The reproduction continental kit, though accurately emulating a factory kit, is constructed of better materials. Mick Fuson noted in his research that most surviving original continental kits had suffered damage in the center section at one time or another. He decided to use 20 gauge sheet metal in the end pans and 18 gauge in the center pans. Ford used the thinner 20 gauge throughout.

The phrase "continental-type kit" was used by Ford in its installation instructions, says Fuson. Yet Ford's name for the kit was "Sport-Spare Wheel Carrier."

The efforts of people like the Fusons and Lyle Hutchins who are instrumental in reproducing obsolete parts for the collector car market are encouraging. Such endeavors, when they are successful, obviously contribute to the enjoyment of old cars for thousands of hobbyists, as well as helping to continue the collector car hobby.

The continental kit was installed on Vicky by Dale Sotzing and Dave Myers, owners and operators of D & D Classic Auto Restoration, Troy, Ohio. First cousins, they have worked together since they were children. Since both loved to work on cars, it was only natural that they would open their own body shop some day. That day finally came in June 1985. Since that

7

8

9 10

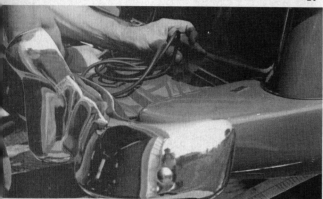

12

14

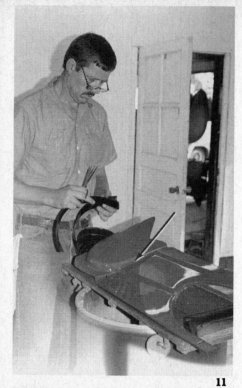

11

13

9. *Some straightening of dented edges (possibly from shipping) was necessary to produce flawless lines along the end pans.*

10. *A revelation is just about to occur. After Myers tightened the lug nuts, we discovered that the non-original tire that came with Vicky was too fat and the band and disc would not fit. We would need an original-size 7.10 x15 or 6.70 x 15 tire!*

11. *Short strips of vinyl fenderwelt (see arrow) were inserted between the center and end pans to achieve a more finished look.*

12. *Kit comes complete with all sheet metal and brackets plus rubber moldings for use along the sharp edges. Kit can be modified to fit a 1954 Ford.*

13. *Bob "Doc" Anderson and Myers carefully lift the painted sheet into place.*

14. *Small holes are drilled into the lower edges of the end pans to secure them to the fenders.*

15. *Installation is complete, except for mounting a lamp above the license plate.*

time, a stream of quality restorations from cosmetic to frame-off types have received the benefit of D & D's combined 50 years of experience in body repair and painting. Attesting to the quality of the work performed by the two-man shop is the fact that a 1987 Hershey class-winning Bentley they restored has been invited to show at the prestigious 1988 Pebble Beach Concours.

D & D offered to install the continental kit between other pressing jobs. Myers and Sotzing began by scanning copies of instruction sheets supplied by Ford to its dealers back in the '50s, and also supplied with the Fuson kit. Then they removed the rear bumper and started the installation. Follow along in the photographs as the D & D team gives Vicky's rear end a new look that leaves a lasting impression.

THE RESURRECTION OF VICKY

Restored at last!

1. *Sporting a fresh, vibrant restoration of professional caliber, Miss Vicky, the 1955 Ford Crown Victoria project car, was intended to serve its new owner as a driver, but she's truly a show quality automobile.*

The resurrection of Vicky is complete. She's a "born again" fifties cruiser, with the jewels back in her crown and the snap back in her step. In fact, she's better than new. But it hasn't been easy coaxing the old girl back to health. To the contrary, it's been an emotional roller coaster.

In what certainly has been the most ambitious project ever undertaken by an automotive hobby publication, the "resurrection of Vicky" has consumed thousands of hours of work, thousands of dollars, and substantial space in more than a dozen issues of *Cars & Parts* Magazine.

The project has demonstrated a healthy appetite right from the start, but the *Cars & Parts* staff has persevered. The result is the restored '55 Ford Crown Victoria depicted on the pages of this article.

The Crown Victoria was the top of the line in the Ford offerings for 1955. In fact, it competes successfully with that year's Sunliner convertible for attention among Ford fans. That's not too bad for a car that began life as a standard two-door hardtop. What a difference some brightwork and special accents can make!

The 1955 Ford Crown Victoria was stylish enough, with its sporty trend-setter lines and elegant trim, that a red and white example appeared on the cover of *Motor Trend's* December 1954 issue, in which all the new '55 U.S. models were reviewed.

In *Motor Trend's* "Spotlight on Detroit," a Crown Victoria was pictured, with the following caption: "A custom car? No, 'just' the most elegant '55 Ford — the Fairlane Crown Victoria." *MT's* Detroit editor, Don MacDonald, was obviously quite impressed with the Crown Vic's styling. He noted in his report that all of the new Fords shared some of the sporty theme found in Ford's new two-passenger Thunderbird. He also observed that chassis alterations gave the new '55 full-size Ford a lower silhouette without infringing on the car's ground clearance.

But the most important single contributing factor to the '55 Crown Victoria's rakish appearance was a factory lowering job. "The Fairlane is an inch lower than standard Fords and a good 2.4 inches lower than any previous Ford," MacDonald said.

Although he seemed taken by the entire Ford line for '55 as many auto writers were, he reserved his greatest praise for the premium offering with the bright strip of stainless steel running full width across the top — the fashionable Crown Victoria. "The Crown Victoria on our cover is cheesecake personified, with or without the optional transparent plastic top. The non-structural chrome tiara across the top is standard on both versions," he wrote.

The Crown Victoria is a good reflection of the company it represented. It was a

2. *The three-quarter rear view of the Crown Victoria with the extreme rake of the back glass long has been a favorite with Ford fans, but the addition of a continental kit sweetens the view.*

3. *A continental kit originally was a $111 dealer-installed option, though Vicky's is a high-quality reproduction unit. Dual exhaust pipes had to be extended.*

4. *A shapely chrome band accents the new headliner. The interior is a kaleidoscope of chrome and color.*

5. *The trunk has been completely refurbished, including the addition of a new trunk mat. When not*

protecting Vicky's beautiful paint and chrome, a top-quality car cover is stored on the right side.

6. *Miss Vicky, despite having a Fordomatic and V-8, wears new 6.70 x 15 reproduction whitewalls instead of the more correct 7.10 x 15 four-ply tires. But the whitewall width is correct, whereas her old tires were not. Hubcaps needed nothing more than polishing and new plastic centers.*

7. *The hood is a bit cluttered, with the hood ornament, Ford crest and Fairlane script vying for attention. However, visual clutter was a hallmark of fifties styling.*

brightly-colored, forward-looking and well-balanced automobile. Ford itself was also in very good shape. After a healthy recovery in the early postwar period, the Dearborn auto maker had forged ahead to strengthen its number two position in the industry. Profits were mounting, expansion was progressing, new product development was receiving appropriate attention, and the public had renewed its faith in a traditional favorite. The '55 model lineup wouldn't do anything to damage that rebuilt reputation. In fact, it would nearly set an all-time record.

Ford Division model year production for 1955 amounted to 1,451,157, which was a bit short of rival Chevrolet's 1,766,076 for the same period. But it was still a very good performance. It was second best in Ford history, trailing only 1923 when the

Model T was at its peak. Our featured model, the Crown Victoria, made its own contributions to that total, with production hitting 35,164, including 1,999 with the transparent roof panel, better known as the glasstop, model.

The Crown Vic was a stylish number but, as always, the fun had to be paid for. In the case of the sporty Crown Vic, that meant a price premium of about $107 over a standard Fairlane two-door hardtop in the V-8 series. V-8 production, incidentally, virtually dominated the Ford line in '55, running about seven to one over the six-banger. Although the Crown Victoria was available with either a six or a V-8, at least according to Ford literature, spec books, etc., few if any were made with the I-block six. A Crown Vic with a six would be a rare bird indeed.

With a starting price of $2,302 for the V-8-powered Crown Victoria ($2,202 for a six), or $2,372 for the V-8 glasstop model ($2,272 with the inline-six), the Crown Victoria's price moved rapidly upward as the options were added. For instance, Vicky is only scantily clad with a few basic options, and a couple of frills, yet they hiked her retail price to $2,926. The options include: Fordomatic, $178; AM pushbutton radio (six-tube with antenna), $87; heater, $71; whitewall tires, $27; power brakes, $32; backup lights, $8; windshield washer, $10; full wheel covers, $15; turn signal indicators, $15; electric clock, $15; and twin outside rear-view mirrors, $10.

A few other options that really "make" the Crown Victoria the dazzling beauty it is are fender skirts ("rear fender shields" in Ford's language) which listed for $18, and the gorgeous Style-Tone paint, the two-tone paint option that sold for $27. A dealer-installed continental kit, which Ford dubbed a "Sport-Spare Wheel Carrier," sold for a hefty $111, but Vicky wouldn't be such a nifty fifties Ford without it.

Other optional equipment marketed by Ford in '55 included air conditioning, which listed for $435, overdrive three-speed manual transmission at $110, power steering at $91, and the V-8 power pack for $15. The latter consisted of a four-barrel carburetor that improved the 272-cid, 162-hp V-8's performance with 20 additional horses.

A really fashionable accessory for '55 was a set of wire wheel covers, which retailed for $34. Power convenience options included electric four-way front seat at $65 and power windows for $102. The deluxe radio, with eight-tube construction and chrome pushbuttons, sold for $100, complete with antenna. Tinted glass helped keep the sun's hot rays at bay for an extra $23.

The '55 Crown Victoria buyer also had a rainbow of exterior paint options from which to select a finish coat for the Crestmark body. Only a single solid color was offered with the Crown Vic, the basic

8. *Trunk lid ornamentation reminds viewers that the Crown Victoria is a Fairlane model of Ford. New badges add much to Vicky's sharp appearance.*

9. *Crown Victoria nameplates and Ford emblems grace the doors. The Fairlane model was nicely trimmed, but the Crown Victoria package added even more pizzazz.*

10. *The most distinguishing feature on the front end is the hooded headlamps, a Ford trademark for years.*

11. *Vicky's "Y"-block ohv 272-cid V-8 engine received a complete overhaul, including conversion for operation on lead-free fuel. New decals completed the engine compartment detailing.*

10

8

9

white vinyl bolsters in the cloth and vinyl combination. All were very appealing and durable, and nicely complemented the exterior paint treatment. Interior decoration, including a liberal dose of chrome, is befitting the car's high-line image. Vicky's interior is red and white vinyl.

Vicky's beauty is much more than skin deep, of course, as one look under the car or in the engine compartment or in the trunk will verify. The detailing on this Crown Vic is extraordinary, even if a few items are not 100% original, such as the 12-volt electrical system. Painstaking care was exercised wherever and whenever possible to retain as much of Vicky's authenticity as possible.

The original 272-cid V-8 with two-barrel Holley-built Ford carburetor and dual exhaust was thoroughly rebuilt, although some minor modifications were rendered to permit a lead-free diet without danger of valve problems. The engine runs strongly and is a credit to the engineering behind Ford's famous Y-block V-8.

The cast iron Ford V-8 has a bore and stroke of 3.62 x 3.30 inches, a compression ratio of 7.6 to 1, a horsepower rating of 162 at 4,400 rpm, and a torque rating of 258 ft.-lbs. at 2,200 rpm. The optional Power Pack four-barrel Holley boosted the power rating to 182 at 4,400 rpm.

The standard transmission with the 272 V-8 was a three-speed manual transmission, with overdrive and the three-speed Fordomatic available as options. Rear end ratios varied, depending on the engine and transmission combination. Vicky's V-8 and Fordomatic team called for a standard 3.30 rear end, with 3.55 optional.

The V-8 power team, regardless of the transmission specified, was ample for the typical '55 Ford buyer, although performance would improve substantially in the years ahead as more powerful engines and various speed options would appear. But Ford, and others, had finally entered the era of the modern overhead-valve V-8, though Ford beat the competition by introducing its version in 1954.

The fabulous fifties were unique. After the Korean conflict had ended, Americans busied themselves enjoying peaceful prosperity. What better way to do that than keep up with the Joneses by parading around town in flashy, brightly-colored new automobiles with powerful V-8 engines?

The automobile as a status symbol has always been very prominent in 20th century American society, but that was never more true than in the fifties. It helped fuel the incredible trend toward fins, tons of chrome, multi-colored interiors, tri-tone paint jobs, and other assorted trademarks of automotive styling in the '50s. There were many winners and losers in that game. The Ford Crown Victoria of 1955 was not only one of the winners, but it also was an undisputed champion.

Now, thanks to *Cars & Parts* Magazine and the many suppliers, craftsmen and readers who supported the Vicky restoration project, another splendid example of the Crown Victoria has been restored to her former glory.

SPECIFICATIONS
1955 FORD CROWN VICTORIA

GENERAL DATA:
Body style: 2-dr.
Passenger capacity: 5-6
Base price: $2,302
  (V-8 model)
Price as equipped: $2,926
  (w/options: Fordomatic, $178; AM radio (6-tube w/antenna), $87; heater, $71; whitewall tires, $27; power brakes, $32; continental kit, $111; backup lights, $8; windshield washer, $10; full wheel covers, $15; skirts, $18; Style-Tone paint, $27; dual outside mirrors, $10; electric clock, $15; and turn signal indicators, $15)

BASIC SPECIFICATIONS:
Wheelbase: 115.5"
Length: 198.5"
Width: 75.9"
Height: 59"
Weight: 3,318 lbs.
Front tread: 58"
Rear tread: 56"
Ground clearance: 8.1"

INTERIOR DIMENSIONS:
Headroom: 35.1"
Legroom (front): 41.9"

ENGINE:
Type: Y-block 90° V-8

Features: Overhead valves, 5 main bearings, aluminum pistons, full-pressure lubrication
Displacement: 272 cu. in.
HP @ RPM: 162 @ 4,400
Torque @ RPM: 258 ft.-lbs. @ 2,200
Compression ratio: 7.6 to 1
Bore x stroke: 3.62" x 3.30"
Carburetion: 2-bbl. duplex downdraft

TRANSMISSION:
Std.: 3-spd. manual
Clutch: 10" single-plate dry type
Opt.: 3-spd. manual w/overdrive; Fordomatic 3-spd. automatic (1st, 2.40; 2nd, 1.47; 3rd, 1.00; reverse, 2.00)

REAR AXLE:
Type: Semi-floating hypoid
Ratios: 3.30 (3.55 opt.)

SUSPENSION:
Front: Transverse link type with ball joints; coil springs; 3-piece stabilizer; hydraulic shocks
Rear: Semi-elliptic, 5-leaf springs; hydraulic shocks

FRAME:
Type: Double-drop w/5 cross members; K-bar const.; special design on Crown Victoria

STEERING:
Type: Worm-and-roller
Ratio: 25.3 to 1
Turning circle (diam.): 41'
Opt.: Power

BRAKES:
Type: 4-wheel hydraulic, 11" drums
Lining area: 192 sq. in.
Opt.: Power

TIRES:
6.70 x 15 (7.10 x 15 w/Fordomatic)
Type: 4-ply blackwall

ELECTRICAL SYSTEM:
Type: 6 volt; 17-plate, 90-amp./hr. battery; 35-amp generator

CAPACITIES:
Cooling system: 20 qts. (21 qts. w/heater)
Gasoline tank: 17 gals.
Engine oil: 5 qts. (6 qts. w/filter)
Manual trans.: 3 pts. (4½ pts. w/overdrive)
Automatic trans.: 9½ qts.
Rear axle: 3½ pts.

11

snowshoe white. But it could be mixed with raven black, aquatone blue, sea sprite green, regency purple, torch red or tropical rose in a two-tone scheme with the main body always snowshoe white. This rarely seen conventional two-tone arrangement had the body one color and the top another, while the daring Style-Tone option on Crown Victorias placed the same accent color on the lower body and top, with white on the upper body. This is the case with Vicky's torch red and snowshoe white combination.

Interior combinations included red, green or rose with white bolsters in the vinyl interior; and black flake pattern with

THE RESURRECTION OF VICKY

Post-restoration reflections

Vicky's restoration is at an end. Today, she sits under her car cover in a collector's garage here in Sidney, Ohio, alongside a couple of other beauties. Her clock, restored to perfect working condition, ticks quietly, counting off the minutes and hours until the day in June when she will be awarded to the winner of *Cars & Parts'* Crown Victoria Sweepstakes at the magazine's Springfield '88 annual car show and swap meet.

The staff of the magazine has mixed emotions about Vicky's departure. Our feelings are somewhat akin to those of parents watching their beloved children leave home to make their own way in the world. We're happy that the demanding task is over, proud that we've done our best. But we're also relieved that now, thank goodness, Vicky's on her own. On the other hand, we're sad to see her familiar shape leave. And we regret that we couldn't have had a bit more time to prepare her even better for her life ahead. But we know Vicky's time at *Cars & Parts* has almost come to a stop, and we both must move on.

It's been an amazing project — long, tiring, taxing, even exhausting, but always challenging. Somehow, we managed to accomplish all we set out to do despite the fact no old car hobby publication had ever done it before.

Any project the magnitude of the Vicky "resurrection" effort saddles its mentors with a series of expensive problems, a few insurmountable challenges, and enough frustration to make everyone involved question their sanity. Every old car hobbyist has suffered through at least some of the trials of restoration: Locating a decent, restorable automobile of the desired year, make and model; combing the swap meets and roaming the junkyards in desperate search for those rare pieces; starting a freshly built engine only to hear a persistent rap from a bad lifter and then get soaking wet feet because the rebuilt water pump's failed; resorting to a hammer to "install" a part that should have bolted into place; enduring all the skinned knuckles and bruised egos left in the wake of the project as it steams ahead to an unknown conclusion.

In *Cars & Parts'* case, luckily, the conclusion was one beautiful automobile, an exciting series of restoration articles showing how the professionals do it, a compilation of the series into book form, and a burning desire to "do another one." Yes, despite the ups and downs of the last two years, the consensus of opinion among staff members is that we will do more.

Sure, some things might be handled a little differently (make that less expensive), but the project was worthwhile and the net result is definitely positive. Though the magazine benefited by gaining many new readers, our readers also benefited because many of the restoration techniques described and portrayed in the preceding pages can be applied to other cars of the postwar period, which is where most of the hobby action is these days. Yet the experience alone was worth the price of admission, as the old saying goes.

The extent of the *Cars & Parts* coverage of Vicky's ground-up restoration (which, ironically, was not our initial goal, as explained earlier in this book) is unique among hobby publications. We recorded in both words and photographs the restoration skills of a host of vintage car professionals. We hope that we have helped to educate novice car collectors as well as expand the knowledge of old-timers. If Vicky's restoration has given someone the inspiration and encouragement to purchase an old car and plan a restoration, that's a bonus that pleases us very much.

Now that Vicky's restored, we're going to miss that pile of Vicky parts, new and old, pictured here that always seemed to inhabit a corner in Art Director Ken New's office. That corner's empty now, but maybe not for long. It seems we've got our eye on a '63 Chevy Impala Super Sport convertible that is up for adoption. Maybe we could do this one completely by ourselves! Hmmmmmm....

APPENDIX

Restoration Products & Services Guide

AUCTIONEERS & APPRAISERS

A.B.C. Auctions, Ltd.: Marrill MacDonald, P.O. Box 2311, Oshawa, Ontario, Canada L1H 7V5. Telephone 416-725-1171, 9 a.m. to 5 p.m. Collector car auctions, sales, shows and flea markets.

ACS International Collector Car Auctions: Ron Christenson, 3701 Minnehaha Ave. S., Minneapolis, MN 55406. Telephone 612-724-0059. Nationwide auction service.

Antiques, Inc.: James C. Leake, P.O. Box 1887, Muskogee, Okla. 74401. Telephone 918-683-3281. Holds annual antique and classic car auction in Tulsa, Okla.

Antique & Special Interest Car Appraisals: F.B. Hemeon, 22 Shipman Rd., Andover, MA 01810. Telephone 617-475-7707, nights-weekends. Appraisals are complete with condition report, historical data, narrative, bound, required insurance copies. Specializing in cars of the 30's through the 60's. No classics but do some foreign cars. Recognized by insurance companies. 20 years experience.

Antique Winter Festival: Bud and Marion Josey, P.O. Box 1929, Zephyrhills, FL 34283. Telephone 813-782-0835. Holds swap meet, car show and auction.

Auto Book Center: See listing under Literature.

Barrett/Jackson Scottsdale 80's: Thomas W. Barrett III and Russell C. Jackson, 5530 East Washington, Phoenix, Arizona 85034. Telephone 602-273-0791. 9:00 a.m. - 5:00 p.m. World's largest Classic Car Auction. Highest in sales, highest in percentage. Great Cars - Great People - Great Times.

Bay Cities Collector Car Auction: Arnie Addison, 29900 Auction Way, Hayward, CA 94544. Telephone 415-788-4500. Northern California's largest antique, classic & special interest collector car auction. Spring/Summer sale with over 500 classic automobiles.

Blair-Collectors & Consultants: Walter R. Blair, 2821 S.W. 167th Pl., Seattle, WA 98166. Telephone 206-242-6745, 10 a.m.-10 p.m. Pacific. Collector car appraisals; cars & parts locating service, technical & restoration advice, car importing advice/assistance, data packages for all cars, buy/sell literature. Cover vintage, classic, high performance, street rods & imports.

Brooks Motors Auction Co.: 186 E. Nacogdoches, New Braunfels, Tex. 78130. Telephone 512-629-1961. Holds collector car auctions.

Dr. Art Burrichter & Sons & Associates: See listing under Collector Car Dealers & Locators.

Charleston Auctioneers: Charles K. Charleston, 5936 E. State Blvd., Fort Wayne, IN 46815. Telephone 219-493-6568, 8:00 a.m. - 6:00 p.m. We specialize in the following auctions: ''Big Daddy'' Don Garlits AUTOGANZA held the first week of March in Ocala, Florida; AUBURN IN THE SPRING held in May in Auburn, Indiana; April in Rockford in Rockford, Illinois; 3 Rivers Collector Car Auction held in July in Fort Wayne, Indiana.

Rick Cole Auctions, Inc.: Rick Cole, 10701 Riverside Dr., No. Hollywood, CA 91602. Telephone 818-506-6533, 9-5. California's largest collector car auction firm for a decade. Auctions in Los Angeles, Newport Beach, Monterey and Palm Springs. Call or write to be placed on our mailing list.

Collector Auto Auction Co., Inc.: Ron Hilen, 5020 N. Main Street, Dayton, Ohio 45415. Telephone 513-275-7450. Holds collector car auction in Dayton. Buys, sells and appraises collector cars.

Dutch Wonderland Collector Auto Auction: 2249 Lincoln Hwy., Rt. 30 East, Lancaster, Pa. 17602. Telephone 717-291-1888. Holds annual collector car auction.

H. K. Klassics: Hy Kusnetz, 16 Hausmann Ct., Maplewood, N.J. 07040. Telephone 201-761-6642, 10 a.m. to 4 p.m. Appraisals for banks, estates, insurance, loans and dealers. Also auctions and shows.

Hudson & Marshall, Inc.: 717 North Ave., Macon, Ga. 31211. Telephone 1-800-841-9400 (Nat.), 1-800-342-2666 (Ga.), 912-743-1511. A full service auction company with an antique & classic car division. For complete information on selling 1 car or a complete collection contact Wm. H. Bonbrake.

Brian Nelson Jones: 3610 Sowder Square West, Bloomington, Ind. 47401. Telephone 812-334-0581. Licensed and bonded auctioneers and appraisers.

Kruse International: Dean Kruse, P.O. Box 190, Auburn, Ind. 46706. Telephone 219-925-5600, 9 a.m. to 5 p.m. Auctioneers and appraisers. Auction guide booklet available.

Lazarus Motor Sales & Museum: Lazarus Motors, 211 Walnut, Box 368, Forreston, Ill. 61030. Telephone 815-938-2250 or 815-938-2668, 11 a.m. to 5 p.m. weekdays. Antiques, classic, special interest and sports-type automobiles, antique, collector car auctions and appraisal service.

Lordship Antique Auto, Inc.: Kevin Biebel, 5 Prospect Dr., Stratford, Conn. 06497. Telephone 203-377-3454, 7 a.m. to 4 p.m. Monday through Friday. Appraisals, brokering, restoration, transporting, and sales.

New England Autosport Associates: 64 North Ave., Wakefield, MA 01880. Telephone 617-246-2427. 9 a.m. to 5 p.m., Monday through Friday. Stated value appraisers and purchase consultants.

New England Old Car Barn: U.S. Route 1, North Hampton, N.H. 03862. Telephone 603-964-7100. Appraiser with over 40 years experience in collecting, selling, buying and restoring collector automobiles.

Rader's Relics: See listing under Collector Car Dealers & Locators.

Von Reece Auctioneers: Von Reece, 4400 Bunny Run, Austin, TX 78746. Telephone in Texas 1-800-222-5132. Outside Texas, 1-800-531-5274, 9-5, M-F. Antique, classic & special interest auto auctions, mainly in Texas and the southwest. Featuring same-day pay with auction company check. 32 page auction handbook available for $3.00 postage paid. Call or write for free info about any of our sales.

James T. Sandoro Collector Car Appraiser: James T. Sandoro, 24 Myrtle Avenue, Buffalo, NY 14204. Telephone 716-855-1931, by appointment Mon. thru Sat. 8 a.m. to 6 p.m. Appraiser. Expert Court Testimony. Bonded & insured. 25 years experience as restorer, auctioneer & appraiser. Available Nationwide. 716-855-1931.

Spectrum Vehicle Auctions (A Division of Spectrum Car Bazaar Corp.): Kurt Hazard & Drew Donen, 18000 Devonshire St., Northridge, CA 91325. Telephone 818-368-6233, M-TH 9-5, F 9-7, Sat.-Sun. 8-5. Antique, classic, exotic, special interest and collector car auctions! Over 500 cars at every auction! Call for California's largest collector car auction dates! Call for free color brochure! Don't miss out!

Swanson Auction Service: Swanie Swanson, CAI, 144 E. Church St., Sandwich, IL 60548. Telephone 815-786-2363. 24 years experience selling autos, new and old. Shop equipment a specialty. Fully licensed and bonded. Equipment and personal to handle the largest sales. Over 3100 sales conducted to date.

Williams Contemporary Classic Cars: See listing Collector Car Dealers.

AUTOMOBILIA

Accent Models, Inc.: S. Richardi, 26 Diamond Spring Road, Denville, New Jersey 07834. Telephone 201-625-0997, Tuesdays thru Fridays 10-5, Saturdays 10-1. Mail order and open shop. Authentic auto models, both factory assembled and kits. Die casts and plastic. Brooklin, Solido, Limited Edition promotional models, one-of-a-kind items, etc. Antique, classic, contemporary models.

The Atlanta Gallery of Automotive Art: PLC Inc., P.O. Box 420024, Atlanta, Ga. 30342. Telephone 404-351-9100. 9 a.m. to 5 p.m., Mon.-Fri. Mail order supplier of gallery-quality lithographs of automotive art; also walk-in gallery.

Audio-Visual Designs: Carl H. Sturner, P.O. Box 24, Earlton, NY 12058. Telephone 518-731-2054. Publisher and supplier of antique and classic automobile post cards to museums, gift shops and other retail outlets. Custom made post cards and calendars in color available for customer's needs!

Auto Dimensions: Manager: D. Merrigan, P.O. Box 133, Mountain Lakes, N.J. 07046. Telephone 201-625-4388, Tues. thru Friday 10-5. Saturdays 10-1. Unique items for auto lovers and drivers. Auto T-Shirts, Color posters, gift items. As usual . . . The Unusual ®.

Autofocus Photographic Services: Directors: David Phillips, Rob. Atherton, David Griffiths, David Loviska, Box 8119, Rego Park, NY 11374-8119, 92-24 Queens Boulevard, Rego Park, New York, NY 11374. Postal Only. Autofocus Photographic Services specialize in producing full-color self adhesive photo labels in four sizes from your automobile slides, negatives or photographs. They stick to every dry surface and are ideal for letters, sales information sheets, auction lists etc. They can be overprinted with your name & address or business message.

Automobilia: Lustron Industries, Inc., 44 Glendale Rd., Park Ridge, NJ 07656. Telephone 201-573-0173, 9-5. Mail order sales of Automotive Miniatures in 1:43, 1:25 & 1:16 scale diecast and pewter by Polistil, Brumm, Collector's Case & others. Also steel toy cars of the 50's, car badges & cruise ship models.

Auto Motif, Inc.: Milton S. Hill, 2968 Atlanta Road, Smyrna, GA 30080. Telephone 800-367-1161, 10 a.m. to 6 p.m. Monday through Saturday. Automotive-theme gifts and collectibles, including books, prints, models, apparel, glassware, magazines, posters, puzzles, lamps, candy, office accessories, original art, telephones, key rings - well over 10,000 different items in stock at all times. Catalog, gift wrap, and worldwide shipment available.

Automotive Emporium: Frederick Z. Tycher, Turtle Creek Village, Dallas, TX 75219. Telephone 214-521-1930, Weekdays and Saturday 10 a.m. - 6 p.m. The complete shopping experience for the enthusiast. From original literature to the latest in motoring books, from Ford to Ferrari, fine original artwork or posters its all at the Automotive Emporium. Everything featured in a museum like atmosphere. Miniatures, memorabilia, jewelery and motoring apparel. No catalog.

Automotive Fine Art: Tom Hale, 37986 Tralee Trail, Northville, MI 48167. Telephone 313-476-9529, by appointment. Original automobile paintings; signed and numbered, limited edition automotive prints; automobile painting commissions accepted.

Auto World Model Shoppe: Mail Corp. Ltd. Ray Berry, Pres., 701 N. Keyser Ave., Scranton, PA 18508. Telephone 717-344-7258. 9 a.m. to 5:30 p.m. Mon.-Sat. Model cars, slot cars, radio control cars and supplies. Serving modelers mail order since 1958. 132 page catalog $3.00 postpaid USA, $5.00 overseas.

Benkin Pump Co.: Ben Staub, 3488 Stop 8 Rd., Dayton, OH 45414. Telephone 513-890-8636, 8-5. The Benkin pump is a reproduction of the ''American'' visable gas pump. It is made of aluminum so it will never rust. It is made in 10' and 8' height. Call or write for free literature.

Beverly Hills Motoring Accessories: See listing under Car Covers.

Broussards: 408 Rivermont Drive, Sheffield, AL 35660. Information Phone 205-383-7915. Prints from original professional photographs; very high quality black and white, sizes 8x10, 11x14, 16x20. We have over 90 different scenes, from 1900 thru 1950. Pictures depict Old cars. Old Service Stations, Downtown Scenes. Car Lots, Wrecks, Coke-Advertisements, Motorcycles, Junkyards, etc. One day service. We also buy, sell or trade Gas-Oil-Automobile Memorabilia - Parking Meters-Signs-Globes, etc.

Car Collectables: Richard Shapleigh, P.O. Box 1500,Madison, CT 06443. Telephone 203-245-2242, 9-5. Antique car Christmas cards; car related gifts.

Carswell's Creations: Megan Carswell, 3476 Alward Rd., Dept. CPA, Pataskala, OH 43062. Telephone 614-927-5224. Mail order - wholesale & retail since 1980! Auto related buttons, magnets, mirrors, bumper stickers, rubber stamps, award certificates and note cards! Custom services available for clubs & business! Full catalog of delightful creations that express ''pride of ownership'' - $1.00! It shouldn't cost a lot to have a little fun!

Cobweb Collectibles: Sheldon Halper, 205 South Ave. West, Westfield, NJ 07090. Telephone 201-233-5777, 11 a.m. to 5 p.m. 6 days. Always a large stock of sales catalogs & owners manuals. Also auto company lapel pins and memorabilia. Please send SASE. For prompt reply to your inquiry.

Comet Products: Marv Schwartz, 1141 Alton Place, Phila., PA 19115. Telephone 215-673-7237, 9-5. Car grill emblem badges - these beautifully made grille badges are a stylish way to dress up your car & make a personal statement at the same time. 500 types are available. Made of brass, nickel-plated with radiant baked on enamel colors. Send $3.00 for full color cat. Dept. CC.

Concept 1.2.3.: P.O. Box 1086, Minnetonka, MN 55345. "Gallery Corvette" poster. A high quality, color reproduction of today's newest automotive masterpiece. Artist signed editions & unsigned versions.

Mike Cornwell, Commercial Art: Mike Cornwell, 14 Owl Creek Road, Fisher, IL 61843. Telephone 217-897-6459. Art prints of original pen and ink drawings showing various special interest cars. Prints available include Corvettes, 55-60 Chevrolets, 55-57 T-Birds, Shelby Mustangs, Z-28's and Trans Ams.

DFR Restorations: Jeff Gillis, 2700 Timber Lane, Green Bay, WI 54303-5899. Telephone 414-499-8797 (evenings). DFR Restorations provides a restoration service for cloisonne emblems from antique automobiles and other such uses. Reproductions can also be made if sufficient demand is shown. Special medallions for clubs, events are possible. Contact for details with your plans or ideas.

Jo & George Domer: Old Paradise School-House, Bantam Avenue, R.F.D. Rte. 2, Milton, PA 17847. Telephone 717-742-8005, anytime. Nickel-silver rings crested with colorful and authentic miniature replicas of the world's familiar & honored hallmarks. Also necklaces and money clips.

Donovan Uniform Co. 171 Parkhouse St., P.O. Box 10184, Dallas, TX 75207. Telephone 214-741-3971, 8 a.m. to 4:30 p.m. weekdays. Dusters, Duster Caps, Googles.

50's Auto Art: Phil Schroeder, Freda Wise, P.O. Box 13061, Kansas City, MO 64199. Telephone 913-888-5761, 8-6 p.m. Nostalgic auto-art sculptures created from parts of classic cars of the big-fin era (1955-1962). Love seats, chairs, A/V entertainment centers, tables, desks, bars, etc. are part of the CAR'S THE STAR® collection produced by 50's AutoArt. Fintastic!

Gee Gee Studios, Inc.: Gary E. Geivett, 6636 S. Apache Dr., Littleton, CO 80120. Telephone 303-794-2788, 8 a.m. to 5 p.m. Monday thru Friday (calls till 9 p.m.). Custom pen-and-ink drawings of your favorite collector cars, home, etc. plus lithograph numbered editions prints of over 28 specific cars. All are fine-line, highly detailed drawings that are available framed or unframed. Catalog available for $1.00 (refundable with print or art purchase).

Richard Hurlburt: 27 West St., Greenfield, Mass. 01301. Telephone 413-773-3235. Hours by phone: 8:30 a.m. to 11 p.m. License plates: Sold, bought, collect, appraised; vast, varied stock U.S., Canada 1905-80, all types for collectors, or your restored vehicle; also bulb horns, hand Klaxons, advertising signs, vehicle aircraft collectibles, vehicle sales, service literature, toy vehicles, head gaskets, hub caps, SASE for reply please. Prefer phone calls (no collect!)

Charles Kacsur/Graphics: Charles Kacsur, 431 N. Center Ave. (Office), 319 W. Fairview (Studio/Shop), Somerset, PA 15501. Telephone 814-445-7779. Hours 10 a.m. to 10 p.m. Design & manufacture dash plaques and awards for auto shows and meets, also auto logo wall clocks and custom auto logo license plates - special automotive artwork and custom framing at studio.

Miniature Cars: Eric Waiter, Box 567, Bernardsville, NJ 07924. Telephone 201-267-5612, 8-8 EST. Retail & wholesale supplier scale model autos. Over 5200 different models presently in stock. Catalog $2. Also distributor British magazines "Classic & Sportscar", "Motor Sport" etc.

Miniature Toys: P.O. Box E, Westboro, MA 01581. Telephone 617-366-8121. 9:00 a.m. to 5:00 p.m. Your mail order firm specializing in miniature vehicles from around the world. We offer such well known names as Matchbox, Brooklin, Nostalgic Miniatures, Rio, Brumm, Lledo, etc. and little known names such as Schabak, Mini Marque 43, Idea 3, etc. Serving the collectors needs since 1968. Send $3.00 for current catalog.

Model Car Collectables: Dick Knaack, 5743 S. Willowbrook Drive, Morrison, CO 80465. Specializing in 1/43 and 1/24 new scale model diecast cars including Mini Marque, Brooklyn; Western; Precision Miniatures etc. Also dealer showroom color and upholstery books. Send SASE for free listing.

Model Expo, Inc. 23 Just Road, Fairfield, NJ 07007. Telephone 201-575-6253. Miniature cars and car kits. Finely detailed, accurately scaled models of legendary automobiles.

The Model Shop: Leonard A. Kulas, W7867 County Z, Onalaska, WI 54650. Telephone 608-783-6687, Mon.-Sat. 8-6. The Model Shop is a mail order business that sells all types of model car and truck kits. We also have a complete line of hard to find modeling supplies including Decals, Engine Wiring Kits, Styrene, Paint, Tools and Discontinued Kits. Send $3.00 for our new 1987-1988 Catalog, Dept. A.

Motorwerks: C. Schneider, 4th King, La Crosse, WI 54601. Telephone 608-784-9280, 8:30 a.m.-5 p.m. Automobile paper memorabilia; poster, prints, pictures, folders, brochures and hood ornaments, bought sold and traded.

Munchkin Motors: Westford Road, P.O. Box 266, Eastford, CT 06242. Telephone 203-974-2545. For the very best deal on your next car . . . Automobiles in miniature, 1/87 to 1/2 scale. Open 7 days a week. Call or write for free brochure. "We want to be your car dealer."

Narcon Imports, Inc.: Stanley Narwid, President, 6 Madison Ave., Kearny, NJ 07032. Telephone 201-998-2994, 6 p.m.-11 p.m. EST. International car badges, car marques, zodiac's etc., badge bars and accessories, plastic touring plaques and flags.

The Painted Post Calliope Company: Robert & Laurel Bruce, 24 Hillcrest Drive, P.O. Box 88, Painted Post, NY 14870. Telephone 607-962-0002, anytime - machine takes off-hour calls. Genuine porcelain enameled signs with automotive themes - early motoring signs, Ford signs, Chevrolet signs, etc.

Pelham Prints: Clarence O. Pelham, 1619 North 6th St., Clinton, Iowa 52732. Telephone 319-242-0280, 8 to 5 daily. Antique and classic auto art. 30 different designs available on notecards. Mail order only. Also pen and ink and scratchboard drawings of antique and classic autos. Complete information and free literature available.

Sea-Tac Specialties: Don & Jan Guilbault, 12040 Standring Ct. S.W., Seattle, WA 98146. Telephone 206-246-5397. 8:00 a.m.-5:30 p.m. Mail orders, car shows, swap meets, hat pins, key chains, posters, antenna flags, Gatsby hats & patches.

Sinclair's Auto Miniatures Inc.: David Sinclair, P.O. Box 8403, Erie PA 16505. Serving miniature car collectors since 1964. 1/43 scale die casts and ready-built hand-made models. Over 300 U.S.A. cars! Retail catalog $1.00. New! "Precious Toys" - Auto motif tie tacs, key chains, charms and cuff links in sterling silver, 10K, 14K gold. Dealer inquiries invited. Write on business letterhead.

Trumbull Nameplates: Frank Tisler, 1101 Sugar Mill Drive, New Smyrna Beach, FL 32069. Telephone 904-423-1105. 8:00 a.m. to 11:00 p.m. Manufacturers of dash plaques for auto meets and tours.

The Tin Type Press: Mr. Hayne, P.O. Box 11781, Albuquerque, NM 87192. Publisher: The World Automobile Stamp Album. The comprehensive source illustrating over 700 stamps depicting autos of all kinds. Yearly issue of new pages with index by country, year, make and number of stamps issued. If you like cars, you are going to enjoy this album.

Vette Vues Enterprises, Inc. See listing under Literature.

Weber's: Marsha Lovelace & Mitch Stenzler, 1121 S. Main, Ft. Worth, TX 76104. Telephone 817-335-3833, 8:30-5:00 Monday-Saturday. Gas globes, vinyl decals & other supplies for gas pump restoration. Large selection of porcelain signs, model cars, old photos, posters, Disney items. Lots of gift & novelty items in these lines. We have all you need in one place. We ship immediately. Catalog $4.00, refundable or free with order.

Wilson Enterprises: Dick and Billie Wilson, 8703 Lansdown Dr., Stockton, CA 95210. Telephone 209-474-9690, 9:00-5:30. Personalized license plate frames, decorative auto tags, auto tag clocks, and brass key chains.

BRAKES

Allied Power Brakes: Dave Jones, 8730 Michigan Ave., Detroit, MI 48210. Telephone 313-584-8208, 8 a.m. to 5 p.m. weekdays. Power brake boosters for every make cars & truck.

Cliff's Classic Chevrolet Parts Co.: See listing under Parts Suppliers.

Huck Brake Springs & Accessories: Al C. Petrik, 10436 Crockett St., Sun Valley, Calif. 91352. Telephone 818-768-4867, 9 a.m. to 7 p.m, weekdays. Specializes in rebuilt Ranco/Harrision heater control valves, restored 36-46 GM & Chevrolet, and 39-46 Dodge & Powerwagon truck windshield regulators, 1936-50 Chevrolet truck brake parts.

Muskegon Brake & Dist. Co., Inc.: 848 E. Broadway, Muskegon, MI 49444. Telephone 616-733-0874, M-F 7:30-5:30, Sat. 9-12. Brake, spring and suspension specialists. Corvette brakes, springs, front and rear suspension parts. Also, most other marques, complete service facility including spring manufacturing, brake bonding and rebuilding service. Same location since 1945.

N/C Industries Antique Auto Parts: See listing under Parts Suppliers.

Plasmeter Corporation: Jim Nydigger, 173 Queen Avenue S.E., Albany, OR 97321. Telephone 503/928-3233, 8:00-4:30. Cast iron brake drums for Model A Fords, 1928-1931. Available for both front and rear; mount on original hubs using standard lug studs. Front spoked drums also available; supplied complete with bearings and lug bolts swaged in place.

Stainless Steel Brakes Corp.: H. George Jonas, President, 11470 Main Rd., Clarence, N.Y. 14031. Telephone 716-759-8666, toll free (except N.Y.) 800-448-7722, 8:30-5:00 Mon.-Fri. Disc brake systems, upgraded to stainless steel for Corvette, Mustang (Ford) 64-1/2 to 73, MOPAR 66-71, AMC 65-71, Jaguar (and other imports using Dunlop-Girling brakes). Drum brake to disc brake conversion kits for Mustang, Cougar, Fairlane 64-1/2 to 67. Rear wheel drum to disc conversion kits for 8" and 9" axles.

Street Specialty Products, Inc.: 871 N. Hanover Street, Pottstown, PA 19464. Telephone 215-327-0152, 9:00-5:30 M-F. Corvette Parts & Accessories, Corvette Distributors and Stainless Sleeved Corvette Calipers; Dot 5 Silicone Brake Fluid, dealers please inquire.

Ernie Toth: 8153 Cloveridge Rd., Chagrin Falls, Ohio 44022. Telephone 216-338-3565, Specializing in silicone brake fluid for DOT 5, Qts. $9.00, Gallons $32.00.

CAR COVERS

Beverly Hills Motoring Accessories: 200-CPA S. Robertson Blvd., Beverly Hills, Calif. 90211. Telephone 213-657-4800, 9 a.m. to 6 p.m. weekdays, 10 a.m. to 5 p.m. Saturday. The world's finest automotive accessories are in this full color catalog from Beverly Hills Motoring Accessories. Everything to pamper your collector car can be found within this 64 page catalog. If your car means more to you than just basic transportation, you'll want a copy . . . it's loaded with the finest products from around the world. $3.00 (refundable with purchase).

Circle City Mustang: See listing under Parts Suppliers.

Cobra Restorers Ltd.: See listing under Parts Suppliers.

Stan Coleman, Inc.: See listing under Upholstery.

Pine Ridge Ent.: John Schoepke, 13165 Center Rd., Bath, MI 48808. Our product is Omnibag. A large bag (not a cover) for storing an automobile. Keeps the car perfectly dry and clean. Omnibag seals out moisture then removes moisture from inside, therefore a dry storage environment is created. For long term storage such as over winter. For indoor use only.

Prestige Thunderbird, Inc.: See listing under Restoration Firms.

Reliable Motoring Accessories: Jack Rosen, 1751 Spruce St., Riverside, Calif. 92507. Telephone 714-781-0261, 8 a.m.-5 p.m. Mon.-Fri. & 10 a.m.-4 p.m. Sat. Trend-setting products for the automotive enthusiast include sheepskin seat covers, steering wheels and covers, front end masks, car covers, carpet mats, sunglasses, Recaro Seats, Alarm systems, grille badges, cassette carriers, wheels, louvers, dashboards.

Wayne Rowe - Classic Cars & Parts: See listing under Parts Suppliers.

What's Your Bag: Katherine L. Brown, 1535 Valota Rd., Redwood City, CA 94063. Telephone 415-366-6383, 8 a.m. to 8 p.m. Specializing in custom fit covers and masks.

CAR TRANSPORTERS

Classic Express: 3111 S. Valley View, S-101, Las Vegas, NV 89102. Telephone 702-362-8688, 5 a.m.-5 p.m. Transport of automobiles. Specially built enclosed air ride vans - door to door delivery.

Horseless Carriage Carriers, Inc.: Frank Malatesta, Pres., 61 Iowa Ave., Paterson, N.J. 07503. Telephone 800-631-7796, in New Jersey 201-742-2692, 8 a.m. to 6 p.m. Transporters of antique, classic, new cars, trucks, boats and airplanes.

Lordship Antique Auto, Inc. See listing under Auctioneers & Appraisers.

Northland Auto Transporters, Inc.: 26711 Woodward Ave., Huntington Woods, MI 48070, Telephone 313-544-8330, 800-521-0928. Interstate auto transporter serving all 48 states. Single vehicles to full loads. Fully insured, I.C.C. regulated.

Passport Transport Ltd.: 2551 Metro Blvd., Maryland Heights, Mo. 63043. Telephone 314-997-6777, 8 a.m. to 4:30 p.m. Transports classic and antique vehicles throughout the U.S.

Wayne Rowe - Classic Cars & Parts: See listing under Collector Car Dealers.

CHROME PLATING

A-1 Plating: Dale Carter, 2170 Acoma St., Sacramento, CA 95815. Telephone 916-927-5071, 7 a.m. to 5 p.m. Custom chrome plating, job shop work plus production. Show chrome a specialty. Copper, nickel, brass, chrome & gold. Two week turn around time.

Classic Chrome: Fred Saltzberg, 2430 Washington St., Boston, Mass. 02119. Telephone 617-444-4974, 8 a.m. to 10 p.m. Specializes in polishing, buffing and plating of metals using copper, nickel, chrome, cadmium, tin and silver. Clear-color anodize coatings available.

CustomChrome Plating, Inc.: Jon E. Wright, 963 Mechanic St., P.O. Box 125, Grafton, Ohio 44044. Telephone 216-926-3116, Mon.-Fri. 8:00-12:30 & 1:30-5:00 EST Sat. by appt. Custom Chrome offers high quality polishing, buffing and electroplating. Finishes include chrome, brass, nickel, copper and black chrome.

Duncan Electroplating: Geary H. Duncan, 2459 County Line Rd., York Springs, PA 17372. Telephone 717-432-9873, 8 to 5 Mon. thru Fri. Plating - nickel, chrome, 24 K. Gold. Specialize in antique car parts.

Gary's Plastic Chrome Plating Inc.: Gary & Kerry McKeon, 39312 Dillingham, Westland, MI 48185. Telephone 313-326-1858, 6 days - 8 a.m. to 6 p.m. The service we offer you is to professionally replate your plastic interior parts using the original vacuum metalizing process. If your car was manufactured between 1957 and 1972, your parts were plated using the same process. Normal turn-around time is 3 weeks. Guaranteed workmanship - satisfying customers for six years.

G. E. Antique Creations: 10721 Forest St., Santa Fe Springs, CA 90670. Telephone 213-946-2664, Monday, Tuesday, Thursday - 6 p.m. to 8 p.m., Wednesday - 9 a.m. to 5 p.m., Saturday - 9 a.m. to 4 p.m. Expert refurbishment in stainless. Repairs and polish pot metal straightening. Pot metal welding. 30 yrs. experience.

Graves Plating Co.: P.O. Box 1052, Industrial Park, Florence, Ala. 35631. Telephone 205-764-9487. 7 a.m. - 3:30 p.m. weekdays, 8 a.m. - 12 noon Saturdays. Specializing in custom chrome, nickel, brass and gold plating automobile parts.

J.P. Custom Plating Co.: 1750 N. Campbell Ave., Chicago, IL 60647. Telephone 312-486-0466, 6:30 a.m.-4:30 p.m. Mon.-Fri. 100 point show chrome. All phases of repair & finishing offered. 15,000 sq. ft. devoted to show chrome. Established 1944.

The Khrome Shoppe: 509 Grace St., Poteau, Okla. 74953. Telephone 918-647-9973. Specializing in quality chrome plating.

Qual Krom: George W. Fluegel, 301 Florida Avenue, Fort Pierce, FL 33450. Telephone 305-465-7900, 8:30-5:00. Premium quality automotive and marine restoration metal plating: chrome, brass, copper, gold, silver. Exclusive SUPER-CHROME® finish carries limited lifetime warranty on most parts. Normal services include metal welding and repair, pot metal restoration, wire wheel restoration, cloissone and engraving.

Triple Chrome Plating - Ron Monte Inc.: Ron Monte, 25 Roseland Ave., Caldwell, NJ. Telephone 201-226-6184, 9 a.m. to 4:30 p.m. Our show quality chrome plating is triple plated copper, nickel and chrome. We also do brass, silver and gold plating.

COLLECTOR CAR DEALERS & LOCATORS

Albers Rolls-Royce: 360 South First Street, Zionsville, IN 46077. Telephone 317-873-2360/2460, M-F 9-5. America's oldest exclusive authorized Rolls-Royce dealer. Officially appointed vintage spares specialist by Rolls-Royce Motors Inc. For pre-1955 models. Also huge inventory for all post-1955 motor cars. Largest Rolls-Royce parts dealer in the USA.

Autoland, Inc.: Charles H. Coney, 9605 S.E. Fed Hwy., Hobe Sound, Fla. 33455. Telephone 305-546-6079, 1 p.m. to 4:30 p.m., Monday thru Saturday. Offers antique, classic and special interest cars. Cars for sale and on display. Major magazines sold. Steam cleaning service.

British Motor Brokers: British Motor Brokers U.K., Ltd., 1003 Park Blvd., Massapequa Park, N.Y. 11762. Telephone 516-799-9250, 9 a.m. to 6 p.m. Specializing in retailing antique and prestige automobiles.

Art Burrichter & Sons, "Special Cars For Special People": Dr. Arthur Burrichter, Box 2045, Boca Raton, Florida 33432. Business location, 150 NW 1st St., Deerfield Beach, FL 33441. Telephone 305-426-3417, 10 a.m. to 4 p.m. daily, others by appointment. Specializing in quality original or restored classic and antique cars. We buy, consign, and sell. Appraisals, estate settlements, etc. a specialty. We provide safe and reasonable hauling anywhere, open or closed. Call us first. "INTEGRITY SINCE 1950".

Car Bazaar (A Division of Spectrum-Car Bazaar Corp.): Kurt Hazard & Drew Donen, 18000 Devonshire St., Northridge, CA 91325. Telephone 818-368-6233, M-TH 9-5:00, F 9-7, SA-SU 8-5. Owner direct auto sales every weekend! Hundreds of cars and thousands of buyers! Car covers, front end masks, floor mats and other selected auto accessories.

Car Connections, Inc.: 89 Massachusetts Ave., Boston, MA 02115. Telephone 800-341-CARS/617-383-CARS, 9-6 M-F, 10-3 Sat., 12-5 Sun. Car Connections has a FREE car buyer locating service. Call us with the details about the car you're looking for. Car Connections matches buyers with sellers of all makes, models and years of vehicles. Since we have BUYERS WAITING, Car Connections is the perfect place to sell your car too. CALL TODAY!!!

Chandler Classic Cars: 1308 14th St. West, Bradenton, Fla. 33505. Telephone 813-747-3441.

The Classic Automobile Company: Tom Mack, Jr., 213 Thompson Blvd., P.O. Box 338, Union, S.C. 29379. Telephone: 803-427-0645, 803-427-0463, 8 a.m. to 4:30 p.m. Anytime. Muscle Car Dealer.

Classic Car Centre: R.R. 7, Box 43, Warsaw, IN 46580. Telephone 219-267-2565. Specializing in collector cars of all ages. Complete restoration facilities.

Coachworks - Classic Cars Inc.: Paul Zimmerman, 1401 N.W. 53 Ave., (P.O. Box 1186), Gainesville, FL 32602. (904) 376-0660, 10 a.m.-5 p.m. We sell antique, collector and special interest cars. Also appraisals.

Collector Auto Auction Co., Inc.: See listing under Auctioneers & Appraisers.

Collector Carousel: Carrol Varney Sales Manager, Laird Ave Drive, Wetbrook, Maine. Telephone 854-0343 by appointment. High quality antique & classics, trucks and investment autos.

Collector Cars Inc.: 56 West Merrick Rd., Freeport, NY 11520. Telephone 516-378-6666, 9-6 p.m. M, T, W, Sat.; 9-8 p.m. Th., F; 9-5 on Sunday. One of the largest dealers in antique, classic and special interest autos, we always have about 50 restored cars for sale on our showroom floor. We also offer complete or partial restorations at our full service facility with craftsmen skilled in mechanical, body and trim work of the finest level. Worth a special trip.

Dragone Classic Motorcars, Inc.: Manny Dragone - George Dragone, 1797 Main St., Bridgeport, CT 06604. Telephone 203-335-4643, Mon.-Sat. 8-6. Specializing in convertibles of the 1930's-60's, 55-57 T-Birds, 55-57 Chev's, etc. Restoration by master craftsmen. Financing available. We also collect and restore Delage, Delahaye and Talbot-Lago. Please stop in to see us.

Duffy's Collectible Car Connection: Wm. "Duffy" Schamberger, 711 Center Point Road NE, Cedar Rapids, IA 52402. Telephone 319-364-3467, 8:30-5:30 M-Fri, Sat. 9:00-4:00. Sales, restoration, transportation, appraisals of classic and collectible cars, specializing in cars of the 40's-50's-60's and 70's. Mostly convertibles, hardtops and muscle machines. Trades and financing.

Euro-Cars: Bob Boston, 701 Atlanta Street, Roswell, Georgia 30075. Telephone 404-993-7653. 9-6 Mon.-Fri. Auto importers since 1968, D.O.T. conversion shop dealing mostly in Mercedes, BMW & Porsche.

Exotic Motor Cars Co.: Earl L. Budro, 482 Amherst St., Nashua, N.H. 03060. Telephone 603-889-0386. Hours by appointment. Specializing in Cadillac motor cars.

H K Klassics: See listing under Auctioneers & Appraisers.

Horsepower Sales & Leasing Co.: Dave Bellon Jr., 39-23 27 St., Long Island City, NY 11101. Telephone 718-786-8973, 9-5. Sales of pre-owned limousines & stretch limousines.

G&B Jackson: P.O. Box 2, Wigton, Cumbria, CA7 9JT England. Telephone 0965-43273, 24 hr. answering service. Austin A40, A70, A90, Sheerline & Princess cars, spares & service. Motoring literature bought & sold for all types of vehicles.

Jim's Motor Service: Jim Jones, Rt. 27, Washington Pike, Knoxville, Tenn. 37918. Telephone 615-522-0009 or 615-637-4029. Hours 7 a.m. to 4 p.m. Liquidation of 532, antique, classic, special interest cars, trucks and motorcycles. For free list write Cars, Box 5567, Knoxville, Tenn.

Kirkwood Classic Motorcars: Owner John F. Bacheldor, 317 Wild Forest, Ballwin, MO 63011. Telephone 314-391-8687. 8:00 a.m. - 5:30 p.m. Kirkwood Classic Motor Cars has served St. Louis Metropolitan area for seventeen years, offering sales, service and parts for antique, classic and special interest motor cars. We are also licensed appraisers.

Lazarus Motor Sales & Museum: See listing under Auctioneers & Appraisers.

Lion Auto Gallery: Lee Janotta & Bob Roeper, 4766 W. 130th St., Cleveland, OH 44145. Telephone 216-884-3932, by appointment. Sales and service of classic and specialty autos. Specializing in southern rust free cars and parts. Also restoration.

Martin's Automotive: See listing under Restoration Firms.

Mausolf Museum or Automotive History: Kenneth and Eileen Mausolf, 4651 South Broadway, Englewood, CO 80110. Telephone 303-761-4680, 8-6 Mon.-Sat. Special Interest Autos and memorabilia. Specializing in Rolls Royce autos and Celebrity autos. President John F. Kennedy's Lincoln, Pres. Eisenhower's '56 Chrysler, Elvis Presley's '56 Lincoln Mark II and other rare one of a kind autos. Large selection of new & used stretched limousines - we represent 21 mfg. of new limos.

Robert Melvard: 7819 South Yakima Ave., Tacoma, Wash. 98408. Telephone 206-474-8322 days or 206-474-8725 nights. Buying and selling of antique and classic cars.

Memory Lane Motors: Chuck Dimon, 2608 SE Holgate Blvd., Portland, OR 97202. Telephone 503-231-1940, 9-5. Specializing in quality affordable collectibles - 30 cars in stock - rust free fine original Oregon cars. If memory lane has it - it's nice. Buy - sell - consign & appraise.

Mershon's World of Cars: Dan Mershon, 2141 E. Main, Springfield, Ohio 45505. Telephone 513-324-8009/8899, 9-7 M-F, 9-5 Sat. Specializes in Vettes, Muscle and Collector cars.

Amos Minter: Dallas, Tex. Telephone 214-248-4446. Specializing in 55-57 T-Birds, also handles other collector cars.

J. Morrison Better Cars Inc.: J.W. Morrison, 117 Third St., Garden City, N.Y. 11530. Telephone 516-741-1322. Dealer in antique, classic and spec. interest cars. Cars available as movie or advertising props. Packard specialist. Literature & some car parts. Restoration advice, east coast. Retired VW dealer.

Mustang Madness: 64 North Ave., Wakefield, MA 01880. 64-84 Mustang sales, service, restoration, buy, sell, trade. V8 conversion specialists.

New England Old Car Barn: U.S. Route 1, North Hampton, NH 03862. Telephone 603-964-7100. We buy and sell antique, collector and special interest cars. Specializing in showroom quality automobiles. We feature any make from A Fords to Volkswagens. Large showroom.

The New Old Stock Market Corp.: (A.M. Milbruk, Pres.), Box 439, Bryans Road, MD 20616. Telephone 301-283-2143, 8-4 p.m. NOS parts locator services, consultants, catalog services for NOS parts suppliers, publications.

Page's Model A Garage: Haverhill, N.H. 03765. Telephone 603-989-5562.

Porsche Auto Recyclers: See listing under Parts Suppliers.

Rader's Relics: Robert E. Rader, 2601 W. Fairbanks Ave., Winter Park, FL 32789. Telephone 305-647-1940, 9-5 M-F. Buying and selling and consigning classics and antiques 10 years same location, 25 minutes from Walt Disney World, year round market. An excellent reputation in the business community and the hobby.

Wayne Rowe Classic Cars & Parts: Wayne Rowe, R.R. 2, Carp Rd., Carp, Ontario, Canada K0A 1L0. Telephone 613-836-2997, 9 a.m. to 6 p.m. Video tapes available of 50 Arizona rust free cars and basic shells in stock at all times. Car Locator Service - Restorations - new and used parts 61-66 T-Birds. Show chrome plating and buffing. Appraisals. Antique classic car transporting from Arizona to Ontario PCV licensed and bonded Canadian Carrier.

James T. Sandoro: See listing under Auctioneers & Appraisers.

O.B. Smith Classic Cars & Parts, Inc.: O.B. Smith, P.O. Box 11703, Lexington, KY 40577. Telephone 606-253-1957, Mon.-Fri. 8-5, Sat. 9-3. We carry chrome, trim parts, weatherstrip, interiors, manuals & etc. for 55-57 Chevys, 58-64 Impalas, 67-69 Camaros, 64-72 Chevelles & 62-74 Chevy II/Novas. Parts catalog $1.00. We also keep in stock 20-25 restored Chevys, mostly 55-57's, also Camaros & Chevelles.

Solid Southern Cars 1582 Austell Rd., Marietta, GA 30060. Telephone 404-427-2727. Very special cars for very special people.

Volo Auto Museum & Sports Car Store: Greg G. Grams, 27640 West Highway 120, Volo, IL 60073, On Route 120 - ½ mile west of 12 in Volo. Telephone 815-385-3644, everyday 10 to 5. Largest nostalgic auto market place in USA under roof. 80 to 100 antique and collectible cars for sale at all times. Appraisals. Buy, Sell, Trade and Consign. Price range $5000 through a quarter of a million dollars. Car model years 1900 through 1975.

Williams Contemporary Classic Cars: Thomas P. Williams, President, 4140 South Lapeer, Lake Orion, MI 48057. Telephone 313-373-2500, 9:00 a.m.-5:00 p.m. Williams Contemporary Classic Cars - AUTOFINDER - If you're buying or selling a collector car . . . let AUTOFINDER do the work for you. Our auction company has built a nationwide, computerized network of active buyers and sellers. Save time and money. For information contact - AUTOFINDER, 4140 Lapeer, Pontiac, MI 48035, 313-373-2500.

Kermit H. Wilson & Co.: Kermit H. and LaVonne E. Wilson, P.O. Box 1169, Minneapolis, MN 55440. Telephone 612-941-1700, outside Minnesota 800-328-6138. 8 a.m. to 4:30 p.m. Specializing in reconditioned collector cars, primarily Lincoln-Ford products of Arizona origin. Arizona phone: (602) 837-3243.

Wiseman Motor Co., Inc.: Bill Wiseman, P.O. Box 848, Marion, N.C. 28752. Telephone 704-724-9313. Hours by appointment only. Buy, sell and trade antique and special interest cars.

Bill Ziegenbein: 23375 Dequindre, Hazel Park, Mich., 48030. Telephone 313-548-8911. Offers a selection of late model limos, luxury, and sports cars for sale.

HUBCAPS & WHEELCOVERS

Agape Auto: Gordeon W. Secrest, 2825 Selzer, Evansville, IN 47712. Telephone 812-423-7332, 9 a.m to 5 p.m. Wheelcovers and hubcaps 1949 thru 1980; fender skirts for 1935 thru 1972.

California Classic Chevy Parts: See listing under Parts Suppliers.

Hub Cap Annie (Jacksonville, Florida): Tom Brolliar, Save 40-70% on new & used hub cars. Buy 1, 2, 3 or 4. Big stock of late model original equipment, plain, deluxe & locking wire wheel covers for U.S. & import cars & trucks. Dualie wheel liners. Use MasterCard or VISA & your order goes out immediately by U.P.S. Telphone 1-800-624-7179 & 1-800-824-9712 in Florida, 6905 Atlantic Blvd., Jax, FL 32211, M-F 9-5:00 & Sat. 10-2.

Radios & Wheelcovers: See listing under Radio Repair.

Wheelcovers - Robinson's Auto Sales: Charles V. Robinson, 200 New York Ave., New Castle, IN 47362. Telephone 317-529-7603, Mon.-Fri. 8:00 a.m.-6 p.m., Sat. 8:00 a.m.-4:00 p.m. Late 40s to 86 wheel covers, hub cap sets, misc. NOS & used auto parts.

INSURANCE

American Collectors Insurance: P.O. Box 8343, 385 N. Kings Hwy., Cherry Hill, NJ 08034. Telephone 800-257-5758, in New Jersey 609-779-7212. Collector car insurance.

Alan M. Blay - Collector Car Insurance: Alan M. Blay, 2204 Jerusalem Ave., P.O. Box 206, Merrick, NY 11566. Telephone 516-223-4264, 800-223-4264, 9 a.m.-7 p.m. eastern time. Free comparison of collector car programs to find the one that suits your situation the best. Insurance for all types of collector and special interest cars, including antiques, corvettes, sports, street rods & replicars. In NY, NJ, PA, CT only.

James A. Grundy Agency Inc.: 145 Willow Grove Ave., P.O. Box 68, Glenside, PA 19038. Telephone 215-887-8100, 9 a.m.-4:30 p.m. Insurance program for collector vehicles.

K&K Classic Insurance Agency: 1615 Vance Ave., Ft. Wayne, IN 46801. Telephone 1-800-423-5548, Indiana residents 1-800-552-1976. Specializing in classic and antique auto insurance.

New England Autosport Associates See listing under Leasing.

J. C. Taylor Antique Auto Insurance Agency, Inc.: 320 South 69th Street, Upper Darby, Pa. 19082. Telephone 800-345-8290, in Pennsylvania 215-853-1300. Insurance for antique and classic autos.

LEASING

Esprit Leasing, Inc.: Bill Towart, 8 Chichester Rd., Huntington Station, N.Y. 11746. Telephone 516-673-3100, 9 a.m. to 5 p.m. Automobile leasing for all makes and models of cars, new and used, classics and collectibles. Financing available.

New England Autosport Associates: See listing Auctioneers & Appraisers.

LITERATURE

Accelerated Trends: 1711 Corinthian, Suite 323, Newport Beach, Calif. 92660. Tax consultants, authors of *Tax Guide for Automotive Collectors and Restorers*, also *Tax Guide for Racers*.

Applegate and Applegate: Shelby C. Applegate, Box 1, Annville, PA 17003. Telephone 717-964-2350, 9 a.m. to 5 p.m. EST, Monday thru Friday. Automotive sales literature, owners manuals, photographs, paint charts, stock certificates, American and foreign, cars and trucks.

Arnold-Porter Publishing Co.: Box 646, Keego Harbor, Mich. 48033. Book publisher.

Auto Ads+: 1501 Franklin St., Little Chute, WI 54140. Telephone 414/788-9232 evenings. AUTO ADS+: A brand new name for an established literature dealer with 19 years of serving the needs of auto enthusiasts worldwide. Auto Ads+ has magazine ads for cars & trucks & dozens of other product lines & auto dealer literature & road tests. An SSAE brings prompt response.

Auto Book Center: 48 Appleton Rd., Auburn, MA 01501. Telephone 617-832-3081, 9-6. Mail & phone only. Factory manuals for many U.S. & foreign cars. Shop, service, parts, owners manuals. Many are original, rest are top quality reprints of factory manuals. Send large SASE for catalog.

Automotive Emporium: Frederick Z. Tycher, 100F Turtle Creek Village, Dallas, Tex. 75219. Telephone 214-521-1930, 10 a.m. to 6 p.m., Monday through Saturday. Specializing in new books, original literature, art gallery, memorabilia, 1/43 miniatures, gifts, bronze sculptures and modern driving apparel.

Automotive Information Clearinghouse: Box 1746, La Mesa, Calif. 92041. Telephone 619-447-7200, 7 a.m. to 10 p.m. PST everyday. Publishes automotive survival figure guides and computer assisted value and appreciation figures. Distributor of Hollander interchange manuals 1926 to present.

Automotive Obsolete: See listing under Parts Suppliers.

Automobile Quarterly Publications: 245 West Main St., Kutztown, Pa. 19530. Publishers of *Automobile Quarterly* and automotive books.

Aztex Corporation: President: W. R. Haessner, P.O. Box 50046, Tucson, AZ 85703. Telephone 602-882-4656, 8:30-4:30 M-F. Books - transportation and how-to-do-it subjects. Send large SASE for current list.

Bassett's Jaguar: See listing under Parts Suppliers.

Bitz and Frost: P.O. Box 2010, 788 Commerce St., Sinking Spring, PA 19608. Telephone 215-678-7733, 8-5 p.m. Publishers & distributors of books, posters & automotive related material. Also owners & shop manuals.

Michael Bruce Associates, Inc.: Michael B. Antonick, P.O. Box 396, Powell, OH 43065. Telephone 614-965-4859. 9 a.m. to 5 p.m. Automotive book publisher specializing in Corvettes and Camaros. Titles include Corvette Black Book; Camaro White Book; Best of the Corvette Restorer; Secrets of the Showcars; Secrets of Auto Photography; Corvette! America's Only; Corvette! Sportscar of America; Corvette Restoration: State of the Art. Wholesale and retail.

Francis Burley: Rt. 7, P.O. Box 1281, Moultrie, GA 31768. Telephone 912-985-6860. Shop manuals, parts catalogs, owner's manuals, promo models, also have a full line of Chrysler parts.

Catalog Creations: 1654 Mardon Drive, Dayton, OH 45432. Telephone 513-429-5642, 9 a.m. to 5 p.m., Monday thru Friday. We provide businesses in the special interest auto field with cost effective quality catalogs. Typesetting, photography, printing, artwork & design, etc.

Chewning's Auto Literature, Ltd.: Carlton L. Chewning, P.O. Box 727, 123 N. Main Street, Broadway, VA 22815. Telephone 703-896-6838, Monday thru Friday 9:00 till 5:00, Saturday 9:00 till 12:00 noon. We have the largest in stock inventory of shop manuals, owners manuals, sales catalogs and part books. Send a SASE stating year and model for a complete computer listing of what I have. We accept VISA & MasterCard & COD orders. I also buy literature.

Classic Motorbooks: T. Warth, P.O. Box 1, Osceola, WI 54020. Telephone 800-826-6600, 24 hr./day. We carry over 7,000 different titles on everything for the auto enthusiast. We feature books on antiques, classics, collectables, restoration and much much more. Our 152 page catalog is sure to have just what you've been looking for.

Cobweb Collectibles: See listing under Automobilia.

Crank'en Hope Publications: Doris & Dave Cummings, Jr., 461 Sloan Alley, Blairsville, Pa. 15717. Telephone 412-459-8853. Specializing in originals and reprints of shop manuals, owner manuals, parts books, sales literature and hardbacks, at discount prices.

Crestline Publishing: 1251 North Jefferson Ave., Sarasota, Fla. 33577. Automotive book publisher.

Davis Antique Auto Literature: Paul & Gladys Davis, 1740 S.E. 17th La., Silver Springs, FL 32688. Telephone 904-625-3555, anytime. Automobile sales literature 1909-1987, owners manuals, magazine ads, rare automotive hardback books, Antique Auto, Vintage Ford, MAFCA & Mod. A Restorers club magazines, Road & Track, Car & Driver & other magazines.

The Discount Book Company: P.O. Box 1529, Ross, CA 94957. Telephone 800-348-2665. Carry over 1600 different automotive books. Prices are generally discounted at least 15%.

John Dragich Discount Auto Literature: 1500 93rd Lane N.E., Minneapolis, MN 55434. Minnesota callers please use 612-786-3925, Toll-free 1-800-328-8484. For immediate quotes on shop manuals - owners manuals - parts books. Most orders shipped within 24 hours. American Express, Visa, MasterCard, COD's accepted.

Tom W. Dunaway, Jr.: See listing under Parts Suppliers.

The Evergreen Press: Box 1711, Oceanside, Calif. 92054. Order line 619-757-5976. Publisher of the Ford Road series and the Chevy Chase series.

The Foner Co.: P.O. Box 505, Lake Jem, Fla. 32745. Publisher of *Tax Savings on Automobiles.* Authoritative book on all of the tax saving techniques available to collectors and investors in antique and collector automobiles.

Dave Graham: See listing under Parts Suppliers.

Highland Enterprises: Box 7000, Dallas, Tex. 75209. Telephone 214-358-3456, 9 a.m. to 5 p.m. Publishes automobile books.

Hollander Publishing Co.: P.O. Box 9405, Minneapolis, Minn. 55440. Publishers of parts interchange manuals.

Carl Hungness Publishing: Carl Hungness, Publisher Indianapolis 500 Yearbook, P.O. Box 24308-CP88, Speedway, IN 46224. Telephone 317-244-4792, M-F 9-3. Our speed reading catalog contains the world's largest selection of auto racing books and videos. Please enclose $1 for postage.

International Directory of Automotive Literature Collectors: John Lloyd, 29 Froelich Ave., Mountville, PA 17554. Telephone 717-285-4647. Since 1968 the directory has helped hundreds in over two dozen countries buy, sell or trade literature and automobilia. $5 includes your listing and a copy. 1987 edition entries must be in by Nov. 1986.

Dan Kirchner: 404 N. Franklin, Dearborn, MI 48128. Telephone 313-277-7187, 6-9 p.m. EST. Selling shop manuals, owner manual, sales catalog, etc. Send SASE with wants, also always buying.

Lamm-Morada Publishing Co., Inc.: Michael Lamm, Box 7607-CP, Stockton, CA 95207. Telephone 209-931-1056. 9:00 to 5:00 PST. We publish hardcover books about Camaros, Corvettes, and Firebirds. Free catalogue available on request.

License Plate Data: Robert Gilbert, 1446 N. Martel, Unit 3, Los Angeles, Calif. 90046. *License Plate Data* covers the data, research and history of U.S. license plates from their beginning (1903) to the present. Published a book in color on license plates, 1928-1931 for U.S. and Canada.

Jere V. Longrie: 3651 Hwy. 38, Grand Rapids, Minn. 55744. Specializing in Pontiac, Chevrolet and other GM dealer albums, sales literature, parts books, shop manuals, etc. Also handles Pontiac and Chevrolet NOS, used and repro parts.

Louisville Literature: Box 32262-CP, Louisville, KY 40232-2262. Mail order service - original sales literature on most all American made cars and trucks. Send SASE with needs for computer print out listing.

Miniature Cars: See listing under Automobilia.

Ken McGee: 232 Britannia Rd. W., Goderich, Ont., Canada N7A 2B9. Telephone 519-524-8391, 9-5. Shop, owners and parts manuals, sales brochures. North America only. Lots of real old obsolete make owners manuals - all reasonable. Send SASE with your wants. Also have many 20's to 50's data and facts books, mostly for GM products.

Walter Miller: 6710 Brooklawn Pkwy., Syracuse, NY 13211. Telephone 315-432-8282. Automobile sales catalogs and manuals for all makes of cars, domestic and foreign from earliest time right up to the present.

Obsolete Chevrolet Parts Co., Inc.: See listing under Parts Suppliers.

Obsolete Ford Parts Co., Inc.: See listing under Parts Suppliers.

Glen Pancoma: 1205 Melrose Way, Vista, Calif. 92083. Sales catalogs, owners & shop manuals & misc. Also magazine ads. Trades made on parts for 1929 & 1949 Chevy, 1952 Plymouth suburban wagon, or any literature I don't have. Satisfaction guaranteed.

Performance Listing: Thomas S. Von Drashek, P.O. Box 2708, Washington, D.C. 20013. Telephone 703-548-5597. Mail order. 100 page book listing. 1,155 wholesalers to open your own shop with catalogs and decals free from. $11.95 guaranteed or money back. Also 40 pages of inside tips on retail auto parts sales and shop set-up.

Paul I. Politis Automotive Literature: Paul I. Politis, Box 335, HCR 75, McConnellisburg, PA 17233. Telephone 717-987-3702. (Best times, Mondays, Tuesdays, Wednesdays, 6:30 a.m. to 9 p.m.) We maintain a huge, constantly changing inventory of original and reproduction shop and owner manuals, paint chips, showroom literature, postcards, press photos and miscellaneous, automotive paper for U.S. and import cars and trucks. Reasonable prices. Mail order and swap meets. Also active buyers. Serving the hobby since 1974; full-time since 1983.

Post Publications: Dan R. Post, Box 150, Arcadia, CA 91006. Telephone 818-446-5000, 9-5. Under substyles Post-Era Books and Post Motor Books firm specializes in publication of standard archival and service manual references for the collector or enthusiast associated with antique and special interest cars and early aircraft. Rare collector interests like pioneer typewriters, vintage slot machines and classic comic strip creators are also covered.

Professional Accounting Offices: Don Walden, 18021 Sky Park Circle, Suite J, Irvine, CA 92714. Telephone 714-786-3066, 8-5 M-F. Publishers of the "Tax Guide for Automotive Collectors and Restorers," anyone involved with automobiles can save $1,000's annually $19.95 ppd.

Pro West: C Gayle Warnock, 7355 East Citrus Way, Scottsdale, AZ 85253. Communication services and publisher of complete reference book on Edsel, the car, its management and what went wrong: "The Edsel Affair."

Quicksilver Communications, Inc.: Martyn L. Schorr, President, 167 Terrace St., Haworth, NJ 07641. Telephone 201-384-1910, 9 a.m. to 5 p.m. Publisher of marque series enthusiast books - Quicksilver Supercar Series. Retail and wholesale distribution, all popular makes, 25 titles.

David N. Rosen: 364 Tompkins St., Cortland, NY 13045. Telephone 607-753-6235. 9:00 to 9:00 Mon.-Sat. Lucas Parts Identification and Interchange Manuals. These fine manuals provide correct factory part numbers, give multiple breakdowns and interchanges for all British automobiles. Why pay Aston Martin prices when Hillman parts are identical? Save time and money locating those hard to find parts.

Wayne Rowe - Classic Cars & Parts: See listing under Parts Suppliers.

Specialty Auto Prints: See listing under Miscellaneous.

Standard Auto Parts: See list under Parts Suppliers.

Sueeds Enterprises: Ed Booker, Rt. 1, Box 212A, Pauls Valley, OK 73075. Telephone 405-665-2518, 10 a.m. to 6 p.m. Mail order 228 page book covering 56 Chevrolet. $10.00 ea. postpaid.

Paul Wiesman: 48 Appleton Rd., Auburn, MA 01501. Telephone 617-832-3081, 9-6. Original sales, shop, owners manuals and literature for sale. Send large SASE for list.

Bill White: 2443 Mt. Carmel Ave., Glenside, PA 19038. Telephone 215-887-4791. Automobile literature: sales catalogs, owners manuals, shop manuals, magazines, NADA, Red books, etc.

John W. Wimble: 1407 Stoneycreek Dr., Richmond, VA 23233. Telephone 804-740-0652, before 9 p.m. Postwar sales literature - comprehensive list with over 10,000 selections available. Five loose stamps appreciated, but not necessary. Prompt, friendly service, low prices, satisfaction guaranteed. Serving the hobby since 1977.

MISCELLANEOUS

Aero Locksmith, Inc.: Roger Beebe, P.O. Box 16434, Memphis, TN 38186-0434. Telephone 901-398-8708, 8-5 Mon.-Sat. Keys fit to original or replacement locks on foreign or domestic autos. Locks changed (re-keyed) to new keys or set to match existing keys. Locks repaired, broken keys removed and duplicated.

Muneef Alwan Co.: Muneef Alwan, P.O.B. 862, Meadow Vista, CA 95722. Telephone 916-637-4236. Antique car wall clocks and decorative wall plaques. Wall clocks available: Model A, T, 1937, '38, '39, '40 Fords and 1956 Corvette. All sculptured in 3-D with gold hands, numerals and solid oak frames 10½" x 10½". Fitted with precision quarts movements. Also have black walnut wall plaques w/goldplate medallions of Mustang, Model A, '50 Ford.

American Pie: Janet Volat, P.O. Box 66455, Los Angeles, CA 90066. Telephone 213-391-4088, 8 a.m.-6 p.m. Tues.-Fri. All your favorite 45rpm oldies can be delivered directly to you by American Pie. Our huge catalog lists thousands of smash singles from the 1940's to today's hit records. Pop, classic rock, R&B, country and jazz hits are included. Our service is prompt and courteous. Please send $2.00 for comprehensive catalog.

Anderson's: Elmer Anderson, 2527 D West, 237th Street, Torrance, CA 90505. Telephone 213-530-6744, 9 a.m. to 5 p.m., Monday thru Saturday. Car door monograms. Die cut and prespaced for immediate fool-proof installation. Cost for set of two three-initial monograms in either block or script lettering is $9.50 PPD. Unconditionally guaranteed.

Anderson's: Box 7, Houtzdale, Pa. 16651. Telephone 814-378-8571. Auto emblem caps and crest. Send for free catalog.

Antique Classic Limousine Service: Jim Schild, 933 Strodtman Rd., St. Louis, MO 63138. Telephone 314-355-3609. Antique classic offers a 1929 Cadillac Town car, 1931 Cadillac, 1940 Packard and 1960 Cadillac Limousines for the finest in specialty limousine service while in St. Louis.

Automotive Information Clearinghouse: P.O. Box 1746, La Mesa, CA 92041. Telephone 619-447-7200, 7 a.m.- 10 p.m. 7 days a week. Suppliers of the "How Many Are Left?" services. Verify the existence of every year/make/model of U.S. automobile, 1930 to 1980.

Auto Upholstery Institute: 2118 S. Grand, Santa Ana, CA 92705. Get started making big $$$ in auto upholstery. Write for free information today.

Auto World Models: See listing under Automobilia.

Bills Lock Shop: Bill Walker, 3605 Robin Rd., Toledo, OH 43623. Telephone 419-475-0027, eve's and weekends. Locks and keys for 95% of all cars, some Script, Hurd, GM, Briggs & Stratton, Yale from $1.50 and up. Send SSAE with needs.

Car Tronics Inc.: Guy Stuart: P.O. Box 1077, Owosso, MI 48867. Telephone 800-426-6832, 24 hours. Auto accessories, performance timers, radar detectors, car alarms, cruise controls, trip computers, etc. at discount prices.

Warren C. Christensen: See listing under Parts Suppliers.

CompuHeat Inc.: 1625 F. Sycamore Ave., Bohemia, NY 11716. Telephone 516-563-1080, 8 a.m.-5:30 p.m. Alternate fuel heating systems for business and home. Build it yourself engine oil and wood heaters in kit form, no fabricating or welding anything. Clean in less than 2 minutes, heat up to 6,000 sq. ft. as low as $98.00.

Mike Cornwell, Commercial Art: Mike Cornwell, 14 Owl Creek Rd., Fisher, Ill. 61843. Telephone 217-897-6459. 6 p.m. to 10 p.m. Automotive Art, prints of classic Chevrolets and Corvettes

E. Gene Dawes: 3209 Erie Dr., Orchard Lake, MI 48033. Plans, with directions, for building a 28' x 34' garage for up to 8 cars. Also plans for building your own car hauling trailer. SASE for more information.

Donovan Uniform Co.: 171 Parkhouse, Dallas, Tex. 75207. Telephone 214-741-3971, 8 a.m. to 5 p.m., Monday through Friday. Dusters, caps, goggles for men and ladies.

Foilers: Monique Industries Inc., 6317 Capricorn Ave., Agoura Hills, CA 91301. Telephone 818-889-3374, 8 a.m.-5 p.m. mail order only. Mon-Fri 8 to 5. Mfgr of FOILERS for 1970-86 Firebird, Camaro, Trans-Am and Z-28 cars. Auto accessories for foreign and domestic cars, including louvers, masks, car covers, car trays, headlight covers, FOILERS and other accessories. Catalog, send 50 cents or 2/22¢ stamps.

Gee Gee Studios, Inc.: See listing under Automobilia.

Hagstrom's Sales: Wayne Hampton, 2 Dunwoody Park, Atlanta, GA 30338. Telephone 404-393-0363. 8:30 a.m. to 5:00 p.m. Miniature classic cars for up to 1 adult and 1 child: Model T's, '75 Corvette, '32 Ford Roadster. Great birthday gifts!

William F. Harrah Automobile Museum: 970 Glendale Avenue, Sparks, NV 89431. Telephone 702-355-3500, 9:30 a.m.-5:30 p.m. Hundreds of antique, classic, vintage and special interest automobiles displayed in the museum, including fashions of bygone eras, a research library, snack bar and gift shop.

Imperial Palace Hotel & Casino: Ralph Engelstad, 3535 Las Vegas Blvd. So., Las Vegas, NV 89109. Telephone 702-731-3311, 9:30 a.m.-11:30 p.m. daily. The Imperial Palace Auto Collection has over 200 antique, classic and special-interest autos on display daily in a plus, gallery-like setting on the fifth floor of the hotel's parking facility from 9:30 a.m. to 11:30 p.m. Included in the collection are automobiles once owned by entertainers, political figures and famous people.

MISCELLANEOUS

International Society for Vehicle Preservation: Ex. Dir. Walter R. Haessner, 1126 N6 Ave., P.O. Box 50046, Tucson, AZ 85703. Telephone 602-622-2201, 8:30-4:30 M-F. Dedicated to restoration and preservation of self-propelled vehicles. Magazine with how-to, history, resource articles, news bulletins, actively opposing EPA in lead phase out. Museum & library collections in progress. Educational, 501(c) 3 organizations. Dues $15.00 annually, donations tax deductible. Send large SASE for brochure.

Charles Kacsur/Graphics: See listing under Automobilia.

The Key Shop-Locksmith: Wayne Finney, 144 Crescent Dr., Akron, OH 44301. Telephone 216-724-3822, 9 a.m. to 9 p.m. N.O.S. keys and locks for modern, classics and antique autos. Locks repaired, key made by code or duplicated. Codes changed. Complete locksmith service.

Knoxgun International: Loren Peterson, 301 N. Cedar St., Dept.CCA, Abington, IL 61410. Telephone 309-462-3248. Digital watch sales. Auto insignia, stainless steel. Satisfaction guaranteed. Dealers and clubs ask for low rate sheet. Many styles, Corvette, Mustang, Studebaker (over 150 styles).

Kozak Auto Drywash, Inc.: President Edward R. Harding, 6 S. Lyon St./P.O. Box 910, Batavia, NY 14020. Telephone 716-343-8111, M-F 8:30 a.m.-4:30 p.m. Manufacturing since 1926, a line of Auto Drywash cleaning and polishing cloths for fine automobiles. Kozak cloths are the choice of thousands of antique car owners, funeral directors, auto museums and discriminate car owners for safely keeping their cars always looking showroom clean and shiny. Write for free catalog with these and many other fine car and home car products.

Langston-Smith Company: Hoover Langston, Jr. and David Smith, 5221 Central Avenue, Unit 6, Richmond, CA 94804. Telephone 415-528-0341, 8 a.m.-5 p.m. Distributor-Sunshield Dashcovers. Dashcovers are made of a soft fade-resistant velour developed by DuPont, and are custom made with your car's logo. Each cover is tailored to protect your entire dash and steering wheel plus conceals audio equipment and stays in place without hooks or fasteners. Available for import and domestic cars, trucks & vans.

P. Lehmann Co.: Paul Lehmann, 2041 Yarnall Rd. Pottstown, Pa. 19464. Telephone 215-326-8928, 9 a.m. to 6 p.m. Handcrafted walnut and oak wall and desk clocks with solid brass face and car logo plates.

License Plate Restorations: A. V. Polio, 746 N. Greenbrier Dr., Orange, Conn. 06477. Telephone 203-795-6434, 9 a.m. to 5 p.m. Professional restoration of antique license plates, political tags, city tags. 16 years servicing the hobby-collectors and commercial auto restoration shops. USA and overseas.

The Louver Press: Kurt McCormick, 238 S. Old Orchard, Webster Groves, MO 63119. Telephone 314-962-7981, evenings and weekends. Louvers punched in hoods and other sheet metal. Careful work, low prices.

Milan Convertibles, Inc.: P.O. Box 661, Fillmore, CA 93015. Telephone 805-584-3409, 7 a.m. to 5:30 p.m., Monday thru Saturday. Convertible conversions on '79 Cadillac Seville. '79-'84 Cadillac Eldorado, '79-'84 Mustang, and many others. Two factory locations, California and New York.

Miniature Cars: Eric Waiter, Box 221, Bernardsville, N.J. 07924. Telephone 201-267-5612, 8 a.m. to 8 p.m. EST. Over 3500 different scale model autos. Catalogs $2. Also US distributor for British magazines *Classic & Sportscar, Motor Sports, Model Auto Review* and *Modeller's World.*

Model Car Collectables: P.O. Box 19337, Denver, CO 80219. Specializing in 1/24 and 1/43 scale new diecast model cars, posters and caps.

Barry D. Mueller: R.D. 1, Box 201-B, Washington, NJ 07882. Telephone 201-689-4236. Business cards custom printed for the car dealer or collector. Our own original designs. Order as few as 100. Send $1.00 for samples and price list.

Mustang Parts Corral of Texas: See listing under Parts Suppliers.

Narcon Imports, Inc.: Stanley K. Narwid, Pres., 6 Madison Ave., Kearny, N.J. 07032. Telephone 201-998-2994, after 6 p.m. International car badges, badge bars, badge bar clips and collector badges.

National Corvette Owners' Assn.: Joseph R. Salta, Pres., 900 S. Washington St., Falls Church, VA 22046. Telephone 703-533-7222, 9-5. Membership 14,000. Dues $28 per year. Publishes monthly newsletter. Recognizes 1953 to present Corvettes only. Purpose is to bring Corvette owners together to qualify for group benefits.

NOB Industries: A. Seleznov, P.O. Box 43444, Tucson, AZ 85733. Telephone 602-887-1470. Manufacture and distribute accessories for radar detectors. Products include a mount with suction cups that adheres to the windshield, coil cords, power cords, dual outlet adaptors, plug adaptors, and hook and loop.

Mary-Don Noska: 133 Juniper, West Covina, Calif. 91791. Telephone 818-966-0150. Fender protectors of all kinds. Special dealer prices in quantity lots of 50 or more.

Jim Osborn Reproductions, Inc.: 3070-A Briarcliff Rd., N.E., Atlanta, Ga. 30329. Telephone 404-325-8444. Offers restoration decals for a wide variety of makes and models, plus shop manuals, owner's manuals, etc. All new catalog available at $2.00.

Parts Duplicators: 7133 Newton St., Westminster, CO 80030. Telephone 303-428-7181, 8 a.m. to 5:30 p.m. weekdays. Wholesale manufacturer of plastic emblems and chrome ornaments.

Polishing Systems: Butch Caiazza, 1808 W. Washington St., New Castle, PA 16101. Telephone 412-658-2832, 9 a.m. to 5 p.m. Machines and chemicals for car cleaning and waxing.

Pop Top Mini: Ed Caffrey, 31200 La Baya Drive, Suite 303, Westlake Village, CA 91362. Telephone 818-707-0505, 8-5, M-F. Pop Top Your Mini! Enjoy the best of both worlds - a truck and a sports car. Your pop top kit comes ready to install. Don't worry about matching colors. Your own top becomes the pop top. Warranty and instructions included.

POR-15: See listing under Upholstery.

Professional Accounting Offices: 18021 Skypark Circle, Suite J, Irvine, CA 92714. Tax consultant firm, authors of the *Tax Guide for Automotive Collector and Restorer.*

Relaxo-Bak Inc.: 319 E. California, P.O. Box 812, Gainesville, TX 76240. Telephone 1-800-527-5496 or 1-817-665-6601, 9 a.m. to 5 p.m. (DST). Relaxo-Bak is a thin form-fitting auxiliary seat for the relief of lower back pain.

Seelig's Custom Finishes: 10456 Santa Monica Blvd., Los Angeles, Calif. 90025. Telephone 213-475-1111. Specializes in custom finishes. Sixty colors of pearl available. Gold leaf and pinstriping supplies. Catalog available at $2, $3 outside U.S.

James D. Sheridan: P.O. Box 468, Poughkeepsie, NY 12602. Telephone 914-462-5807. Fire extinguishers. Hand held, remotes, and automatics. Dry chemicals and halons. Red or chrome.

Specialty Autoprints: Michael Kaufman, 705 Westmoreland Rd., Charleston, WV 25302. Telephone 1-304-344-5580, 11:30 a.m. to 3:30 p.m. Muscle car posters and original design t-shirts.

Standard Auto Parts: See listing under Parts Suppliers.

Swain Tech Coatings: Daniel B. Swain, 35 Main St., Scottsville, NY 14546. Telephone 716-889-2786, 7-5. Coatings automotive, metal, ceramic, teflon etc. coatings, rebuild crankshafts and worn parts with metal, steel, stainless, bronze, copper etc. Thermal barrier coatings for pistons, heads, exhaust systems. Corrosion coating. Rebuilding of worn parts.

Tamara, Ltd.: 21 Holden St., Providence, R.I. 02908. Telephone 401-274-4736, 9 a.m. to 5 p.m. Car badges, belt buckles, keytags and medallions.

Terco Supply: Ted Robinson, P.O. Box 1164, Pleasanton, CA 94566. Telephone 415-462-6865, 24 hrs. Plastic bags for storage of parts and supplies, tools, Dayton equipment, air compressors, office supplies and printing.

Total Filter Systems: Daniel Grasso, 1175 Harvard Road, Waldorf, MD 20601-9218. Telephone 301-645-3625, after 3 p.m. weekdays - mail order only. Total Filter Systems handles the full line of Frantz filters, the "toilet paper" filters for oil, fuel, and transmissions including marine oil units. These partial flow filters including the fuel filters filter out all contaminates for 100% clean fluid guaranteed or your money back. Send 50¢ for brochure.

T.S.A.: Ernest L. Howell, P.O. Box 835092, Douglasville, GA 30135. Telephone 404-489-1860. The shirt-pocket size FILLER FINDER powered by a replaceable 9 volt battery, features a sophisticated electronic circuit capable of detecting plastic filler or lead as little as 1/16" thick. This product is designed to assist the car enthusiast by accurately locating and measuring the amount of plastic filler used in body repair. Its use is much quicker and more accurate than any other previously used method.

Unique 'N Useful Products, Inc.: Charles Robbins, P.O. Box 1055, Des Plaines, IL 60017. Telephone 312-699-1335. 9:00 to 5:00. KAR KRASH KIT© Vehicle Accident Recording and Reporting Information System. The Kit contains necessary items and forms to logically cope with a "fender bender" or a "disabled" vehicle. Further information on request.

VACO, Inc.: Floyd Andrus, P.O. Box 6, Florence, MA 01060. Telephone 413-586-0978, 10-6. Upper cylinder lubricators help pre-'75 car owners reduce engine wear from unleaded gasoline. Manufactured for internal combustion engines, easy-to-install unit is designed to supply constantly metered, finely dispersed oil vapor-spray to engine's critical heat/wear friction zone where high temperatures cause wear and damage to parts.

Vintage Varieties: 240 Greenridge, Grand Rapids, MI 49504. Telephone 616-784-6640, Evenings. Posters, reprints of old pictures.

West Star Enterprises, Inc.: John Duck, 9420 Reseda Blvd. #293, Northridge, CA 91324. Telephone 818-365-9824, 12 to 8 p.m. Valve Guard - lead replacement, power plus - octane booster, all vehicle wash - super car wash. Send $3 for complete product catalogue flier, do-it-yourself tune-up spec and maint guide, inside door sticker-refundable on 1st order.

Wilson Enterprises: Richard and Billie Wilson, 8703 Lansdowne Dr., Stockton, CA 95210. Telephone 209-474-8017, 8:30 a.m. to 5:30 p.m. Personalized license frames - we print anything. Also large selection of decorative auto tags.

Wirth & Associates Advertising: 1654 Mardon Drive, Dayton, OH 45432. Telephone 513-429-5642. 8 a.m. to 5 p.m., Monday thru Friday. Marketing and advertising services especially for business and events in the collector car world. Offering ad design and placement, display work, packaging, catalog printing and sales increases.

X-EL Products: P.O. Box 4666, Detroit, Mich. 48234. Assembled promotional cars. Price list, $1.00.

PAINT STRIPPERS RUST REMOVERS

Ace Enterprises, Inc.: 820 N.W. 144th St., Miami, Fla. 33168. Telephone 1-800-327-5721, 8 a.m. to 5 p.m. "Sand-All" sand blasters. Siphon or pressure sand blasters, blasting cabinets, suction type blasters and all related accessories.

Dura Finish of San Mateo: 726 S. Amphlett Blvd., San Mateo, CA 94402. Chemical stripping, derusting and metal prep of auto body parts, fenders, door, hoods, wheels, etc.

East Coast Auto/Stripping: John, Joe, Larry Arena Bros., 209-211 E. Main St., Norristown, Pa. 19401. Telephone 215-277-7538, Monday to Friday, 9 a.m. to 5 p.m., and Saturday, 9 a.m. to 12 noon. Paint stripping and rust removal from cars, parts and complete bodies. Also strip, refinish furniture.

The Eastwood Co.: See listing under Tools.

Lions Automotive: See listing under Tools.

Redi Strip Co., Inc.: 11007 Forest Pl., Santa Fe Springs, Calif. 90670. Telephone 213-944-9915. Paint and rust removal by safe alkaline immersion processes. Dozens of convenient locations in U.S. and Canada.

Restoration Specialists Inc.: Robert Brostowicz, 6846 S. 112th Street, Franklin, Wisconsin 53132. Telephone 414-529-1515, 8-5 wkdays, 8-12 Sat. Paint stripping and rust removal using chemical immersion process. Tanks large enough to accomodate frames and body shells. Prompt, professional service with over ten years experience.

TIP Sandblast Equipment: Truman's, Inc., 7075 State Rt. 446, Canfield, OH 44406. Telephone 216-533-3384, 9-5:30 Mon.-Fri., 9-12 Saturday. Mfg. of pressure & siphon fed sandblasters and glass bead cabinets. Thousands of units, parts & supplies always in stock. Also specializing in sales & service of 5 h.p. compressors. Wide variety of body shop, wood working, electric and air tools. Everything in sandblasting. FREE 76 page catalog.

PARTS SUPPLIERS

A-1 Auto Wrecking: John Hazelrigg, 13818 Pacific Ave., Tacoma Wash. 98444. Telephone 206-537-3445. 9:00 a.m. to 5:00 p.m. 6 days a week. Since 1948, same location, same owner, transmission parts, new and used. Good used axles, drums, fenders, hubcaps, cylinder heads, starters, generators from 1928 and newer.

A-1 Shock Absorber Co.: Mark Lincenberg, 2241 So. Cottage Grove, Chicago, IL 60616. Telephone 312-225-0700 or 800-344-1966. Shock absorber specialists: heavy duty, extra heavy duty, loadleveler and air shocks for all vehicles. Rebuilder of lever action shocks on all American cars. Steering systems rebuilt on an R&R basis.

Agape Auto: Gordon W. Secrest, 2825 Selzer Rd., Evansville, IN 47712. Telephone 812-423-7332, 9 a.m. to 5 p.m. CST. Reproduction fender skirts for U.S. cars from 1935 thru 1970; good original wheelcovers; 1949 thru 1980.

Albers Rolls-Royce: 360 South First St., P.O. Box 222, Zionsville, Ind. 46077. Telephone 317-873-2460 and 873-2560, Monday through Friday, 8 a.m. to 4:30 p.m. Authorized Rolls-Royce dealer. Extensive stock of post-war parts. Advise needs and chassis number when ordering.

Jim Alexandro: Box 144, Maspeth, NY 11378. Telephone 212-899-0136, 7 to 10 p.m. Carburetor rebuilding service, carburetor rebuilding kits, 1916-50

Alfa Ricambi: Brad Bunch, 6644 San Fernando Rd., Glendale, CA 91201. Telephone 818-956-7933, M-F 8-5, Sat. 9-12. Over $2,000,000 inventory of 10,000 parts for Alfa Romeo along with select accessories. We also stock a large supply of parts for Lancia, Ferrari and other exotic Italian autos.

All Cadillacs of The 40's: Ed Cholakian, 12811 Foothill Blvd., Sylmar, CA 91342. Telephone 818-361-1140, 8-4:30. Specializing in 1940 and 1950 parts. Good used and reproduction parts. Service also available by appointment only.

Bill Alprin: 184 Rivervale Rd., Rivervale, NJ 07675. Telephone 201-666-3975. NOS Ford Mustang; T-Bird; Falcon; Fairlaine; Galaxie; Mercury; Cougar; Comet; Montego; Torino; Capri; Maverick; Pinto; Granada; LTD; Lincoln Mark II to VII; Continental; Van, F1-7; Bronco. 1949-1984.

A&M SoffSeal Inc.: 104 May Drive, Harrison, OH 45030. Phone 513-367-0028. Monday thru Saturday 9 a.m. to 5 p.m. Weatherstripping and rubber items for 50's, 60's and 70's Chevy, Camaro, Chevelle, Chevy II, Nova, GTO, 442-GS.

American Arrow Corp.: Don Sommer, 625 Redwood Dr., Troy, MI 48083. Telephone 313-588-0425, 8 a.m. to 11 p.m. Manufacturer of stainless steel radiator mascots, wire wheels, pilot ray lights, sportlights, Tonneau windshields, automotive art castings.

American Motor Haven: Charles Ackel, 1107 Campbell Ave., San Jose, CA 95126. Telephone 408-246-0957, 9 a.m.-5:30 p.m. & 7:30-9 p.m. Parts & service for all American motors related makes from 1949 through current. Includes Hudson, Nash, Willys, Jeep & later model Renault. Specializing in obsolete & hard to find parts.

American Mustang Parts: Nick Dressler & Andy Jarwin, 8345 Sunrise Blvd., Rancho Cordova, CA 95670. Telephone 916-635-7271, 9-6. 1964½-1970 Mustang restoration parts. Complete interiors, exterior sheet metal, rust repair panels and chrome interior & exterior accessories. One of America's oldest and largest supply stores.

Ames Performance Engineering: Steve Ames, Bonney Road, Marlborough, N.H. 03455. Telephone 603-876-4514. Open 24 hours. NOS, reproduction and factory original post-war Pontiac parts, specializing in GTO.

Antique Auto Fasteners: Nadine & Guy Close, 13426 Valna Dr., Whittier, Calif. 90602. Telephone 213-696-3307, 10 a.m. to 6 p.m. PST. Clips for canvas and chrome; molding bolts, bumper bolts and special screws; inside door handles, locking G.M. trunk handles; lock cylinder retainers; lock springs; striker plates; rubber door checks and pedal pads; assist straps and robe rail - new and old stock. Catalog $2.00.

PARTS SUPPLIERS

Antique Auto Parts: John and Richard Kuimann, 449 West Main St., Waterbury, CT 06702. Telephone 203-755-0118. 8:00 to 5:00 weekdays, 9:00 to 1:00 Sat. Mechanical parts - Chrysler Prod., Ford and GM 1930-1960.

Antique Auto Parts Cellar: Tom Hannaford, Jr., P.O. Box 3, S. Weymouth, MA 02190. Telephone 617-335-1579, 9 a.m. to 5 p.m., weekdays. We supply new old stock, new old replacement stock, and our own top quality reproductions of wearing mechanical parts for all makes from 1909 to 1965 specializing in fuel pump kits, new fuel pumps; pistons; engine valves; valve guides; valve springs; timing gears and chains; oil pumps and kits; water pumps and kits; suspension parts, gaskets and all things mechanical. We guarantee our parts and we ship promptly.

Antique Auto Stable, Inc.: Paul Zimmerman, 1501 N.W. 55 Pl., Gainesville, Fla. 32606, or P.O. Box 384, Gainesville, Fla. 32602. Telephone 904-377-7951, Monday through Friday, 8 a.m. to 6 p.m. Large inventory of new and rebuilt parts for cars and trucks, 1970 and older. Hundreds of parts, cars and trucks. Large inventory of restored and restorable cars for sale.

Antique Cycle Supply, Inc.: Cedar Springs, MI 49319. Telephone 616-636-8200. 9:00 to 5:00 EST Mon.-Fri. Harley Davidson parts, literature, accessories for all models. Government surplus and obsolete parts a speciality. $5.00 for huge catalog. Write or call.

Apple Hydraulic Motors Inc.: 610 Nostrand Avenue, Uniondale, NY 11553. Telephone 516-481-8111, Toll Free 1-800-882-7753. Knee action shock absorbers rebuilt. Delco, Armstrong, Houdaille, Buick,Chevy, Cadillac, Plymouth, Packard, Rolls/Bentley, Dodge, Olds and more. Five day turnaround. Heavy duty rebuilts also available. To ship: Wrap in plastic bag. Pack securely, Visa, MasterCard, COD orders welcome. Free catalog.

Arizona Mustang Parts: Tom Adams, 10147 Grand Ave., Suite B-6, Sun City, AZ 85351. Telephone 602-933-1777, 8 to 5. Mustang parts, Mustang sales brochure and postcards. Many obsolete parts. Evenings call 602-978-2955.

Ausley's Chevelle Parts: Roger W. Ausley, 700 Oakley St., Graham, NC 27253. Telephone 1-919-228-6701. 8:30 a.m. to 6:30 p.m. EST. We are a full-time parts supplier since 1981. We carry a complete line of new old stock parts, the latest in reproductions, and a large inventory of used parts. Send $1.00 stating year for an updated list.

Auto Hardware Specialties: RR 1 Box 12A, Sheldon, Iowa 51201. Specializes in hardware for 1929-41 GM cars; original type screws, bolts, nuts, hinge pins, bumper bolts, hose clamps, clips and more, new & reproduction. Illustrated catalog $2.00.

Auto Hardware Supply: William Slavik, 906 Broadway, Bedford, OH 44146. 10:00 a.m. to 5:00 p.m. 28-31 Model A Ford hardware, fasteners and small parts. Catalogue $1.

Automated Recycled Auto Parts and Service: William J. Zimmerman, N86 W16350 Appleton Avenue, Menomonee Falls, WI 53051. Telephone 414-251-1900, M-W-F 8:00 to 8:00, T-T 8-6:00, Sat. 8-3:00. We have a complete line of used parts, rebuilt parts, reproduction parts, includes fenders, door, rockers, etc. All your automotive parts under one roof. Also, a complete service department and body shop. We restore old cars in our shop. Also, do complete body straightening.

Automotive Obsolete: Lois & Russ Steele, 1023 East 4th Street, Santa Ana, CA 92701. Telephone 714-541-5167. Counter sales Tuesday through Saturday after 11 a.m. Mail order Monday through Saturday after 8 a.m. Parts and literature for all cars. Catalogs available $3.00 refundable with purchase. Inquiries (714) 541-5167 order line only 1-800-CARS-USA.

Auto World Motorsports: Mailcorp, Ltd., Ray Berry, Pres., 701 N. Keyser Ave., Scranton, PA 18508. Telephone: 717-344-7258. 9:00 a.m. to 5:30 p.m. Mon.-Sat. Accessories and performance parts including racing safety equipment for vintage and current sports and performance cars. 132 page catalog $3.00 pp. - $5.00 overseas.

Bassett's Jaguar: William E. Bassett, P.O. Box 145, 48 Kersey Rd., Peace Dale, R.I. 02883. Telephone 401-789-9378, 8 a.m. to 4 p.m. EST. Full restoration facility, complete interiors, wide range of parts and supplies from brakes - wood, etc., exhaust systems, wiring harnesses and more!

Baumgarten's Vintage Auto Parts: John & Joan Baumgarten, P.O. Box 305, Voorheesville, NY 12186. Telephone 518-765-3695, 10 a.m.-8 p.m. M-F, 8 a.m.-Noon Sat. (E.S.T.) Ford Model T parts & literature. New, N.O.S., used & rebuilt. Depot hack bodies. Bonar's famous floating hubs, brakes that work, fourth main bearings & ball bearing D.S. spools. We accept MasterCard & VISA. Fast UPS service including C.O.D. Catalog $1.00. Mail order only.

B&D Motors: Bob Moser, 1138 Landgraf, Cape Girardeau, MO 63701. Telephone 314-334-7310, 8 a.m.-8 p.m. Reproduction parts for 37-38-39 Chevys - we have chrome - stainless - rubber - smoothie "steel" runningboards - also, some "NOS" & "used" parts.

Beam Distributors: 231 South St., P.O. Box 524-CP, Davidson, N.C. 28036. Telephone 704-892-5205. 9 a.m. to 5 p.m., Monday through Thursday. Wholesale, retail, manufacture of Ford parts 1909-48. Specializing in Model A wood and metal Model A bodies. Serving the old car hobby since 1968.

Blaser's, Nash, Rambler, AMC Parts: 1224 4th Ave., Moline, Ill. 61265. Telephone 309-764-3571. We specialize in new old stock factory parts, for only Nash, Rambler and AMC products. We also have all kinds of Rambler service and dealer related items. Over 30 years experience as a dealer for these fine automobiles.

Blower Drive Service: 12140 Washington Blvd., Whittier, CA 90606. Super charges & components.

Bob's Antique Auto Parts: P.O. Box 1856, 7826 Forest Hills Rd., Rockford, IL 61110. Telephone 815-633-7244, 9 a.m. to 4:30 p.m. Monday thru Friday, 9 a.m. to 12 noon Saturday. Specializing in Model T Ford Parts, 1909-27. We are the largest supplier of Model T parts in the Midwest, with large quantity of new old stock parts. Catalog available $1.00.

Bob's Automobilia: Beverly Carrubba, Box 2119, Atascadero, CA 93423. Telephone 805-434-2963, 9 a.m. to 8 p.m. Monday through Saturday. The largest supplier specializing in BUICKS 1919-1953. Parts, Supplies, Rubber, Literature, Upholstery Fabric and Hardware. Reproduction, New Old Stock and Used Parts. Phone and Mail Orders promptly shipped. Our Catalog is $2 Or Free with an order.

Bob's Bird House: Bob Mench, 124 Watkins Ave., Chadds Ford, PA 19317. Telephone 215-358-3420, 7 a.m.-5:30 p.m. 58-69 T-Bird parts, cars - buy, sell, trde, service on mech. and body work.

Bob's Pontiac Parts, Inc.: Bob Antelman, P.O. Box 333-P, Simpsonville, MD 21150. Telephone 914-735-7203. N.Y. Store M-F 9:00-6:00 p.m., Sat. 9:00-12:30. G.T.O. and Firebird, Comprehensive Catalogs of restoration parts. Interiors, sheet metal patch panels, trunk floor sections, chrome emblems, weatherstrips, tri-power parts, decals, books, moldings, carpets, detailing items, suspension and mechanical parts, much more. Send $2.00 for G.T.O. or $1.00 for Firebird. Specify which catalog you want.

Bob's T-Birds: See listing under Upholstery.

Roger Bond: 303 Bank St., Attleboro, MA 02703. Telephone 617-222-3252. Call in advance. Running board side moldings for cars in the mid 1930's to 1941 - made to order. Reproduction Packard parts 1935-1941 descriptive literature upon request.

Borla East: Robert C. Auten, 600A Lincoln Blvd., Middlesex, NJ 08846. Telephone 201-469-9666, 8:30 a.m. to 4:30 p.m. Specializing in the manufature of exhaust systems for Rolls-Royce and Bentley cars. Also custom-made exhaust systems for cars of all kinds. Turbo mufflers and glasspacks available. Custom installations.

Tony D. Branda Shelby and Mustang Parts: 1434 E. Pleasant Valley Blvd., Altoona, PA 16602. Telephone 814-942-1869, 8 a.m. to 6 p.m. Shelby and Mustang parts and accessories; for restoration, emblems, stripe kits, sheet metal, fiberglass, decals, apparrel, catalog available send $3.00.

The Brassworks: 1031 S. Soderquist, Turlock, Calif. 95380. Telephone 209-668-8825. Manufacturer of authentic and correct radiators for 1910-40 Ford cars.

British Auto: Mark Voelckers, 703 Penfield Rd., Macedon, NY 14502. Telephone 716-377-1160, Monday thru Friday 8 a.m. to 5 p.m. Only English cars, 1950 to present. Austin Healey, MG, Triumph, Jaguar. Also have parts for lots of obscure cars. Unbelievable English auto parts supply.

Brock Supply: P.O. Box 1000, Tempe, AZ 85281. Telephone 602-968-2222.

Brothers Automotive: Steven Kenny, 1435A S. 38th St., St. Joseph, MO 64507. Telephone 816-364-2594, 9-6 M-F, 11-5 Sat. Cutlass/44a parts 64-72 correct # carburetors, N.O.S. sheetmetal, presewn seat upholstery kits, weatherstrips, red fender wells, wiring harnesses, carpets, bumpers, grilles, ramair parts, lenses, chassis & suspension, sway bars, hood pins, exhaust extensions, trunk paint, correct high heat blue 455 engine paint, new, used or reproduction, your satisfaction is guaranteed. MC, VISA & COD orders are accepted.

Brown Carburetor Co., Inc.: Jim Cofield, 272 W. Cottage Ave., Sandy, UT 84070. Telephone 801-566-3334, 9 a.m. to 5 p.m. The Fish Carburetor can be installed on any vehicle from a model T to a HI Grain truck, runs on 100's or organic chemicals, won't spark, knock on high compression engines, not made out of pot medal and plastic all for under $300.00. Write for free info. Box 89, Draper, UT 84020.

Buchingers: George Buchinger, P.O. Box 66114, Chicago, IL 60666. Telephone 312-678-6140 or Toll Free 1-800-435-7002, Ill. 1-800-892-8636, 8:30-5:00. New windshields, back windows and curved side glass for cars and trucks of the 1940's, 50's, 60's and 70's. Your source for hard to find auto glass. Everything new, nothing used.

Bugeye Ltd.: Don Janda, Main Street, Homestead, IA 52236. Telephone 1-319-622-3937. Specializing in hard to find restoration parts for 1958-1961 A.H. Sprite.

Buick Barn: Box 49, Weymouth Landing, Mass. 02190. Telephone 617-337-9151, Monday through Friday, 3 p.m. to 6 p.m. Buick parts, 1937-1941 and 1949-1956. Many parts and parts cars. Partial restoration services. C.O.D. orders.

The Buick Nut: Joe Krepps, 2486 Pacer Lane South, Cocoa, Fla. 32926. Telephone 305-636-8777, evenings or weekends. Buick reproductions and NOS parts sold, 1916 thru 1970.

Burchill Antique Auto Parts, Inc.: Robert C. Burchill, President, 4150 24th Avenue, Port Huron, MI 48060. Telephone 313-385-3838, Monday, Tuesday, Thursday, Friday 9 a.m. to 3 p.m., Wednesday, Saturday 9 a.m. to 12 noon. Parts and information on most American-made cars to 1960. Rebuilds and repairs clutches, vacuum tanks, temperature gauges, water pumps, oil pumps and carburetors. Custom welding on cylinder heads, engine blocks and manifolds. Catalogs available. Inquire.

Caddy Shack Cadillac: 2410 Harvard St., Sacramento, Calif. 95815. Telephone 916-921-2575, Mon.-Fri. 8 a.m.-5 p.m., Sat. 9 a.m.-3 p.m. Over 250 cars inventory for parts. New rebuilt and used mechanical and body parts. Complete restoration and repair facility. We buy and sell cars. Call us for all your Cadillac needs. We ship anywhere.

Cahill Automotive: Gary & Janice Cahill, 890 Stanford, Elyria, Ohio 44035. Telephone 216-365-0138. 8 a.m. to 6 p.m. - Monday thru Friday, 9 a.m. to 2 p.m. - Saturday. Body repair panels for domestic & foreign cars & trucks also collision parts and 1955-64 Chevrolet restoration supplies.

California Classic Chevy Parts: Ken McBridge, 13545 Sycamore Ave., San Martin, CA 95046. Telephone 408-683-2438, 9:30 to 6:00. Manufacturers - wholesale distributors and retail sales of 55 to 57 Chevy and 67 to 69 Camaro parts. We stock a full line of new and used and reproduction parts, interior, exterior, chassis, weatherstrip, manuals and more. 24 hour service on phone and mail orders. Dealer inquiries invited.

California Mustang Parts and Accessories: Bob Twist, 18435 Valley Blvd., La Puente, CA 91744. Telephone 818-964-0911, M-F 8-5, Sat. 9-3, closed Sundays. Over 6000 original Mustang parts & accessories in stock. Authentic upholstery, weatherstripping, body panels, engine & transmission parts, electrical items, decals, fashion apparel, etc. Catalog available, send $2 for postage & handling. Order parts toll free 1-800-854-1737, in California call 818-964-0911.

Camaro Country, Inc.: Jerry and Karen Buller, 14386 - 21½ Mile Road, Marshall, MI 49068. Telephone 616-781-2906, M-F 8-5, Sat. 8-1. 1967-1981 Camaro parts and accessories. We offer new, used and reproduction.

Canadian Mustang: Mike Pickering, 3142 Cedar Hill Rd., Victoria, B.C. Canada V8T 3J6. Telephone 604-385-7161. Mon.-Fri. 9 to 5. Manufacturer and distributor of 1965-73 Mustang parts. Catalog $4 (refundable on purchase). Vancouver branch at 10354 Scott Rd. Surrey (604-585-1577). Also most makes 1946-87 carpets.

Can Am Restoration Supply: 1964 W. Eleven Mile Rd., Berkley, MI 48072. Original Chevrolet interiors and parts, 1955-64, also selected 1967-69 Camaro parts.

C.A.R. Distributors: Bernard Baumann, 12375 New Holland St., Holland, MI 49423. Telephone 616-399-6783, 8:00 to 5:00 Mon.-Fri. Sat. by appointment. We are a full time Mustang and Model A parts dealer. We handle a full line of Mustang and Model A parts, with most all parts in stock. We also have thousands of used 64½ to 73 Mustang parts. We do Mustang restorations with conv. frame repair our specialty.

Carlin Mfg. & Dist. Inc.: Jack F. Carlin, 830 Fannin St., P.O. Box 3591, Beaumont, TX 77704. Telephone 409-833-9757, 8 a.m. to 4:30 p.m. Manufactor of Model T and A Ford parts (wood; sheet metal; and seat springs). We also distribute engine and chassis parts.

Dennis Carpenter Ford Reproductions: Dennis Carpenter, P.O. Box 26398, Charlotte, N.C. 28221. Telephone 704-786-8139, Monday-Friday 8:00 a.m. to 5:00 p.m. Sat. 10:00 a.m. to 1:00 p.m. Rubber parts for Ford 1932-64, T-Birds 1958-66, Falcon 1960-65. Pickup parts 1932-72. All parts Mfg. U.S.A.

CARS: Pearl St., Neshanic, NJ 08853. Telephone 201-369-3666. 8-5. CARS offers the largest selection of new, used and reproduction parts for restoring and maintaining 1936-1976 Buicks. We offer a computerized & illustrated catalog. To receive the catalog send $2 and state the year of your car.

Central Mass. Antique Auto Parts: Francis A. Delisle, 56 Franklin Rd., Fitchburg, Mass. 01420. Telephone 617-343-7817, 6 p.m. to 9 p.m. - Monday, Wednesday and Thursday. Complete line of Model A parts.

Chevelle Classics, Inc.: Dave Leonard, 16602 Burke Ln., Huntington Beach, CA 92647. Telephone 800-CHEVELLE, Info 714-841-5363, 8-5 M-F, 10-2 Sat. Comprehensive selection of original GM, Chevelle/El Camino parts. Also many parts authentically reproduced by Chevelle classics that are no longer available from G.M. Catalog free.

Chevelle World: See listing under Upholstery.

Chev's of the 40's: Ron Wade, 18409 NE 28th St., Vancouver, WA 98662. Telephone 206-892-1191, 8:30 a.m.-5:00 p.m. West Coast time. The most complete supplier in the world of 37-54 Chevrolet car and truck parts. Bringing together the very best quality part at the best price!

Chevy Craft: 3414 Quirt, Lubbock, Texas 79404. Telephone 806-747-4848. New and used parts/accessories, 1955 up Chevrolet passenger models. Includes Impala, Chevelle, Corvette and all factory hi-performance items. 400 car inventory. Show quality replating available. Open by appointment. Catalog $3. VISA/MC/COD/UPS. (No Corvair, Vega or six cylinder). V8 Chevrolet only. Our 23rd year. "Hometown of Buddy Holly."

Chevy Duty Pickup Parts: Mark Jansen, 4600 NW 52nd, Dept. CPA, Kansas City, MO 64151. Telephone 816-741-8029, 8:00 a.m.-6:00 p.m. Weatherstrip, bed parts, door parts, manuals & literature, lamps & lenses, electrical, steering, brakes, chassis parts, patch panels, glass, mirrors, etc. Complete line of parts for 1947-1966 Chevy & GMC pickups.

Chicago Camaro & Firebird Parts: 900 S. 5th Ave., Maywood, IL 60153. Telephone 312-681-2187, 10 a.m.-8 p.m. Specializing in Camaro & Firebird parts 67-69. New, reproduction, used. Sheet metal, weather stripping, glass, interiors, carpet, all types of brackets, options, conv. parts, leaf springs, lens, tachs, consoles, etc.

Chicago Vette Supply: 8260 Archer Ave., Willow Springs, IL 60480. Telephone 312-839-5671, Open Monday-Saturday. Specialists in mechanical parts for Vettes to include custom part rebuilding. Fast dependable service at a reasonable price. Full line new and reproduction parts.

Warren C. Christensen: 30 Pomeroy St., Wilbraham, Mass. 01095. Telephone 413-596-4873. Manufacturer of Model A Ford Deluxe trunk racks, side mount mirrors and antique car name rubber stamps.

Circle City Mustang: Rt. 1, Box 27, Midland City, Ala. 36350. Telephone 205-983-5450, 8 a.m. to 6 p.m. CST Monday thru Friday. Complete one-stop Mustang parts and literature marketplace.

City Motor Company: 944-6th Street, Clarkston, WA 99403. Telephone 509-758-6262, 9-5 P.S.T. Ford new original and top quality reproduction parts for 65-73 Mustang, 62-71 Fairlane, 64-67 Comet, 67-73 Cougar, 60-65 Falcon, 60-66 Galaxie, 62-66 Dagenham 4 speed transmissions.

Clark's Corvair Parts, Inc.: Calvin M. Clark, Jr. & Joan Clark, Rt. 2, Shelburne Falls, MA 01370. Telephone 413-625-9776, Mon.-Fri. 8:30 a.m. to 5:00 p.m.. Specialize in Corvair parts only, over 4500 different parts in a 400 page catalog ($4 charge) - Upholstery, manuals, gaskets, seals, engine & trans parts, suspension, trim, tools, paint, weatherstrips, chrome, door panels, carpets, body panels, technical "hot line." Mail order only.

Classic Auto Air Mfg. Co.: Al Sedita Jr. (Pres.), 2020 W. Kennedy Blvd., Tampa, FL 33606. Telephone 813-884-3681 & 251-2356, 10-6 M-F. Mail order and open shop. Manufactures air-conditioning parts and complete systems for 1949-69 Rolls-Royce & Bentley and 1965-68 Ford Mustang. Provide remanufacturing service on all under-dash units, A/C, clutches, and filter-driers. Proto type and custom systems designed.

Classic Auto Parts: Kenneth L. Johnson, 550 Industrial Drive, Carmel, IN 46032. Telephone 317-844-8154, 9 a.m. to 5 p.m. by appointment only and/or invitation only! Specializing in Cadillac, LaSalle, Pierce Arrow, Packard, and other genuine Classic Parts from 1928 thru 1941. Also Non-Classic from 1928 thru 1960.

Classic Auto Parts Unlimited: S. Batrik, 2331 Cranmore Rd., Victoria, B.C. Canada V8R 1Z5. Mercedes-Benz parts for restoration and maintenance of the 180, 190, 190SL, 220S, 220SE models, and selected newer M-B models.

Classic Auto Supply Co., Inc.: See listing under Restoration Firms.

Classic Buicks, Inc.: 4738 Murietta St., Chino, Calif. 91710. Telephone 714-591-0283. Sales, service, restoration and parts for post-war Buicks, 1946-73.

Classic Camaro: 16651 Gemini Lane, Huntington Beach, Calif. 92647. Telephone 714-894-0651. Camaro parts and accessories. Free catalog.

Classic Cars, Inc.: Robert E. Turnquist, Maple Terrace, Hibernia, NJ 07842. Telephone 201-627-1885. 7 a.m. to 5 p.m., Monday thru Friday. Manufacturer and supplier of Senior Packard parts for engine, brake system, cooling system, chassis, beauty accessories, electrical parts, rubber grommets, upholstery fabrics, cloisonne medallions refinished and many used parts.

Clermont Auto Wholesalers: Carmella Maffucci, Rd. #1, Box 699, Germantown, NY 12526. Telephone 518-537-4619. Weekdays after 8 p.m. and weekends. Sell obsolete NOS, used and reproduction parts for '49-'60 Lincoln and '49-'72 Mercury (no Comet or Cougar).

Cliff's Classic Chevrolet Parts Co.: Cliff Waldron, P.O. Box 16739, Portland, OR 97216-0739. Telephone 503-667-4329, 9-5:30 Monday-Saturday. Exclusively 55-56-57 Chevrolet Parts. Quality used, new & reproduction. Currently have over 100 parts cars. Catalog $3.50. Mirror resilvering (all makes). Triadle & hydra-vac power brake rebuilding. Satisfaction guaranteed.

The Clip Manufactory: Lewis D. Hutchison, P.O. Box 100, Moravian Falls, NC 28654. Moulding, upholstery, chassis and engine compartment clips, bolts and plates, individually or in sets, for FoMoCo, GM, MoPar, IHC, Hudson, Packard and Nash autos, 1928-1965. Small appointments for classic marques, particularly Pierce Arrow and Cunningham.

Cobra Restorers Ltd.: 3099 Carter Drive, Kennesaw, GA 30144. Telephone 404-427-0020, 9 a.m. to 5 p.m. - Monday thru Friday, 9 a.m. to 2 p.m. - Saturday. Large stock of parts & accessories for AC and replica Cobras, Shelbys & Mustangs. Restoration service for original Cobras, replica Cobras built to customer specs. Cobra engine dressup kits for Ford engines.

Coil Spring Specialties: David Pflum, 2322-N Bates Avenue, Concord, CA 94520. Telephone 415-827-1575, 8-5 p.m. M-Fri. Suspension Coil Springs, 1934-1986, all makes and models, standard and custom manufactured, truck, van, motorhomes, limousines.

Collectors Car Parts of Britain: David Griffiths, 2nd Floor, Cunard Buildings, Water Street, Liverpool L3 1ER, Great Britain. UK code 051-236-7413. Telex: 628052 24 hour service. New and reconditioned parts for British cars and commercials at lowest possible rates and shipped direct to North American customers by cheapest or quickest means dependent on customers preference. British military and jeep parts also obtained. CAR INSPECTION carried out in Britain/Europe for prospective American buyers - full report inc. color photographs supplied.

Collector's Helper: 216 Rt. 17 N., Upper Saddle River, N.J. 07458. Telephone 201-327-8904. Mon.-Fri. 9:30 to 5:00, Sat. 9:30 to 3:00. Restoration parts for Chevrolet Corvettes, stainless steel brakes, interiors, N.O.S., new, used, reproduction parts. Restoration service.

Connecticut Antique Ford Parts: 985 Middlesex Tpk., Old Saybrook, Conn. 06475. Telephone 203-388-5872. Model A Ford parts.

Continental Enterprises, Ltd.: 1673 Cary Ave., Kelowna, B.C. Canada V1X 2C1. Telephone 604-763-7727. Continental kits for most Ford and GM cars, 1949-current.

Convertible Service: Paul Terry, 5106 Valley Bl., Los Angeles, CA 90032. Telephone 213-222-9922, 8:30-5:00 Mon.-Fri. New & rebuilt convertible parts: top pump/motors, lift cylinders, hose assemblies, top latches, hydraulic window & seat cylinders, folding top frames. Mechanism service & repair. Call (213) 222-9922 or send us a 22¢ stamp and we'll send you our catalog.

Bob Cook Ford Classic Parts: Hazel, Ky. 42049-0165. The largest new and reproduced Ford products mail order parts company in the world. Catalogs charged for. 1955/72 Fords, 1958/72 T-Birds, 1958/60 Edsels, 1964/72 Mustangs, 1960/72 Lincoln & Marks.

Corvette Central: 16 Sawyer Rd., Sawyer, MI 49125. Telephone 616-426-3342, 9-6. Corvette parts for 53-82, new used and reproduction. Americas leader in Corvette parts.

Corvette Rubber Co.: Robert Stanhope, C533 N. Park, Lake City, MI. Telephone 616-839-7200, 8-5:30. We specialize in Corvette weatherstripping and related rubber products for Corvettes.

Corvette Specialties of Maryland: Brian W. Tilles, 3422 Pine Circle S., Westminster, MD 21157. Telephone 301-795-3180, 800-638-6450, 9 a.m.-8 p.m., Mon.-Fri. Now in our 11th year. New used and reproduction parts. Specializing in 53-67. Wiring harnesses, chrome, interiors, weatherstripping, clocks, gauges, etc. Restoration service for clocks, gauges, wiper motors, and instrument clusters. Toll free order line. No catalogs. Try us and compare prices. You will be plesaed that you did.

C & P Chevy Parts: 50 Schoolhouse Rd., Box 348, Kulpsville, PA 19443. Telephone 215-721-4300. 9:00 a.m. to 5:30 p.m. Mon.-Fri. Restoration supplies for 55-56-57 Chevys. Free 132 page catalog available.

Crossroads Classic Mustang: Norm Stepnick - Paul Nusbaum, 12421 Riverside Avenue, Mira Loma, CA 91752. Telephone 714-986-6789, M-F 8:00-5:00, Sat. 8:30-2:00. Crossroads sells new, used, and reproduced 1965 and up Mustang parts. Over 200 Mustangs are in our 5 acre inventory, adding more cars weekly. For those "hard-to-find" parts, we offer a free teletype-hot line locating service to locate the desired part. Toll-free ordering (800) 443-3987.

Custom Mold Dynamics, Inc.: Richard H. Miller, 1689 Woodville Pike, Loveland, OH 45140. Telephone 513-722-1404, 8 a.m. to 5:30 p.m. 1953-67 Chevrolet & Corvette, 1967-69 Firebird reproduction emblems and trim parts.

Dallas Mustang Parts: 9515 Skillman, Dallas, TX 75243. Telephone 214-349-0991, 8 a.m. to 5 p.m. - Monday thru Friday, 8 a.m. to 2 p.m. - Saturday. Parts for 1964½ to 1970 Mustangs.

Danchuk Manufacturing Inc.: Art/Dan Danchuk, 3221 So. Halladay St., Santa Ana, CA 92705. Telephone 714-751-1957, M-F 7-4, Sat. 8-3. Closed Sunday. We specialize in manufacturing 1955-56-57 Chevrolet passenger car parts. Dealer inquiries invited! We also now stock 64-72 Chevelle/El Camino parts. 55-57 Catalog - $4.00, Chevelle/El Camino catalog - $3.00.

Len Dawson: 3990 St. Andrews Drive,Reno, NV 89502. Huge inventory of NOS Mopar parts and accessories, middle 1930's to late 1970's. Mail order only. SASE and Chrysler Corp. part numbers requested with inquiries.

Dayton Carrier Company: Jerry Walko & Jake Woelfle, 2276 Old Mill Road, Maineville, Ohio 45039. Telephone 513-683-2813 or 513-791-4125. After 5:00 p.m. preferred. Model A trunks & trunk repair hardware. Specializing in straight back reproduction trunks for Model A chrome rack. Wood construction with black vinyl covering. Also available - individual high quality hardware items to build or restore antique auto trunks. SASE please for flier.

Daytona Carburetor Parts Co.: Ron Hewitt, P.O. Box 247, New Smyrna Beach, FL 32070. Telephone 904-756-1386, 8 a.m. to 5 p.m. Newly manufactured carburetor repair kits for American cars 1932-61. Also complete line of upholstery, covers, headliners, carpet, yard goods, etc. 1927-1980.

Delorean Service & Parts: Troy Adams, 10728 N. 96 Ave., Peoria, AZ 85345. Telephone 602-979-2673, 8:00 to 6:00. Specializing in Delorean service and parts, sales brochures.

D & G Valve Mfg. Co., Inc.: Ansel Grose Jr., 8 Mt. Vernon St., Stoneham, MA 02180. Telephone 617-438-1773 & 1789. 8 a.m. to 6 p.m. Grose-Jet replaces that leaky needle and seat in your carburetor. Antique, import, domestic, racing or pleasure. Grose-Jet controls fuel level best. Call or write for catalog.

Diamond Auto Glass Corp.: 105 Emjay Blvd., Brentwood, NY 11717. Telephone 800-645-3180 Coast to Coast, 800-832-5181 N.Y. state, 8 a.m. to 5 p.m. Automobile glass for all domestic and foreign cars and trucks.

Dick's Chevy Parts: Dick Moffit, 4358 Bosart Rd., Springfield, OH 45503. 513-390-1008, 325-7861, 5 to 11 p.m. Hood and trunk ornaments & emblems - body side mouldings - complete interiors 1953 to 64 - door S.11 plates 49-64 - most all rubber parts 1937 to 64 - body panels & etc. Many N.O.S. reproduction - replated parts, grilles. In business since 1965. 28 to 64 parts & etc.

Don's Obsolete Auto Parts: Don Leask, 13059 Rosecran's, Santa Fe Springs, CA 90670. Telephone 213-921-0666, 9 a.m. to 5 p.m. Mon. to Fri., Sat. 9 to 4, Closed Sun. Obsolete auto parts bought and sold, mail order and open shop, heavy in Chevy.

Tom W. Dunaway, Jr.: P.O. Box 5074, Anderson, S.C. 29623. Telephone 803-226-8693, 7:30-9:00 p.m. All 6v headlight, tail light, interior, other light bulbs. Heater switches. 1930-1948 NOS windshield wiper blades and arms. Refinished Trippe lights and driving lights. Trippe lenses, brackets, switches, bulbs, parts. Old automobile literature, factory parts manuals. Specializing in Automobile Quarterlies.

Early Ford Parts Co.: 2948 Summer Ave., Memphis, TN 38112. Telephone 901-323-2179, 9:30 a.m. to 5:30 p.m. New parts for 1928-1959 Fords. Retail store hours 9:30 a.m. to 5:30 p.m. weekdays, 9 a.m. to 2 p.m. Saturday. Telephone orders taken 24 hours a day (901-323-2179). Big 80 page catalog for 1932-1959 Fords $3.00, refundable on first order.

Egge Machine Co.: 8403 Allport, Santa Fe Springs, Calif. 90670. Telephone 213-945-3419. The parts house for old cars.

Erb Repair Shop: Elmer Erb, Box 158, Bazine, Kan. 67516. Telephone 913-398-2455, 8 a.m. to 6 p.m. Specializes in antique car and tractor parts. Small engine and lawn mower repair.

English Motors: Paul Bell, 410 Saint Francis St., Mobile, Ala. 36602. Telephone 205-433-0385, 8 a.m. to 5 p.m., daily. Sports and foreign car garage. English car specialty. Appraisal service.

Larry Evenson's Concours Parts & Accessories: P.O. Box 1210, 3563 Numancia St., Santa Ynez, Calif. 93460. Telephone toll-free outside Calif. 800-722-0009, inside Calif. 800-872-3313, or call 805-688-7795. Specializes in 1955-57 Ford Thunderbird new and used parts. Call for free 72-page illustrated catalog.

Ezra Welding Shop: Paul Ezra & Les Ezra, R.R. 2, Box 309, Winamac, Ind. 46996. Telephone 219-278-7219, 8:00-4:30. Model A and T Ford pickup beds, top bows, etc. Bumpers 1927 to 1940. Luggage racks 1932-36, braces for running boards, fenders and bumpers. Much more.

Fairlane Co.: Keith Ashley, 210 E. Walker St., St. Johns, Mich. 48879. Telephone 517-224-6460, 9 a.m.-9 p.m. Mon.-Sat. (mail order). Manufacturer and distributor of fiberglass fenders and running boards for 1948-1956 Ford pickup trucks, cardboard headliners and interior panels for 1938-1956 Ford pickups, and 1949-50 Mercury Tudor and Convertible fiberglass quarter panels. Mail order and warehouse pickup by appointment.

Faspec British Cars & Parts: Stan Huntley, 1036 SE Stark Street, Dept. CA, Portland, OR 97214. Telephone 503-232-1232, toll free 800-547-8788, 9-6 M thru F Pacific time. New and used parts and accessories for MGA, MGB, Sprite-Midget Austin/Healey 100-4, 100-6, 3000, Triumph TR2-3-4-6 (new parts only). MG/Sprite-Midget/Austin-Healey/TR catalogs (free-specify model).

Fatsco Transmission Warehouse Inc.: 81 Rt. 46, Fairfield, NJ 07006. Telephone 201-227-2487, 8-5 5 days. Automatic & manual transmission parts for cars & trucks 1930 to date, also transmission rebuilding service.

Fellwocks Mopar Motion: Ron Fellwock, 10004 Darmstadt Road, Evansville, IN 47710. Specializes in restoration and detailing parts for 1966-74 Performance Mopars. We offer personalized service, thorough knowledge of Mopars, large inventory of NOS parts, immediate shipping by COD. Catalog: $3.00. Call Ron, afternoon and evenings at 812-867-3658, or write.

Maceo Felton: 132 Tejah Ave., Syracuse, NY 13210. Telephone 315-428-6905 days, 478-0846 evenings. Chevrolet parts 1932-54. Interior and radio knobs, lenses, emblems and reproduction items.

Fiberglass & Wood Co.: Jim Tygart, Rt 3, Box 119, Nashville, GA 31639. Telephone 912-686-3838, 800-CHV-TRUK. 8:00 to 9:30 Let ring till you get an answer. Chevrolet car and truck parts. Fiberglass, body wood, rubber goods, electrical wiring, body panels, truck pick up beds and parts, engine and chassis parts, door glass channel kits, etc. We also install body wood in the older cars and doors on a custom basis. Call on our toll free order line.

David Ficken Auto Parts: David Ficken, Box 11, Babylon, NY 11702. Telephone 516-587-3332. TRICO windshield wiper motors, arms and blades. Ignition parts for American cars. Hershey/Carlisle Fall Show Directory of Vendors.

The Filling Station: Steve & Jerry Kassis, 6929 Power Inn Road, Sacramento, CA 95828. Telephone 916-381-6810, M-F 10 a.m.-6 p.m., Sat. 9 a.m.-5 p.m., closed Sunday. Chevrolet & GMC quality reproduction parts for 1929-54 cars & 1929-66 trucks. Rubber products including: windshield & rear window seals, door & trunk seals; pickup bed parts including: wood beds & strips, bolt kits, tailgates; shop manuals, suspension & brake parts, hubcaps, trim rings, dash & radio knobs, floormats, headliners, decals & trim items, mirrors & brackets, and much more! Catalog $4.00.

Florida 4-Wheel Drive & Truck Parts: 6110 17th Street East, Bradenton, FL 34203. Obsolete Jeep and Willys parts.

Five Points Classic Auto Shocks: Jack White, 7471 Slater, Unit G, Huntington Beach, CA 92647. Telephone 714-842-0707. 9 a.m. to 5 p.m. Rebuilding lever type shocks, Armstrong, Girling, Delco & Houdaille for American & British classic cars. Offer shock fluid link bushings and links.

Ford Parts Obsolete Inc.: Wayne B. Peterson/R.C. Carlson, 1320 W. Willow St., Long Beach, CA 90810. Telephone 213-426-9501. Tues. thru Sat. 9 a.m. to 5 p.m. Full stock T, A, V8, F-100 & Mustang. Dealer program available - direct importers & distributors - worldwide.

The Ford Parts Specialists: 98-11 211th St., Queens Village, NY 11429. Telephone 212-468-8585, 8 a.m. to 4:45 p.m. - Monday thru Friday, 8 a.m. to 12 noon - Saturday, except July and August, closed national holidays. 1909-69 mechanical parts - brakes, front ends, steering, engine, electrical, transmission, motor mounts, rear end, drive line, exhaust, radiators, water pumps, fuel pumps, fuel systems, generators, starters, distributors and all components to keep Ford vehicles on the road.

Ford Parts Store: Toby and Sandy Gorny, 4925 Fort Rd., P.O. Box 226, Bryan, OH 43506. Telephone 419-636-2475. Mon.-Sat. 9:00 to 9:00. We specialize in 1954 thru mid 60's. Ford passenger car new and reproduced parts.

PARTS SUPP. CONT.

King & Wesley Obsolete Parts Co.: Courthouse Square, Liberty, Ky. 42539. Telephone 606-787-5031. Monday through Friday, 8 a.m. to 5 p.m. Large inventory of NOS and reproduction parts for Ford, Mustang, Thunderbird and pre-1970 pickups. COD (cash only), Visa and MasterCard welcome.

Ford Truck Parts Division: Obsolete Chevrolet Parts Co., Inc., 200 North Taylor St., Nashville, Ga. 31639. Telephone 912-686-7230. Monday through Thursday, 9 a.m. to 6 p.m.; Friday, 9 a.m. to 5 p.m. NOS and reproduction parts for 1948-60 Ford trucks, F-1 and F-100.

Garton's Auto Ford Parts & Accessories: 5th & Vine, Millville, New Jersey 08332. Telephone 609-825-3618. Mail order. 1932-1960 Genuine Ford parts bought & sold. Have in stock: fenders, grills, trim, ornaments, mechanical & chassis parts. Over 1,000,000 NOS parts in stock!

Gaskets: Gerald J. Lettieri, 132 Old Main Street, Rocky Hill, CT 06067. Telephone 203-529-7177. Mail order. Gaskets - head, manifold, oil pan, full sets.

Gasket King Company Limited: Michael Lynch, 18 Hastings Ave., Toronto, Ont., Canada M4L 2L2. Telephone 416-466-6775, 7 p.m. to 11 p.m. nights only. New old stock, engine gaskets for cars, trucks, tractors and marine engines 1909-1950 only! Over 25,000 in stock headgaskets.

Gaslight Auto Parts, Inc.: 1445 S. State Rte. 68, P.O. Box 291, Urbana, OH 43078. Telephone 513-652-2145, 8:30 a.m. to 5 p.m. Monday thru Friday. We supply a complete line of replacement parts for Ford, Model T, Model A, and V-8.

Girtz Industries, Inc.: Elmer Girtz, R.R. #3, Box 264, Monticello, IN 47960. Telephone 219-278-7510. Mon.-Thurs. 8:00 to 5:00. Model A & V-8 reproduction antique auto parts, sheet metal, fender braces, chrome top irons, stanchion post, and other misc. parts. All parts manufactured in our factory. 25 years experience.

Glazier's Mustang Barn, Inc.: 531 Wambold Rd., Souderston, Pa. 18964. Telephone 215-723-9674. Large inventory of 1964½-70 Mustang parts.

G.M. Hardware & Parts: James T. Mackin, 150 Garden Street, Bedford, OH 44146. Telephone 216-232-2498, 9:00 a.m.-9:00 p.m. Specializing in obsolete G.M. hardware such as hinge pins, bushings, clutch head screws, door ferrules, rubber products, body nails, trim screws, etc. Send $1.00 for catalog or S.A.S.E. with inquiries.

Golden State Pickup Parts: 618 E. Gutierrez St. Santa Barbara, CA 93103. Telephone 805-564-2020, 9 a.m. to 6 p.m. Mon.-Sat. '47-'72 Chevy/GMC truck parts. If we don't have the part your looking for, we'll help you find it. Satisfaction guaranteed for the life of your truck. Toll-free order line 800-235-5717

Gordon Imports, Inc.: Hugh and Jeani Gordon, 14330 Iseli Rd., Santa Fe Springs, CA 90670-5296. Telephone 213-802-1608, 8-6 p.m. M-F, some weekends also. Complete parts inventory for the Amphicar all years. In depth restoration or mechanical advise available. Amphicar Club plans under preparation. Parts price list available for $5.00 refundable with order.

GP Fiberglass: Gerald Phillips, 5101 Mockingbird Road, Greensboro, NC 27406. Telephone 919-674-0245. Fiberglass Fender skirts & sun visors for 1960 to 1988 trucks, all makes.

Dave Graham: 1655 Hunters Way, Orange, CA 92669. Telephone 714-547-0139, 8:00-5:00 Mon.-Fri. Manufacturer and wholesaler of shop manuals, owners manuals, engine decals, truck sun visors, arm rests, door panels, headliners, seat kits, send for free catalog.

John K. Griffith/Antique Car Shades: John K. Griffith Jr., 308 Washington Ave., Nutley, NJ 07110. Telephone 201-667-1474, 8:30 a.m. to 5:30 p.m. We manufacture original style window shades for any closed car. Many colors are available in cotton poplin and silk. We will also mount new material on customers old rollers. New rollers are also available as well as original duplicate Shade Tassels and Chrome Plated Mounting Brackets. This is the only service we provide as we deal retail and wholesale to the trade.

Harmon's Inc.: Highway 27 North, Geneva, IN 46740. Telephone 219-368-7221. Hours: 8-5 Mon.-Fri., 9-3 Sat. Showroom and mail order Chevrolet restoration parts and accessories for 1955-67 passenger, 1962-72 Nova, 1964-72 Chevelle, and 1967-80 Camaros. Interiors, sheetmetal, emblems, chrome, rubber, books, and car care products. Catalog $2.00.

Harmon's Inc.: Centerpoint Mall, 2655-B Saviers Road, Oxnard, CA 93033. Telephone 805-483-3369, 10-6 Mon.-Thur., 10-9 Fri., 10-6 Sat.-Sun. Showroom sales (only) Chevrolet restoration parts and accessories for 1955-67 Passenger, 1962-72 Nova, 1964-72 Chevelle, and 1967-80 Camaros. Interiors, emblems, chrome, rubber, books, and car care products.

Headlight Headquarters: Donald I. Axelrod, 35 Timson St., Lynn, MA 01902. Telephone 617-598-0523, by appointment only. Specializes in complete headlight units, lenses and parts for 1914 to 1939 American cars (no Fords). Maintains want list for headlights and parts not in stock.

Heavy Chevy Pickup Parts: P.O. Box 650, Siloam Springs, AR 72761. Telephone 501-524-4873, Tuesday through Saturday. Offers 1948-59 Chevrolet and GMC truck parts, including a complete headlight to taillight wiring harness with instructions. Catalog available at $2.

Helgensen Antique & Classic Auto Parts: Rt. 6, Hwy. 14W., Janesville, WI 53545. Telephone 1-800-356-0006, In WI 608-756-0469, 7:30 a.m. to 4 p.m. Mainly domestic mechanical parts from 1930's to 1960's.

James Hinshaw Reconditioning: James C. Hinshaw, 100 Bell St., Burlington, NC 27215. Telephone 919-226-8242, Mon. & Wed.-Fri. 10 a.m.-6 p.m., Sat. 9 a.m.-4 p.m. We are a full-time operation with a showroom specializing in Chevelle and Monte Carlo parts. We offer quality parts and other services. Installation and reconditioning of parts are just two of our services. We also manufacture quality parts to try to meet our customers needs.

Bill Hirsch Auto Parts, Inc.: Bill Hirsch, 396 Littleton Ave., Newark, NJ 07103. Telephone 201-642-2404. Restoration materials include leather, broadcloth, mohair, bedford cloth, carpet, engine enamels, nitrocellulose lacquers, convertible tops, fabric, wheel trim rings, hub caps, etc.

Hoover's Camaro Classics. See listing under Restoration Firms.

Tom Horne Reproductions: 23032 Hatteras St., Woodland Hills, CA 91367. Telephone 818-348-0332, 9 a.m. to 6 p.m., Monday thru Friday. Mustang reproduction parts and accessories, wholesale and retail. Mail - phone orders, weatherstrip, mirrors, kick panels, floor mats, die cast plated accessories, rubber pads and small hardward.

J. K. Howell: 465 No. Grace St., Lombard, IL 60148. Telephone 312-495-1949. Cord parts. Mail order only. Catalog available $1.00.

Huck Brake, Springs & Accessories: See listing under Brakes.

Hydro-E-Lectric: Paul Wiesman, 48 Appleton Rd., Auburn, MA 01501. Telephone 617-832-3081, 9-6. Convertible top and power window parts, motor pumps, cylinders, motors and hoses. Send SASE for list. Call to place MasterCard, VISA or C.O.D. orders.

I & I Reproduction: Wendy S. Ikari, 15513 Vermont Avenue, Paramount, CA 90723. Telephone 213-531-8117, 9 a.m.-6 p.m. 1925-54 Chevrolet reproduction parts, chrome/rubber and accessory items.

IMCADO Manufacturing Co.: W. George Chubaty, Eng., Director, P.O. Box 452, Dover, DE 19901. Telephone 302-734-4177. 9 a.m. to 5 p.m. Monday through Friday. Exclusive manufacturer in the field since 1956 and production of most complete line of leather equipment for any motorcar ever built from 1896 on. Hood belts, top straps, crank holsters, fan belts, axle straps, gaiters, joint boots, etc. Original replacement authenticated and approved, prime grade cowhide with select hardware and full 12 month warranty.

Imperial-Mopar: Box 439, Bryans Road, MD 20616. Telephone 301-283-2143. NOS and good used parts for Imperials and other MoPar products.

Jahns Quality Pistons: Louis Mascola, Kurt Jacobi, Albert Jelenic, 2662 Lacy St., Los Angeles, CA 90031. Telephone 213-225-8177, 7:30-5. Specializing in custom forged and cast pistons for all internal combustion engines. Also have complete engine kits.

J.B.'s Corvette Supplies: Joseph Bastardi, 1992 White Plains Rd., Bronx, NY 10462. Telephone 212-931-2599, Mon. thru Fri. 9:00-5:30. Complete line of Corvette Parts & Accessories 1953-86 - fiberglass, interiors, automotive parts - 1986-87 parts catalog available $3.00.

The Jeepsterman: Morris Ratner, 572 Ramtown Road, Howell, NJ 07731. Telephone 201-458-3966. 7 days a week - weekdays 9-5, Sat. Closed Sunday. Willys-Jepster, st. wg., panel delivery truck CJ2A-3A - CJ3A-5 - MB, surry - DJ3A jeep, hard to find parts, new, old, bought, sold, sheet metal; new, used, st. wg. tailgate repair kit, hub caps, complete exhaust system, pickup beds new, wire harness headliners, manuals, rubber parts, mechanical parts - send 60¢ - state model with SASE - Free list.

Jim's Motor Service: Jim Jones, K#27, Washington Pike or Box 5567, Knoxville, TN 37918. Telephone 615-637-4029. After 6:00 p.m. Have in stock 600 to 800 vehicles from 1917 to 1970, autos, trucks, motorcycles, parts new and used in stock from 1921 to 1970 will ship or deliver any item. Mechanical, body or trim parts.

Jim's Mustangs: Pony Corp., 1399 N. Cuyamaca, El Cajon, CA 92020. Telephone 619-562-0912. 64½-73 Mustang - new, used, NOS reproduction parts. Rebuilt steering gear boxes. Full service shop.

Joblot Automotive, Inc.: 98-11 211th St., P.O. Box 75, Queens Village, NY 11429. Telephone 212-468-8585. Monday through Friday, 8:30 a.m. to 4:45 p.m., Saturdays 8 a.m. to 12 noon except July and August. Closed National holidays. Ford parts specialists. Complete line of parts for Model T, Model A, Early V-8's, Nifty-Fifties, Thunderbirds, Pickup Trucks 1948-64, and the sixties Ford cars.

John's N.O.S. Chevelle Parts: John Raumikaitis, P.O. Box 1445, Salem, NH 03079. Telephone 603-898-9366. Chevelle, El Camino, N.O.S. and repro, thousands in stock, chrome, emblems, grilles, rubber, etc. 87 illustrated 40 page catalog. $3.00 refundable. U.S. funds. Try us first for your Chevelle parts.

The Judge's Chambers: Robert J. McKenzie, 114 Prince George Drive, Hampton, VA 23669. Telephone 804-838-2059. Devoted to the 1969-1971 Pontiac GTO Judge with parts such as all 1969-1971 Judge Stripe Kits, decals, front & rear spoilers, glovebox emblems, Ram-Air parts & seals, hood tachometers, videos, Judge and GTO memorabilia and recordings.

The Junk Yard Dog: Box 439, Bryans Road, MD 20616. Telephone 301-283-2143, 8-4 p.m. Used parts locator services. Salvage yard consultants, catalog services for used parts, suppliers, publications.

Just Suspension: Bill Kanouse, Gary Kunits, P.O. Box 167, 640 Rte. 202, Towaco, NJ 07082. Telephone 201-335-0547, 8:30 a.m. to 5:30 p.m. American cars 1936-1986. Ball joints, tie rod ends, center links, pin kits, bushings, pitman arms, idler arms & kits, stabilizer links, king pins, strut bushings, shaft kits, control arms, rebound bumpers and coil springs, stabilizer bars front & rear with polyurethane bushings.

Kanter Auto Products: 76 Monroe St., Boonton, NJ 07005. Telephone 201-334-9575, 9 a.m. to 5 p.m., Monday thru Friday. Kanter Auto Products has been supplying fellow car collectors with service, value and the quality parts and products they need since 1960. Offering suspension, brakes, shocks, carpeting, upholstery, leather, convertible tops, exhaust systems, batteries, and much more. Call or write for free catalog.

John Kepich Exhaust: John Kepich, 7520 Clover Bldg. 6, Box 1365 (shop), Mentor, OH 44061. Telephone 216-942-0908 shop, Home 352-7990, Mon.-Fri. 9-5, Sat. 9-2. Manufactures heavy duty steel and lifetime type 304 stainless exhaust systems. Specialty Y-pipe & H-pipes. We can supply most original American car & truck systems 1920-up. Can make most any size steel or stainless muffler.

Keystone Mustang: Barbara Mowery, RR 2, Box 19, Belleville, PA 17004. Telephone 717-935-2683, 7 a.m.-9 p.m. All Mustang parts. 64½-73 sheet metal upholstery, trim items, UPS shipping, discount prices.

King & Queen Mufflers: Box 423, Plumsteadville, PA 18949. Telephone 215-348-1284. Specializes in NOS exhaust parts for cars and trucks from 1926 and up.

Lakeview Vintage Distributing: Richard Culleton, West Lake Rd., Lane 33, Skaneateles, NY 13152. Telephone 315-685-7414, 9-4 weekdays. Phone orders 9-9 M-F. Model A Ford interiors, reproduction parts for 1928-48 Ford & Chevrolet. We mail order as well as attend most major meets on the East Coast.

Larry's Thunderbird and Mustang Parts: Ted Money, 511 S. Raymond Ave., Fullerton, CA 92631. Telephone 714-871-6432. Larry's provides the highest quality of parts and upholstery to fit every need for your 65-73 Mustang, 55-57 Thunderbird, or 1958-66 Thunderbird. We are the source for all your needs in parts and upholstery. Call and talk to our experts! Free catalogs available.

Michael Lawson: 59 Leader Drive, Jacobus, PA 17407. Telephone 717-428-3408 Evenings. Replacement hydraulic hoses manufactured for all makes of convertibles and other automobiles with hydro-electric power systems. Rebuilding service for most types of hydro-electric system pumps. Quality work and reasonable rates.

LeBaron Bonney Co.: See listing under Upholstery.

Legendary Corvette, Inc.: Lisa & Larry Williams, 903 Easton Rd., Warrington, PA 18976. Telephone 215-343-2424, 9-5 M-F. Corvette body panels 56 to 87. Manufacturer of bonding strips, stock panels, one pc. fronts, custom panels.

Jere V. Longrie: 3651 Hwy. 38, Grand Rapids, MN 55744. See complete listing under Literature.

Lo-Can Glass International: Alan Tankel, P.O. Box 45248 - 693 McGrath Highway, Somerville, MA 02145-005. Telephone 800-345-9595 - 617-396-9595, 9-6 a.m.-p.m. Auto glass. Specializing in hard to find glass for past & current models - Locator service.

W. H. Lucarelli: 14 Hawthorne Ct., Wheeling, WV 26003. Telephone 304-232-8906 or 304-232-3263. Specializes in mechanical parts for 1931-33 and 1935-36 Auburns, Ford Model As and 17-inch Ford wire wheels.

Mack Products: Box 278, 100 Fulton Ave., Moberly, MO 65270. Telephone 816-263-7444, 7 a.m. to 5 p.m., Monday thru Friday. Worlds largest mfg. of antique pickup parts. New beds for 1934-53 Chevys and 1928-56 Fords. Books on pickups.

Mac's Antique Auto Parts: Doug McIntosh, P.O. Box 238, 1051 Lincoln Ave., Lockport, NY 14094. Telephone 800-828-7948 or in New York 716-433-1500. Hours 9 a.m. to 5 p.m. weekdays, Saturdays 9 a.m. to noon. Complete line of parts for Ford Model T, A & V-8 from 1909 to 1948. Includes new, NOS, used, reproduction, books & literature. Free catalogs. Outside U.S. send $2.00 per catalog.

Made-Rite Auto Body Products, Inc.: 869 E. 140th St., Cleveland, OH 44110. Telephone 216-681-2535, 8 a.m. to 4:30 p.m., Monday thru Friday. Steel replacement panels.

Mainly Vettes: Jim Olson & Rich Peting, 3511 Illinois #90, Lansing, IL 60438. Telephone 312-895-6024, 12:00-5:00. New & reproduction parts & literature for the restoration of all Chevy's, G.T.O.'s, Firebirds, Skylarks & Cutlass.

Mal's 'A' Sales: L.M. Staley, 4968 Pacheco Blvd., Martinez, CA 94553. Telephone 415-228-8180, 10 a.m. to 5 p.m. - Closed Sunday and Monday. New antique Ford parts & supplies '09-'48 and early Mustang parts to '68 - catalog $3.00

Marv's Auto Sales: RR 2, Box 32, Gaylord, MN 55334. Telephone 612-237-5211. Has large assortment of N.O.S. and used parts and cars from the late 20's thru early 60's for sale.

Masonville Garage - Model "A" Ford Parts: Craig Starr, Box 57 (600 Gordon), Masonville, IA 50654. Telephone 319-927-4290, 8-5 Monday-Friday; 8-12 Saturday. Model "A" Ford Parts, Books, Accessories, Wood & Sheet Metal Parts, Seat Springs, Top & Trim Parts, Wescott's Fiberglass Fenders & Bodies, Pickup Parts, Restoration Supplies. New All-"A" Catalog, $2, Refundable.Full Line, Fast Service, Since 1967.

MAS Racing Products: Richard Kohn, 2538 Hennepin Av. S., Minneapolis, MN 55405. Telephone 612-377-6707, 9 to 5. Manufacturers of '23 Ford T bodies and suspension components - every part is available from MAS to build a complete, full fendered T replica or the conventional and popular '23 T Ford "Hot Rod."

McDaniel Old Ford Parts: George E. Williams Jr., 3685 Chamblee-Dunwoody Road, Chamblee, GA 30341, outside GA 800-445-2154, 404-452-0422, 9-5 M-F; 9-1 Sat., closed Sunday. Model A parts (new and used) and Firestone tires.

McDonald Ford Parts Co.: R.R. # 3, Box 94, Rockport, IN 47635. Telephone 812-359-4965, Mon.-Fri. 8 a.m. to 5 p.m., Sat. 8 a.m. to 12. We specialize in body parts, mouldings, ornaments and also have mechanical parts for '42-'82 Fords. Call or write (SASE) with needs.

Mercury Research Co.: 639 Glankler St., Memphis, TN 38112. 1949-1959 Mercury parts. Mail order only. 45 page catalog $4.00, refundable on first order.

Metro Moulded Parts Inc.: Douglas Hajicek, President, 11610 Jay St. N.W., Minneapolis, MN 55433. Telephone 612-757-0310. 8:30 a.m. to 4:30 p.m. Monday through Friday. We manufacture thousands of rubber parts, weather strips, sponge products for the vintage car hobby, all makes of cars & trucks '29-'72. The oldest & largest. Ill. catalog available for $2.00. Dealer info available on request.

MG Bits & Spares: Don Bridger, P.O. Box 864, 105 Azalea Ln., Jonesboro, AR 72401. Telephone 501-932-7150, 8 a.m. to 5 p.m. Monday thru Saturday. Complete line of parts for MGB and MGB-GT.

M & G Vintage Auto: George Medynski, 265 Route 17, P.O. Box 226, Tuxedo Park, NY 10987. Telephone NY 914-753-5900, all others 800-631-8990, 9:00-6:00. Complete inventory of T, A & B series MG parts. Mail order specialist. Catalogs available upon request. Please specify model. Orders placed before 1:00 p.m. get same day shipping. Complete service & restoration available.

Mid-America Corvette: Jeff Leech, 210 42nd St., Moline, IL 61265. Telephone 309-764-1578, 8 a.m. to 5 p.m. Monday thru Friday. Grand Sport II conversions and components, stock replacement components, custom building services.

Mid America Corvette Supplies: Mike Yager, P.O. Box 1368, Dept. CPA5, Effingham, IL 62401. Telephone (217)-347-5591, 8-5 central time. CORVETTE CATALOG for the serious enthusiast and those who own a Corvette just for fun. Send $2 for the most complete grouping of sportswear, exciting interior and exterior accessories, books, decorator products and artwork.

Mid-Atlantic Performance Parts: Bob Antelman, P.O. Box 333-PC, Simpsonville, MD 21150. Telephone 301-596-0357. Cutlass 4-4-2,Skylark, G.S. Comprehensive catalog of restoration parts, interiors, sheet metal patch panels, trunk floor sections, chrome emblems, weatherstrips, decals, books, moldings, carpets, detailing items, suspension parts. Send $2.00.

Midwest Muscle Cars & Parts: Kurt Nauman, 1301 Drexel Blvd., So. Milw., WI 53172. Telephone 414-764-6669, 7 a.m.-10 p.m. Wisconsins only one stop full line muscle car parts dealer. Handling all lines of Chevrolet plus Buick G.S., 442 and G.T.O. Everything from interior kits, weather strips, mouldings and sheetmetal to hard to find accessories, gauge sets, cowl induction and ram air parts. One call does it all!

Mike's Auto Parts: Mike Porter, 121 East Ford Street, Ridgeland, MS 39157. Telephone 601-856-7214, 8 to 5. New, rebuilt and new old stock parts for most old cars. Water pumps, fuel pumps, universal joints, hydraulic brake parts, bearings, ignition - starter - generator parts, belts, filters, 6 volt bulbs and Chevrolet transmission gears are our specialties. Largest supply of N.O.S. MoPar and Jeep in this area.

Mitchell Motor Parts, Inc.: Frank Mitchell, 2467 Jackson Pike, Columbus, OH 43223. Telephone 614-875-4919, 8:00-5:30 M-T 8:00-5:00 F, 9:00-1:00 Sat., Closed Sunday. Mitchell Motor Pts., Inc. is dedicated to the preservation & restoration of Chrysler built vehicles 1928 to current model year with over 40,000 sq. ft. of inventory located 3 miles from the intersection of Interstate 70 & 71 and specializing only in MoPar pts.

Moss Motors Ltd.: P.O. Box MG, Goleta, CA 93116. Telephone 805-968-1041. Specializes in quality parts and accessories for pre-1967 British sports cars.

Mr. G's Mustang City (Also) Mr. G's Rechromed Plastic: Glenn Garrison, 5613 Elliott Reeder Rd., Ft. Worth, TX 76117. Telephone 817-831-3501, 9 a.m. to 5 p.m. Monday thru Friday, 9 a.m. to 2 p.m. Saturday. Complete line of Mustang new, used, and reproduction parts. Rechroming of all type of plastic parts, auto, toy, motorcycle, etc. Full line of fasteners, screws, nuts, bolts, grommets, rubber bumpers, clips, etc. We are a distributor for Au-Ve-Co., Car-Pak and other fastner companies.

Mr. Mustang, Inc.: 5088 Wolf Creek Pike, Dayton, OH 45426. Telephone 513-275-7439, 9 a.m. to 5 p.m., Monday thru Friday. Manufacturing, wholesales and retail sales of all types of parts and products for Ford Mustangs 1964½ to 1972.

Mr. Plymouth: Neil Riddle, 452 Newton, Seattle, WA 98109. Telephone 206-285-6534, anytime. Plymouth parts for years '46 thru '54 only, N.O.S., used & repro. Hard to find parts and detail items my specialty. Overdrive transmission conversions. Send SASE for free catalog featuring Moparmania products.

Mr. Thunderbird Classic Parts: Carl H. Maroney, 4015 Heatherhill Dr., Huntsville, AL 35802. Telephone 205-536-1956, 7 a.m. - 11 p.m. Monday thru Friday, 9 a.m. - 11 p.m. Saturday. Specialize in parts for 55-57 Thunderbirds. Over 1,400 different new and reproduced parts in stock. Write or call for prices and availability. No catalog is available.

Moose Motors: Jeff Adkins, 1805 2nd St., Berkeley, CA 94710. Telephone 415-548-8411, 9:30-5:00 M-F, 12:30-4 Sat. Moose Motors Antique Auto Parts and Service has been serving the old car community since 1976. The auto parts store provides new mechanical parts, plus weatherstripping and lenses for older American cars, from the 1920's through the 1960's. Our repair shop does mechanical work on these cars too.

Muck Motors Ford: William F. Muck, 10 Campbell Road, Getzville, NY 14068-1299. Telephone 800-228-6825, 716-688-5464, 8:30-4:30 M-F. Ford parts - current & obsolete - specialists in 58-66 Thunderbird. Largest selection of N.O.S. & repro parts. Rebuilding services for many parts. Interiors, carpets, sheetmetals, engine, chassis etc. Some used pieces available. Credit card and COD sales. Ford Motorsport parts distributor.

Muscle Car Corral: Gary R. Hall, RR 3, Box 218, Paris, IL 61944. Telephone 217-465-8386, 8 a.m.-5 p.m. Tuesday-Friday. Specializing in fine quality 1965-1968 Mustang parts new & used; quick service & a personalized business trying to meet your restoration needs. We handle the finest items on the market at the best prices.

Musclecar Specialties: Jack & Emily Olcott, 51 Glenwood Drive, Hauppauge, NY 11778. Telephone 516-864-2254, evenings. N.O.S. and used parts, accessories and options sales. Specializing in 1962 to 1972 Chevrolet (Nova, Camaro, Chevelle, Impala). Also many NOS 1929-1961 Chevrolet and Pontiac parts. Reasonable prices w/money back guarantee if not satisfied. Mail order and C.O.D. welcome. Try us before you buy. No reproduction parts carried.

Mustang of Chicago: 1321 Irving Pk. Rd. (West of Rt. 83), Bensenville, IL 60106, Division of Deluxe Ford Parts Ltd. Telephone 312-860-7077, M-F 9 a.m.-8 p.m., Sat. 8:30-5 p.m. Complete line of 1965-87 Mustang SVO, Motorsport parts. Frame and floor restoration, complete interior restoration. Also 1909-1973 Ford car and truck parts.

Mustang Corral: Tim & Shawn Harville, Rt. 6, Box 242, Edwardsville, IL 62025. Telephone 618-656-5428, Mon.-Sat. 9-6. Parts & supplies for 65-73 Mustangs - new & used. Complete Mustang rust - repair and restoration service. Used Mustangs - restored or unrestored, bought and sold.

Mustang Country: Donald R. Chambers, 14625 Lakewood Boulevard, Paramount, CA 90723. Telephone 213-633-2393, 10-5 Tuesday-Saturday. Mustangs (1965-1973) parts, interiors, and auto sales.

Mustang Headquarters: Don Johnson, 1080 Detroit Avenue, Concord, CA 94518. Telephone 800-227-2174, 8 a.m. to 5 p.m. - Monday thru Friday, 8 a.m. to 12 p.m. Saturday. We offer a complete line of parts for the 1965 thru 1973 Mustang, including upholstery, sheet metal, rubber products, suspension parts and interior paints and dyes. Catalogs are $1.00 or will be shipped free with order.

Mustang Mart Inc.: B. Malachek, 655 McGlincey Ln., Campbell, CA 95008. Telephone 408-371-5771, 9:30 to 5:30 Mon. thru Sat. closed Sun. We serve 65 to 70 Mustangs. Complete line of new used and reproduction parts complete interior restoration send $3.00 for catalog refundable on 1st order. Doing business in the same location for over 9 yrs.

Mustang Parts Corral of Texas: June Kelty & Dave Kelty, 3533 S. Ledbetter, Dallas, TX 75236. Telephone 214-296-5130, Mon.-Fri. 8:00 to 5:00, Sat. 9:00 to 1:00. Mustang parts - new, used, reproduction, specialty parts, rechromed bumpers, carpet, upholstery, weatherstripping, consoles, inner fenders, radiator supports, interior trim, recoverable seats, quarter panels, deck lids, shock towers, rechromed plastic, 4-barrel intakes, 4-barrel heads, rear glass, quarter extensions, steering wheels, interior trim, Mach I/fastback parts, exhaust manifolds. Free catalog.

Mustang Parts of Oklahoma: Rex Beagley, 6505 South Shields, Okla. City, OK 73149. Telephone 405-631-1400, 9 a.m. to 5 p.m. We have the largest "Mustang Parts Catalog" in the U.S.A. Over 4000 parts listed in our new 162 page catalog with over 600 pictures and illustrations. Each item individually priced. Send $4 today for your catalog.

Narragansett Reproductions: Ed and Miki Pease, P.O. Box 51, Woodville Rd., Wood River Junction, RI 02894. Telephone 401-364-3839, 9 a.m. to 5 p.m., Monday through Friday. Mail order service offering complete parts line for 1936-48 Lincoln, 1956-57 Lincoln Continental, Lincoln Zephyr and 1932-48 Ford. Specializing in wiring harnesses, rubber and mechanical parts for Ford Model As and other models through 1960. Wiring harnesses made to order for any American or foreign cars. Catalogs available. Please specify year model of your car to receive proper catalog.

National Parts Depot: 3101 S.W. 40th Blvd., Gainesville, FL 32608. Telephone 904-378-2473 in Fla. or 800-874-7595, Monday through Friday, 8 a.m. to 9 p.m., and Saturday 8:30 a.m. to 5 p.m. Specializes in complete stock of parts, upholstery and restoration supplies for 1955-57 Ford Thunderbird and 1965-73 Ford Mustang.

National Spring Company, Inc.: Bob Guthrie, 630 Grand Ave., Spring Valley, CA 92077. Telephone 619-697-3544 - CA residents, 8 a.m. to 5 p.m. Monday through Friday. A complete automotive spring service. New leaf springs for all American cars, pickups and most foreign autos. Coil springs, shackle kits, bushings, spring liner & u-bolts. In business since 1947. Leaf springs are custom manufactured. Club discounts available with membership number.

N/C Industries Antique Auto Parts: Kevin & Bob, 215 So. Thomas Ave., Sayre, PA 18840. Telephone 717-888-6216. We reproduce Plymouth & Dodge parts from 1931 to 1937. We also reproduce steering and brake parts for Ford Model A's and 1935-36 Ford closed car windshield frames.

New England Mustang Supply Inc.: 4 Research Drive, Stratford, CT 06497. 203-377-6186 M, T, Th, Fr 9-6, W 9-3, Sat 9-4:30. Full line of 65-73 new & used Mustang parts. Huge inventory in stock for immediate shipping. Also supplying new parts for other special interest autos from 50's, 60's & 70's era.

New England Old Car Barn: U.S. Route 1, North Hampton, NH 03862. Telephone 603-964-7100. We offer a large supply of parts; reproduction, NOS and used, for a wide range of popular marques from Model T to Mustang, from early Chevrolet to Corvette and Imports from MG to Jaguar. Authorized Dealers for many major collector car parts suppliers. Telephone and mail orders promptly shipped by United Parcel Service or Common Carrier.

New Ford Goodies: Ed McMullen, 18008 St. Clair Ave., Cleveland, OH 44110. Telephone 216-531-8685. 9 a.m. till 5 p.m. Genuine Ford parts and quality reproductions (no used parts) 1949 and up for Ford, Mercury, Lincoln, Thunderbird, Falcon, Fairlane, Mustang, Comet, Cougar, Torino, Marks, Cyclone and even trucks.

Northstar Commemoratives, Inc.: P.O. Box 803, Lakeville, MN 55044. Telephone 612-469-5433. Specializes in cloisonne badges, reproduction parts, and reproduction manuals.

Northwest Classic Falcons: Ron & Jean Boesl, 1964 N.W. PEttygrove, Portland, OR 97209. Telephone 503-241-9454, 9 a.m. to 6 p.m. PST, M-F. We buy/sell obsolete car parts from the Ford product line. Our primary specialty is Falcons from 1960-1970 with a sub-specialty in Mercury Comets. We have a very good supply of new, quality used, reproduction and NOS parts from nuts and bolts to sheet metal. Credit cards accepted.

Northwest Transmission Parts: John Dobbins, 13500 US Rt. 62, Winchester, OH 45697. Telephone 513-442-2811. 8 a.m. - 5:30 p.m. Monday thru Friday. Automatic transmission master overhaul kits available for any car ever made in the USA, also Rolls Royce, Jaguar, Mercedes-Benz. Pumps, drums, bands, bushings, and hard parts in stock, back to 1940. Also stock standard transmission parts for General Motors and Chrysler products, call for availability, friendly prices, and immediate delivery.

NOS Locators: 587 Pawtucket Ave., Pawtucket, RI 02860. Telephone 401-725-5000. Surplus and/or obsolete original new parts. Offers only those products that can be sold below wholesale. Motto: Good stuff cheap! Mail or phone orders only.

Oakcrest Machine Shop: Elster C. Hayes, 2110 Boda St., Springfield, OH 45503. Telephone 513-399-8435, 9 a.m. to 5 p.m. Specializes in all clincher rims, Ford Model T rims and split rims for some cars.

Obsolete Chevrolet Parts Co., Inc.: Tim Tygart and Jerry Kelley, 504 Hazel Ave., P.O. Box 68, Nashville, GA 31639. Telephone 912-686-5812 or 912-686-5227, Monday through Friday 8 a.m. to 6 p.m. and Saturday by appointment only. We buy and sell NOS parts and reproduction parts for Chevrolet only 1929-mid 60's. NOS and reproduction sheet metal, chrome, mechanical and rubber parts.

Obsolete Ford Parts Co., Inc.: C.A. Jones, 311 E. Washington Ave., Nashville, GA 31639. Telephone 912-686-5101, 8 a.m. to 5 p.m. Monday thru Friday, 8 a.m. to noon Saturday. Large comprehensive line of Ford parts, NOS & reproduction for 1949-1968 Fords, 1960-70 Falcon, Mustang, 1962-76 Fairlane/Torino and 1948-72 ½ ton Ford Trucks. Full line including sheet metal, bumpers, trim, rubber, books, mechanical parts, etc.

Obsolete Ford: Dale Bliss, 6601 S. Shields, Oklahoma City, OK 73149. Telephone 405-631-3933, 9-5 M-F. We carry full line of automotive parts ranging from 1909-27 Model T, 1928-31 Model A; 1932-48 Pass. & Pickup; 1949-59 Passenger car; 1948-66 Pickup, to 1960-72 Ford, Falcon, Fairlane & T-Bird. Catalog available for each era. Inquire (405) 631-3933.

Ol '55: Ted Wieckowski, Rd. 3, Box 68, New Hope, PA 18938. Telephone 215-598-3186, 9:00 to 5:30 Mon.-Fri., Sat. 9:00-12:00 noon. 24 hour answering machine. 55-56-57 Chevy parts our specialty, complete inventory A to Z, now stocking for popular models 58-70. Daily UPS service. Knowledgable personal service, 10 years service to the hobby.

Olcar Bearing Co.: George Bachleda, 5101 Fedora, Troy, MI 48098. Telephone 313-879-7916, 8 a.m. to 10 p.m. Bearing and seals for: axle, diff., pinion, clutch, transmission, wheels. All years, most models.

Old Car City, USA: Dean Lewis, Hwy. 411, White, GA 30184.

Jim Osborn Reproductions, Inc.: Jim Osborn, 101 Ridgecrest Drive, Lawrenceville, GA 30245. Telephone 404-962-7556, 8:00 a.m.-5:00 p.m. World's largest selection of automotive restoration decals for AMC, Chevrolet, Camaro, Corvette, Chevelle, Chevy II, Nova, Corvair, Ford, Lincoln, Mercury, Falcon, Mustang, Thunderbird, Chrysler, Plymouth, Dodge, Pontiac, GTO, Firebird, Oldsmobile, 442, Cutlass and other American made cars. Large selection of owners and shop manuals. Catalog $3.00 refundable.

Packard Farm: Bill McDowell, 97N 150W, Greenfield, IN 46140. Telephone 317-462-3124, 8 a.m. to 5 p.m. M-F, Sat. by appointment. Specializes in Packard and Studebaker engine and transmission parts, exhaust systems, Chevrolet exhaust systems, fender welt, hood lacing, etc.

Packard Reproductions: Roger Bond, 303 Bank St., Attleboro, MA 02703. Telephone 617-222-3252. Evenings or telephone ahead. Runningboard side moldings made to order. Packard oil filters and air cleaner decals. Packard front suspension bushings. Clipper rear view mirrors.

The Paddock, Inc.: 221 W. Main, Knightstown, IN 46148. Telephone 317-345-2131. 8 a.m. to 5 p.m. Specializes in Mustang, Camaro, Chevelle, GTO and Firebird parts.

PARTS SUPP. CONT.

Papke Enterprises Inc.: Bill Papke, 16178 Shasta St., Fountain Valley, CA 92708. Telephone 714-839-3050, by appointment & weekends. Specializing in parts & parts cars for 1949-51 Ford & Mercury. Have 20 parts cars on hand along with large inventory of hard to find parts.

Par-Porsche Specialists: Paul Resnick, 206 S. Broadway, Yonkers, NY 10705. Telephone 914-476-6700. 8:30 a.m. to 5:30 daily, Sat. 9 a.m. to 1 p.m. Complete inventory of Porsche parts & accessories at discount prices. Largest used parts inventory in United States. Sales of new, used & rebuildable Porsches. Complete engine & transmission rebuilding - custom turbo modifications. Full performance & race preparation shop.

Parts Duplicators: 7125 A Newton St., Westminster, CO 80030. Telephone 303-428-7181, 8 a.m.-5 p.m. week days. Manufacturers of plastic emblems for 1950 thru 1970 automobiles. Distributors of auto body repair panels for 1949 & up Ford and Chevrolets. Wholesale and retail.

Patrick's Antique Cars & Trucks: Patrick H. Dykes, P.O. Box 648, Casa Grande, AZ 85222. Telephone 602-836-1117. Per customer (feel free...) Specializing in early speed and appearance accessories for flathead Fords, Chevy & GMC '6'. Manufacturer of Fenton cast iron headers for those, and Wayne rocker & side cover for the Chevy '6'. 30 years experience also with '47-'54 Chevy trucks.

Pease Cable & Harness Co., Inc.: Ed and Miki Pease, P.O. Box 51, Woodville Rd., Wood River Junction, RI 02894. Telephone 401-364-3839, 9 a.m. to 5 p.m. Monday through Friday. Manufacturer of antique-type braided and lacquered wiring harnesses, plastic and taped wiring harnesses for all makes of autos, American and foreign. Dealer inquiries invited.

Penn Ball Bearing Co.: Paul Small, 3511 N. American St., Philadelphia, PA 19140. Telephone 215-423-3105, 9 a.m. to 5 p.m. Specializes in ball and roller bearings, oil seals and grease retainers for antique and classic motor vehicles, trucks, motorcycles and all types of motive vehicles, including aircraft. Our 41st year.

Perfect Plastics Industries, Inc.: 14th St., New Kensington, PA 15068. Telephone 800-245-6520, in Pennsylvania 412-339-3568. Manufacturer of quality body parts for MGA, MGB, Midget, Austin Healey, Triumph TR-4, TR-6, BMW, Datsun Z and Fiat.

Perogie Enterprises: Randy & George Porubski, 827 Route 526, Robbinsville, NJ 08691. Telephone 609-259-7057, 9 to 9. Mustang & Ford performance parts. 1965-73 Mustang, 1966-1971 Fairlane/Torino and 1967-73 Cougar parts. Many hi performance engine and drive train parts. Boss 302 specialty.

A. Petrik, Huck Brake Springs & Accessories: See listing under Brakes.

P&M Fastner & Supply: Arthur E. Medeirs & Joseph Peters, P.O. Box M-315, New Bedford, MA 02744. Mail order. Mail order of Auto Hardware, rubber goods and supplies interior washers of all types. Stainless steel, chrome and nickel products. We can also make up some special fasteners. We may have that special what-cha-ma-call-it you need. Send $1.00 for new larger catalog.

Jack Podell Fuel Injection Specialist: Jack Podell, 106 Wakewa Ave., South Bend, IN 46617. Telephone 219-232-6430, 8 a.m.-10 p.m. Monday thru Saturday. Specializing in Rochester Fuel injections for 57-65 Corvettes. Complete rebuild/restoration service, massive parts inventory, rebuilt/detailed units available, and original air cleaners. Now rebuilding distributors. Your one stop fuel injection center.

POR-15: See listing under Upholstery.

Precision Sportscar Servicing: Michael C. Salter, 307 Enford Rd., Richmond Hill, Ont., L4C 3E9. Telephone 416-883-3676, 8:30 a.m. to 5:30 p.m. Mon.-Fri., Sat. 9 a.m. to 1 p.m. Canada's biggest Austin Healey Specialists mail order and open shop Mon.-Fri. 9-5:30, Sat. 9-12:30. Parts service, restoration service for Austin Healeys frame rebuilding jigs, new, used and reconditioned parts, assemblies catalogue $4.50. "Our parts fit because we have to fit them"

Prestige Thunderbird Inc.: See listing under Restoration Firms.

PRO Antique Auto Parts: 50 King Spring Rd., Windsor Locks, CT 06096. Open 9 a.m. to 5 p.m., weekdays. Thousands of new parts available for 1929-1964 Chevrolet and GM cars, Chrysler products, Ford & Mercury. Illustrated catalogs available for $2.00 per make, refundable on order.

P & R Parts Unlimited: Dick Rutherford, Box 608, Park Rapids, MN 56470. Telephone 218-732-5668, after 5 p.m. We make the Mullins fiberglass trailer kits and fender for F-100 Ford pickup and for just about all 27-48 Ford cars & pickup. We have running boards for 33-34 cars, 39-40 cars, 48-56 Ford pickup.

Quality Thunderbird Parts & Products: Stan Brown, 1501 Reisterstown Rd., Baltimore MD 21208. Mail order only, no over the counter sales. Quality used, re-chromed, re-finished and NOS parts for 1964, 1965 and 1966 Thunderbirds. Free detailed catalog available at no charge.

Rankin Auto Parts: J. L. Rankin, P.O. Box 341, Anderson, SC 29622. Telephone 803-226-7947, after 6 p.m. We have some parts, accessories for most cars 1928-1960, ignition bulbs, gaskets, brake kits and lining, misc. other parts, SASE.

RB's Obsolete Automotive: 7130 Hwy. 2, Snohomish, WA 98290. Telephone 800-426-6607, Washington residents call 1-206-568-5669. No. 1 line of rubber parts. Catalog available.

Redden's Relics: Gerald L. Redden, P.O. Box 300, Boiling Springs, PA 17007. Telephone 717-245-2200. By appointment. N.O.S. Pontiac, GTO & Firebird parts. We stock moldings, emblems, bumpers, ignition, brake, front end, electrical & interior parts. Send $1.00 with year & model # for a computerized list of parts we have in stock for your car.

Regent Trading Corp. - "Parts By Paul": Paul T. Brensilber, 245 East 54th Street, Suite 7P, New York, NY 10022. Telephone 212-319-9753, call anytime. Presently we offer exact reproduction striker plater for Ford Passenger Cars and Ford Trucks. Striker plates currently available are Ford Passenger Cars 1949-54, 1955 and 1956 and Ford Trucks 1953-55 and 1956. Write or Call Anytime. Look for other items in the coming year.

Restoration Specialties & Supply, Inc.: David A. Mihalko, R.D. 2, P.O. Box 328, Windber, PA 15963. Telephone 814-269-3304 or 814-467-9282, 9 a.m. to 5 p.m. Window channel; belt weatherstrip, rubber weatherstrip, chrome trim screws, moulding clips & fasteners, trimming sundries, misc. hardware. Catalog $2.00.

Rhode Island Wiring Service, Inc.: John H. Pease, P.O. Box 3737, Columbia Street, Peace Dale, RI 02883. Telephone 401-789-1955, Mon.-Sat. 9:00-5:00. Show quality wiring harnesses for American cars through the late fifties and foreign cars through the late sixties. Exact reproductions of the originals with soldered connectors and full installation instructions. 100% satisfaction guaranteed or 100% refund of all charges.

Rick's Antique Auto Parts: Box 662, Shawnee Mission, KS 66201. Telephone 800-228-5657. Specializes in over 7,000 auto parts and accessories. Free catalog available.

Rik's Corvette Shoppe: Rik and Laurie Craig, Rt. 4, Box 778, Morganton, NC 28655. Telephone 704-433-6506, 9 a.m.-5 p.m. Mon.-Fri., 9 a.m.-3 p.m. Sat. (except weekends when we are away at car shows). Complete line of Corvette parts and accessories for all years of Vettes. Makers of original Astro-Ventilation windows for '68-'74 Vettes. We also stock the original disc brake rally wheel centers for Corvettes and Camaros. Everything at low competitive prices. Specify year model for free price sheet.

Roberts MOtor PARts Inc.: Gary L. Roberts, 17 Prospect St., West Newbury, MA 01985. Telephone 617-363-5407, 617-363-5881, 9 a.m. to 6 p.m. weekdays, 9 a.m. to 12 noon Saturday. New and N.O.S. for Chrysler, Dodge, Plymouth & Desoto passenger cars & Dodge, Plymouth, Fargo & Power Wagon trucks. Also now supplying GMC & Chevrolet truck parts. Car catalog 28-75, $3.00, Mopar truck catalog 28-80 $3.00, GMC & Chevrolet truck list $2.00.

Rochester Fuel Injection: Jack Podell, 106 Wakewa, South Bend, IN 46617. Telephone 219-232-6430, 8 a.m. to 5 p.m. Monday thru Friday. Complete line of reproduction fuel injection parts, massive supply of NOS parts. Complete rebuilding service. Completely rebuilt, restored units available for sale!

Rock Valley Antique Auto Parts Ltd.: David Southwick & Donald Johnson, Rte. 72 & Rothwell Rd., Stillman Valley, IL 61084. Telephone 815-645-2271 or 645-2272, 9 a.m.-9 p.m. We manufacture stainless steel gas tanks for early Ford, Chev., also Corvette and 55-57 Chev. tank. We special build custom tanks. Chev. bumpers and a full line of 1928-48 Ford parts - full line of street rod parts.

Mary Jo Rohner: 15847 Avenida Lamego, Rancho Bernardo, CA 92128. Telephone 619-451-1933. I sell 1953-62 Corvette parts. I specialize in original restored parts. I have rare hard to find parts. Specializing in 1953-55.

Ron's Restorations Inc.: Ron & Janet Brewton, 2530 Shakespeare Drive, Indianapolis, IN 46227. Telephone 317-881-3660, 10 a.m.-7 p.m. We specialize in Ford retractable hardtop parts, new, reproduction and used.

Rootlieb, Inc.: Henry A. Rootlieb, 815 So. Soderquist, P.O. Box 1829, Turlock, CA 95381. Telephone 209-632-2203, Monday through Friday, 7:30 a.m. to 4:30 p.m. Manufacturer of vintage Ford sheet metal and speedster kits. Hoods, fenders, splash aprons, running boards, early Model T bodies and speedster kits for Model Ts and Model As.

Wayne Rowe - Classic Cars & Parts: See listing under Collector Car Dealers.

R&B Classics: Randy & Rick Donovan, 10014 Old Lincoln Trail, Fairview Heights, IL 62208. Telephone 618-398-3477, Mon.& Fri. 9-6 Tues., Wed., Thurs. 9-5, Sat. 9-12. Specialize in Chevy parts for 55-56-57 Chevrolets, Large in stock inventory, Carries all reproduction and G.M. parts available. Daily UPS service, free catalog, toll free order phone.

JIM CARTER, 1500 E. Alton, Independence, MO 64055. Telephone 816-833-1913. 9 a.m. to 5 p.m. Monday-Friday. Chevrolet and GMC trucks - mid 1930's to late 1950's. We provide personal service for the GM truck restorer. Detail items for the perfectionist. Most items always in stock. This is our full time business. May we help you?

Scarborough Faire Inc.: 1151 Main Street, Pawtucket, RI 02860. Telephone 401-724-4200. Importer/exporter, manufacturer and world wide distributor of classic British car parts. Wholesale and retail mail order. Specializing in MGA, MGB, Midget/Sprite, Austin-Healey, Jaguar and Triumph. Largest North American importer of Dunlop wire wheels. Largest worldwide distributor of Heritage Manufacturing (TM) products. Open 6 days, 9 to 5:30. Orders 800-556-6300.

Service Motors: Clarence Kapraun "Kap", Box 8, U.S. 24 West, Lake Cicott, IN 46942. Telephone 219-722-1152, anytime someone answers the phone. Crosley cars and parts - bought - sold - and traded - new and used.

Shell Valley Motors, Inc.: Bob, Jim, and Steve Swoboda, Rt. #1, Platte Center, Neb. 68653. Telephone 402-246-3455, M-F 8-5. Manufacturer of fiberglass Cobra bodies, tubular car frame retail distributor for various aftermarket car parts. Specialists in Shelby Cobra 427 bodies & 1929 Model A Ford reproductions. In house facility towards designing, engineering & completion of fiberglass molds.

Sickafus Sheepskins: P. H. Sickafus, Rt. #78, Exit #7, Strausstown, PA 19559. Telephone 215-488-1782. Retail store open seven days a week 8 a.m. to 8 p.m., Factory hours 10 a.m. to 4 p.m. Monday thru Friday. Sheepskin seat cover, natural shaped skins, semi custom or full custom fit, mail order catalog, manufacture, wholesale, retail.

Small Marine Products: Peter Lindgren, 2700 N.E. 7th Ave., Pompano Beach, FL Telephone 305-945-4265. 8 a.m. to 5 p.m. Mon.-Fri. Stainless steel luggage racks for 1968-77 Corvettes.

O. B. Smith Classic Cars & Parts: P.O. Box 11703, Lexington, KY 40577. Telephone 606-253-1957, 8 a.m. to 5 p.m. Parts for 55-56-57 Chevy, 58-64 Impalas / Camaros / Chevelles / Novas / Corvettes

Smith & Jones Distributing Company: W. Harold Jones - Gary P. Smith, #1 Biloxi Square, West Columbia, SC 29169. Telephone 803-794-0875, 9 a.m. to 5 p.m. We specialize in reproduction parts for Fords 1909-31. We are a full line distributor with mail order and walk in business.

SoCal Pickups Inc.: Clark Beaumont, 6412 Manchester Blvd., Dept. ACP, Buena Park, CA 90621. Telephone 714-994-1400 or 213-941-4693. 9 a.m. to 5:30 p.m., closed Sun. & Mon. '53/'56 Ford F100 parts specialists. Power steering kits, oak bedwood, stainless bed strips, complete instrument panels, new gauges, disc brake kits; motor & tranny mounts, weather stripping. Shop manuals and much more.

Southeast Antique Auto Parts: R.R. #3, Box 160, Pittsburgh, KS 66762. Telephone 316-232-2319 for 24-hour ordering service. Specializes in selling reproduction Ford Model A parts by mail order or open shop.

Special Interest Cars: John Baum, 5891 Westminster Ave., Westminster, CA 92683. Telephone 714-892-6083, 8-5. 1960-1979 Ford parts and accessories, 1958-1974 Thunderbird parts and accessories for sale.

Specialized Auto Parts: Tommy Traylor, Manager-Ken Barker, 7130 Capitol, P.O. Box 9405, Houston, TX 77261. Telephone 713-928-3707, 9:00-5:30 Mon.-Fri. 9:00-1:00 Sat. Established in 1959, we carry a full line of 1909-1948 Ford parts and growing line of 1928-48 Chevrolet parts. Each year we add many new parts to our line. Our catalog is 87 pages, well illustrated, and only $4.00. VISA/MasterCard accepted. COD orders by phone only, please. All orders shipped within 24 hours of receipt.

Speedway Automotive: Phil Hertel, 2300 W. Broadway, Phx, AZ 85041. Telephone 602-276-3200, 8:30-5:30 weekdays, Sat. 9 to 3. Buick parts & service. Over 300 Buick parts cars, Rivieras, Convertibles & full size, a large selection of Skylarks including GS models. Turbo Regals & Grand Nationals. Most cars '61-'81. Also new, NOS & reproduction parts including GSX spoilers front & rear, wood grain dash, engine parts & restoration supplies.

Sports & Classics, Inc.: 512 Boston Post Road, Darien, CT 06820. Telephone 203-655-8731/8732, M-F 9-6, Sat. 10-2. British sportscar parts - Austin Healey, MG, Triumph, Jaguar. Complete selection of restoration parts and accessories. Interior, body, engine and electrical parts. 400 page catalog $7.00.

Standard Auto Parts: Ernie Hemmings, P.O. Box 3906-ACP, Quincy, IL 62305. Telephone 217-224-1078. Ford 1903-31 parts, books, supplies from nations oldest supplier of vintage Ford parts, established 1923, owned by Ernie Hemmings. Catalogue 25¢. Mail order only, phone will be answered when available 7 days a week from 7 a.m. - 9 p.m. central time, if no answer try again.

Duane Steele, Inc.: Duane & Johneva Steele, 920 Mica Dr., Carson City, NV 89701. Telephone 702-883-0766, 8:00 a.m.-5:00 p.m. Monday-Saturday. Duane Steele specializes in mechanical parts, rubber items, trim & emblems and literature for Chevrolet cars and trucks 1914-70, and GMC truck 1934-60. In addition to a full line of restoration supplies, Duane provides free technical and restoration advice based on 40 years of experience in the automotive field and he has a catalog of parts available from his mail order firm.

Lynn H. Steele Reproduction Rubber: Lynn H. Steele, Route 1, Box 71W, Denver, NC 28037. Telephone 704-483-9343. Mon.-Fri. 8 a.m. to 12, 1 p.m. to 5 p.m.; Sat. 8 a.m. to 12 EST. Top quality repro rubber parts for non-Ford American makes, circa 1925-55, up to mid-sixties in the GM line. Extensive line of interior and exterior rubber, vulcanized glass channel, reserviced motor mounts, and runningboard matting. Comprehensive catalogs available for $1.00 per make.

Street Specialty Products, Inc.: 871 N. Hanover Street, Dept. 1117, Pottstown, PA 19464. Telephone 215-327-0152, 9:00-5:30 M-F; 10:00-1:00 Sat. Corvette Parts & Accessories. Corvette distributors and stainless sleeved Corvette calipers; Dot 5 Silicone brake fluid, dealers please inquire. Street Specialty Products, Inc. 871 N. Hanover St., Dept. 1117, Pottstown, PA 19464.

Stoddard Imported Cars, Inc.: 38845 Mentor Ave., Willoughby, OH 44094. Telephone 216-951-1040, Mon./Thurs. til 9:00, T-W-F til 6:00, Sat. 1:00 p.m. Stoddard Imported Cars is internationally known for its specialization for restoration parts for the Porsche Automobile. Strong involvement with the 356 series including reproduction of nose and hood panel for the 356 T-6. Many other items are reproduced for Stoddard from original molds. Mail order catalog, $5.00.

Sunbeam Spares: Box 5172, Kansas City, MO 64132. Telephone 913-541-8500. Specializes in 1946-71 Alpine and Tiger parts.

PARTS SUPP. CONT

Super Sport Restoration Parts, Inc.: William J. Koivu, 2370 Stone Mountain Lithonia Rd., P.O. Box 7, Lithonia, GA 30058-0007. Telephone 404-482-9219, 9-5 M-F, 9-2 Sat. Retail parts dealer. New (N.O.S.), reproduction and used parts. 1962-75 Chevy II/Nova. 1964-75 Chevelle/El Camino. 1967-75 Camaro.

Syverson Cabinet Company: 2301 Rand Rd., Palatine, IL 60074. Telephone 312-358-8428, 9 a.m. to 5 p.m. Monday thru Friday. Specializes in Ford Model T Ford bodies, fenders, radiators, dashboards and firewalls.

T-Bird Nest: P.O. Box 1012, Grapevine, TX 76051. Shop address: 2550 E. Southlake Blvd., Southlake, TX. Telephone 817-481-1776. Full time family business selling parts, making repairs and doing restorations. Servicing 1958-1966 Thunderbirds (others considered).

Tee-Bird Products Inc.: Box 153, Exton, PA 19341. Telephone 215-363-1725. 1955 and 1956 Ford Passenger car parts, parts list $2.00. 1955, 1956, 1957 Thunderbird parts. Catalog $2.00.

Texas Mustang Parts Inc.: Rt. 6, Box 996A, Waco, TX 76706. Telephone 817-662-2790, 8-5:30 5½ days. Complete line 64½-73 Mustang parts. Free 98 page catalog - Free calls for orders - Free shipping over $150.00 - Free information - Satisfaction guaranteed. New parts only.

Terrill Machine Inc.: Feltz Terrill Jr., Rt. 2, Box 61, De Leon, TX 76444, Mon.-Fri. 8 a.m.-6 p.m. CST. We handle engine overhaul parts for 37-58 Buick, 36-62 Cadillac, 29-51 Chevrolet, 37-54 Chrysler, Dodge, Desota, 37-60 Oldsmobile, 35-56 Packard, 37-56 Pontiac, 33-52 Plymouth. S.A.S.E. required for inquiry.

Thunderbird Headquarters: Don Johnson, 1080 Detroit Avenue, Concord, CA 94518. Telephone 800-227-2174. 8 a.m. to 5 p.m. Mon. thru Fri., 8 a.m. to 12 p.m. Sat. We offer a complete line of parts for the 1955 thru 1966 Thunderbird, including upholstery, sheet metal, rubber products, suspension parts, paints and dyes. Catalogs are available for $3.00 or will be shipped free with order.

Tioga Stainless: Walter H. Grove, 6 Deborah Dr., Apalachin, NY 13732. Telephone 607-625-4425. Quality stainless steel nuts, bolts, screws, washers, rivets, cotter pins, nails and buffing supplies. Many hard to find fastener sizes. Model "A" Ford fastener sets a specialty. (Sorry, no metric nor British Whitworth).

Tom's Obsolete Chevy Parts: Tom Hunter, 21 Terrace Ave., Pawtucket, RI 02860. Telephone 401-723-7580, 1-9 p.m. EST. New & reproduction Chevrolet parts 1955-1972. Camaro, Nova-Chevy II, Chevelle, Impala, Belairs & Monte Carlo. Chrome trim, emblems, mouldings, weather stripping, electrical parts, mirrors, lenses, trunk mats, spare tire covers, outside door handles, wheel covers, etc. Call between 1-9 p.m. Monday-Saturday EST.

The Truck Shop: Donald L. Sumner, P.O. Box 5035, 102 West Marion Ave., Nashville, GA 31639. Telephone 912-686-3833, Mon.-Fri. 8:00 to 5:00. Chevy & GMC Truck Parts 1927-72. NOS & Reproduction parts. All type of parts available for above. Satisfaction Guaranteed.

U.S. Mustang Inc.: 24 East Aurora St., Waterbury, CT 06708. Telephone 203-573-0900, 9 a.m. to 6 p.m. Monday thru Friday, till 8 p.m. Thursday, 9 a.m. to 4 p.m. Saturday. New, reproduction, used parts and accessories for 1964½ thru 1973 Mustangs. MasterCard, Visa and COD orders accepted. UPS shipping available.

UVIRA, Inc./UVIRA Laser Optics Corp.: P.O. Box 610, 310 Pleasant Valley Road, Merlin, OR 97352. Telephone 503-474-5050, 9:00 a.m. to 6:00 p.m. Pacific std. time. Original headlights with sealed beam efficiency. High reflectance, protected aluminum coating of your original headlight reflectors. Vacuum deposited aluminum yields reflectance equal to best obtainable with silver. Coating looks like authentic, freshly polished silver in every way, but will never tarnish. SASE for more information.

Valley Ford Parts-AKA: Valley Obsolete Ford: 11610 Van Owen St., No. Hollywood, CA 91605. Telephone 213-982-5303, Monday through Saturday, 9:30 a.m. to 5 p.m. Specializes in 1928-70 Ford parts, 1965-73 Mustang and Shelby parts. Full line of new and used stock parts. Dealer inquiries invited.

Vintage Automotive: Mr. & Mrs. Jim Hines, Box 626, Mtn. Home, ID 83647. Telephone 208-587-3743, 9 a.m. to 6 p.m. Monday thru Friday, 9 a.m. to 5 p.m. Saturday. Full line of new and used parts of all kinds for all older cars and trucks, 1920's - 60's. Over 700 parts cars on hand.

Vintage Auto Parts: 24300 Highway 9, Woodinville, WA 98072. Telephone 206-486-0777, 1-800-426-5911, 9:30 a.m. to 5:30 p.m. Monday thru Friday, 9:30 a.m. to 4:00 p.m. Saturday. Specializing in auto parts from 1920-1970, very good stock of mechanical parts.

Vintage Auto Parts: 11318 Beach Blvd. Stanton, CA 90680. Telephone 714-894-5464. Specializes in new parts for Ford Model T, Model A, early V-8, 1949-56 and 1948-56 pickups.

Vintage Brass Works: Art Hart, R.R. #1, Box 91-B, Chester, NJ 07930. Telephone 201-584-3319. Mail order only. Specializes in pre-1912 reproduced parts for one-cylinder Cadillacs, Curved Dash Olds', Stanley Steamers and other early cars.

Vintage Car Corral: Paul Zimmerman, 1401 N.W. 53 Ave., P.O. Box 384, Gainesville, FL 32602. Telephone 904-376-4513, 10 a.m.-5 p.m. Many new mechanical parts for older cars. Some trim & sheetmetal.

The Vintage Garage: North Brookfield, MA 01535. Telephone 617-867-2892 or 617-867-9210. Specializes in hard-to-find parts for many Rolls-Royce models.

Vintage Specialists: P.O. Box 772, Hobe Sound, FL 33455. Telephone 305-546-3177. MG Parts 1929-70's, new and used. Interior tops, chrome, body, mechanical and accessories. Catalog $2.00 each. Credit cards or COD.

Virginia Vettes: Richard Barron, 110 Maid Marion Place, Williamsburg, VA 23185. Telephone 804-229-0011, 9 a.m.-9 p.m. EST. A one stop source for your '57-'82 Corvette parts and accessories. Virginia Vettes specializes in Corvette weatherstrip, window felt, fasteners, complete interiors, carpeting, door panels, fiberglass front ends, spoilers. We have a 6000 square ft. warehouse full of new and used Corvette parts.

Volunteer State Chevy Parts: Don Trivett, Highway 41 South, Greenbrier, TN 37073. Telephone 615-643-4583. Mon.-Fri. 8 a.m. to 6 p.m. weekends by chance. One of the largest Chevrolet parts sources available today. 1935-69 Chevy's all makes and models. New old stock (millions of parts), complete line of reproductions, plus rechromed and mint used!! Largest combined Chevy parts inventory in the world!!

Volunteer Vette Products: Ronnie Martin, 400 Young High Pike, Knoxville, TN 37920. Telephone 615-573-4843, 9-6. Reproduction of discontinued Corvette parts. Also, full line of GM Corvette parts and repro parts,including interior, mechanical, detail, etc.

V & V Supplies: 23 Alma Rd., Reigate, Surrey, RH2 0DJ, England. Telephone 011-44-7372-43534. Rare sales catalogs 1890's-1920. Covering European and American cars. Also, the complete Automobilist Ltd. Vintage Accessory catalog, over 1,000 items. List/catalog airmailed $5.00 each, cash.

Burton Waldron, Antique Auto Parts: Burton Waldron, 25872 M-86 Box C, Nottawa, MI 49075. Telephone 616-467-7185, 9:30-4:30. We do most cars & trucks 1924 to late 60's. We do many pipes in stainless steel #409. No "Y"s or mufflers in stainless. All inquiries answered.

Ken Walls: R. #6 Box 47, Harriman, TN 37748. Telephone 615-882-2561. VHSA video tapes of junkyards in the South. Parts cars, restorable cars, restored cars and trucks. Also have old stock rubber floor mats and trunk mats for most cars of the 1940's, 50's, 60's. Moulded carpets from 1960's-86.

Ed West: 1941 Jan Marie Pl., Tustin, CA 92680. Telephone 714-832-2688. Jaguar parts, XK120, 140, 150, Mark I, II, VII, VIII, IX. Over 10,000 items! New/used reproductions.

Wheel Covers - Robinson's Auto Sales: See listing under Hubcaps & Wheelcovers.

J.C. Whitney: 1917-19 Archer Ave., P.O. Box 8410, Chicago, IL 60680. Telephone 312-431-6102. 24 hours - 7 days. Automotive catalog - save up to 50 per cent on more than 100,000 automotive parts & accessories in this catalog from J.C. Whitney. Components for motorcycles, vans, pickups, RV's and off road vehicles are included. Free catalog.

Windy Hill Auto Parts: Pat, Allan & Larry Bajari, Box 179, New London, MN 56273. Telephone 612-354-2201. 8 a.m. - 5 p.m. 7 days a week. We have over 150 acres of older cars and trucks for parts. We ship parts all over the country. Customers are welcome to browse through the yard. We are open 365 days a year.

Year One, Inc.: Box 450131, Atlanta, GA 30345. Telephone 404-493-6568. 10 a.m. to 7 p.m. weekdays, 12 noon to 5 p.m. Saturday. Restoration parts for '64-74 American made performance cars, Mopars, GM, AMX. Interiors, exteriors, trim, upholstery, chrome, nameplates, decals, books, etc.

Y n Z's Yesterdays Parts: Gene Zdunowski, 1615 W. Fern Ave., Redlands, CA 92373. Telephone 714-825-3614 or 714-822-7317. 9 a.m. to 6 p.m. PST. Antique and classic car wiring harnesses. Over 650 patterns from 1919-1957. Duplications of originals. Lacquer coated braided wire. Terminals are crimped and soldered. Color coded. Simplified installation instructions. Harnesses are guaranteed to fit. Quality of workmanship is guaranteed to please. Send $1.00 for catalog.

The Zierden Co.: Peter F. Zierden, 7355 S. 1st St., Oak Creek, WI 53154. Telephone 414-764-6630, 8-4:30. Exhaust pipes, tailpipes, mufflers, stainless & conventional steel.

Z Power Plus: Amy Chan, 3405 Belle River Dr., Hacienda Hts., CA 91745. Telephone 213-333-1718, 24-hour line. Specializes in fiberglass custom parts, suspension, interior and mechanical parts for Datsun Z, ZX, and 510. Also Capris, Porsche and Mazda RX-7.

PERIODICALS

A&B Investments Ltd.: Bob Kroupa, P.O. Box 2273R, Morristown, NJ 07960. Telephone 201-898-9110, 8 a.m.-8 p.m. Publishes a Corvette Pricing Guide and Appraisal service. Summarizes the prices of 19,000 Corvettes covering all years and body styles. Includes original base price, number manufactured, high, low and average resale prices, and the all important change in average price from previous year - excellent indicator of investment potential.

Auto Collector News: P.O. Box 286, Whiting, IA 51063. Telephone 712-458-2402, 8 a.m.-5 p.m. M-F. Publishes monthly magazine that features the Parts Finder - listings of parts from salvage yards nationwide, updated monthly.

Automobile Quarterly: P.O. Box 348, Route 222 and Sharadin Rd., Kutztown, PA 19530. Telephone 215-683-8352, 8 a.m. to 4:30 p.m. EST. Publishers of *Automobile Quarterly Magazine*, Library Series Books, and Automobile Quarterly Car Portrait Posters.

British Car & Bike Magazine: D. Destler, Publisher, P.O. Box 1045, Canoga Park, CA 91304. Telephone 818-710-1234. 9 a.m.-5 p.m. British Car & Bike magazine is the definitive publication for the enthusiast of English vehicles of all ages and types. Every big, colorful issue is packed with roadtests, historical articles, technical and instructive features on British automobiles and motorcycles. Published quarterly.

Cars & Parts Annual: P.O. Box 482, 911 Vandemark Road, Sidney, OH 45365. Telephone 513-498-0803, 8 a.m. to 5 p.m., Monday through Friday. The once-a-year guide to the collector car hobby with comprehensive directories for car clubs, antique auto museums and automotive salvage yards specializing in vintage car parts. Included are special features on various aspects of owning, operating and maintaining collector cars, as well as in-depth articles on restoring vintage cars and trucks. A valuable year-round reference edition for both the armchair enthusiast and the active do-it-yourselfer. Produced by the publishers of *Cars & Parts Magazine*.

Cars & Parts Magazine: P. O. Box 482, 911 Vandemark Road, Sidney, OH 45365. Telephone 513-498-0803. 8 a.m. to 5 p.m., Monday through Friday. The Magazine Serving the Car Hobbyist, *Cars & Parts* is a monthly magazine with entertaining and informative editorial features, attractively presented display advertising and a massive classified ad section with thousands of vintage cars, parts and related items for sale, and wanted. Editorial features include in-depth series on the history of the automobile, pioneers in the industry and individual manufacturers and marques. Full-color car features on specific models include detailed photography and complete specifications, plus vital information on the car's development, impact on the market, innovations in engineering, etc. Regular monthly columns include: Ford Country by noted Ford authority David L. Lewis; Free Wheeling, a special column devoted to the history of various makes and makers, by the legendary Menno Duerksen; show and swap meet calendar with a full preview of upcoming hobby events throughout the U.S. and Canada; Tool Bag, a technical question and answer column by veteran hobbyist and talented restorer Ken New; Reader Forum, a letters to the editor column where readers can air their gripes and voice their opinions about anything automotive; and In the Headlights, a news and events column reporting on current activities in the hobby. Rounding out the most popular editorial package in the old car hobby are regular restoration features emphasizing "how-to" techniques for the novice and veteran restorer. Annual subscription $18.00.

Chrysler Power Magazine: Roland Osborne, P.O. Box 1210, Azusa, CA 91702. Telephone 818-303-6220, 8 a.m.-5 p.m. M-F, Sat. by appt. Who to, where to and how to. Chrysler Power emphasizes a broad range of vintage, muscle and hi tech info for restorers, collectors and enthusiasts.

Classic Publishing, Inc.: 8601 Dunwoody Pl., Suite 144, Atlanta, GA 30338. Publishers of *Car Collector and Car Classics*, a monthly magazine.

Collector Car News: P.O. Box 5279, Long Beach, CA 90805. Telephone 213-492-1563, 8:30 a.m. to 5:00 p.m. The West's oldest and largest complete "collectible car" magazine.

CSK Publishing Co. Inc.: 175 Hudson St., Hackensack, NJ 07601. Telephone 201-440-2770, 9:30 to 5. Publisher of the following automotive magazines: Vette-Edited for the Corvette Enthusiast; Pontiac-Covering Great Pontiacs of the Past Plus Today's High Tech Performers; Musclecars. The Monster Stockers of the Sixties vs. Modern Muscle of the Eighties; Cars Illustrated - Street Action at its Best. Burnout Contests, Power-shifting and MOPAR - featuring Chrysler power of yesteryear.

Dobbs Publications: 3816 Industry Blvd., Lakeland, FL 33807. Telephone 813-646-5743, 9 a.m. to 5 p.m. Publishes *Mustang Monthly Magazine, SuperFord, Car Exchange & Car Review.*

Ficken Antique Publications: See listing under Parts Suppliers.

Hemmings Motor News: P.O. Box 100, Bennington, VT 05201. Telephone 802-442-3101, 9 a.m. to 5 p.m. World's largest, and largest circulation, old auto hobby magazine, over 600 pages monthly of ads for cars, parts, supplies, services, and everything else the hobbyist needs. "The bible" of the old auto hobby since 1954.

Krause Publications, Inc.: Iola, WI 54990. Publisher of *Old Cars Weekly*, a weekly tabloid newspaper, and *Old Cars Price Guide*, a bi-monthly.

Locator: P.O. Box 32, Whiting, IA 51063. Telephone 712-458-2213, 8 a.m.-5 p.m. M-F. "The World's largest used auto and truck parts magazine." Published monthly since 1957, features listings of parts from salvage yards from classic to contemporary.

Miniature Cars: Eric Waiter, Box 221, Bernardsville, NJ 07924. Telephone 201-267-5612, 8 a.m. to 8 p.m. EST. Over 5000 different scale model autos. Catalogs $2. Also US distributor for British magazines *Classic & Sportscar, Motor Sports, Model Auto Review.*

Model Car Trader: Lester Sturtevant, 75 East Grove St., Middleboro, MA 02346. Telephone 617-947-7214. Bi-monthly publication for miniature car hobbyist. Classified ads for plastic kits, promotionals, diecast, slotcars, parts, literature, plus a comprehensive guide of toy show dates & locations.

New England Autosport Associates: See listing under Auctioneers and Appraisers.

Off-Road Advertiser: Fred C. Horton, P.O. Box 1154, Arcata, CA 95521. Telephone 213/860-7007, 9 a.m.-5 p.m. Magazine for four wheel drive and dune buggy owners. Major off-road races, events, calendar, driver profiles and large classified ad section.

Professional Publications: P.O. Box 505, Lake Jem, FL 32745. Publishes "Tax Saving Techniques for Antique, Collector and Investor Automobiles," the "Bible" of tax information on this subject since 1980.

Quicksilver Communications, Inc.: Martyn L. Schorr, President, 167 Terrace St., Haworth, NJ 07641. Telephone 201-384-1910, 10 to 5 p.m. Publisher of marque series high performance auto books dealing with 50s, 60s & 70s. Wholesale & retail.

Randolphs' Special Services: Steve Randolph, 112 N. Main St., Lowell, NC 28098. Telephone 704-824-1619. 5 p.m. to 9 p.m., Monday thru Saturday. AUTODEX - Nations largest late model parts locator. Many special interest cars included. Over 10,000 wrecks and rebuildables listed monthly. Our 29th year.

Restoration Magazine: I.S.V.P., P.O. Box 50046, Tucson, AZ 85703. Telephone 602-622-2201, 8:30-4:30 M-F. A magazine for the collector/restorer - featuring how-to, history, sources, types and more - Send SASE for brochure and subscription information.

Special Interest Autos, P.O. Box 196, Bennington, VT 05201. Telephone 802-442-3101, 9 a.m. to 5 p.m. Bi-monthly, glossy magazine featuring in-depth articles, driving impressions, comparison tests on cars from '20s through '60s; very well illustrated.

Sport & GT Market: P.O. Box 99414, San Diego, CA 92109. Monthly sports car magazine.

Vintage Auto Almanac P.O. Box 945, Bennington, VT 05201. Telephone 802-442-3101. 9 a.m. to 5 p.m. Hobby's most complete guide to dealers, vendors & other sources, plus clubs, museums, publications and salvage yards. Over 3,000 listings. Organized for easy use.

Vette Vues Enterprises, Inc.: Jim Prater, 5064 Roswell Rd., Suite B-102, Atlanta, GA 30342. Telephone 404-252-2575, 9 a.m. to 4:30 p.m. Monday thru Friday. We publish two magazines for car enthusiasts. *Vette Vues* monthly, for Corvettes; *Street Vues*, bi-monthly, for street rods & street machines. Both feature classified & display advertising for cars, parts & services, articles, coming events, news of new products and services, etc.

PROMOTIONS

Antique Winter Festival: See listing under Auctioneers and Appraisers.

Automotive Ventures Inc.: Wm. H. Bonbrake, 717 North Ave., Macon, GA 31211. Telephone 912-743-5913. Automotive Ventures is involved in all aspects of promoting car shows & events. We maintain a small inventory of quality cars & also do appraisals.

Barrie Automotive Flea Market: Box 841, Barrie, Ont., Canada L4M 1Y6. Telephone 705-722-4421, anytime. Canada: Barrie Automotive Flea Market June - Annual Spring Flea Market: Car sales, R.V. sales, general sales. September - annual automotive flea market: antique and classic cars and parts, car show, car sale and auction, car competition.

Chevy & GMC Truckin' Nationals: Seth Doulton, P. O. Box 119, Santa Barbara, CA 93102. Telephone 805-962-4514, 10 a.m. to 6 p.m. Chevy truck show held in Ogden, Utah each year on Father's Day weekend.

Classic Auto Productions: Robert Barrett, Richard Demberg, Rd. #5, Box 546-A, Middletown, NY 10940. Telephone 914-386-3962, after 5:00 p.m. Eastern. Mid-September, Middletown '88, fourth annual show. Middletown, New York/Antique autos, streetrods, customs, steam & gas engines, antique tractors, auto flea mkt., car corral, arts & crafts, addt'l. attractions.

The Flea Marketeers: Chip & Bill Miller, 1000 Bryn Mawr Rd., Carlisle, PA 17013-1588. Telephone 717-243-7855, 9-5 weekdays. Promoters of Carlisle Collector Car Flea Markets, April, July & October, Import Festival May & Corvettes @ Carlisle in August. Also publishers of Car Events Almanac.

Hershey In The Spring: Jerry Doney & Larry Stalnecker, P.O. Box 234, Annville, PA 17003. Telephone 717-867-4810, Mon., Wed., Fri. 6-9 p.m. EST. Automotive Flea Market, Car Mart (cars for sale by their OWNERS) Arts & Crafts, Saturday & Sunday, Car show, Peoples Judging, Trophies awarded, Sunday only.

Michigan Antique Festival: Saginaw Strokers Auto Club, 3519 Westview, Saginaw, MI 48602. Telephone 517-793-8389, 7 p.m.-9 p.m. Mon.-Fri. Michigan Antique Festivals, Midland Mich. Fairgrounds, June 4-5, July 16-17, Sept. 24-25, 1988, Antique & Special Interest Auto Show, Sales Lot, Swap Meet.

Pomona Swap Meet: George Cross & Sons, P.O. Box 12311, Santa Ana, CA 92712. Telephone 714-547-5257, 8 a.m. to 8 p.m. West Coast Largest Antique Auto, Corvette & Porsche Swap Meet, held six times a year at the Los Angeles County Fairgrounds in Pomona, CA.

Portland Swap Meet: Committee, P.O. Box 23722, Portland, OR 97223. Telephone 503-244-2296, anytime. April 9 & 10, 1988 - Expo Center - Largest meet west of the Mississippi. 3500 stalls - 40,000 buyers.

Rainbow City: Frank Martino, 1418 Broadway, Ft. Wayne, IN 46802. Telephone 219-422-7790. 9:30 a.m. to 5:00 p.m. Promoter of automobile & motorcycle swap meets & toy shows & car shows.

RADIATORS

American Honeycomb Radiator Mfg.: Neil Thomas, 1281 Arthur Kill Rd., Staten Island, NY 10312. Telephone 212-948-7772, 8:30 a.m. to 5 p.m., Tuesday through Saturday. Manufacturer of cartridge type Honeycomb radiators and cores. Catalog available.

The Brassworks: Greg Gouveia, 3523 So. Higuera, Unit E, San Luis Obispo, CA 93401. Telephone 805-489-6560, 8:00 a.m.-4:30 p.m. Manufacturer of exact reproduction radiators for Fords 1909-1927 round tube and flat tube.Model A replacement radiators. Restoration of radiators for classic cars. Pressurized radiators for Street Rods.

Glen-Ray Radiators, Inc.: Ray Schirmer, 2105 Sixth St., Wausau, WI 54401. Telephone 715-842-3352, 7 a.m. to 5:30 p.m. Mon.-Fri. Radiator rebuilding and recoring. Mail order and open shop.

Mustang Parts Corral of Texas: See listing under Parts Suppliers.

Vintage Radiators: P. D. Stevenson, Main Street, Abthorpe, Towcester, Northants, England NN12 8QN. Telephone 0327-857726, anytime. Manufacturers of radiator cores and complete radiators for antique autos.

RADIO, CLOCK, SPEEDOMETER REPAIR

Auto Clock Shop: Rick Graham, 1801 Bladensburg Rd. N.E., Washington, DC 20002. Telephone 202-399-0699, 8:30-5:00 M-F. Auto Clock Repair - all American models, any year U.S. car - Send SASE for price quote - free estimates.

Auto Radio Specialists: Marvin Paul, 405 S. Willow, Sioux Falls, SD 57104. Telephone 605-332-5168, 8:30 a.m.-5:30 p.m. Mon.-Fri., 8:30-Noon Sat. Auto radio service for the car collector. All work done by craftsman, 33 years experience in tube type radios, wonderbar tuners, vibtator rebuilding, simple repair work to complete restoration done. Also, full service department for transistor radios, 8-track, cassette units. Many original equipment radios available from 1939. Estimates cheerfully given.

Bill's Speedometer Shop: Bill Heidemann, 3353 Tawny Leaf Ct., Sidney, OH 45365. Telephone 513-492-7800. Restoration, repair and calibration of all types of mechanical speedometers and tachometers. Cables made to order. Speedo and gauge faces refurbished.

G. A. Brooks, Watchmaker: R.R. 1, Box G25, Lee, MA 01238. Telephone 413-243-3367, 9 a.m. to 5 p.m. Repair of Waltham and Elgin auto clocks.

The Clock Shop: Frank Fulkerson, 4141 Monroe St., Toledo, OH 43606, Telephone 419-472-4421. Auto clocks repaired, all work guaranteed. We also can cut, drill and grind glass to your sample frame or specifications. 25 years experience.

Corvette Specialties of Maryland: See listing under Parts Suppliers.

Charles Ivey Speedometer Service: Charles Ivey, 2144 Wallace Drive, Wichita, KS 67218. Telephone 316-683-6765, 9:00 a.m.-4:00 p.m. Mon.-Fri. central time. Repair and restoration, Ford speedometers, 1928-1937, with dial and odometer re-facing. Try us for later Fords and other makes. We will try to help you if we can. Many thanks to all who sent us speedometers in the past thru Cars & Parts Annual listings!

Custom Autosound Mfg.: Carl Sprague, 808 West Vermont Ave., Anaheim, CA 92805. Telephone 714-535-1091, 8 a.m.-6 p.m., six days. Custom Autosound specializes in custom converted AM-FM cassettes remanufactured to fit OEM into original radio openings of the great American cars such as: 1965-73 Mustang, 1955-57 Chevy, T-Bird, 1958-82 Corvette, 1967-68 Camaro, Firebird, 1964-72 Chevelle, Monte Carlo. Also available are custom fitted dual speaker assemblies (replacing singles) for above cars as well as other speaker configurations. Over 400 parts and restoration dealers handle their products.

International Speedometer & Clock Co.: 3017 W. Irving Park Rd., Chicago, IL 60618. Telephone 312-463-3680. Contact Jack Pustil.

Midsouth Speedometer: 1633 Midland Blvd., Fort Smith, AR 72901. Telephone 501-785-5662. Speedometer, tachometer, clock and gauge repair.

Mustang Parts Corral of Texas: See listing under Parts Suppliers.

Ole 'Doc' Clock: P.O. Box 2234, Byrd Road, Salisbury, NC 28144. Phone him at 704-279-6019. Ole 'Doc' Clock Board Certified Clockologist is a real people, not just a mail box. So that you may personally know who you are sending your valuable auto clock to, and to better serve a growing family of satisfied customers, 'Doc' and his mobile clock shop appear at over 15 car shows each year to offer you a larger stock of N.O.S. and rebuilt clocks, free advice, expert repair and quartz conversions for all clocks. All other times 'Doc' is in his North Carolina clock shop taking care of your mail orders. Ole 'Doc' Clocks is the specialist. He deals ONLY in automobile clocks. "No Tick-Tock, Call on 'Doc." Call or write 'Doc' and send your sick clocks today.

Prestige Thunderbird, Inc.: See listing under Parts Suppliers.

Radio Doctor: 202 Lexington Pl., Uniontown, PA 15401. Repairs old car radios, tube type a specialty. Over 40 years experience. Ship via UPS insured. Seven day service.

Radios and Wheelcovers: John and Ruth Sheldon, 2718 Koper Drive, Sterling Hts., MI 48310. Telephone 313-977-7979, 9 a.m. to 6 p.m. EST. We specialize in Radios and Wheelcovers. We buy, sell, restore radios from 1926 to 1986. We specialize in conversion of radios from AM to AM-FM with 100% original appearance. We also sell and restore record and tape players, speakers, grilles, etc. We have the worlds largest selection of Wheelcovers and Rally Wheels from the 50's, 60's, 70's and 80's.

Marvin Roth Antique Radios, Parts, Service: Marvin Roth, 14500 LaBelle St., Oak Park, MI 48237. Supplier of parts and service for domestic brand tube type radios. Repair, Rebuilding. Specialist: Wonderbar Town/Country, power tuners. Help for "do-it-yourselfers" service diagrams re-build kits. T-Bird radio switches etc. "Mirrormatic" electronic mirrors (MoPar).

Seckman's Antique Radio & Speaker Repair: Zeke and Ginger Seckman, 5340 Sandra Dr., Ravenna, Ohio 44266. Telephone 216-297-1816, 11 a.m. to 8 p.m., Tuesday through Saturday. Rebuild car radios up to 1971. One-year guarantee. Speakers reconed for any radio to date. 1932-48 Ford and Mercury and 1936-48 Lincoln distributors strobed and serviced using original Ford Stroboscopic equipment.

The Speaker Shop: C. C. Orme, 2409½ West Colorado Avenue, Colorado Springs, CO 80904. Telephone 303-634-7358. Rebuild speakers for auto radio.

The Temperature Gauge Guy: A. R. (Dick) Evans, 521 Wood St., Dunedin, FL 33528. Telephone 813-733-6716, when caught. "The Temperature Gauge Guy" more than thirty years of tinkering temperature gauges. Yours probably will be no problem. Non-electric and non-radiator-cap only. A. R. (Dick) Evans. May-October, 45 Prospect St., Essex Jct., VT 05452 (802-878-2811. October-May, 521 Wood St., Dunedin, FL 33528 (813) 733-6716.

West Hill Auto Clocks: William G. Dexter, West Hill Road, Wolcott, VT 05680. Telephone 802-888-2820, 7:00-5:00. West Hill Auto Clocks specializes in auto clock repair of all types except electronic. Most repairs $27 includes parts, labor, shipping. String-wind, stem-wind, eight-day, foreign, and Motochron, $37.

John R. Wolf: 4741 Sherwin Rd., Willoughby, OH 44094. Telephone 216-942-0083. 9 a.m. to 9 p.m. Service repair of all non-electric temp. gauges, motormeters, oil pressure gauges, etc. Guaranteed, plus 3 day turnaround. Also repair of many electric gauges. Call first.

REPLICARS

Antique & Classic Automotive, Inc.: 100 Sonwil Industrial Park, Buffalo, NY 14225. Telephone 800-245-1310/NY State and Canada: 716-684-1167, Monday-Friday 8:30 a.m.-5:00 p.m., Saturdays by appt. Full size, authentic replicas of 1937 Jaguar SS-100 and 1952 Jaguar XK 120. SS-100 available as a VW or front engine kit, XK 120 as a front engine kit only. All kits engineered for assembly by the home do-it-yourselfer, no welding, no fiberglassing for assembly. Free brochures.

British Coach Works, Ltd.: Arnold, Pa. 15068. Telephone 800-245-1369, PA 412-339-3541. Manufacturer the BCW 52 replica (MG-TD replica) highly detailed & very authentic kit designed for the average D.I.Y. Use with GM drivetrain or VW Beetle chassis.

California Custom Coach: Cecil Gold, 1285 E. Colorado Blvd., Pasadena, CA 91106. Telephone 818-796-4395. Mon.-Fri. 9 a.m. to 6 p.m., Sat. 11 a.m. to 4 p.m. We build the Auburn Speedster replica and the California Daytona Spyder. We also restore vintage, classic, and exotics. We import European automobiles and federalize European automobiles. We have a 3500 sq. ft. showroom we use for sale and display of classic, exotic and vintage automobiles.

Classic Cars Ltd. Joseph Fricano, Manager, RD #1, Box 141-E, Chatham, NY 12037. Telephone 518-392-9636. Sales representatives for Classic Roadsters Ltd., with the 1939 Jaguar SS-100, 1952 M.G.T.D., 1962 Austin Healey "3000" and also 1929 Mercedes Beanz

Cobra Restorers Ltd.: See listing under Parts Suppliers.

Elegant Motors, Inc.: Del O. Amy, P.O. Box 30188, Indianapolis, IN 46230. Telephone 317-253-9898. By appointment. Manufacturer of the Auburn & Cord, Cobra & Cheetah reproduction kits, packages, and assemblies, as well as a line of off-shore yacht kits, packages & assemblies.

Experi-Metal, Inc.: 6345 Wall St., Sterling Heights, MI 48077. Telephone 313-977-7800, 8 a.m. to 5 p.m. Reproduction body, in steel, of '32 Chevrolet roadster.

Handcraft Motorcar Company: Orville A. Feikema, 4620 26th Avenue, West, Bradenton, FL 33529. Telephone 813-749-1355, 9 to 5. Manufacturers of the Cormorant Rumble Seat Roadster. The Cormorant is not a replica, but the styling is strongly reminiscent of the classic Packards of the 1930's. The car utilizes a full-size rear drive Cadillac chassis of 1977 or newer vintage. Available in kit, partially completed and completed forms.

Lazarus Motor Sales & Museum: See listing under Auctioneers and Appraisers.

Milan Convertibles: Milan Daniel, 1467 E. Main St., Santa Paula, CA 93060. Telephone 805-584-3409. 9:00 - 5:00, 24 hr. answering service. Milan Roadster convertible 4-door 1976-79 Cadillac Seville converted into 2-door custom convertible. Cadillac Eldorado convertible conversions.

Perfect Plastics Industries Inc.: 14th Street, New Kensington, PA 15068. Telephone 800-245-6520, PA 412-339-3568. Manufacture body parts for Datsun Z, MGB, MGA, MG, Midget, Sprite, Austin Healey 100-4-6-3000. BMW, Triumph TR-4-6.

RESTORATION AIDS

Anover Sales: 3445 S. Hanover St., Baltimore, MD 21225. Telephone 301-355-3664, 8:30-5:00. Spray dye for carpets. Plastic window spray cleaner (anti-static). Spray dye for leather & vinyl.

ATTACK: Dr. Howard Rosenthal, 18 North Walling, St. Louis, MO 63141. Telephone 314-434-7825. Attack is a rubber, vinyl, and leather protectant suitable for new cars or classics, superior in nature to products sold in discount stores. Attack also manufactures an exotic non-abrasive, no soap, high suds car wash as fine as any available anywhere.

Automotive Paints Unlimited: Rt. 1, Roxboro, NC 27573. Telephone 919-599-5155, 9 a.m. to 5 p.m. Mail-order supplier of acrylic enamel and acrylic lacquer finishes for 1904-present automobiles.

Blue Star Inc.: Paul Sawczyc, 569 Anderson Ave., Wood-Ridge, NJ 07075. Telephone 201-933-4435, 8-5. Automotive laundry, sandblasting, glass beading, hot tanking, acid dipping. Cylinder heads resurfaced, rebuilt blocks, bored & honed. All work done on premises.

RESTORATION AIDS

Bugeye Ltd.: See listing under Parts Suppliers.

California Classic Chevy Parts: See listing under Parts Suppliers.

Calyx Corporation: George F. Albright, Jr., P.O. Box 39277, Cincinnati, OH 45239. Telephone 513-923-1154. Calyx® Manifold Dressing the finishing touch. Easy to use and non-toxic. Won't burn off. Leaves manifold with a silver luster.

Champion Lubricants, Inc.: A. J. Wichita, 605 Laguna Dr., Richardson, TX 75080. Telephone 214-231-5464, 9:00-5:00. Champion products has developed oil and fuel treatments with the only known undersurface lubricant that migrates into metals and "sweats" out under operational heat. Our products have been sold directly to the major oil companies for use in their own equipment for the 41 years specifically to reduce downtime.Life extension of equipment from 2 to 3 times has been documented with QX-500 Fuel Lubricant and QX-700 Moly Oil Blend.

C.M. Laboratories, Inc.: Eugene B. McGurl, P.O. Box 8002, Portland, ME 04101. Telephone 207-772-3689, 8-5 p.m. Manufacturer of automotive reconditioning products. Products that are of interest, Blue Diamond Paste Wax, Vinyl Sheen Detergent Resistant Protectant, Spike and Wire Wheel Cleaner, Pink Stuf® All Purpose Cleaner and Degreaser, (water base). Wash and Wax Car Wash Liquid. Miscellaneous cleaners and reconditioning products.

Color-Plus: Joseph L. Maliszewski, P.O. Box 404, Kearny, NJ 07032. Telephone 201-659-4708, 8:30 to 4:30. Manufacturers of SURFLEX Flexible Colorant (dye) for refinishing leather and vinyl; SOFFENER - the most potent leather conditioner available for old and new leather; FLEX-FILL Crack Eliminator for leather and vinyl. Free detailed booklet "About Leather" for restoring and refinishing leather and vinyl at a fraction of the cost of replacement!

Competition Chemicals, Inc.: P.O. Box 820, Iowa Falls, IA 50126. Telephone 515-648-5121. 8 a.m. to 5 p.m. Central Time Zone. We are distributors of Simichrome Polish, the finest all-metal polish in the world. Simichrome cleans and protects while it polishes chrome, brass, copper, pewter, silver, gold...virtually any metal surface.

The Eastwood Co.: See listing under Tools.

FASPEC British Cars & Parts: See listing under Parts Suppliers.

Fluoramics, Inc.: Franklin G. Reick, President, 103 Pleasant Avenue, Upper Saddle River, NJ 07458. Telephone 201-825-8110, 8:00 a.m.-4:30 p.m. TUFOIL FOR ENGINES . . . FIGHT ENGINE FRICTION TUFOIL is a patented lubricant and friction modifier that has resulted from over 14 years of scientific research. Lab tests show that TUFOIL, which is a blend of synthetic and mineral oils carrying a complex additive system that uses PTFE (polytetrafluorethylent), has the lowest surface friction of any known lubricant. BROCHURE FREE.

Ft. Morgan Slick 50: Van M. Polowchak, Pres., 407 Del Rio Rd., Berthoud, CO 80513. Telephone 800-227-5425, 8:00 a.m.-5:00 p.m. Slick-50 Engine Treatment - one treatment added to your oil coats your engine with "poly" - the slipperiest substance known to man. By reducing friction Slick 50 can save you gas, increase horsepower and save your engine.

4-D Chemicals Co.: Mike Roe, 5640 S. Whipple St., Chicago, IL 60629, Telephone 312-722-5243. 8:30 a.m. to 4:30 p.m. Polytect "The Liquid Garage" is a petroleum base, siliconized exterior finish sealant containing polytetrafluoroethylene. When applied according to simple instructions, penetrates automotive paint, forming a resilient chemical shield.

Hawk Laboratories Co.: Box 112, Station 27, Lakewood, CO 80215. Telephone 303-447-0239, 8-5 weekdays. New Rustop 3 - removes - stops rust, increases paint adhesion. Rustop 40 - long term 10 yrs. & protection. Meets military specs. Brush or spray both products. Most effective products available.

Bill Hirsch: See listing under Parts Suppliers.

J. R. Pride Automotive Accessory Centers: Lawrence S. Eaton, 1118 West Market Street, Akron, OH 44303. Telephone 1-216-253-9668. 8:00 a.m. to 5:00 p.m. Rustproofing, fabric protector, paint sealant, sunroofs, vinyl tops, simulated convertible tops, sound systems, rear window defoggers, cruise controls, body side moldings, pinstripes, splashguards, luggage racks, reconditioning.

Kaleidoscope: Box 86, Mt. Ephraim, NJ 08059. Telephone 609-779-0012, 10 a.m. to 5:30 p.m. Windshield scratch remover kit, $14.95 · $1.50 postage.

Kanter Auto Products: See listing under Parts Suppliers.

Kozak Auto Dry Wash, Inc.: 6 S. Lyon St./P.O. Box 910, Batavia, NY 14020. Telephone 716-343-8111, 8:30 a.m. to 5 p.m., Monday thru Friday. Kozak drywash cleaning & polishing cloths, for fine automobile finishers. BJR - Bug and Tar Remover. MUO - Mak-ur-own, grime & dull film remover for chrome & paint. Misc. auto cleaning aids/catalog available (free).

Lowe Oil Co.: Ralph Lowe, 510 Price Lane, Clinton, MO 64735. Telephone 816-885-8151, 8-5. Valve Shield - valve & valve seat protection for gasoline engines designed to run on leaded fuel.

NSE Sales & Service, Inc.: President: R. Kenneth Edwards, 4823 S. Sheridan Road, Suite 311, Tulsa, OK 74145. Telephone 918-663-7336, M-F 9:00 a.m. to 5:00 p.m. Gas Tank Sealer - Alcohol and additive proof! Not just resistant, but unaffected by gasohol, fuel additives, aviation fuels and octane boosters. Drys to a smooth, hard tack-free surface. Blended for the sole purpose of sealing gas tanks. Complete instructions provided. You will never have to worry about your tank again!

Polishing Systems: Tully Caiazza, 1808 W. Washington St., New Castle, PA 16101. Telephone 412-658-2832. 9 a.m. to 5 p.m. We sell polishers, steam cleaners, pressure washers, and chemicals for car cleaning from the backyard hobby to the professional detail shops.

Porcelain Patch & Glaze Co., Inc.: Ask for Dan or Glen, 966 86th Ave., Oakland, CA 94621. Telephone 415-635-2188. 6:00 a.m. to 4:00 p.m. Mon. - Fri. Porcelain enamel cast iron intake and exhaust manifolds, also repair and weld cracked or broken manifolds. Allow two weeks for processing. Superior workmanship.

Pratco, Inc.: See listing under Tools.

Professional Auto: Rt. 94, Vernon, NJ 07462. Telephone 201-827-2203. Vacu-shine cleaning cloths, mail order tires, and AMS/oil products.

Race Glaze: Dennis P. Smith, 19725 W. Edgewood Dr., Lannon, WI 53046. Telephone 414-255-3880, 8-5. Manufacture Race Glaze auto polish & sealant. Premium auto polish & sealant used by collectors, racers, rod & custom professionals, auto museums and demanding do-it-yourselfers.

Restoration Products, Inc.: President: Walter R. Haessner, P.O. Box 50027, Tucson, AZ 85703. Telephone 602-624-8786, 8:30-4:30 M-F. Specialty chemicals to economically protect your investment in either collector vehicles or new diesel or gasoline powered cars or trucks. Send large SASE for current brochures.

Ramcote Products, Inc.: P. O. Box 42785, Evergreen Park, IL 60642. *Ramcote* restores color to upholstery, tops, headliners, rug and floor mats.

Shine Enterprises: Rich & Jackie Warner, 22 Pellridge Dr., Hopewell Jct., NY 12533. Telephone 914-226-7057. Distributor for Race Glaze, polish and sealant and Rain-X (the liquid windshield wiper). Dealer for Top Brite metal polish. Mail order available on Race Glaze and Rain-X. We are at major north east shows, including Carlisle and Englishtown.

SPRI Marketing: P. O. Box 231, Lake View, NY 14085. Non-toxic, non-flammable rust remover. Aerosol heavy duty anti-rust. Aerosol paint/decal remover.

Terco Supply: See listing under Miscellaneous.

Top International: Conrad Longval, P.O. Box 4610, Bedford, NH 03108. Telephone 603-472-3307, 8 to 5. National distributor of TopBrite metal polish. The new polish everyone is asking for, great for magnesium, aluminum, chrome, brass, copper, silver, etc. sold at shows, shops, auto parts. etc.

Treatment Products: Charles Victor, 7137 N. Austin, Niles, IL 60648. Telephone 312-647-8300, 9-5. Manufacturer of performance car care products. The line features unique packaging and an unconditional money back guarantee. The first car wax in a tube. The treatment.

W. T. Tyrrel: Box 98, East Northport, NY 11731. Telephone 516-261-5380, 6 p.m. to 8 p.m. PF-47 rust remover. Send stamped self addressed envelope for complete details.

VACO, Inc.: Floyd Andrus, P.O. Box 6, Florence, MA 01060. Telephone 413-586-0978, 10-6. Upper cylinder lubricators help pre-'75 car owners reduce engine wear from unleaded gasoline. Manufactured for internal combustion engines, easy-to-install unit is designed to supply constantly metered, finely dispersed oil vapor-spray to engine's critical heat/wear friction zone where high temperatures cause wear and damage to parts.

World Class Show Car Glaze: 10440 Liberty St., St. Louis, MO 63132. Up to 200% more shine than ordinary polishes. Made from actual cosmetic ingredients. 396 day guarantee. 16 oz. $6.00.

RESTORATION FIRMS

Jim Alexandro: Box 144, Maspeth, NY 11378. Telephone 718-899-0136, 7-10 p.m. Carburetor rebuilding service. 72 hour turnaround on most rebuilding jobs. Cosmetic restoration is part of rebuilding process.

Antique Auto Restoration: Joe Batthauer, R.R. 1 Rd., 700 West, Yorktown, IN 47396. Telephone 317-759-8687, 8 a.m. to 5 p.m., Monday through Friday. Body restorations, complete or partial. Majority of paint work performed with DuPont Imron.

The Antique Auto Shop: Fred & Ray Vagedes, 603 Lytle Ave., P.O. Box 217, Elsmere, KY 41018. Telephone 606-342-8363, 8-5 Mon. thru Fri. From the smallest dent or engine tune up to the most comprehensive restoration, we do it all with pride. The skilled craftsmen in our upholstery, paint, body, mechanical and machine shops do their work with patience and an eye to detail that will insure your pride and pleasure.

Antique & Classic Restoration Enterprises Inc.: 618-622 Morse Ave., Schaumburg, IL 60193. Telephone 312-894-0881. 8 a.m. to 5 p.m. Mon.-Fri., Saturday by appointment only. Antique & Classic can help you give it a bright future. For years, we've been providing collectors, car buffs and show competitors with a full range of services from fine detailing to complete body-off restorations. If you have a treasured antique, classic or milestone, a rare special interest vehicle or an automobile with special sentimental value, we can restore and renew it to meet the most demanding show specifications, or your own high personal standards.

Automotive Restorations, Inc.: Kent S. Bain, 1785 Barnum Ave., Stratford, CT 06497. Telephone 203-377-6745. Complete or partial restorations for foreign and domestic automobiles.

Automotive Restorations Unlimited: Raymond Winstead, Rt. 1, Roxboro, NC 27573. Telephone 919-599-5155, 9 a.m. to 5 p.m. Complete restoration on pre-1960 automobiles.

The Babbitt Pot: Zigmont G. Billus, Rd. #1, E. River Rd. (Route 4), Ft. Edward, NY 12828, 518-747-4277. 9 a.m. to 5 p.m. Specialize in rebabbitting & machining of auto bearings (mains, rods, cam bearings) also do custom engine rebuilding.

The Barn: Jack Sutherland, P. O. Box 1211, Martinsburg, WV 25401. Telephone 304-263-1444, 7 a.m. to 7 p.m. Restoration of Rolls-Royces and other collector cars. Consignment sales for private owners.

Bassetts Jaguar: See listing under Parts Suppliers.

Batista Automotive, Inc.: Paul Batista, President, 5642 Mission Blvd., Ontario, CA 91762. Telephone 714-983-8810, 8:30-4:00 California time. Monday-Friday. Complete restoration of CCCA-approved classic automotives. Full line of services including machine work, electrical, mechanical, upholstery, wood, glass, body and paint.

Beckley Auto Body: David Ten Brink, 4405 Capital Ave., SW, Battle Creek, MI 49017. Telephone 616-979-3013, 7:00 a.m.-5:00 p.m. Antique classic restoration service complete.

Blue Star Inc.: See listing under Restoration Aids.

Burchill Antique Auto Parts, Inc.: See listing under Parts Suppliers.

Clapper Restorations: Stan Clapper, Box 74, Clinton, WI 53525. Telephone 608-676-5186, 7 a.m. to 4:30 p.m. Complete or partial restorations. Nearly 40 years in business.

Classic Auto Restoration: Buck Varnon, technical advisor, 22456 Orchard Lake Rd., Farmington, MI 48024. Telephone 313-477-4767. Shop open 7:30 a.m. to 5 p.m., Monday through Friday. Complete restorations, specializing in antiques and classics, including Rolls-Royce and Bentley. Complete wood shop. Body, paint, mechanical and upholstery restoration. Also engine and individual component rebuilding, plus Rolls-Royce and Bentley parts. Mail order services available on parts and rebuilt components.

Classic Auto Supply Co., Inc.: W. W. Brown, President, 795 High St., P.O. Box 810, Coshocton, OH 43812. Telephone 614-622-8561, 8:30-5:00 M-F, Sat. by appt.: Full line supplier of paints for 1955-1957 Thunderbirds - free catalog. Also restores classic T-Birds for street or show.

Classic Car Centre: See listing under Collector Car Dealers.

Clean Sweep - (Windshield Wiper Motor Service): Kent Jaquith, Rt. 1, Box 1401, Zillan, WA 98953. Telephone 509-865-2481, day-night - mail order. Specializing in vacuum wiper motor rebuilding, all types of vacuum motors for all years. Have many rebuilt motors in stock, some N.O.S. Also rebuild other vacuum auto related items. 24 to 48 hour turnaround on most motors. All work guaranteed.

Cobra Restorers Ltd.: See listing under Parts Suppliers.

Cobb's Antique Auto Restoration, Inc.: 717 Western Ave., Washington C.H., OH 43160. Telephone 614-335-7489. Mon.-Fri. 8 a.m. to 5 p.m., Sat. by appt. Complete restorations, sheet metal and aluminum fabrication, woodwork, mechanical, wiring, sandblasting, show quality painting.

Concours Auto Restoration Services: Ed. West, 1941 Jan Marie Pl., Tustin, CA 92680. Telephone 714-832-2688, 8:00 a.m.. Jaguar parts Mark 1-2-7-8 & 9, XK 120-140 & 150 new, used, reproduction. Help on your problems by phone, what to look for, who can do what, how you can do your own repairs, etc.

Daku's Antique & Classic Coachworks: 1135 Howertown Rd., Catasauqua, PA 18032. Telephone 215-264-5507. Total or partial restorations.

D. Dennis: 708 Pineview Dr., Valdosta, GA 31601. Model A and T engine rebabbitting service.

D & G Valve Mfg. Co., Inc.: Ansel B. Grose, Jr., 8 Mt. Vernon St., Stoneham, MA 02180. Telephone 617-438-1789. Grose-Jet, replaces needle and seat in carburetors.

The Electroplate-Rite Corporation Restoration Shop: John W. Dickerson, President, Rt. 11, P.O. Box 160, Dublin, VA 24084. Telephone 703-674-6156. 8:00 a.m. to 4:00 p.m. The antique car restoration specialists, we detail the nuts and bolts. Total restoration complete detail of car, motor and chassis, 50% restoration paint, chrome and upholstery. Antique or classics cars. Special interest and street machine cars. Cars of the forties or the nifty fifties. We welcome the high performance decade or the sixties which brought our Mustang, Chevelle and GTO.

F & R Import Ltd.: James M. Rickel, 2300 W. Hampden Ave., Englewood, CO 80110. Telephone 303-761-5806, 8 a.m. to 5 p.m. Monday to Friday, 9 a.m. to 1 p.m. Saturday. Jaguar parts, service and restoration.

Gassaway Auto Restorations: Stephen Babinsky, 519 Main St., So. Amboy, NJ 08879. Telephone 201-721-2260, 8 a.m. to 8 p.m. Antique and classic auto restoration, full or partial mechanical restoration, full body restoration and panel fabrication. Parts for Duesenberg and classic era Cadillac. Honeycomb radiator fabrication and restoration.

G.E. Antique Metal Restoration: Gonzalo-Esparza, 10721 Forest St., Santa Fe Springs, CA 90670. Telephone 213-946-2664, Tue.-Fri. 9 to 5, Sat. 9 to 3. We specialize in stainless steel moldings. Grills, hub caps. Major damage accepted. 30 years experience.

Gene's Auto Rebuilding: Gene Kolupski, 9811 Deering Avenue, Suite F, Chatsworth, CA 91311. Telephone 818-341-7500, 8 a.m.-6 p.m. Complete and full restoration of any vehicle import or domestic, auto research service, specializing in authentic rebuilding.

Grey Hills Auto Restoration Inc.: Marty Beron, P.O. Box 630, Vail Rd., Blairstown, NJ 07825. Telephone 201-362-8232, 8 a.m. to 5 p.m. Complete or partial restorations of antique, classic or collectible automobiles. Also general maintenance, collision repair and pin striping on antique, classic or collectible automobiles.

Harkin Machine Shop: Terry Harkin, 115 1st Ave. NW, Watertown, SD 57201. Telephone 605-886-7880, 8 a.m. to 12 noon and 1 p.m. to 6 p.m. Rebabbits engine bearings and rebuilds complete engines.

Hibernia Auto Restorations, Inc.: Robert E. Turnquist, Maple Terrace, Hibernia, NJ 07842. Telephone 201-627-1882, 7 a.m. to 5 p.m., Monday thru Friday. Restorations and maintenance of all types of vehicles, partial or full. Manufacture Nitrocellulose Lacquer for all types of vehicles.

Jack Hoovers Camaro Classics: Jack Hoover, 383 Whalom Rd., Fitchburg, MA 01420. Telephone 617-342-8092, 9-7 weekdays, Sat. 9-2. Specializing in 67-68-69 Camaros. Complete inventory of new, used, reproduction parts. I also do complete restorations, sell quality used cars especially low mileage, clean, rust free muscle cars.

Hudson Wagon Works: Rt. 1, Box 28, Bridgewater, IA 50837. Telephone 515-369-2865. Commercial wood bodies and plans for pre-1932 cars and trucks.

Jim's Motor Service Inc.: Robert Murr & Jim Jones, R. #27, Washington Pike, Knoxville, TN 37918. Telephone 615-522-0009, 637-4029, 24 hrs. Complete auto restoration of imports, domestic vehicles, trucks & motorcycles, parts body and mechanical for all above from 1917 to 1970. Also 562 assorted autos, trucks & motorcycles 1914 to 1982.

J K Restorations: Jim Kakuska, 12 W. Jackson, Oswego, IL 60543. Telephone 312-554-2120, 8 a.m. to 5 p.m. Monday through Friday, 8-12 Sat. Antique auto restoration. We specialize in body and paint work for the particular collector. XK Jaguars a house specialty.

Ken's Klassics: Mr. Ken Stadele, RR 1, Hwy. 60, Muscoda, WI 53573. Telephone 608-739-4242, 8 a.m. to 5 p.m., Monday thru Friday. Specializing in meticulous partial or total frame-up, body-off restorations of all models of antique, classic and special interest automobiles. Fiberglass repairs and handrubbed lacquer painting is a specialty.

L & N Olde Car Co.: Fred Livers, 9992 Kinsman Rd. Box 378, Newbury, OH 44065. Telephone 216-564-7204, Tues. thru Fri. 7:30-6:00. Total or partial restoration. Concours or to custom specifications. Show quality. Sheet metal and aluminum fabrication including complete bodies, floor and panel fabrication. Wood fabrication and coachwork. Mechanical, electrical, upholstery, wood refinishing, leadwork, show paint and finish. Machine work and parts fabrication. Maintenance work and repairs.

Lordship Antique Auto, Inc.: Kevin Biebel, 5 Prospect Drive, Stratford, CT 06497. Telephone 203-377-3454, 7:00 a.m. to 5:00 p.m. Mon.-Fri. Complete restoration shop, appraiser, broker, offering European technology, featuring the latest downdraft spray booth and oven for the refinishing of vintage automobiles. Specializing in vintage Mercedes Benz.

The Louver Press: Kurt McCormick, 238 S. Old Orchard, Webster Groves, MO 63119. Telephone 314-962-7981, evenings and weekends. Louvers punched. Also have repro Barris crests.

Lozano's Custom Paint & Body Shop: Sonny Lozano, 1721 Lorraine, Houston, TX 77026. Telephone 713-237-8688. Complete or partial restorations.

Jerry Martin Shop: Jerry Martin, Box 28, Rock Lake, ND 58365. Telephone 701-266-5340. M-F 8-5, Sat. 8-12. Engine rebuilding, drive train repair, welding, body work, etc. 11 yrs in the business.

Martin's Automotive: Daniel F. Martin, RR 2, Waits Rd., Kendallville, IN 46755. Telephone 219-894-4666, 10 a.m. to 6 p.m. Complete restoration for classic, antique and special interest automobiles. We also buy and sell classic, antique and special interest autos. Martin's Automotive was established in 1970.

Memoryville U.S.A./Carney's Restoration Shop: George L. Carney, 1008 West 12th Street, Rolla, MO 65401. Telephone 314-364-1810. Shop: M-F 8:00 a.m.-4:30 p.m. Museum: M-F 8-5, Sat. 9-5, Sun. 12-5. Memoryville: Antique Auto Museum, Gift Shop. Carney's Restoration Shop: Largest restoration shop in U.S. Professional restoration, from ground up. Lowest hourly rates. Many show cars restored here.

M & G Vintage Auto: 265 Route 17, P.O. Box 226, Tuxedo Park, NY 10987. Telephone 914-753-5900, 9 a.m. to 6 p.m. Manufacture, sales, service and restoration of 1945 to 1980 MG.

Mill Creek Motors: Highway 136 West, R.R. 2, Box 55B, Clinton, IA 52732. Telephone 319-242-5090. Complete facilities for every phase of auto restoration. All types of body, mechanical and upholstery work welcome.

Mustang of Chicago: See listing under Parts Suppliers.

Mustang Corral: See listing under Parts.

Mustang Madness: See listing under Collector Car Dealers.

Oak Bows: 122 Ramsey Ave., Chambersburg, PA 17201. Telephone 717-264-2602, 8 a.m. to 6 p.m. Complete top restoration. Make steambent top bows for convertible tops. No glue nor lamination. We repair and make new irons and sockets for any year.

The Old Car Shop: Eugene Marocco, 2605 Huffman Blvd., Rockford, IL 61103. Telephone 815-962-4724, 7 a.m. to 5:30 p.m. Monday thru Friday, 7 a.m. to 12 noon, Saturday. Complete or partial restoration of antique or special interest automobiles.

Old Crafter Wood Work: Gary Van Dyken, 5821 43rd Ave., Red Deer, Alberta, Canada T4N 3E5. Telephone 403-347-5341, 8 a.m. to 5 p.m. Fabricating and installing new wood in all makes of antique autos.

Old Spokes Home: Ronald L. Orr, Rt. 1 Box 96, Junction of Rts. 40 and 49, Casey, IL 62420. Telephone 217-932-4538, 7 a.m. to 7 p.m. Complete auto restorations, all types of welding, wood graining, sand blasting, painting, etc.

A. Petrik Restoration & Rebuilding Services: Al & Lynda Petrik, 3704 S.W. 110th, Seattle, WA 98146. Telephone 206-248-0402, 10 a.m. to 7 p.m. P.S.T. Services offered specializes in rebuilding Ranco/Harrison heater control valves. Complete restoration of Truck windshield regulators: (G.M. 36-46, Dodge 36-46. Powerwagons.) 33-35 MoPar Passenger car windshield regulators. Full-Service business since 1977.

Anthony V. Polio: 746 N. Greenbrier Dr., Orange, CT 06477. Telephone 203-795-6434, 9-6 p.m. Restoration of license plates, political tags & raised stamped metal signs. Finest reputation for excellent workmanship throughout antique car hobby. 15 years experience w/thousands of satisfied customers worldwide. Ask the man who has one. Isn't it time you send yours?

Porcelain Patch & Glaze Co., Inc.: Ask for Dan or Glen, 966 86th Ave., Oakland, CA 94621. Telephone 415-635-2188, 6:00 a.m. to 4:00 p.m. Mon.-Fri. Porcelain enamel cast iron intake and exhaust manifolds, also repair and weld cracked or broken manifolds. Allow two weeks for processing. Superior workmanship.

Precision Sportscar Servicing: Michael C. Salter, 307 Enford Road, Richmond Hill, Ontario, Canada L4C 3E9. 416-883-3676, Mon.-Friday 9:00-5:30, Sat. 9-12:30. Mail order and open shop. Monday-Friday 9:00-5:30, Saturday 9:00-12:30. Parts, service and restorations for Austin-Healeys and Sprites from 1953-71 and postwar British sports cars. "Expert attention to parts requirements, tune-ups or full restorations."

Prestige Thunderbird, Inc.: James Moomaw & Jerry Bird, 10215 Greenleaf Ave., Santa Fe Springs, CA 90670. Telephone 213-944-6237, 8:30-5:30 M./Fri. 8:30-4:00 Sat. Restoration / Upholstery / Body & Paint / Repair & Service / Parts, New & Used / Hard & Soft Tops / T-Birds for Sale / Catalog Available, $1.00 - The only catalog you'll need!

Proper Motor Cars: Woody Richey, 1811-11th Av. N., St. Petersburg, FL 33713. Telephone 813-821-8883, 8-4:30. Full service facility, service shop, body shop with metal working equipment, trim shop specializing in leather & fine fabrics. Our specialty is Rolls-Royce & Bentley with large stock of new & used parts for sale.

Prestige Mustang, Inc.: See listing under Collector Car Dealers & Locators.

Prestige Thunderbird, Inc.: See listing under Parts Suppliers.

R.C.M. Inc.: R.C. Middendorf, 620 Spring St., Elsmere, KY 41018. Telephone 606-727-3113, 8-6. Body & frame - Ky. license plate collector.

Realistic Auto Restorations, Inc.: Stephen & Jana Samuels, 2519 6th Ave. S., St. Petersburg, FL 33712. Telephone 813-327-5162. Full service restoration shop specializing in show quality paint & body, upholstery & complete mechanical services. Other services include stainless steel repair, sheet metal fabrication, sandblasting, woodwork, wiring, welding, periodic maintenance, research & photography.

The Restoration Shop, Inc: Earl Lewis, Pres., Rt. 1 Box 228, Jamesburg, NJ 08831. Telephone 201-521-1128. Complete facilities for partial or total restoration of antique and classic automobiles.

Restoration Specialists Inc.: Robert L. Brostowicz, 6846 S. 112th St. Franklin, WI 53132. Telephone 414-529-1515. 8 a.m. to 5 p.m. weekdays, 8 a.m. to 12 noon Saturdays. We are a paint and rust removal service serving hobbyists and professionals alike. Our process is an immersion type that can accept any size piece, and any type metal, including aluminum and die cast. We have been serving Wisconsin for ten years.

Rods, Babbitt & Machine Works, Inc.: Edward B. Rubin, President, 712 East 135th St., Bronx, NY 10454. Telephone 212-585-2445. 8:00 a.m. to 5:00 p.m. Mon.-Fri. Rods & Babbitt insures a high quality product by combining modern technology with time proven workmanship. It is our intent to produce the finest connecting rod and babbitting service available anywhere. This continual policy of excellence is always applied to both modern and antique applications.

Wayne Rowe - Classic Cars & Parts: See listing under Collector Car Dealers.

James T. Sandoro: See listing under Auctioneers & Appraisers.

Schaeffer & Long, Inc: 210 Davis Rd., Magnolia, NJ 08049. Telephone 609-784-4044. Antique and classic automobile restoration.

Stafford Restorations: Gilbert S. Stafford, Ph.D., P.E., 771 Old Post Rd., R.R. 5, Wakefield, RI 02879. Telephone 401-789-6540, anytime. Specializing in precision reproductions and research. Also restoration and sales of antique, milestone and classic cars. Over 50 cars in stock from 1899 through 1973. Consignment cars considered.

Steering Wheel Restoration: Jack Turpin, Route 2, Peaceful Valley, Box 327B, Cleveland, GA 30528. Telephone 404-865-2242. 9 a.m. to 9 p.m. Full time not a hobby 40 years in old cars. Spoke in hub repair and partial remolding, complete rim circle replacement on brittle or bare frame in hard rubber for about half of what the others charge from 30's to 60's. All work spindry painted to completion, please send SASE.

Stutz Specialty: Paul Freehill, 1931 Sovereign Dr., Ft. Wayne, IN 46815. Telephone 219-745-5168 shop, 219-749-0297 home. Hours 8 a.m. to 6 p.m. Complete restoration and maintenance of Stutz and all other collector cars. Expert mechanical repair and parts fabrication.

Swain Tech Castings: Daniel B. Swain, 35 Main St., Scottsville, NY 14546. Telephone 716-889-2786, 7-5. Coatings automotive, metal, ceramic, teflon etc., coatings, rebuild crankshafts and worn parts with metal, steel, stainless, bronze, copper etc. Thermal barrier coatings for pistons, heads, exhaust systems, corrosion coating. Rebuilding of worn parts.

T-Bird Nest: P.O. Box 1012, Grapevine, TX 76051. Shop address: 2550 E. Southlake Blvd., Southlake, TX. Telephone 817-481-1776. Full time family business selling parts, making repairs and doing restorations. Servicing 1958-1966 Thunderbirds (others considered)

The Valley Forge Restorations: Bob Williams, P.O. Box 1133, Apache Jct., AZ 85217. Telephone 602-463-2298, 7 a.m.-7 p.m. Mon. thru Sat. Probably the best equipped small shop in the country for complete or partial restoration of classic & antique autos. Specializing in engineering & making parts that are not available. We are a 3-man operation with a total of 106 years of auto experience, 47 of those years spent with antique car restoration.

Vintage Car Restoration Center: Fred J. Clark, 2160 N.W. Vine St., Grants Pass, OR 97526, Telephone 503-474-1957, 9:00 a.m. to 5:00 p.m. Mon. thru Sat. Largest car restoration in the United States. 92,000 feet under roof. Large retail parts department, complete chrome shop, diptank rooms, upholstery shop, transmission, brake and tire, paint and body shop, glass shop, 12,500 foot showroom on I-5. Entire plant done in colonial style structure. 200 car parking.

Vintage Restorations: J. E. Marks, The Old Bakery, Windmill Street, Tunbridge Wells, Kent, England TN2 4UU. Telephone 0892-25899, 8:30 a.m. to 6 p.m., closed Thursdays. We restore, supply and manufacture instruments and dash fittings for classic and vintage vehicles.

Ed West Concours Auto Restoration Services: See listing under Parts Suppliers.

White Post Restorations: Billy Thompson, White Post, VA 22663, Telephone 703-837-1140, 7:00 a.m.-4:00 p.m. EST. Brake cylinders better than new sleeved with brass to standard size - wheel cylinders, calipers, master, slave and clutch cylinders. Send disassembled cylinders to White Post Restorations, White Post, VA 22663. Also, complete frame-up restorations on 1948 and older automobiles.

Ed White Head & Block Repair: Ed White, P.O. Box 968 or Hwy. 33 East, Chouteau, OK 74337. Telephone 918-476-5684, call day or eve. shop hrs 8-5 p.m. I do cold worked, stress free repairs of cracked heads, blocks & housings on antique autos - classics and also industrial machinery repairs are tested before leaving my shop and my work is reasonably priced. This is not a sideline, this is my occupation. 25 yrs. experience.

Wilkinson & Sharp: George M. Gottschalk, 233 Philmont Ave., Feastersville, PA 19047. Telephone 357-8090, 8:00 a.m. til 4:30 p.m. Complete restoration of antique and classic cars. Thirty years in business. Over four hundred restored.

John Worden Garage: John Worden, Box 573, Green Mountain, IA 50637. Telephone 515-474-2313, 8 a.m. to 5 p.m. Antique and classic auto restoration.

W W Motor Cars & Parts, Inc.: Jack P. Wenger, P.O. Box 667, 132 N. Main Street, Broadway, VA 22815. Telephone 703-896-8243, 8:00 a.m.-4:30 p.m. W W Motor Cars & Parts, Inc. is a full service restoration facility located in scenic downtown Broadway in a remodeled 100 year old building.All cars and trucks are economically restored to original specifications with all work guaranteed.

Ye Olde Carriage Shop: Lloyd Ganton, 151 2nd St., Spring Arbor, MI 49283. Telephone 517-750-4300, open weekdays. Collects and restores Jackson, Mich. made autos.

SHEET METAL

Auto Body Specialties Inc.: Nancy and Roger Hersey, Route 66, Middlefield, CT 06455. Telephone 203-346-4989, 9-5:30 M-W-F, 9-8 Tues. & Thurs., 9-3 Saturday. Distributors of 1950-86 reproduction and original quarter panels, fenders, repair panels, grills, bumpers, carpets, emblems, for domestic and foreign cars, pickups and vans.

Autosteel, Inc.: Warren E. Damman, 22959 Rasch Dr., Mt. Clemens, MI 48043. Telephone 313-791-0220, 9-5. We are a manufacturer of after market universal auto body repair panels. We manufacture flexedge for wheelwells and carry a full line of flat sheet metal for collision damage or rust thru damage on any car.

Beam Distributors: See listing under Wood.

Bill's Speed Shop: 13951 Millersburg Rd., SW, Navarre, OH 44662. Telephone 216-832-9403, 9 a.m. to 5 p.m. Replacement body repair panels for cars & trucks. Specializing in obsolete panels, also limited number of NOS quarters and fenders.

Cahill Automotive: See listing under Parts Suppliers.

California Classic Chevy Parts: See listing under Parts Suppliers.

C.A.R.S. Inc.: See listing under Upholstery.

Circle City Mustang: See listing under Parts Suppliers.

Classic Reproductions G.T.O. Chevelle Mopar: Tom Jeffers, P.O. Box 74, 11467 Dayton-Greenville Pike, Phillipsburg, OH 45354. Telephone 513-884-7059, Mon.-Fri. 9 a.m.-6 p.m., Saturday 10 a.m.-3 p.m. Manufacturers of quality sheet metal reproduction parts for G.M. A-body, 64 thru 72, Mopar 70-74 E-body parts. American tooling and U.S. steel trunk floors, body floors, filler extension panels, patch panels, body panels and quarter panels, 64-72 A-body cars Buick, Chevelle, G.T.O., and Oldsmobile, 70-74 E-Body cars Barracuda and Challenger.

SHEET METAL

The Eastwood Co.: See listing under Tools.

Experi-Metal Inc.: Contact Sonny Rinke, 6345 Wall St., Sterling Heights, MI 48077. Telephone 313-977-7800, 8:00 to 5:00 M-F, 8:00 to 12:00 Sat. 1932 Chevrolet roadster bodies in steel - fender - aprons - rad. shells. All in steel. 1931-32 Chevy - kits or complete cars available.

Ezra Welding Shop: See listing under Parts Suppliers.

Fortiers Auto Body Benders Ltd.: Ron Fortier & Eugene Julian, P.O. Box 562, Long Sault, Ontario, Canada K0C 1P0. Telphone 613-931-1352, 8 to 5 p.m. Worlds best built body bending hand brake. Bends 3 edges on the angle as per door skin. Fully adjustable industrial quality tool bends full 5'0" lg. x 18 ga. steel built to last a lifetime. Build your own rocker panels door & rocker & lower fender repair panels. MasterCard accepted.

Gaslight Auto Parts, Inc.: See listing under parts suppliers.

Girtz Industries, Inc.: Elmer Girtz, R.R. #3, Box 264, Monticello, IN 47960. Telephone 219-278-7510. Mon.-Thurs. 8:00 to 5:00. Model A & V-8 reproduction antique auto parts, sheet metal, fender braces, chrome top irons, stanchion post, and other misc. parts. All parts manufactured in our factory. 25 years experience.

Howell's Sheetmetal Co.: David Howell, P.O. Box 179, Nome, TX 77629. Telephone 409-253-2478, 9-5 Mon.-Fri. Sat. appointment only. Manufacturer of 09-34 sheetmetal, body panels, seat risers, patch panels, running board shields, show quality reproduction stone guards for model "A" best quality sheet metal parts at any price.

The Louver Press: See listing under Miscellaneous.

Mack Products: See listing under Parts Suppliers.

Made-Rite Autobody Pro: Gary Krupa, 869 E. 140th St., Cleveland, OH 44110. Telephone 216-681-2535. 8 a.m. to 4:30 p.m. Mon.-Fri. Die-stamped steel replacement panels, car, trucks, vans from 1949-87.

Mal's 'A' Sales, Inc.: See listing under Parts Suppliers.

Met-Del Enterprises: Daryl & Lyn Elliott, 134 Hieber Ave., Pittsburgh, PA 15229. Telephone 412-364-7425. We sell plain sheets of sheet metal: 22 ga. for body rust repair and panel fabrication and 18 ga., heavy duty, for floorboards. We also have universal wheel lip and door bottom repair aids. Brochure on request for $1.50.

Mustang Parts Corral of Texas: See listing under Parts Suppliers.

Obsolete Ford Parts Co., Inc.: See listing under Parts Suppliers.

O. B. Smith: See listing under Parts Suppliers.

TABCO: 30500 Solon Industrial Pkwy., Cleveland, OH 44139. Telephone 216-248-5151. 8 a.m. to 5 p.m. TABCO has steel rust repair parts for cars, trucks and vans. The Cleveland, Ohio stamping plant manufactures parts for the Ford, Chevy & Dodge vans and pickups. $3.00 for illustrated catalog.

Valley Forge Restoration: See listing under Restoration Firms.

Vintage Automotive Engineering: Everett Smith, P.O. Box 1440, Bandon, OR 97411. Telephone 503-347-9116, 9-5:00 p.m. Manufactures sheet metal repair panels for "Big" Austin Healeys (100-4, 100-6 & 3000).

Howard Whitelaw: 6067 Richmond Rd., Solon, OH 44139. Telephone 216-721-6755, 216-232-0235. N.O.S. fenders, quarter panels for Chrysler, Dodge, Desota, Plymouth cars from 1933 through 1976. Wrapped for shipping. Reasonable prices.

TIRES & WHEELS

Calimers Wheel Shop: Bill and Bob Calimer, 30 E. North St., Waynesboro, PA 17268. Telephone 717-762-5056. 8 a.m. to 5 p.m. Mon.-Fri., Sat. 8 a.m. to Noon. Custom building of wood spoke wheels of all types for antique cars using the customers old metal parts. All wheels are hickory. Top bows are custom bent duplicating them from your old patterns in oak.

Coker Tire: 1317 Chestnut Street/P.O. Box 72554, Chatanooga,TN 37407. Telephone 800-251-6336, 615-265-6368 Tenn. and International Calls. 8-5 M-F, 8-12 Sat. Tires, tubes and flaps for antique autos. Full line of USA made B.F. Goodrich Silvertowns. Firestone Super Sport Wide Ovals for muscle cars.

Dayton Wheel Products: 1147 South Broadway Street, Dayton, OH 45408. Telephone 513-461-1707, outside Ohio 800-862-6000. Mon.-Fri. 8:00-5:00. Manufacturer of wire wheels since 1916. Custom made wire wheels for nearly any vehicle. Show quality restoration services for all wire wheels.

Harry Johnson: 2570 Pioneer Dr., Reno, NV 89509. Telephone 702-826-8832. Firestone N.O.S. split rims and felloe bands sizes 23" to 27".

Kelsey Tire, Inc.: Box 564, Camdenton, MO 65020. Telephone 800-325-0091, 8 a.m to 5 p.m. Tires and tubes for vintage automobiles.

Lucas Automotive: Two Stores: 2850 Temple Ave., Long Beach, CA 90806. Telephone 213-595-6721. 2141 W. Main, Springfield, OH 45504. Telephone 513-324-1773. Tires & tubes for collector cars. World's largest vintage tire source. Firestone, Dunlop, Denman, Goodyear, Goodrich, Insa, Aerolon, Custom Classic, Avon, Universal, Lester and more. Free catalog.

Mustang Parts Corral of Texas: See listing under Parts Suppliers.

Oakcrest Machine Shop: Elster C. Hayes, 2110 Boda St., Springfield, OH 45503. Telephone 513-399-8435, 8:00 a.m.-5:00 p.m., closed Thursday. New rims for all Model T Fords and some other cars, split rims for cars in the twentys. Rims for wire wheels, with a flat base and side ring to be dimpled and punched for adjustable spokes.

Professional Auto: Route 94, Vernon, NJ 07462. Telephone 201-827-2203, evenings. Antique and standard tires.

Wayne Rowe - Classic Cars & Parts: See listing under parts suppliers.

O. B. Smith: See listing under Parts Suppliers.

Universal Tire Company: E. Ann Klein, 987 Stony Battery Rd., Lancaster, PA 17601. Telephone 800-233-3827, in PA call 717-898-0291, 8 a.m. to 5 p.m. Monday thru Friday. Universal Tire Company stocks more than 300 types of antique and classic car tires, under the Universal, Lester, Dunlop and Denman brands. The exclusive USA agent for The Complete Automobilist catalog, Universal also carries a full line of collector car accessories including Lucas Electric parts (spares), wheel hardware and moldings.

Wallace W. Wade - Wholesale Tires: Wallace W. Wade, 4303 C. Irving Blvd., Dallas TX 75247. Telephone 214-688-0091, 8 a.m.-5:30 p.m. M-F, 9 a.m.-1 p.m. Sat. Antique & Classic tires & tubes - We are the only vintage tire dealer that stocks all four major brands of antique & classic tires. "If we don't have it - We'll get it."

Wheel Repair Service Inc.: 317 Southbridge St., Auburn, MA 01501. Telephone 617-832-4949. Specialists in wire wheel rebuilding and disc wheel straightening on antique, classic, domestic and foreign automobiles and motorcycles. Our Complete wheel service includes: sandblasting, refinishing, chrome plating and alloy wheel polishing. Distributors of Dayton, Tru Spoke and Appliance wire wheels. Pintos to Rolls Royces, Street Rods to Replicars, we fit them all!

Willies Antique Tires: William Drozd, 5257 W. Diversey Ave., Chicago, IL 60639. Telephone 312-622-4037, M-F 8:30-5:30, Sat. 9-2. New tires for antique cars. 75 sizes in stock. Also tubes & flaps & tire values. Tru Spoke & McLean wire wheels.

TITLE SERVICE

Jim Parkinson: 18 Maple Ave., Friendship, NY 14739. Telephone 716-973-2690, 24 hours. Titles - all cars, trucks & motorcycles, 1900-1971 satisfaction guaranteed.

Titles Unlimted: G. Ross Barnette, P.O. Box 36904, Birmingham, AL 35236. Telephone 800-325-8136, 9 a.m. to 5 p.m. CST. Title service for pre 1975 vehicles, no previous paperwork required, legal vehicles only. A service to the collector and restorer.

TOOLS

A&I Supply: Preston Windom, 2125 Court St., Pekin, IL 61554. Telephone 309-353-3002, 800-553-5592, 8-5. Professional tools and equipment for restoration. Hand tools, power tools, air tools, specialty tools, Mig welders, air compressors and supplies.

Arco Electric Products Corp: P.O. Box 278, Shelbyville, IN 46176. Telephone 317-398-9713, 8 a.m. to 5 p.m. Phase converters, single to 3 phase.

Accurate Tool Supply: George Huber, 1675 Shoreline P.O. Box 274, Hartland, MI 48029. Telephone 313-632-7504, 9 a.m.-5 p.m. Hand tools for the hobbyist and the professional i.e. Dial calipers, micrometers, sheetmetal tools, magnetic and offset screwdriver sets and specialty tools. Brand name tools with warranty and 30 day return privilege on all purchases. Send for free tool brochure.

B-Clean: Wayne Carlson, N59 W14508 Bobolink Ave., Menomonee Falls, WI 53051. Telephone 414-252-3230, 8 a.m. to 5 p.m. Parts cleaners designed for economically cleaning parts with solvent, B-Clean parts cleaners are ideal for use in shops ranging from the home mechanic's garage to heavy industry. All B-Clean units, while inexpensive to own and operate, have the same rugged construction and convenient design features usually found on much more expensive units. For more information, write or call toll free.

The Eastwood Co.: Curt Strohaeker, 147 Pennsylvania Ave., Box 296 PCAN, Malvern, PA 19355. Telephone 215-644-4412, 9-5 M-F, 9-12 Sat. Free auto restoration catalog. The Eastwood Company, leading supplier of auto restoration tools and techniques, offers a FREE CATALOG covering stitch welders, spotweld guns, buffing, body and fender, body solder, pinstriping, sandblasters, engine tools and much more.

Fortiers Auto Body Benders Ltd.: See listing under Sheet metal.

Hoosier Distributing: Stan Szklarek, 3009 W. Sample, South Bend, IN 46619. Telephone 219-232-0033, 8:30 a.m. to 4:30 p.m. Tools: "Makita," "Chicago Pneumatic," "Ingersoll Rand," "Astro," "Norton," "Wright," "Kett" Shears, "Channellock," "Vise Grip," "Hanson," "Ken Tool," "Rimac," "Eklind," "Adjustable," "Easco." Free tool catalog.

Johnson's Engineering: 10124 Copeland Drive, Manassas, VA 22110. Telephone 703-361-1601. Engine stands, hoists, compressors, tow bars, etc.

KorenCare, Inc.: James T. Koren, President, 214-R, Route 13, Bristol, PA 19007. Telephone 215-785-3389, 8:00-5:00 p.m. KorenCare, Inc. manufactures "Lug-Loose," a product designed to aid the user in loosening or tightening the lug nuts of a light truck or automobile by providing a fulcrum for which the lug wrench acts as a lever. "Lug-Loose" also serves as a traffic-hazard warning device (triangular flare).

Lions Automotive: Box 229 CPA, Lyons, IL 60534. Telephone 312-484-2229, 9 a.m. to 5 p.m. Mon.-Fri. Lions Automotive Autobody Restoration Equipment & supplies has been serving the restorers needs since 1974. Complete catalog covers Sandblasters, Polishing pads, Fiberglassing Products, Body Repair, Maskers, Sheet Metal Products, Primers, Putties and more.

Mid-America Engineering Corp.: Box 310, Hwy. 34 E., Mt. Pleasant, IA 52641. Telephone 319-385-3817, 8:00 a.m. to 5 p.m., Manufacture and direct sales of jack stands, engine stands and hydraulic floor cranes.

Seacliff International, Inc.: Charles R. Muirhead, 2210 Santa Anita Avenue, South El Monte, CA 91733, Telephone 818-350-0515, 7:30 a.m.-5:30 p.m. THE WASHBOARD - Portable parts washer. No electricity, plumbing or compressed air required. AIR-N-LITE - portable air conpressor and spot light. 135psi, operates from vehicle cigarette lighter. PUMP & LIGHT - 165psi Air compressor/spot light with exclusive battery powered flashlight. "D" BOOSTER - 12 volt battery charger. Start your car with flashlight batteries.

Solar Electric: Gary Starr, President, 175 Cascade Court, Rohnert Park, CA 94928. Telephone Toll Free 1-800-832-1986, in Calif. 707-586-1987, 8-5. We manufacture The Maintainer solar battery charger to prevent your 12 or 6 volt starter battery from losing energy while in storage or in between use. Larger solar independent power systems also available - RVS, boats, cabins, mobile homes.

Terco Supply: See listing under Miscellaneous.

Tip Sandblast Equipment: See listing under Paint Strippers.

Tool Tech: C. L. Potter, 345 S. Wabash Ave., Brewster, OH 44613. Telephone 216-438-9230, 1-800-321-0888, 9 a.m. to 5 p.m. Complete line of sand blasting equipment & accessories. Metal bending brakes and other auto body repair equipment.

Wheeler Industries: Ernest Wheeler, 7887 Dunbrook Road Suite "H", San Diego, CA 92126. Telephone 619-549-4206, 8-5. Wheeler Industries offers a new revolutionary welding machine that weighs 18 lbs., is smaller than a car battery (6"x6"x8") and is powered by 115 vac, 20 amp service, capable of welding 3/3L rod on 3/16 mild and stainless steels, it comes with a 1-year warranty and is great for home use or maintenance.

K. Woods, Inc.: Ken Woods, Rt. 2 Box 230, Washington, MO 63090. Telephone 314-239-7415, 8-5. Dillon MK III welding & cutting torch, welds copper, brass, cast iron, lead, stainless steel, mild steel, bronze, aluminum, chromolly and magnesium. Works on 4 PSI oxygen and 4 PSI acetylene, oxidations elminated. Cuts up to 1 inch thick steel, 4 PSI oxygen, 20 PSI Acetylene.

TRAILERS

E. Gene Dawes: See listing under Miscellaneous.

D & D Trailers, Inc.: G. Douglas Reside, President, 100 Lexington Ave., Trenton, NJ 08618. Telephone 609-771-0001, open 6 days, 60 hours. Manufacter and distributor of utility trailers for 1,000 to 10,000 lbs., both open and enclosed. Specializing in trailers to carry automobiles.

Haul-Lite Trailers: 1275 E. Cross, Ypsilanti, MI 48198. Telephone 313-483-3935. Our frame hitch and fifth wheel enclosed trailers are Super Star (car storage & work space & living accomodations), Haul-Lite (car storage & work space) and Car Vault (car storage). Our open trailer is Formula Star.

Jensen Enterprises Ltd.: Walter Jensen, 1301 9th Ave. N., Humboldt, IA 50548. Telephone 515-332-5963. Manufacturers of custom built enclosed car trailers sold at factory direct prices. Also offering a full line of utility trailers in sizes from 6'-40', and a variety of open trailers. Call or write for free literature.

M & R Products: W. Virgil Brown Jr., 2979 S. Delsea Dr., Vineland, NJ 08360. Telephone U.S. 1-800-524-2560, NJ 1-800-232-6619, 8:00 a.m. to 6:00 p.m. Auto tie-down strap assemblies, related hardware and supplies.

Owens Classic Trailers: P.O. Box 628, Sturgis, MI 49091. Telephone 616-651-9319. 9 a.m. to 5 p.m., Monday thru Friday. Manufacturers of top quality open car trailers and related accessories with dealers and distributors all over most of the US.

Pask Inc.: Rick D. Fox, P.O. Box 1023, Albertville, AL 35950. Telephone 205-593-8932, 8 a.m. to 4 p.m. CST. Wholesale axles, fenders, wheels, hitch couplers, trailer drawings, trailer jacks, light kits, small gas engines to 22-hp, hydraulic pumps and hydraulic cylinders.

QQ's Trailers Inc.: James A. Cular, P.O. Box 166 (Route 15), Lafayette, NJ 07848. Telephone 201-579-1223. 8 a.m. to 6 p.m. 6 days. Trailers, Owens open trailers, enclosed trailers, lightweight. Delivery available anywhere. Financing available. We are the largest car specialty dealer in the Northeast. We will not be undersold.

R-D-T Plans and Parts: R. D. Toney, P. O. Box 2272, Merced, CA 95344-0272. Telephone 209-383-4441, 8 a.m. to 5 p.m. Trailers, trailer plans, windshields and windshield frames, parts for Packard, Ferrari, Mercedes, American underslung.

Don Randall: 5614 S. Logan St., Lansing, MI 48910. Telephone 517-882-1250. Nationwide Sales - Wells Cargo Trailers. Car carriers, open and enclosed - Concession trailers - Enclosed motorcycle carriers - Contractor's job site office and tool trailers - Ultralight Aircraft enclosed carriers.

Tommy's Trailers, Inc.: Thomas O. and Pat Hudson, 1505 W. 29th St., Ada, OK 74820. Telephone 405-332-7785. Tommy's Aluminum Trailers, nylon rachet tie downs and axle straps.

Trailer World: Richard Feldman, P.O. Box 1687, Bowling Green, KY 42102-1687. Telephone 502-843-4587, 8-5 M-F, Sat. 8-3. Enclosed and open car trailers, vendor trailers, parts and service.

Trailex, Inc.: K. W. George, 60 Industrial Park Dr., P. O. Box 553, Canfield, OH 44406. Telephone 216-533-6814, 8 a.m. to 5 p.m. weekdays, 8 a.m. to 12 Saturdays. Trailex manufacturers aluminum car hauling trailers and two wheel tow dollys. The use of special designed extruded aluminum shapes permit the reduction of weight by as much as 50% and eliminates the need for painting.

Wells Cargo, Inc: Jeffrey M. Wells, President, McNaughton St., P. O. Box 728-683, Elkhart, IN 46515. Telephone 219-264-9661, Toll Free 800-348-7553, 8 a.m. to 5 p.m. weekdays. autoWagon® van type trailer for transporting collector automobiles. Easily towed by most any vehicle equipped with ball-type hitch. Fifth-wheel units also available. Quality structured for 15 years life expectancy.

UPHOLSTERY

ABC Auto Upholstery Co.: Ronald M. Murray, 4289 Paul St., Philadelphia, PA 19124. Telephone 215-289-0555, 9 a.m. to 5 p.m. NOS upholstery goods and services. Specializes in 1955 through '58 Fords.

Auto Custom Carpets, Inc.: 316 J Street, P.O. Box 1167, Anniston, AL 36202. Telephone 1-800-633-2358, 8:00 a.m. to 5:00 p.m. Mon.-Fri. CST. World's largest selection of original style automobile carpets.

Auto-Mat Co.: Eric Browner, 225A Park Ave., Hicksville, NY 11801. Telephone orders 800-645-7258, in NY 516-938-7373, M-F 8-5, Sat. 8-1. Auto interiors & accessories. Custom fit, ready to install carpet sets, upholstery sets, tops, headliners, trunk mats, floor mats, rubber floors, dashes, sheepskins, car covers, car masks, logo jackets & gifts, steering wheels, Recaro & Flofit seats & matching interiors & much more. All cars & trucks! Send $3 for 80-page color catalog - receive $10 off purchase.

Autosheep: Div. of Wheel Repair Service, Inc. of New England, 317 Southbridge St., Auburn, MA 01501. Telephone 617-832-5267, 9 a.m. to 5:30 p.m. Manufacturer of tailor made sheepskin seat covers. Catalog and sample $2.00.

Auto Upholstery Institute: Dept. DW731, 2118 S. Grand Ave., Santa Ana, CA 92705. Telephone 714/546-0886. 9-4:30. Auto interior customizing and upholstery are today's high demand skills - yet easily learned at home! Fabulous profit potential. Send for FREE opportunity kit.

Bassett's Jaguar: See listing under Parts Suppliers.

Bob's T-Birds: Bob Dunn, 4421 NW 9th Ave., Ft. Lauderdale, FL 33309. Telephone 305-491-6652. T-Bird parts, complete interiors for 55-56-57. Also many used parts for 55-56-57. Have many other parts for 58 thru 71, including 61 to 66 T-Birds. No list - too many parts to keep track of.

California Classic Chevy Parts: See listing under Parts Suppliers.

CARS Inc.: Larry Wallie and Bob Chauvin, 1964 W. 11 Mile Road, Berkey, MI 48072. Telephone 313-398-7100 or 800-521-2194. 8:30 a.m. to 5:30, Mon. to Fri. Chevrolet, Chevelle, Nova, Camaro 1955 to 1972 interiors and parts. Worlds largest manufacturer of correct original interiors and sheet metal parts. Thousands of items in stock.

Chevelle World: Henry Nunn, Box 38, Washington, OK 73093. Telephone 405-364-0379, 9-5 Central. 64-72 Chevelle & El Camino parts, door panels, interior kits, carpets, grilles, trim, bumpers, emblems, sheet metal, weatherstrip, body mounts, other rubber items, etc. - Also rubber parts for 55-72 GM car and pick-up.

Ciadella Enterprises, Inc.: David Nora (sales Kathy Johnson), 3757 E. Broadway Rd. Suite 4, Phoenix, AZ 85044. Telephone 602-968-4179, 7:00 a.m.-5:00 p.m. M-F. $3.00 catalog includes 1953-1972 Chevrolet upholstery kits for BelAir, Impala, Del-Ray, 210, Supersport, Camaro, Chevelle, Corvette.

Clark's Corvair Parts, Inc.: See listing under Parts Suppliers.

Cobra Restorers Ltd.: See listing under Parts Suppliers.

Continental Classics: Harry Samuel, 65 Wisner St., Pontiac, MI 48058-1193. Telephone 313-335-1900, 10 a.m.-9 p.m. N.O.S. molded carpets. 1950-1975 headliners, vinyl, seat cloth, package trays, hood pads, trunk mats for GM cars. 1964-1967 GTO door panels and upholstery. Some Ford, Mercury and Chrysler headliners, vinyls, carpets and seat cloth. Send body style, type transmission, color, description, large SASE and samples for matching.

Daytona Carburetor Parts Co.: See listing under Parts Suppliers.

Eagle Ottawa Leather Co.: 200 N. Beechtree, Grand Haven, MI 49417. Telephone 616-842-4000, 8 a.m. to 5 p.m. Manufacturer of automotive leather.

The Eastwood Co.: See listing under Tools.

Electron Top Mfg. Co., Inc.: 135-11 Hillside Ave., Richmond Hill, NY 11418. Telephone 212-739-1940, 8 a.m. to 5 p.m. Convertible tops for all cars 1940 to 1984.

Futterman Auto Specialties & Upholstering: Robert Futterman, 518 Ballough-Bungalow CP, Daytona Beach, FL 32014. Telephone 904-255-1952, 9 a.m. to 5 p.m. Interior restorations, make 1939-50 custom tailored seat covers, NOS 1912 to 1950 ignition parts.

Hampton Coach Inc.: Jim & Pat Roll, 70 High St., P. O. Box 665, Hampton, NH 03842. Telephone 603-926-6341. Vintage Chevrolet Upholstery Kits patterned from the originals are available for over 150 models from 1922-54. Kits come complete; easy to install yourself or use a trim shop. Other hard-to-find items also available. Write or call for free literature; include year and model of your Chevrolet. We guarantee quality & fit.

Harmon's Chevrolet Parts: See listing under Parts Suppliers.

Bill Hirsch: See listing under Parts Suppliers.

Infinite Rainbows Upholstery: Thomas Bridwell, P.O. Box 408, No. San Juan, CA 95960. Telephone 916-292-3106. 8 a.m. to 5 p.m. but you may call on weekends or evenings. Complete handcrafted interiors in one-man shop. Convertible tops, meticulous attention to detail for award winning results. Close to Sacramento, CA and Reno, NV

John's Corvette Care: 23954 Kean Street, Dearborn, MI 48183. Telephone 800-521-4774, 313-277-4700, Mon. thru Sat. 8:30/5:30. John's Corvette Care is a leading manufacturer of original Corvette interiors and fiberglass body parts. John's also designs and manufactures Corvette accessories. Johns' has a complete "in-house" service facility featuring expertise in body, mechanical, and trim work. John's Corvette Care has been servicing both the wholesale and retail market for over 10 years.

Just Dashes, Inc.: Irwin Tessler, 5945 Hazeltine Ave., Van Nuys, CA 91401. Telephone 818-780-9005, 8:30-5:30 M-F. Dashpad and door panel restorations are our main business. We have a heat shrink vinyl reskining process which will make the worst looking part look new again with original grain texture and color restored. All work guaranteed. We ship anywhere in U.S.A.

Kanter Auto Products: See listing under Parts Suppliers.

LeBaron Bonney Company: 6 Chestnut St., Amesbury, MA 01913. Telephone 617-388-3811, 8:30 a.m. to 5 p.m. Monday through Friday, 8:30 a.m. to 1 p.m. Saturday. Ford products include complete interiors and tops for all Model As and most early Ford and Mercury V-8s. Complete top assemblies for Model As and 1932 roadsters. Fabric by the yard for Fords and other makes. General products include fabrics by the yard for many makes, toppings, headlinings, wool broadcloths, bedford cords, mohairs, carpeting, leathers and companion vinyls, and trims. Many fabrics custom-made to duplicate originals.

Midland Automotive Products: 33 Woolfolk Ave., Midland City, AL 36350. Telephone 205-983-1212. 8 a.m. to 6 p.m., Monday thru Friday, 8 a.m. to 1 p.m. Saturday. Chevy carpet, truck mats, Landau tops, convertible top pads, also have literature.

Mustang Parts Corral of Texas: See listing under Parts Suppliers.

POR-15: P.O. Box 1235, Morristown, NJ 07960. Telephone in New Jersey 201-887-1999, 9 a.m. to 5 p.m. Suppliers of upholstery material, carpet, fuel pumps and restoration supplies and materials.

Prestige Thunderbird, Inc.: See listing under Parts Suppliers.

O. B. Smith: See listing under Parts Suppliers.

Charles Wes Sayer Top Upholstery and Fasteners: P.O. Box 438, Kearney, MO 64060. Telephone 816-635-5569. Top upholstery and fasteners for antique and classic cars.

Stitts Supply Co.: Edward W. Stitt, Hwy. 23 P.O. Box 185, Churchtown, PA 17555. Telephone 215-445-6851. By appointment. We are mail order. Upholstery fabrics for antique and classic cars also toppings and bindings, fasteners and other upholstery items. Guidebooks for restoration work as well as gaskets for many of the older model cars.

USA-1 Interiors: P.O. Box 691, Williamstown, NJ 08094. Telephone 609-629-4334. Monday thru Friday 8:30 a.m. to 6 p.m. Sat. 9 a.m. to 2 p.m. Complete upholstery sales and services for 1955 thru 1972 Chevrolet, Camaro, Chevelle, Nova, and Corvette. Mailorder catalog $2 for all models but Corvette (installations only).

Western Hide-Tex: P. O. Box 6478, Santa Rosa, CA 95406. Telephone 707-544-2088. Leather, wool, broadcloth, carpet, top material, mohair, and trim.

Wilkinson & Sharp: Stanley D. Wilkinson, 233 Philmont Ave., Feasterville, PA 19047. Telephone 215-OR-6-7290, 8 a.m. to 4:30 p.m. Restoration of antique and classic auto upholstery, diamond tufting in leather, tops and curtains.

WOOD

Antique Auto Specialties Co.: Barry Shlaes, 729-30 St., Rock Island, IL 61201. Telephone 309-794-0168, 24 hour ans. service. Wood only parts for Fords between 1926 & 1932. Top kits, seats, door posts, belt rails, windows, etc. for many of those cars. We also duplicate your wood. Free estimates.

Bassett's Jaguar: See listing under Parts Suppliers.

Calimer's Wheel Shop: See listing under Tires & Wheels.

Carlin Mfg. & Distr. Inc.: J.F. Carlin, 830 Fannin, Beaumont, TX 77704. Telephone 409-833-9757. Hours 8:00 a.m. to 4:30 p.m. Mon. thru Fri. We manufacture Model A and V8 Ford wood; seat springs, and sheet metal parts. We also stock chassis parts. Send $2.00 for complete listing of all parts.

Dunnville Garage (Restoration): Chester Riggins, P.O. Box 68, Dunnville, KY 42528. Telephone 606-787-7542. Wood - (specializing) in Model A Ford roadster complete interior oak-wood kits, original pattern 1928-29 - 1930-31 - 1928-29 Phaeton. All orders mailed out following day order received.

Hudson Wagon Works: D. H. Feazell, Rt. 1, Box 28, Bridgewater, IA 50837. Telephone 515-369-2865. Depot hack, Huckster wagon and truck bodies for Model A and Model T. Bodies, plans and hardware.

Newood Products: 1404 Broadway, P.O. Box 128P, Monett, MO 65708. Telephone 417-235-5872. 8 a.m. to 4:30 p.m. Monday - Thursday. Top wood and body wood for 1913 thru 1931 Fords. Mail order. Free price list. Please state year and body on request. Will re-wood cars in our shop. Made of oak. COD, VISA, MasterCharge, check, money order.

Oak Bows: Richard Kesselring, 122 Ramsey Ave., Chambersburg, PA 17201. Telephone 717-264-2602. Steambent top bows duplicating your original bow. All bows steambent like the original, not glued. No danger of separation. Have patterns for most cars.

Syverson Cabinet Co.: Ray Syverson, 2301 Rand Road, Palatine, IL 60074. Telephone 1-312-358-8428. 9:00 a.m. to 5:30 p.m. Monday-Saturday. Replacement bodies for Model T Fords, such as speedsters, depot hacks, commercial, also new dashboards, radiators, hoods, fenders, splash aprons, and running boards.

Valley Forge Restoration: See listing under Restoration Firms.

Index